THE
GULF CRISIS:
BACKGROUND AND CONSEQUENCES

Edited by
Ibrahim Ibrahim

Center for Contemporary Arab Studies
Georgetown University
Washington, DC 20057

Tel.: (202) 687-5793
Fax: (202) 687-7001

Published by Center for Contemporary Arab Studies,
Georgetown University, Washington, DC

©1992 Center for Contemporary Arab Studies,
Georgetown University, Washington, DC 20057
All rights reserved.
Printed in the United States of America.

Library of Congress Cataloging-in-Publication Data
The Gulf Crisis: background and consequences/edited
    by Ibrahim Ibrahim.
        p.   cm.
    Includes bibliographical references and index.
    ISBN 0-932568-22-X: $37.95.—ISBN 0-932568-23-8 (pbk.): $15.95
        1. Persian Gulf War, 1991.   2. Middle East—Politics and
government—1979-   . 3. Persian Gulf Region—Politics and government.
I. Ibrāhîm, Ibrāhîm, 1932-
DS79.72.G817   1992   92-41303
956.704′421—dc20   CIP

CONTENTS

Part 4: The Economic Aftermath of the War

ACKNOWLEDGEMENTS

It is my pleasure to acknowledge the contributions of the many friends and colleagues who have made this book possible.

In addition to the time and effort expended by the contributors to this volume, an invaluable role was played by those who helped to organize the symposium from which it is derived. The book originated with decisions by the Executive Committee of the Center for Contemporary Arab Studies that the Center's Sixteenth Annual Symposium in 1991 should be devoted to the Gulf crisis arising from the Iraqi invasion of Kuwait, and that the Center should subsequently publish a book on the crisis. Many thanks are due to the members of the Symposium Steering Committee for their dedicated efforts, as well as to the other faculty members, staff and friends of the Center who cooperated in making the symposium a success. A special debt of gratitude is owed to symposium manager Anne-Marie Chaaraoui for the great organizational skills she displayed, and to the Center's Assistant Director, Mary C. McDavid, for her diligent and capable endeavors to mobilize Center resources in support of the symposium.

Turning the symposium proceedings into a cohesive book required a great deal of effort. Some chapters that were not originally presented as papers at the symposium have been written specially for the book. Another chapter—that by L. Carl Brown on the history of American involvement in the Middle East—was originally delivered at the Center for Contemporary Arab Studies in 1991 as the Kareema Khoury Annual Distinguished Lecture in Arab Studies. Authors have revised and updated their chapters to take account of important developments that occurred after the symposium took place.

Special thanks are due to the Center's Director of Publications, Dr. Michael Simpson, for his insightful and meticulous management of the publications process which resulted in this book. Thanks are also due to Mary E. Kepferle for assistance with copy-editing, to Tim Lake for his work on the chronology, and to Robert Engle for help with research and the index, which he compiled in cooperation with Mary Kepferle. In addition, I would like to acknowledge the valuable assistance in research and fact-checking provided by Lara Friedman, Simone Manigo-Truell, Mary E. Schmidt, and Lucia Volk. The Center for Contemporary Arab Studies is an integral part of the School of Foreign Service of Georgetown University. I would like to take this opportunity to acknowledge with deep gratitude the support of Dr. Peter F. Krogh, Dean of the School of Foreign Service, for the Center's programs and activities since its foundation in 1975.

Ibrahim Ibrahim
Center for Contemporary Arab Studies

INTRODUCTION

Ibrahim Ibrahim

The Gulf crisis of 1990-91 was a watershed for the Arab world, the United States and the rest of the international community. The invasion of Kuwait by Iraq was the first occupation of an oil-producing Arab state by one of its neighbors, and it shook the Arab state system to its foundations. The invasion was a departure from the practices that had prevailed in inter-Arab diplomacy since Arab states had acquired their independence, and was a violation of the principles of the Arab League Charter to which all Arab states were signatories. For Kuwait, its oil-producing neighbors and most of the international community, it represented an attempt at Iraqi hegemony in the Gulf region, and threatened a decisive Iraqi influence on issues of oil pricing and supply.

This unparalleled situation set in motion a chain of events leading to another situation without precedent: a coalition was formed including the United States and three leading Arab states, Saudi Arabia, Egypt, and Syria, to confront the Iraqi occupation of Kuwait. It subsequently fought a war against Iraq that expelled Iraqi troops from Kuwait and restored the Kuwaiti government. The intervention of the United States and some of its European allies in the crisis provoked major divisions in the Arab world, where memories of western colonialism and presumptions that western powers act in their own global interests, not those of the Arab world, run deep. There was opposition to the US-led alliance against Iraq in many of the poorer Arab countries. Saddam Hussein made repeated efforts to convert this to his political benefit by appealing to Arab dissatisfaction with US support for Israel in the Arab-Israeli conflict, and by presenting Iraq as the symbol of support for the Palestinian Arab cause.

The evolution of the crisis showed that Saddam Hussein had seriously miscalculated the international response to the invasion of Kuwait. The international community was not willing to allow Iraq to be the dominant influence over the supply and pricing of the world's oil. The crisis demonstrated how far the world had come since the days of the Cold War, when the Soviet Union, previously Iraq's principal supporter, joined the United States in condemning the invasion and offering diplomatic support in the United Nations for resolutions condemning Iraq, imposing economic sanctions on it, and legitimizing the use of force in the event of an Iraqi refusal to withdraw from Kuwait. The US-Soviet entente resurrected the United Nations—at least for the period of the crisis—as a forum for the effective discussion and resolution of international disputes.

The destructive effects of Saddam Hussein's invasion and the Gulf war were sure to remain with the Arab world for decades to come. The human costs in loss of life because of war, and the deprivation of human rights under occupation, were immense. Kuwait was devastated, and its burning oil wells became a worldwide symbol of economic and environmental damage caused by war. Iraq, once one of the more developed Arab countries, was ravaged by the economic boycott, military bombardments and the civil strife that broke out after the Iraqi defeat. The countries of the Gulf Cooperation Council (GCC) suffered major financial losses as a result of extensive commitments to support the expenses of the confrontation and war. All of this represented the irreparable loss of hundreds of billions of dollars that might otherwise have been spent on development.

Politically, the Gulf crisis sent the Arab world down a path onto which few Arabs wished to venture. The invasion of Kuwait caused deep divisions in the Arab world, and the crisis that it triggered resulted in a massive western military presence of the kind reminiscent of the two World War periods, the kind that many Arabs thought would never recur after the colonial era had passed. The crisis occurred during a period of widespread interest by many Arabs in the changes taking place in the international order—the end of the Cold War, political liberalization and self-determination in Eastern Europe, and the prospect of the unification of western Europe. In Arab countries where there existed some freedom of speech and liberty of the press, the question was frequently raised whether this kind of development would spread to the Middle East. In no region of the world had an ideology of political unification been so powerful as in the Arab world since World War II; yet the Gulf crisis frustrated Arab aspirations, and left Arabs more divided and dependent on external power than before. A strong sense of powerlessness prevailed among the citizenry of Arab countries, a sense that their destinies were guided by forces outside their control. One of the effects of the crisis was likely to be a major revaluation by Arabs of the state systems of the Arab world, with increased questions about why governments were so dictatorial at home, and unresponsive in their regional policies to ideals of cooperation between Arabs.

For the world at large, the crisis demonstrated the overwhelming power of the United States in international affairs, as well as its determination to maintain the supply of world oil predominantly in friendly hands. Some argued that the crisis, by relying heavily on the United Nations, might have opened a new era of development of international mechanisms for dealing with regional conflict. On the other hand, the continuation of conflicts in other regions of the world not affecting the world's oil supply, with little effective international intervention, indicated the limitations of the optimistic view that a new era of conflict resolution was at hand. It was clear that the influence of the United States within the Middle East had increased, but that this was predominantly for reasons of military power. Converting military influence into political influence would be a far more complex operation. In the Middle East, much depended on the ability of the US to assume a positive role in resolving other problems, notably that of the Palestinians. Failure to do this would limit its role in the Middle East to support for Israel and protection of its oil interests, a combination that would guarantee bitter tensions between the United States and most politically conscious Arabs and Muslims.

The Gulf is a region of the world that has received much less academic attention than it deserves. It is underrepresented in almost every domain of social scientific literature—politics, economics, sociology, anthropology and psychology. This book attempts to remedy part of the deficiency by examining the different dimensions of the Gulf crisis: its background, evolution and consequences. Its focus is analytical rather than descriptive; a chronology is provided for those who seek information on the sequence of events. The contributors to the book attempt to explain the causes of the crisis, to analyze the responses of major participants, and to outline the repercussions of the war, which are likely to dominate the politics of the region during the 1990s.

The book originated with a symposium on the Gulf crisis held by the Center for Contemporary Arab Studies at Georgetown University in April 1991. The symposium was designed so that its outcome could be a comprehensive book on the subject; papers were revised, expanded and updated, and four contributions not presented at the symposium were added (Ibrahim, Brown, Dunn, Simpson) to expand the scope of the book.

The book is divided into four parts. The first examines the background to the crisis. The article by Ibrahim Ibrahim on states and borders in the Gulf region focuses on the history of Iraq-Kuwait tensions and traces the eruption of the crisis. It argues that the outbreak of the crisis cannot simply be understood in terms of events getting out of control, but that it reflected structural weaknesses in the Arab state system. These included the lack of mechanisms for the settlement of conflicts over borders, the proliferation of dictators willing to take arbitrary decisions without concern for the future of their peoples, and the failure of relations between Arab states to reflect the widespread aspirations within Arab societies for inter-Arab cooperation and greater participation by citizens in vital decisions affecting national destiny.

Looking at another key historical dimension, the background to American intervention, L. Carl Brown examines the development of American interests in the region. His chapter focuses on the change in the US role in the region since World War II, prior to which the US had only limited interests in the region. In the postwar era, the United States became increasingly involved in the region, as a result of the new importance of Arab oil, the Cold War, the creation of Israel and the rise of nationalist challenges to western control of the Middle East. Brown argues that Operation Desert Storm fitted into "a well-established pattern of American policy," but notes the need to review the costs and benefits to the US of its pre-eminent position in the region.

In the third contribution to the section on the background to the war, Abbas Al-Nasrawi examines the reasons for the Iraq-Kuwait dispute over oil prices and quotas. He shows how the increased importance and value of Middle East oil after 1973 created new possibilities for conflict as the development plans of a number of Middle East countries became tied to assumptions that high oil prices would be set by the members of the Organization of Petroleum Exporting Countries (OPEC). Iraq emerged from the war with Iran in 1988 in a weak, highly indebted economic state. Facing an economic crisis as a result of falling oil prices in 1990, Iraq made it a vital objective to secure higher oil prices through any means. Its dispute with Kuwait's entirely different policies on issues of prices and production escalated into the invasion of Kuwait.

The crisis generated unprecedented international cooperation against Saddam Hussein. In the section of the book dealing with the international dimension of the crisis, Michael C. Hudson examines the "uncharacteristically violent American intervention" to expel Iraq from Kuwait, and analyzes it as a response to Iraq's challenge to two major US interests, the supply of Arab oil to the West, and the security of Israel. Hudson examines in detail the implications of the claim made by President Bush that the United States sought to implement the principles of a New World Order in the Middle East, and outlines the steps that would be necessary to build this order, noting the many obstacles to it.

The Gulf crisis of 1990 demonstrated the dramatic reversal that had taken place in the international policies of the Soviet Union since the Cold War. Yelena Melkumyan interprets the crisis as a shift in the axis of international confrontation from an East-West to a North-South direction. From the start, the Soviet Union adopted a very different policy from that which it had followed in the earlier crisis over an Iraqi claim to Kuwait in 1961. Internal developments were at the heart of the transformation of Soviet policy, notably the tug of war between the three forces represented by Gorbachev, Yeltsin, and the conservatives, and a preoccupation with maintaining good relations with the West at a time when the Soviet Union was taxed by the nationality problem and the call of its republics for greater independence.

The Gulf crisis created particular problems for China, which had traditionally asserted a claim to Third World leadership, and presented itself as a symbol of independence from superpower intervention. During its recent period of internal change, as Xiaoxing Han points out, China had pursued close relationships with many of the countries involved in the Gulf coalition. Unwilling to risk this relationship, it acquiesced in the actions of the US-led coalition and the use of "necessary means" to expel Iraq from Kuwait. The Chinese orientation, though, had been that of a non-aligned peace broker, which forced China to juggle contradicting policies.

One of the most significant effects of the Gulf crisis was its revival of the role of the United Nations as a forum for responding to international crises. Augustus R. Norton shows how a US-Soviet understanding transformed the UN into an effective diplomatic force. Norton asks if the Gulf crisis can be used as a basis for institutionalizing the instruments of collective security, in order to preempt acts of international aggression. One test of UN power in the Middle East region will be whether UN resolutions on Lebanon, the Palestine problem and Arab-Israeli conflict, and Cyprus can be made effective. He notes that resentment in the UN against monopolization by the US may lead to a more explicit orientation to deployment under the UN flag.

Ties between the countries of the GCC and many parts of the

world were forged or greatly strengthened during the occupation of Kuwait. In the aftermath of the war, John Duke Anthony evaluates the conception of regional security held by GCC countries in a situation where they feel a permanent need to balance the power of two larger neighbors, Iraq and Iran. The future diplomacy of GCC countries will be directed by their need to create an extensive system of alliances. Anthony examines their attitudes to and policies on cooperation with the major world and regional powers. He underlines the important implications of developments in Iran for Gulf stability, and notes the need to resolve the Arab-Israeli conflict to consolidate the security of the region.

The third section of the book explores the regional effects of the crisis. The first two articles examine the political impact on the two most affected countries, Iraq and Kuwait. Phebe Marr examines the devastating implications of the war for Iraq's future development, and analyzes the postwar civil strife inside the country. There are a number of possible scenarios for Iraq's political future, and Marr examines these, evaluating the potential strength of the different social and political forces that might play a determining role. Shamlan Al Essa looks at the political structure of Kuwait, noting the importance of a number of non-governmental institutions in the country's politics. One striking effect of the war was the role played by such institutions in the resistance to the Iraqi occupation. Al Essa suggests that they will play a prominent role in attempts to expand political participation in postwar Kuwait.

In the Gulf region outside Iraq and Kuwait, the war also caused many changes. Jo-Anne Hart notes that the extensive damage and expense of the war is sure to affect future inter-Arab relations, because there will not be the abundant supply of oil wealth that was once used by Gulf states as a key instrument of diplomacy. Despite the success of the war, Gulf rulers faced a number of key political challenges in its aftermath, notably demands for political participation at home, and the need to pursue a closer relationship with the United States, which was sure to arouse the concern of nationalist and religious movements.

Despite the decisive defeat of the Iraqi armed forces in the war, maintaining the future security of the Gulf is a complex task. Michael Dunn argues that Iraq was not deterred from invading Kuwait, first because the Gulf states had not created a credible collective defense, and secondly, because the US commitment to Kuwait was vague and uncertain. External guarantees are essential, but not sufficient conditions to ensure future deterrence. Dunn suggests that the prudent defensive posture would be to increase the strength of GCC forces to develop trip-wire early warning capabilities, sufficient to allow external assistance to arrive.

The relationship between the Gulf and the wider Arab world changed during the crisis. Hani Faris notes the failure of the old Arab political order to prevent the Gulf crisis from arising, and examines the strength of the Saudi-Egyptian-Syrian alliance that was forged during it. Faris notes that the three states have significantly different political characters, and questions the plausibility of regarding their coalition as a basis for a new Arab order. All three, he argues, face a dilemma in pursuing close ties with the US in the face of the unpopularity of United States Middle East policies among the most ideologically influential movements in the Arab world.

The Arab-Israeli conflict emerged as a factor early in the Gulf crisis, when Saddam Hussein attempted to link the two issues. Despite the rejection of his position by the United States, US proposals for new Arab-Israeli peace negotiations were quick to follow the war. Two chapters examine the effects of the Gulf crisis on Israel and on the Palestinians. Examining the Israeli response to the crisis, Bernard Reich notes the increasing concern of Israeli officials prior to the crisis with Iraq's strongly anti-Israel orientation. Israel was supportive of US policy during the crisis, and acceded to US requests not to respond to Iraq's SCUD missile attacks. After the conclusion of the war, Israel felt more secure, and had made gains in the political and diplomatic spheres. Its leaders, however, were uncertain how long this new sense of security would last, and did not share in optimistic projections that a New Middle East Order might emerge.

Michael Simpson interprets the PLO refusal to condemn the Iraqi invasion of Kuwait as a reflection of the powerful militant orientation of the organization, which overrode the interest that Palestinians had in maintaining good ties with the Gulf states. After the defeat of Iraq and the subsequent weakening of the Palestinian position, the door was opened for a pragmatic Palestinian tendency that had gathered strength in the years prior to the crisis to move to the forefront of Palestinian politics. He sees the future of Palestinian pragmatism as dependent on whether Palestinian pragmatists can negotiate an agreement with Israel that is acceptable to the majority of Palestinians.

Turkey played a significant role in the Gulf crisis, as might be expected from its close ties with the United States and its proximity to Iraq. As Sherif Mardin notes, however, the Turkish supporting role was not one that generated great enthusiasm in the country, and there was significant public concern about being too closely identified with a war waged by the US against a neighboring country. President Özal's support for the anti-Iraq coalition nevertheless emphasized Turkey's importance in the international arena at a time when it was seeking to expand its influence among former Soviet satellite countries in the Black Sea region.

Economic factors, the long-term determinants of so many historical events, were highly significant in the Gulf crisis. The fourth and final section of the book is devoted to them. Ibrahim Oweiss quantifies the economic cost of the crisis, seen as the opportunity cost of going to war instead of settling matters peacefully. Direct and indirect costs included the loss of remittances from displaced workers, export losses, and the decline of the level of tourism, etc. The magnitude of the cost to the principal participants, i.e. Iraq, Kuwait and Saudi Arabia, can be estimated in the hundreds of billions of dollars, while smaller participants (Egypt, Syria, etc.), felt a secondary burden estimated in the billions.

The reconstruction of the region after the damage caused by war is one of its major priorities. Nemir Kirdar points out how the Gulf crisis interrupted many promising economic developments in the region. Following the end of the great infrastructure boom of the 1970s, there were growing indications that a much-needed industrial diversification was gathering pace. The Iraqi invasion of Kuwait had a negative impact on the confidence of domestic and foreign investors in the area. The banking industry, largely commercial banks, faced massive capital flight. Reconstruction is seen as a burst of economic activity which offers the opportunity to rebuild this confidence. A major need for long-term development in the region is, however, an investment banking system that has so far been lacking.

The Gulf crisis emphasized how crucial the price and supply of oil can be in influencing historical events. In the final chapter of the volume, Charles Ebinger and John Banks note their effect on Saddam Hussein's calculated risk of invading Kuwait, and the devastating consequences of his failure for Iraq. There was close cooperation throughout the crisis between large Western oil consumers, and large-capacity, large-reserve, oil-producing nations, as well as some low oil-producing countries, such as Syria and Egypt. In the aftermath of the crisis, they suggest, the tendency may be toward stability of supply and moderate pricing policies.

PART 1: THE HISTORICAL BACKGROUND

1 SOVEREIGN STATES AND BORDERS IN THE GULF REGION: A HISTORICAL PERSPECTIVE

Ibrahim Ibrahim

The Gulf crisis of 1990–91 had both immediate and long-term causes. Its immediate origins lay in the bitter dispute between Iraq and Kuwait over issues of oil pricing, the repayment of Iraq's debt to Kuwait, and the production of oil from the Rumaila well on the border between the two countries. A major factor exacerbating this dispute was the weakness of the Iraqi economy caused by the Iran-Iraq war, and the difficulties that the Iraqi government experienced in improving economic conditions after the end of the war in 1988.

Iraqi-Kuwaiti tensions were all the more dangerous because they overlapped with a historical dispute about the map of the region drawn by the British after World War I. These tensions highlighted a structural weakness in the politics of the area: the lack of an effective system for the peaceful resolution of conflicts over the borders drawn at that time. The separate territories demarcated by the British Empire became states, a number of which were small, rich, and surrounded by states with larger populations and fewer resources. The dominant political ideology of the Eastern Arab world for most of the twentieth century advocated Arab unification, and challenged the borders established by the British. In the Gulf, the borders were also subject to challenges because they did not coincide with the system of tribal organization that dominated the politics of the area.

The Arab League Charter, signed in 1945, attempted to reconcile the idea of Arab unity with respect for the sovereignty of states whose borders had been drawn during the colonial period. The League was the first supranational political structure embodying the idea of Arab unity, while at the same time recognizing the sovereign rights of each individual member state, including respect for their existing borders. Yet the enforcement of these rights depended on a consensus among states that existed until 1990 that it would be unacceptably disruptive to attempt to change borders by force (or that the local and international balance of power would not permit it). There was no effective system in place to inhibit a determined and authoritarian leader with a large army from using it to invade a smaller neighbor.

The Historical Origins of the Crisis

After World War I, the mandated territories and protectorates that were carved by the British and French out of the Ottoman Empire were new political entities. In 1914, the peoples in the Arab East, including those of Iraq, had been part of the Ottoman Empire. Arabia was a region of diverse emirates, shaikhdoms, and tribal confederations.[1]

After the collapse of the Ottoman Empire and the establishment of British rule after World War I, the idea of establishing new territorial entities in the region, each of which would eventually become a state, possessing internal and external "recognized" authority with legitimate and exclusive power, was created by the occupying forces of the European powers. Immediately after the war, the British government attempted to delineate the borders of its occupied territories, and did so without much regard for the wishes of the leaders and the people of the occupied countries. As Christine Helms has noted,

> From the perspective of the indigenous populations, there was little historical rationale in their formulation . . . . Many of the borders were linear, as if drawn with a ruler, determined by Europeans to further their own ends . . . .[2]

In the Arab East, the partition of Greater Syria and the creation of new territorial entities brought about serious difficulties for the populations. The establishment of borders in Arabia and the Gulf was also very problematic. The idea of the nation or territorial state with fixed borders was a new concept for the nomadic and settled inhabitants of central Arabia and the Gulf. The majority of the nomadic people identified themselves with a particular tribe or a system of tribal alliances, as well as a shaikh or tribal chieftain. One observer has noted:

> The concept of territorial sovereignty in the western sense did not exist in eastern Arabia. A ruler exercised jurisdiction over a territory by virtue of his jurisdiction over the tribes inhabiting it. They, in turn, owed loyalty to him and not to the shaikhdom, amirate or sultanate in which they dwelt. Political allegiance to a territorial unit, such as is implicit in the European states system, is unknown to the Arabian tribesman. His loyalty is personal to his tribe, his

shaikh, or a leader of greater consequence, and not to any abstract image of the state.[3]

The imposition of fixed borders ran counter to the grazing and migration patterns of tribes in the region. Local rulers like Abdul-Aziz Ibn Saud, Sultan of Najd (which would later be unified with the Hijaz to form the kingdom of Saudi Arabia), asserted that the imposition of territorial borders cutting across tribal boundaries would lead to major problems. A number of British officials also anticipated difficulties. As early as 1907, Lord Curzon, one of the architects and masters of British policy in Arabia, had expressed ideas similar to those of Abdul-Aziz on "tribal boundaries" rather than fixed "territorial borders." In his *Romanes Lecture, 1907,* he asserted:

> In Asia . . . there has always been a strong instinctive aversion to the acceptance of fixed boundaries, arising partly from the nomadic habits of the people, . . . but more still from the idea that in the vicissitudes of fortune more is to be expected from an unsettled than from a settled Frontier.[4]

In 1922 and 1923, the British established borders between Iraq, Najd and Kuwait. The Treaty of Muhammara, signed on May 5, 1922, allocated control of the tribes of the region among the leaders of Iraq, Najd and Kuwait on the basis of decisions made by Sir Percy Cox, the British High Commissioner in Baghdad. Ibn Saud, however, refused to ratify the treaty, claiming that some of his tribes had been assigned to the sovereignty of King Faisal of Iraq.

To resolve this problem, and delimit permanent borders, a conference was held at Uqair in November 1922. Cox autocratically reprimanded the delegations for their various claims, and imposed modern borders between Najd and Iraq, and Najd and Kuwait.

> [He] took a red pencil and very carefully drew in on the map of Arabia a boundary line from the Persian Gulf to Jabal 'Anaizan, . . . This gave Iraq a large area of the territory claimed by Najd. Obviously to placate Ibn Saud, he ruthlessly deprived Kuwait of nearly two-thirds of her territory and gave it to Najd, his argument being that the power of Ibn Sabah (the desert title of the Shaikh of Kuwait) was much less in the desert than it had been when the Anglo-Turkish Agreement of 1913 [recognizing British interests in

Kuwait and distinguishing the British and Ottoman spheres of influence in the region] had been drawn up.[5]

The new borders delineated at Uqair were ratified by the parties as Protocols to the Treaty of Muhammara. However, neither Ibn Saud, nor Ibn Sabah, nor the Iraqi government were satisfied with the arbitrary boundaries imposed by the British. The British official who served as translator during the proceedings, Harold Dickson, later observed that ". . . natural lines of trade cannot thus be lightly interfered with or laid aside, and, as a result of this policy, we have seen nothing but trouble."[6]

Immediately after the conclusion of the Uqair Conference, Cox turned his attention to the Kuwait-Iraq borders. The Anglo-Ottoman Convention of July 1913 had included the northern Gulf islands of Bubiyan and Warbah within the frontiers of Kuwait, which was at that time in the sphere of British influence, though the Convention had not been ratified by the Ottoman Parliament. In December 1922, Cox suggested to the Colonial Office "that the 'green' line [the Kuwait-Iraq border agreed between Britain and the Ottoman Empire in 1913] be confirmed as the Kuwait-Iraq boundary."[7] In a letter dictated April 4, 1923 Cox was informed that the Shaikh of Kuwait claimed the territory accorded to him by the Anglo-Ottoman Convention in the demarcation of the Kuwaiti border with Iraq. On April 19, 1923 Cox reaffirmed "that the 'Shaikh could be informed that his claim to the frontier and islands (Bubiyan and Warbah) indicated is recognized in so far as His Majesty's Government are concerned'."[8]

If British agents in Iraq and Kuwait were able to reach some kind of understanding between Iraq, Najd and Kuwait in 1922–23, the three protagonists remained uneasy about the British-sponsored agreement. The newly created state of Iraq was denied territory on the Gulf itself and thus condemned to emerge as a landlocked country (except for a riparian outlet), with Iran in the East, Syria to the West, and Kuwait to the South.

*   *   *   *   *   *

From 1923 onward there existed tensions between the Iraqi government and the British over the delineation of the Iraqi-Kuwaiti border. Neither Iraq nor Kuwait was able to resolve the question of boundaries. In the case of Kuwait, there was a fear of problems from tribes in the

Najd. The borders laid down by the British were not recognized by the Ikhwan, the militant Wahhabi tribal groups based in settlements established by Ibn Saud in different regions of the country, who were a powerful force spreading and consolidating his rule, until a split between them and Ibn Saud led to their rebellion and suppression. In the late 1920s, there was talk in British courts of forging an alliance between Iraq and Kuwait against the Ikhwan. Indeed, Major Hubert Young, Acting High Commissioner in Baghdad, "recommended during the summer of 1930 that Britain should aim at the gradual absorption of Kuwait by Iraq."[9] However, the British government took the stance that Britain should continue to protect Kuwait as a separate entity, free from Najdi or Iraqi influence.

At the start of the 1930s, the Colonial Office sought to resolve the issue of the Kuwait-Iraq boundary before the admission of Iraq as an independent state during the September session of the Council of the League of Nations in 1932. While some British voices in Baghdad were favorable to the idea of Kuwait's absorption by Iraq, other British government departments, particularly the Government of India, were vehemently opposed to the idea. In 1932, the British Government reaffirmed the 1913 Kuwait-Iraq boundary and pressured Iraq to accept a settlement that was favorable to Kuwait, according to which Iraq would be kept landlocked without access to the waters of the Gulf.[10]

Upon its independence and admission to the League of Nations in 1932, Iraq rejected the borders drawn up by Great Britain, maintaining that "as successor state to the Ottoman Empire, it inherited Kuwait, *a fortiori* since the Anglo-Ottoman Convention had never been ratified . . . ."[11] While Nuri al-Said, the Iraqi Prime Minister, was not inclined to enter into a major dispute with the British on the issue, Jaafar Al-Askari, the Iraqi Defense Minister, recommended advancing a claim of Iraqi sovereignty over the islands of Warbah and Bubiyan. From 1932 onward, the Iraqi defense establishment was eager to provide for Iraqi control of the islands to improve Iraq's disadvantageous geographical position regarding access to the Arabian/Persian Gulf.

Both Iraq and Kuwait had very different conceptions of historical rights. For Iraq, the Shaikhdom of Kuwait came into existence as an independent unit when the British carved it out of the Wilayat of Basra and put it under their special protection in the late nineteenth and early twentieth centuries to prevent the Germans from building a railroad with a terminus on the Persian Gulf. The territory of Kuwait then had the status of an "autonomous caza of the Ottoman Empire."[12] Only when the Ottoman Empire signed the above-mentioned convention with the British in July 1913 did the British gain recognition that Kuwait was within the British imperial sphere of influence. Iraq claimed that Kuwait had been an administrative subdistrict of the Iraqi province of Basra in Ottoman times and was therefore historically an integral part of modern Iraq.

The Kuwaiti position, on the other hand, was that Kuwait had not been effectively ruled by the Ottoman Empire, and that the new international map established after World War I made Iraqi claims based on Ottoman times irrelevant in any case. Since the eighteenth century, Kuwait had led an autonomous existence under the rule of the Al-Sabah family, not of the Ottoman administration.

The Iraqi position was asserted in the 1930s, before Kuwait became oil-rich or independent, by King Ghazi (1933–39), under whose rule the Arab character of the Iraqi state became more pronounced. Some of his influential advisors were officers who had fought with King Faisal of Iraq, in the days when he was a leader of the revolt aiming at Arab independence during World War I. They retained an Arabist ideology, and they were highly critical of the constraints imposed on Iraq by the drawing of the border. The growing military establishment influenced the king to assert his claim to Kuwait in 1938.

The British were able to prevent any serious Iraqi threat against Kuwait at that time. Kuwait had assumed a new strategic importance to Britain, since the independent Iraq was experiencing nationalist unrest and showing favorable sentiments toward pan-Arabism and the increasingly prominent cause of the Palestinian Arabs in particular. These sentiments were spilling over into the Kuwaiti opposition, which was developing growing links with the Arab nationalist movement and increasing its criticisms of the government.[13] The winds of war that threatened in Europe made the British all the more concerned with the maintenance of vital strategic interests. The result was that the British favored maintaining Kuwait's key strategic position at the head of the Arab Gulf and on the Arabian coastal routes to the East. This commitment was vigorously maintained once oil was discovered in Kuwait, making it an important supplier to the West.

World War II temporarily ended the tension between Iraq and Kuwait. Yet Iraq never wholeheartedly accepted the British delineation of its border. The monarchy was overthrown in a bloody coup in 1958 in Baghdad. Upon the declaration of Kuwait's independence from Britain in 1961, General Abdul-Karim Qassim, Prime Minister of Iraq, massed troops on the Kuwaiti frontier and announced his intention to annex Kuwait and incorporate it in the newly created

Republic of Iraq. British troops immediately returned to Kuwait and later were replaced by Arab League forces (Egypt, Saudi Arabia and other Arab states).[14] In February 1963, General Qassim was overthrown and killed. On October 5, 1963, the Ba'th Party, which succeeded him as the government of Iraq, publicly acknowledged the sovereignty and independence of Kuwait, although it did not specify any border line that it was willing to recognize. Relations between Iraq and Kuwait improved in the late 1960s, especially after Kuwait terminated its defense agreement with Britain in 1968. But in 1972, relations deteriorated as the Iraqi government became irritated by Kuwait's grant of asylum to Iraqi opponents to the regime in Baghdad. In 1973, Iraq moved troops to the frontier and demanded a draft treaty of friendship and cooperation between the two countries. In northern Kuwaiti territory, this treaty would grant to Iraq " '. . . the right to build, maintain and operate offices, pumping stations, refineries, depots and tanks for the storing of oil and water, bridges, harbors, airports and railway lines' — and all without the payment of dues."[15] In March 1973, the Kuwaiti government rejected the proposed treaty, whereupon, on March 20, Iraqi troops attacked Kuwaiti posts in the north-eastern corner of Kuwait and some military units landed on Warbah and Bubiyan islands. On April 4, 1973 the Iraqi Foreign Minister publicly stated that "Iraq wanted Bubiyan and Warbah islands so that 'Iraq would become a Gulf State'."[16] Arab League intervention brought the crisis to an end. Iraq asserted that it was now ready to renounce its "claim to sovereignty over Kuwait as a whole in return for the cession of Warbah and Bubiyan Islands."[17]

The Iraqi government soon became preoccupied with the Kurdish uprising in the north of Iraq, supported by the CIA, and the Iranian challenge under the Shah. In the late 1970's, Iraq was once again provided with an opportunity to emerge as a leading Arab power, especially after Sadat's visit to Jerusalem and Egypt's subsequent decline as a state with major influence in the Arab world. After the outbreak of the Islamic revolution in Teheran, there were fears in the Gulf of the spread of radical Islam, combined with the possible aspirations of Iran to a dominant role in the Gulf region. In response, an Arab Covenant was proposed by Saddam Hussein in 1980 as a new basis for an Arab regional order. Under this covenant, all members (the Gulf and Arabian Peninsula states, Jordan, Lebanon, and the remaining North African countries) "would abide by the non-use of force in interstate relations, . . ."[18] This proposal seemed to prepare the Arab world for the imminent war with Iran.

In September 1980, the Iraqi leadership launched a strike against Iran. The hoped-for *Blitzkrieg* failed to materialize, and Iraq's initial gains were indecisive. The Iran-Iraq war dragged on for another eight years, without any favorable conclusion for either Iran or Iraq. The Iran-Iraq war set the stage for the later Gulf war. At the time of the ceasefire of 1988, Iraqi finances were in extremely poor condition. Iraq's economic problems were at the heart of the tension between Iraq and Kuwait that gradually built up over the issues of frontier delineation, Iraqi access to the Gulf, the oil production and pricing policies of Kuwait, and the Iraqi debt to Kuwait and other Gulf creditors.

In 1988, the Iraqi armed forces contained a million men. The government of Saddam Hussein was worried about the implications of demobilizing them into a poorly functioning economy. As Roger Owen has pointed out, "it seems reasonable to argue that it was the financial strain which this involved, as well as his inability to re-establish satisfactory control over the leadership of his peace-time army, which drove him on to find compensation in Kuwait."[19]

Tensions arose between Iraq and Kuwait over a spate of economic issues—the price of oil, the right to produce oil from the Rumaila oil well on the border, and the repayment of Iraqi debts to Kuwait. The two countries did not treat the issues equally seriously. The Kuwait government saw them as issues that fell in the normal range of disagreements that states often had with each other. Kuwait had adopted a consistent and established position on them. It had for a long time been among the OPEC countries advocating maintaining a low price of oil, to prevent western consumers from seeking other sources and to protect its massive foreign investments that were dependent on the health of western economies. It had already given billions of dollars in grants to Iraq, and saw nothing wrong with requesting the repayment of outstanding loans. It was willing to have the dispute over the Rumaila oil well mediated.

The language with which the Iraqi leadership addressed the same issues became increasingly inflamed during the summer of 1990. Iraq's economic recovery was seen as dependent on Iraq's ability to sell oil at high prices, yet an oversupply of oil in the international markets had depressed oil prices. In 1990, in the closed session of the Arab heads of state, Saddam Hussein accused Kuwait and the United Arab Emirates (UAE) of producing oil beyond their OPEC quotas as "an act of war" against Iraq. Some six weeks later, his foreign minister, Tariq Aziz, sent a long memorandum dated July 15th to the Secretary General of the Arab League in which he accused Kuwait and the United Arab Emirates of overproduction as part of "an intentional scheme to glut the oil market with a quantity of oil that exceeded their quotas as fixed by OPEC."[20] According to Aziz, "a drop of one dollar in the price of a barrel of oil leads to a drop of one billion dollars in Iraqi revenues annually."[21]

The Aziz memorandum belittled the assistance given to Iraq by Kuwait and other Arab countries during the Iran-Iraq war, stating that it was "only a small portion of the great cost borne by the Iraqi economy and people, who offered rivers of blood in defense of pan-Arab sovereignty and dignity. . . ."[22] The memorandum also asserted that Kuwait had "committed aggression against Iraq and its rights by encroaching on our territories and oil-fields and by stealing our national wealth. Such behavior amounts to a military aggression."[23]

Neither the rulers of Kuwait nor other involved Arab governments believed that Iraq intended to invade Kuwait. As a member of the Arab League as well as the United Nations, Iraq was bound by the Charter of both organizations to respect the sovereignty of other countries. It had recognized Kuwaiti independence in 1963. Moreover, Saddam's Arab Covenant of February 1980 had pledged "the renunciation of the use of force by any Arab country against another and the resolution of all inter-Arab disputes by peaceful means."[24]

At an OPEC meeting of July 1990, Kuwait and the United Arab Emirates agreed, at least temporarily, to reduce the level of production of oil. Attempts were made by Saudi Arabia to arrange for mediation of the other issues. The Iraqi government was not, however, prepared to enter into a long round of bargaining, and was only interested in quick and major concessions by Kuwait on border issues and the problem of the Iraqi debt to Kuwait. An Iraqi-Kuwaiti meeting for negotiations was scheduled in Jeddah on August 1. It was, however, broken off by Iraq when Kuwait rejected the Iraqi demands on the issues of borders and debt repayment. The invasion of Kuwait by Iraq took place on the next day.

The Gulf Crisis and the Arab State System

Beyond the Iraq-Kuwait tensions that were its immediate cause, the Gulf crisis revealed important structural weaknesses in the Arab state system. These included a lack of effective mechanisms for peaceful conflict resolution between states; the promotion by Arab leaders of narrow state interests under the guise of advancing Arab nationalist or Islamic ideals espoused by their populations; and arbitrary international behavior by authoritarian political systems whose leaders took decisions affecting the lives and futures of their peoples without consultation. One of the byproducts of the Gulf crisis was to emphasize that the power of individual Arab states, and their success or failure on the international scene, derived not from their mobilization of the social and political energies of their citizens, but to a much greater extent from their location in the world economy and from the strength and degree of commitment of their powerful international allies.

Most of these problems could be seen throughout the Arab world, but their most dramatic and fateful illustration was the decision of Saddam Hussein to invade Kuwait. Instead of waiting for an Arab mediation process to resolve the dispute with Kuwait, he decided to use force to bring the neighboring country under his control. The decision was taken by Saddam and a small circle of advisors, who had become his advisors partly because they were willing to echo or acquiesce in his views. Once Saddam Hussein had made up his mind on a course of action, there was no mechanism for convincing him that it might lead to disaster. There was no process of consultation or democratic airing of views, and none of the free flow of information and interaction with the outside world that might have allowed the view to circulate that the invasion was a potential disaster.

In his attempts to justify the occupation of Kuwait, Saddam appealed to ideas of Arab and Islamic unity, and spoke of the need for the Arab world to control its resources, and to escape foreign influence. Yet his invasion resulted in the most serious division of the Arab world in recent history, and in a restoration of western power in the region.

The attempt to legitimize the Iraqi invasion by invoking pan-Arab principles was an effort to appeal to a consciousness that was widespread in the Arab world. Arabs everywhere perceive a strong consciousness of Arab identity and close cultural bonds with other Arabs. As Maxime Rodinson has pointed out "These judgements are in fact conditioned by a concrete situation which is the product of social factors informed by thousands of years of history."[25] Movements for Arab unity have aimed to channel these sentiments.

*　*　*　*　*　*

The ideology of Arab unification has deep roots in modern Arab history. The leaders of the Great Arab Revolt of World War I aimed at a unified Arab state. King Faisal I, throughout his reign in Baghdad, continued to cherish the idea of a united Fertile Crescent; his brother, King 'Abdullah in Amman, propagated the idea of Greater Syria. During the 1950s and 1960s, the idea of Arab unity was strongly promoted in the heyday of Nasserism, when Gamal Abdul-Nasser, a charismatic leader, captured the mind and soul of political romantics throughout the Arab East, arguing that there existed an organic unity in the Arab world.

During Nasser's era, interstate Arab relations were dominated by a mutual lack of recognition of the sovereignty of the borders of a number of Arab states. Activities that crossed territorial borders were common. Examples abound: ". . . the Saudi role in the Omani civil war of the 1950s, Iraq's assertion of its claim to Kuwait in 1961, Syrian and Egyptian policy towards Jordan in the mid-1950s and mid-1960s, Syrian involvement in Lebanon in 1958 and Egyptian in Iraq in 1960, Egyptian and Saudi intervention in the Yemen civil war in 1962–7, and the Moroccan-Algerian conflict of 1965."[26]

A major weakness of the pan-Arab movement was that even states ruled by Arab nationalists advanced narrow state interests that were competitive with each other. Attempts at unity between Egypt and Syria, and between Egypt, Syria and Iraq failed. Rivalry between Nasser's Egypt and the ruling Syrian Ba'th Party was a key part of the chain of events leading to the 1967 Arab-Israeli war, as Syrian accusations that Nasser was no longer effectively promoting the Palestinian cause influenced Nasser to a more strongly anti-Israeli posture. The Ba'th Party itself split into different factions, one ruling Syria, the other Iraq, whose bitter hostility placed them on different sides in the Iran-Iraq war, as well as in the Gulf crisis of 1990–91.

After the defeat of Egypt in the 1967 war, and the end of the 'Arab Cold War,' a new Arab solidarity emerged over the Arab-Israeli conflict. Temporarily broken after the Camp David Accord of 1978, it resumed with the return of Egypt to the Arab fold in the 1980s, following which inter-Arab rivalries entered a phase of decline. "Indeed a working consensus now emerged around the sanctity of existing political borders and the inadmissibility of clandestine subversion or military intervention. Above all, the hitherto destabilizing thrust of pan-Arabism was replaced by a general acceptance of the autonomy and legitimacy of the modern state."[27]

The problem that faced the unification movement in the Arab world was elegantly described by an Arab nationalist intellectual in 1973:

> The myth of [an Arab] organic unity has so far fueled most attempts at inter-Arab integration. Because the gap between the postulated myth and reality was great but unrecognized, the premature attempts at integration were necessarily counter-productive. All those attempts, irrespective of whether they were initiated by dynasties, by a pan-Arab party or a charismatic leader—carried hegemonial overtones. Because of that crucial factor, they were strongly resisted.[28]

*   *   *   *   *   *

The Iraqi invasion of Kuwait in 1990 was widely seen as an attempt at Iraqi hegemony in the Gulf region, and the GCC states allied themselves with the United States against the invasion. In the Arab world in 1990 there was no political romanticism concerning Arab unity by force. In this respect, the Iraqi Ba'th was out of touch with the changing mood and realities in the region.

As Walid Khalidi pointed out at the time, by invading Kuwait, Iraq wrested "the right of self-determination of Kuwait from those to whom it naturally belongs—the people of Kuwait. [The Iraqi invasion] sanctions the seizure by one country of the territory, the properties, and the assets of another. It visits upon the weak the anguish of occupation and displacement. It proclaims the primacy of might over right."[29] Even the Arab states that opposed the war against Iraq by the international coalition agreed that a negotiated settlement must be found in which Iraq withdrew from Kuwait. The outcome of the conflict showed that "Arab regimes and boundaries remained sacrosanct and no effort should be made to try to alter them by force."[30]

Despite this emphasis on the individual sovereignty of Arab states, it would be inappropriate to discuss the Arab world as if its state system consisted of a group of nation states in the traditional sense. Notwithstanding the consolidation of the Arab state system, states in the Arab world lack many of the features that have characterized the historical development of the nation state. The populations of the Arab world feel a strong sense of being Arab and Islamic; and these are commitments that go well beyond state borders. There is a widespread belief that Arab and Islamic states should cooperate, and frustration at the failure of these states to do so. The objectives of the Arab League—to encourage Arab unity while respecting the sovereignty of individual Arab states—reflect a strong consensus of opinion throughout the Arab world. There have also been differences in internal development between Arab states and typical nation states. In the West, the rise of the nation state was associated with increasing constitutionalism and democracy. The participation of the different strata of society in the activities of the states gave states a solid social base of support. Control of the state was based on representative institutions, and members of governments were subject to public scrutiny and judicial constraints on their conduct. In the Arab world in the era of independence, control of states has been widely used to promote the power of traditional social groups and formations—families, sects, tribes, and cliques with access to power. Democracy and constitutionalism, while widely sought, have rarely been practiced. Governments have preferred to make their rule dependent on security forces and armies rather than on the mobilization of the social and political energies of their peoples. Small circles of men have made decisions affecting the future destiny of their peoples in secrecy and without consultation.

Arab states have not escaped the need to rely on more powerful states in their efforts to achieve major economic and political goals. When he made the decision to invade Kuwait, Saddam Hussein calculated that other Arab states would not be able to stand up to his invasion, and that the United States would be either unable or unwilling to wage war against Iraq over Kuwait. One of his biggest miscalculations was a failure to understand the continuing interest and commitment of the superpowers in the Arab East. He and his advisors never fully understood the significance of the decline of the Soviet Union, and its consequences for regional and international affairs. Nor did they appreciate the tremendous changes that had taken place in the United States in the 1980s, as the Vietnam syndrome diminished and was replaced by a new willingness to intervene militarily in foreign regions. Saddam Hussein appears to have believed that the end of the Cold War would make the United States less, not more willing to intervene in the Middle East; yet the experience of the region during the twentieth century, including the period prior to the Cold War, had shown that western powers always intervened in the region when interests they considered vital were at stake. Moreover, it was clear that major Arab states such as Saudi Arabia, Egypt and Syria were sure to oppose Iraqi hegemony in the Gulf region. On the same issue in 1961, for example, when Abdul-Karim Qassim advanced the Iraqi claim to Kuwait, even Egyptian President Gamal Abdul-Nasser, the symbol of Arab nationalism, had sided with the British in defense of Kuwait. The reality faced by the Arab world and Arab states was one of dependency. The economic and political importance of the Arab world lay in its oil reserves. Because of the importance of Arab oil to the world, superpower involvement in the region was inevitable, and was likely to tilt the balance of forces. An Arab country's strength in the inter-Arab balance of power thus derived in large part from the power and degree of commitment of its superpower ally or allies. This situation of dependency was not counterbalanced by significant moves toward Arab cooperation that might have established regional institutions for the resolution of conflicts.

Major wars are often the prelude to significant changes. The Gulf crisis of 1990–91 was the most disruptive crisis faced by the Arab world in its era of independence. None of the other major wars—those between the Arab states and Israel, and the Iran-Iraq war—inflicted the same degree of disunity upon the Arab world. Yet the populations of the different Arab states were not prepared to confer legitimacy on a state system of competing authoritarian Arab states looking to the powerful outside world for arms and support in conflicts with their neighbors. There was sure to be a substantial revaluation by Arab public opinion everywhere of the evolution of the Arab state system.

Almost all Arab governments were influenced by the need to be sensitive to Arab or Islamic political ideologies and beliefs that favored close ties between the states and peoples of the Arab world. The fate of the invasion of Kuwait by Saddam Hussein showed that Arab unification could not be achieved by attempts by powerful states to exert hegemony over weaker ones. The question after the invasion was whether the divisions caused could be repaired and a new stage of rapprochement and cooperation worked out, resulting in the creation of a system of inter-Arab relations more in line with the aspirations of the populations. The alternative course for the Arab world would be one of fragmentation and interstate tensions that could be very destructive, with an unpredictable outcome.

Notes

1. Dankwart A. Rustow, *Middle Eastern Political Systems* (Englewood Cliffs: Prentice-Hall, 1971), p. 94. Quoted in Christine Moss Helms, *The Cohesion of Saudi Arabia*

(Baltimore: Johns Hopkins University Press, 1981), p. 196.

2. Christine M. Helms, *The Cohesion of Saudi Arabia,* p. 188.

3. J.B. Kelly, *Eastern Arabian Frontiers* (London: Frederick A. Praeger, 1964), p. 18.

4. Lord Curzon, 'Frontiers', *The Romanes Lecture, 1907* (Oxford, 1907), p. 49. Quoted in J.B. Kelly, *Eastern Arabian Frontiers,* p. 17.

5. H.R.P. Dickson, *Kuwait and Her Neighbors* (London: Allen and Unwin, 1956), p. 274.

6. Dickson, p. 277.

7. Richard Schofield, *Kuwait and Iraq: Historical Claims and Territorial Disputes* (London: Royal Institute of International Affairs, 1991), p. 61.

8. *Ibid.*

9. Schofield, p. 63.

10. Schofield, p. 65.

11. John C. Wilkinson, *Arab Frontiers: The Story of Britain's Boundary Drawing in the Desert* (London: I.B. Tauris, 1991), p. 146.

12. Schofield, p. 46.

13. Jacqueline S. Ismail, *Kuwait: Social Change in Historical Perspective* (Syracuse: Syracuse University Press, 1982), p. 71.

14. J.B. Kelly, *Arabia, The Gulf and the West,* (New York: Basic Books, 1980), p. 277.

15. J.B. Kelly, *Arabia, The Gulf and the West,* p. 283.

16. *Ibid.*

17. J.B. Kelly, *Arabia, The Gulf and the West,* p. 284.

18. Yazid Sayigh, "The Gulf Crisis: Why the Arab Regional Order Failed," *International Affairs,* 67, 3 (1991), p. 496.

19. Roger Owen, "Making Sense of an Earthquake: The Middle East after the Gulf War," in Victoria Brittain, *The Gulf Between Us: The Gulf War and Beyond* (London: Virago Press Ltd., 1991), p. 159.

20. Tariq Aziz, Letter to Arab League Secretary General Chedli Klibi, July 16, 1991, *Foreign Broadcast Information Service* (FBIS-NES-90-138, July 18, 1990), p. 22.

21. *Ibid.*

22. (FBIS-NES-90-138, July 18, 1990), p. 23.

23. *Ibid.*

24. Walid Khalidi, *The Gulf Crisis: Origins and Consequences* (Washington, DC: Institute for Palestine Studies, 1991), p. 8.

25. Maxime Rodinson, *The Arabs* (Chicago: University of Chicago Press, 1979), p. 45.

26. Sayigh, p. 490.

27. *Ibid.*

28. Walid Khalidi, "Towards Adjustment in Political Perception in Arab Society," in Margaret Pennar, ed., *The Middle East: Five Perspectives* (North Dartmouth, MA: Association of Arab-American University Graduates, Information Papers, No. 7, October 1973), p. 17.

29. Walid Khalidi, *The Gulf Crisis: Origins and Consequences, op. cit.,* p. 15.

30. Owen, p. 172.

2 BUILT ON SAND? AMERICA'S MIDDLE EASTERN POLICY, 1945–1991: A HISTORICAL PERSPECTIVE

L. Carl Brown

In 1945 with the end of World War II, the expanded wartime official American presence in the Middle East was scheduled to subside, returning the limited American concern with this region to the private sector—oil and educational activities. Only one other interest might have been predicted at that time: A small number of Americans worried about Palestine, where Arabs and Jews prepared for the next round of an already half-century old confrontation in that tiny territory roughly the size of New Jersey. This American interest was also private and in the tradition of Americans supporting those sharing the lands or languages or religions of their origins. Such concerns might have been expected to have an impact on, but not decisively shape, official policy. The Middle East did not seem likely to figure prominently on the American diplomatic landscape following 1945.

The early weeks of 1991 offered a scene that none of America's few Middle East specialists in 1945 could have imagined: Over a half-million American military personnel—men and women—were in Saudi Arabia engaged in warfare against Iraq. This was not another example of great power confrontation that happened to spill over into the Middle East; nor was it the Allies against Rommel's Afrika Korps, Gallipoli in 1915, or the Crimea in the 1850s. It was, instead, a massive intervention by the United States rallying states of the region and the outside world in response to a regional dispute.

Is there a historical pattern that explains the transition from what Americans expected to be doing in the Middle East in 1945 to what they were doing there in 1991? Or was Operation Desert Storm a radical departure from previous American policies, assumptions, and expectations regarding the Middle East?

The interpretation presented here is that Operation Desert Storm fitted into a well-established pattern of American policy. This is not to argue a simple-minded determinism. Of course, President Bush could have chosen to continue economic sanctions against Iraq after January 15, 1991. He could even have done very little in response to Saddam Hussein's invasion on August 2, 1990, of neighboring Kuwait. Rather, it is suggested that the United States long ago abandoned the minimalist policy of 1945 and approached the Gulf crisis assuming that the US had a need, a responsibility, and a right to orchestrate political arrangements in the Middle East. Even if President Bush had chosen different options, he would have taken steps, sooner or later, consistent with this American policy of full involvement.

Moreover, the ideas underlying American policy in the Middle East—for which Operation Desert Storm offers the most dramatic example of that policy in action—have become so much a part of what both policy makers and the public take for granted that only a major ideological reorientation (such as took place following 1945) is likely to change the American approach to the Middle East.

The American position in the Middle East after the Gulf war was more prominent than ever. Indeed, a case can be made that no great power in modern times has attained such lonely preeminence. It is still not clear precisely what commitments the Bush Administration offered to the many different parties (Arab states, Israel, Turkey and others) drawn into the coalition that confronted Saddam Hussein, but they must have been substantial. It now follows that a great power cannot simply walk away from promises made and bargains struck.

At the same time, it is important to study the likely costs and benefits of America's preemptive position in the Middle East. A country's foreign policy, just like a family budget, needs periodic rigorous cost-accounting audits. As things stand, does the United States get adequate returns on its Middle Eastern diplomatic investment? Would a reduced investment—to be realized by bringing in other "investors"—offer greater promise?

Even as the United States wrestles with problems in the Middle East following the Gulf war it may be useful to pose the question of longterm planning. A retrospective look at American policy and assumptions and action in the Middle East since 1945 may provide a useful point of departure.

*   *   *   *   *   *

The United States took a number of quick and significant steps toward heavy involvement in the Middle East in the immediate post-World War II period, Indeed, the two major arenas of the earliest Cold War sparring were Eastern Europe and the Middle East. What the United States saw as Soviet probes against Greece, Turkey and Iran in the years 1945-1947 led to the first of three post-war Presidential

"doctrines" that had their roots in Middle Eastern diplomatic soil—
the 1947 Truman Doctrine.

Nothing could have been more natural. The Middle East is the one
non-western area that shares a common border with Europe. It has
been the arena of choice for intra-European diplomatic joustings ever
since it became vulnerable to an overwhelmingly stronger European
state system beginning roughly two centuries ago. As I have argued
elsewhere,[1] this political game with its many different European
and Middle Eastern players achieved a measure of durability using
rules that scarcely varied. By the mid-nineteenth century, Europeans
had begun to label this distinctive diplomatic confrontation "The
Eastern Question." The name stuck, and the very continuity of
nomenclature indicates that the phenomenon endured over time with
recognizable features.

The question facing Europe was how to divide up the Ottoman
Empire, "the Sick Man of Europe," in a way that would minimize
shocks to the European state system. The same held for Morocco and
Iran, lying to the West and East of Ottoman lands. From the Middle
Eastern perspective it became a "Western Question" or a question of
how Middle Eastern leaders could defend themselves by playing off
regional and European powers.

Traditional scholarship holds that "The Eastern Question" went
out of existence with the final breakup of the Ottoman Empire after
the First World War, but the basic pattern of Middle Eastern politics—a
continuing kaleidoscopic shifting of alliances among states of the
region as well as outside states involved in the region—scarcely
changed. Indeed, the regional dimension of the distinctive diplomatic
system reached new levels of complexity following the Second World
War as more Middle Eastern states achieved independence and began
to play the old game. Some sought to shore up a shaky independence.
Others set out to expand their sway, an impulse that led in the
following decade to political Pan-Arabism. In a sense, the post-1945
Middle East assumed a role in world politics not unlike that of the
Balkans in the earlier phase of the classic Eastern Question.

The standard interpretation of this early American plunge into
Middle Eastern politics epitomized in the Truman Doctrine is linked
to Cold War historiography, and this is certainly appropriate. The
confrontation of the two superpowers provides the larger framework
within which America's post-war relations with the different regions
of the world can be fitted. At another level, however, what was
taking place was simply the addition of a new player to the old

Eastern Question game. Britain needed to cut back on imperial commitments and hoped to recruit the United States in service of British policy goals. The various players within the Middle East were also working to enlist the United States to their different causes or, failing that, to seek other patrons. By viewing a complex, multilateral diplomatic situation in bilateral Cold War terms, American policy makers and opinion molders often mistakenly evaluated the different Middle Eastern political figures as either "for us" or aligned with the Soviets.

The United States, however, was never totally committed to viewing the Middle East through Cold War spectacles. For example, the strong American official support for the creation of Israel since at least early 1947 can hardly be fitted into Cold War thinking. Major reservations came from the likes of George Marshall, James Forrestal, and George Kennan who, as architects of the Cold War foreign policy, considered support for Zionism to be a deviation from the broader geopolitical approach that they advocated. To them support for Zionism was an especially egregious example of letting domestic political considerations shape foreign policy.

Opinion concerning Middle Eastern oil in those early years following the Second World War can be most appropriately interpreted as an interesting mix of the old and the new in the diplomatic thinking of the United States. The American oil industry had moved energetically into the Middle East in the interwar years, carving out a position of strength epitomized by the Aramco partnership of major oil companies in Saudi Arabia. In those years, oil company representatives had not been bashful about calling on US governmental support when needed as, for example, in challenging the cartel arrangement of the so called "Red Line agreement". In another instance, it was at Aramco's urging during the Second World War that Saudi Arabia became a recipient of American Lend Lease aid.

On the other hand, the oil industry resisted American governmental efforts to get too involved in a way that might lead to partial governmental ownership or control. This, in a word, was the history of Secretary Ickes's abortive bid to bring about direct US governmental involvement in Middle Eastern oil somewhat along the lines of the British government's involvement in the Anglo-Iranian Oil Company.

As a result, the American perspective on Middle Eastern oil in the early years following 1945 was an awkward and not completely consistent blend of (1) the old "Open Door" doctrine which required only that American business have access on equal terms to all markets (a policy compatible with political isolationism); and (2) the new concept of oil as a strategic commodity that had to be protected by sound political ties with the regional powers and by military support if necessary.

Also serving as an American policy determinant in these early years was the conviction that western colonialism was passé and should be replaced by a world of independent states. Admittedly, American pressures on Britain and France to decolonize were counterbalanced by efforts to mollify our colonialist allies in order to strengthen NATO. Indeed, the United States attempted to make decolonization more palatable to its European allies by arguing that independent states in friendly relationships — or even better in alliance — with the West were assets, while insisting that the disaffected colonized held down by force were not.

Traditional American anti-imperialism thus had its limits as a determinant of policy. Metternich once observed that the Tsar wanted everybody to be free provided they freely chose to do what he wished. It can be argued that the United States came close to a similar line of thought regarding Middle Eastern independence. Middle Eastern nations deserved to be free of western colonial rule provided they freely chose to remain part of the western-led alliance system. Such was the story of the 1950s that can be told in terms of three strong personalities: Dulles, Khrushchev, and Nasser.

*   *   *   *   *   *

Dulles, having seen the apparently effective integration of what he called "the Northern tier" of Middle East countries bordering the Soviet Union into western defense arrangements, sought to add strategic depth with Arab participation. Egypt would be given the opportunity to play a leading role, but the alliance caravan would not wait for a reluctant Cairo. Iraq was waiting in the wings.

Nasser saw all such plans as the continuation of western domination. He realized that, divided, the Arabs were no match for outside pressures but, united, their prospects improved. Iraq's willingness to go along with a western alliance and perhaps even bring in other Arab states as well was a direct challenge to Nasser's ambitions.

As for the Soviets, Stalin regarded all "bourgeois nationalist leaders" as western puppets. His successors, especially Khrushchev, realized the strength of anti-colonialism and moved quickly toward positive arrangements with leaders such as Nasser. The 1955 Soviet arms deal with Nasser followed. Nasser had permitted the Soviets to leapfrog over Dulles's northern tier, and a generation of Soviet-Egyptian cooperation was underway. It would end only in the mid-1970s in the wake of Sadat's diplomatic revolution of moving from Soviet to American patronage.

The Anglo-French-Israeli collusion and attack on Egypt in response to Nasser's nationalization of the Suez Canal ended in failure. In one of the more ironic twists of the Cold War, the superpower enemies found themselves on the same side refusing to go along with the plan to defeat, and almost certainly, overthrow Nasser. Even more poignant, indeed disgusting, to the western world, the Soviet stand against aggression in the Middle East was concurrent with the brutal Soviet military repression in Hungary.

All this resulted in a cataclysmic decline in what remained of British and French power and prestige in the Middle East. The perception that only the United States was in a position to frustrate Soviet designs in the Middle East seemed eminently realistic to policy makers after Suez. The second presidential doctrine — the Eisenhower Doctrine enabling allies of the US in the Middle East to request US military intervention against external threats to them — resulted in 1957. Just slightly more than a decade after 1945 the United States was positioned to "go it alone" in the Middle East.

*   *   *   *   *   *

An earlier development had contributed to this mood. This was the growing penchant for secret operations designed to sustain or overthrow governments while concealing the American hand. Official America came late to such covert actions, to use the technical term. The Central Intelligence Agency was created in 1947, the same year that witnessed the creation of the unified Department of Defense and the National Security Council, all part of what one critic was to describe as the "national security state."[2]

Distinctions not always made are important on this point. A strong case can be advanced for intelligence gathering and analysis by all states. To the extent that political leaders possess accurate estimates of their enemies, confrontations stemming from ignorance or misguided fears are reduced. Covert action is a different matter. Having every player in the game seeking such shortcuts hopelessly complicates an already dangerously anarchic Middle Eastern diplomatic scene. Establishment powers have a stake in international stability. Covert action, whatever else might be said about it, is destabilizing. Moreover, in a political climate characterized by leaders having very shallow rooted legitimacy, inclined accordingly to rely on military and internal security forces, and conditioned to expect, upon removal from power, not a presidential library and elder statesman status but exile or assassination, covert actions by well-established states having limitless resources at hand can raise the paranoid level of political leadership to new heights.

Nasser, when asked why he did not allow a multi-party system in Egypt, replied, "If I did that, there would be one party acting as an agent for the CIA, another upholding British interests, and a third working for the Soviets."[3] Such alleged activities would be, in any case, one of the tamer varieties of covert action.

The classic example of covert action in the Middle East was the 1953 CIA operation leading to the overthrow of Prime Minister Muhammad Mosaddiq and the restoration of the shah. This was clearly not an isolated incident. The evidence now available, however unreliable parts may be, presents a convincing picture of persistent and intensive American use of covert action in the Middle East since at least the time of the Eisenhower administration. These activities fostered an illusory sense of power in the American leadership, encouraging its move toward preemptive actions in the Middle East. Covert actions, being usually secret only to the American public, not to those targeted, also increased Middle Eastern suspicions of the United States.

*   *   *   *   *   *

By 1957 America stood virtually alone in defending a vulnerable Middle East against a threatening Soviet Union. Such was the official self-image. The region, not surprisingly, saw it differently. They saw the Eisenhower Doctrine as a challenge to Nasserist Arabism. They saw efforts to change governments in Syria and intervene in Lebanese electoral politics as intended to establish American hegemony. Moreover, the Arab world from the Nasser period on was developing "right-left" and "rich-poor" fault lines, and the United States was increasingly seen, with some justice, as a supporter of the old order, a twentieth-century Metternich.

A closer look at the Middle East in regional rather than Cold War terms should have served to modify the official American self-image. The United States had managed to become the preeminent western power in the Middle East. France was fighting a losing cause in Algeria, and Britain remained in the Gulf with America's blessing. Yet the United States had not been able to bring the Middle East into an effective post-colonial alliance with the West. It was true that Turkey was in NATO and Iran after Mosaddiq seemed secured, but other parts of the area were not so promising. The Baghdad Pact had polarized the Arab world, and Nasser with the 1955 arms deals had opened the door for Soviet intervention. The United States had not been able to broker an Arab-Israeli peace, in spite of persistent open and secret diplomacy during the early 1950s. Most of all, the United States henceforth paid the price of the preeminent in a region long accustomed to play off the powerful. Having captured the strongest position of any outside power in the area (which was certainly the case after 1956) and pushing an activist Cold War policy of resisting further Soviet penetration, the United States had to face the blame for problems not resolved.

*   *   *   *   *   *

Then came 1958 and a military coup overthrowing the Iraqi monarchy. The most important Arab government accepting the American anti-Soviet line was no more. A few months earlier, that same year had brought the union of Egypt and Syria, creating the United Arab Republic. Lebanon's President Chamoun, fearing complete loss in a civil war that his own provocative pro-westernism had created, sought American support. Eisenhower sent American troops to Lebanon, the first instance of their deployment there, but not, alas, the last.

American plans to organize the Middle East had failed. Yet, the other states of the Middle East did not thereafter fall like dominoes to be gathered in by Nasser or the Soviets. Nasser proved willing to go along with a de facto neutralization of Lebanon (territorially intact but no longer a western pawn). By 1959 Nasser and Khrushchev were exchanging harsh words over Nasser's treatment of Egyptian Communists, and in 1961 Syria seceded from the United Arab Republic. There was even an interesting, if ultimately unsuccessful, effort on the part of the United States and Egypt to patch up relations in the early months of the Kennedy administration.

The lesson seemed to be that the United States could secure its minimal goals in the Middle East without controlling the policies of the separate states. Middle Eastern oil continued to reach world markets, ships passed without mishap through the Suez Canal, and the Soviet Union was less passionately sought after by Arab states because it was no longer so pressingly needed to counter threats of western hegemony. The Soviets, having established a stake, henceforth had to parry demands for more support from its regional clients.

The year 1960 brought the creation of the Organization of Petroleum Exporting Countries (OPEC), not that much noticed at the time. Later, it would be realized just how important the creation of this cartel had been. Although Venezuela had played the preeminent role in creating OPEC, the group's real economic strength lay in the Middle East. In a sense, OPEC was the economic equivalent of Nasser's political pan-Arabism, both based on the precept that the weak can increase their bargaining power by uniting. That a commercial cartel proved more successful than political unity is suggestive both as to what the region can achieve as well as what the outside world will accept.

The political watershed of the 1960s was the June War, which left Israel in occupation of the West Bank, the Golan Heights and Sinai. This was a war in which the hot line between the United States and the Soviet Union worked effectively, illustrating that the two superpowers had reached an implicit understanding of the safe limits of Middle Eastern proxy wars. All was fair as long as the game was played by proxies, but the principals must not let the proxies drag them into the fight. The lessons learned would be put to good use in the 1969-1970 War of Attrition and even more so in the 1973 War.

The June War caught the United States heavily committed in Vietnam and thus reluctant to get involved on another front. Observers at the time could detect the relief of the Johnson Administration that Israel won, and won quickly, thus obviating any need for American intervention. June 1967 marked, as well, a decided move toward what has become an informal, but very real, American-Israeli alliance. American official support for Israel had long existed, but was diluted by several factors destined to fade away in the years following the June War. First, Israel in its early years had considered taking a more neutralist stand between the two superpower blocs, a policy well on the way to abandonment by the time of the Korean War. Israel in the 1950s cemented a close military and diplomatic relationship with France that hatched the Suez War and survived until De Gaulle, having brought France to accept Algerian independence in 1962, worked to restore French ties with the Arab world. June 1967 was the occasion for the decisive break. Moreover, for the western world Israel's decisive victory in 1967 brought in its wake a diplomatic loss. The Jewish state could no longer be a beleaguered David hemmed in by a collective Arab Goliath.

From the American side, however, a different lesson was drawn. Earlier American official thinking tended to see an Israel not yet at peace with its Arab neighbors as a diplomatic liability, frustrating American efforts to organize the Arab world in the Cold War alliance arrangements. This perception provided the stimulus for the many different efforts, both open and behind the scenes, to broker an Arab-Israeli settlement following 1948.[4] None had succeeded. Efforts to "do business with Nasser" had failed as had efforts to "line up" anti-Nasser forces. The Iraqi monarchy was no more, Eisenhower's strange idea that King Saud could serve to rally anti-Nasser forces was discredited, and the king himself was replaced by his much more dynamic brother, Faisal. American officials in 1967 looked back at Eisenhower's pressures on Israel (as on Britain and France) to withdraw from Egypt following the 1956 Suez War, and saw that they had not led to a negotiated peace. Finally, Lyndon Johnson simply favored Israel and had little regard for the Arabs.

The results of the June War thus brought forward a more decided official American tilt toward Israel and also stimulated the growing notion (absent in earlier times) that Israel was a strategic asset. Black September, three years later, strengthened this way of regarding Israel and the Arabs. The PLO's military challenge to Jordan's King Hussein was receiving support from Syria. A desperate King Hussein appealed to Britain and the United States, but there was not enough time to get troops there. Israel, asked to intervene, mobilized troops in Northern Israel, inducing a Syrian military withdrawal. The Jordanian Army then defeated the PLO forces. Henceforth, the PLO was reined in not only in Egypt and Syria (where this had always been the case) but in Jordan as well. Only Lebanon with its designedly weak, laissez-faire government and army to match remained as a confrontation state in which the PLO could organize unchecked and carry out militarily negligible but politically explosive actions against Israel. A major contributing factor to the Lebanese civil war that broke out in 1975 had been put in place.

As for the PLO, the smart talk after 1967 had it that the only victors in the June War were Israel and the PLO. This seemed obvious enough in the Israeli case. On the Palestinian side, the defeat of the

Arab states opened the way for strong Palestinian leadership freed of control by the Arab state system. A quarter-century later it might seem more apt to say, instead, that both Israel and the PLO emerged from the June War with the illusion of increased power, but neither of them was able to parlay its strengthened position into the defeat of the other and imposition of terms, or movement toward a negotiated settlement.[5]

*   *   *   *   *   *

The 1960s ended with a pattern of alignments somewhat different from the earlier period. The United States which had presented its policy in terms of general western interests since 1945 became increasingly out of line with its western allies by having become the virtually exclusive patron of Israel. On the other hand, Europe (and for that matter Japan) stressed ties with the infinitely larger and oil-rich Arab world. It is worth noting in this context that Israel and all Palestinians together account for less than 3 percent of the entire Middle East, defined as all the Arab world, Iran, Israel and Turkey. Yet Europe and Japan tended to let the United States take the political initiatives, realizing that they hardly had a choice, given the American penchant for preemptive politics. Moreover, any gains achieved from American actions would be shared by all. Any losses would be attributed to, and largely sustained by, the United States alone.

From 1958 until 1973 the United States remained in this muted Cold War phase. The Soviet Union was still seen as the principal antagonist but not necessarily the chief cause of regional unrest. An awareness had grown that forces in the Middle East itself generated or kept alive most of the crises. Nor was it deemed feasible or necessary to expel the Soviets from the area to restore the status quo ante 1955.

*   *   *   *   *   *

The Nixon-Kissinger years and especially the October 1973 War and its aftermath brought a change. The war itself ushered in another example of tense, but ultimately successful hot-line cooperation on the part of the two superpower rivals. Thereafter, the United States took the lead in breathing new life into the pre-1958 Soviet-American rivalry. In the past, in dealing with the Arab world on an official level, the United States had sought to minimize, explain away, or even deny the close American relationship with Israel. Shrewdly, Kissinger made a virtue of this tie to Israel by asserting that only the United States had the standing with both Israel and the Arabs to be able to play the role of the honest broker. This ploy played right into the thinking of Egypt's President Sadat, who maintained that the United States held 99 percent of the cards in the Middle Eastern diplomatic game. Thus, the basic strategy that would result in the March 1979 Egyptian-Israeli peace treaty, signed at the White House, was in place. Even though Jimmy Carter campaigned against the Kissinger approach and his administration claimed to be different, from one very important perspective the Nixon-Carter years offer considerable uniformity. The United States, muscling aside friend and foe, insisted on the leading role.

Events after 1973 suggested, at least in the opinion of most Arabs who were highly suspicious all along, that while the United States might have the power to pressure Israel and the Arabs to make the hard choices necessary for a genuine settlement it did not have the political will to lean on the former. For this reason plus others (including a strong Arab and regional preference for playing off outside contenders lest any one power get too strong) the United States was not able to bring along enough of the Arab players either. Yet the notion that the United States had all the cards, most of the cards, or at least the best cards, dies hard. A former senior State Department official, Joseph Sisco, writing in the *Foreign Affairs* issue reviewing the diplomatic events of 1982, the year of the Israeli invasion of Lebanon, maintained:

> Developments in the area this year have once again confirmed the centrality of the US role as the only power acceptable to both sides. The strength of America's position in the Middle East and Gulf is based primarily on its capacity and ability to produce positive results.[6]

In fact, the significant, if partial, gain that the American-brokered Egyptian-Israeli peace treaty of 1979 had brought was in that same year offset by the Islamic Revolution in Iran, sweeping the shah from his throne. To the Ayatollah Khomeini and his Iranian followers, there was no doubt about Islamic Iran's principal enemy. America was "the great Satan." A review of US efforts to establish strong ties with Middle Eastern regimes enjoying limited popular support such as the Pahlavi dynasty or the Iraqi monarchy calls to mind Robert Keohane's observation: " 'Keeping the lid on' is an appropriate metaphor: If the lid flies off, the force of the explosion may be roughly proportional to the effort expended in keeping it on."[7]

The year 1979 also brought the Soviet invasion of Afghanistan in December, provoking an American response in the form of the third of America's presidential doctrines with Middle Eastern roots. The January 1980 Carter Doctrine asserted that the United States had a vital interest in the Persian Gulf which would be defended against external aggression by military force if necessary. This led, in turn, to the creation of the Rapid Deployment Force, which provided the organizational matrix of the gigantic Operation Desert Storm.

With the Islamic Revolution in Iran the stage was set for perhaps the most bizarre series of incidents in American diplomatic history: the 444-day American Embassy in Tehran hostage crisis, the abortive April 1980 American military effort to rescue its hostages; the Iran-Contra affair, the first news of which broke in November 1986, and the Joint House-Senate hearings of the following year; the May 17, 1987 Iraqi attack on the *U.S.S. Stark* killing 37, followed two days later by the American agreement to reflag Kuwait ships and provide naval escort in the Gulf; and the downing by the *U.S.S. Vincennes* of an Iranian commercial jet with 290 killed on July 23, 1988, followed on August 20 by a cease-fire in the eight-year-old Iran-Iraq war.

*   *   *   *   *   *

Only a brief respite occurred from the time of the Iran-Iraq cease-fire until Iraqi troops invaded Kuwait on 2 August 1990. The new crisis this presented offers an opportunity to review in broad lines the evolution of American policy toward the oil-rich states of the Arabian peninsula from 1945 to the present. Whatever else can be said about the events set in motion by Saddam Hussein's invasion of Kuwait, it clearly forced all the oil-rich states of the Arabian peninsula (organized since 1981 into the Gulf Cooperation Council) to the center stage of regional diplomacy. Earlier, they had prudently opted for low-profile policies, consistently supporting whatever Arab consensus could be reached on issues ranging from Israel to imperialism, while maintaining good commercial ties to the western world and relying on the United States as the protector of last resort, preferably to remain until that time militarily just over the horizon.

The reasons for this posture were simple and straightforward. Saudi Arabia alone among the GCC states boasts a population sizeable enough to lift it out of the ministate category (officially over 14 million, but much lower according to many estimates). The combined population of all the other GCC states is just one-third that of Iraq. Moreover, only Saudi Arabia has been a properly independent actor in interstate politics since well before the Second World War, all the others having been under one form or another of British influence until as recently as the 1960s. It should also be remembered that the era of fabulous oil revenues now enjoyed by these states began only about a generation ago.

Accordingly, the history of American foreign policy toward what is now the GCC essentially revolves around America's relations with Saudi Arabia. This history is distinctive in important respects. First, until the period of the Second World War the United States was viewed by Ibn Saud, the founder of Saudi Arabia, as a welcome counter to British influence. Second, the formative years of Aramco-Saudi relations were free of host country hatred of the oil company as yet another manifestation of the imperial presence (unlike the case in Iran and Iraq, for example). Moreover, in Aramco's early years, US oilmen and their families appear to have got along well with the Saudis, and Aramco was, generally speaking, somewhat quicker than the oil companies operating in the neighboring states to offer concessions favorable to the host government.

From this there grew up a bifurcated US image of Saudi Arabia. On the one hand, American officialdom developed a somewhat exaggerated notion of Saudi Arabia's power and influence in the area. On the other hand, and largely in response, American supporters of Israel tended to discount Saudi Arabia as a de facto American ally. Both groups, it can be seen, managed to distort both Saudi capabilities and intentions.

President Roosevelt's visit with Ibn Saud aboard the *U.S.S. Quincy* in February 1945 added greatly to this distorted image. His later report on that short visit fostered the impression that Ibn Saud could serve as the principal spokesman for the Arab world or that the needed American ties to the Arab world could most effectively be built on a Saudi base. That Ibn Saud was a political leader of heroic proportions can be granted, but such an American outlook misread both what was feasible for the Saudi state and the preferred Saudi diplomatic style.

Roughly a decade later President Eisenhower had the idea that Ibn Saud's son and successor could be the Arab leader to rally others in the region against Nasserism, an amazing miscalculation given that King Saud was later obliged to abdicate, making way for his more effective brother, Faisal. During the latter's reign, Saudi standing did increase substantially (this was also the period that saw oil revenues skyrocket), but Faisal was much too shrewd to attempt more than indirect behind-the-scenes diplomacy. Even after Nasser was much reduced in power and influence after the June 1967 War, Faisal wisely made no effort to fill the Arab leadership void.

Actual Saudi diplomacy was much more nuanced. The story of Saudi activities in the regional and world "politics of oil" (e.g. the Organization of Arab Petroleum Exporting Countries [OAPEC], the Organization of Petroleum Exporting Countries [OPEC], the 1973 Arab oil embargo, the Saudi role as swing producer in order to control price) is a subject for another occasion. It is more relevant here to encapsulate Saudi diplomacy in the following terms: Saudi Arabia never (1) sought or accepted a break with a regional adversary if an accommodation, sweetened if necessary by a subsidy, could be reached and, equally, (2) never permitted Arab pressures to force a break with the United States, but also (3) never permitted the United States to push Saudi Arabia forward into an Arab or regional leadership position. The Saudi refusal to go along with the Camp David accords or to work with the United States in putting teeth into the Carter Doctrine by granting base rights for the American Rapid Deployment Force illustrated clearly the limits of Saudi diplomacy.

Kuwait was even more inclined to engage in balance of power diplomacy for protective purposes, surrounded as it was by Iraq, Saudi Arabia, and Iran. Kuwait was the first GCC country to establish formal diplomatic relations with the Soviet Union, and later played the two superpowers off against each other in getting its tankers reflagged during the last years of the Iran-Iraq war. In the same spirit, Kuwait later ordered military materiel from both the United States and the Soviet Union.

The Saudi and Kuwait diplomatic style epitomized that of the entire GCC (with partial exceptions here and there such as the more explicitly pro-western orientation of Oman). It was a defensive, reactive diplomacy with "protection money" paid to potential adversaries (to put it crudely, but then it could be argued that realistic diplomacy involves using whatever resources are available), and keeping lines open to all. It was a realistic stance for vulnerable countries that were too rich not to provoke the envy and greed of their neighbors and too weak to defend themselves with their own resources.

The Iraqi seizure of Kuwait and all that followed destroyed this carefully calibrated policy and confronted Saudi Arabia with a harsh either/or choice (after having presented Kuwait with a even more brutal *fait accompli*). The choice was: would Saudi Arabia, Kuwait and the other states of the GCC stay firmly and explicitly aligned with the United States with all the intractable regional problems (especially that of Israel, the Palestinians and the Arabs) still unresolved? Or would they seek to work their way back to their more cautious policies of the past? Would it be in the American interest to have the GCC states remain as closely aligned as they became during Operation Desert Storm? Or would the earlier, looser arrangements that existed before August 2, 1990, be preferable?

*   *   *   *   *   *

This fleeting account of major developments from 1945 to 1991 hardly reveals an America "acceptable to both sides" or able "to produce positive political results" as Joseph Sisco insisted a decade ago. Rather, the Middle East in these years, as in the past, has been characterized by more than two sides, and none of the parties, regional or outsiders, present very impressive records of positive political results. In this situation of regional near-anarchy, time after time new events heralded as opening a window of opportunity have had a distressing way of fizzling out.

The impressive Palestinian uprising—the *intifada*—against continued Israeli occupation beginning in December 1987 provoked an intense diplomacy leading a year later to the United States agreement to talk with the PLO. Then on May 30, 1990 an abortive raid against Israel by a PLO splinter group, which the PLO leadership disavowed but would not denounce, caused Bush to break off talks with the PLO the following month. For that matter, nothing significant had been accomplished in the previous 18 months of the US-PLO dialogue. Another example, the strange alliance of outside supporters of Lebanese breakaway General Michel Aoun, with Israel and Iraq on the same side for a time, revealed the ever-changing kaleidoscopic alliance pattern in the Middle East.

Thus, the continuation of the old Eastern Question system is dangerous enough, presenting formidable obstacles to peace. Still, the Middle Eastern diplomatic scene might well pass as no more wasteful of human resources in its time than was Machiavelli's Italy, but for a number of other factors that raise the stakes of the game to intolerable levels. Middle Eastern oil makes the area too attractive to outsiders and provides the capital to fund one of modern history's largest arms races. Middle Eastern military expenditures as a percentage of GNP are more than double the world average. Middle Eastern armed forces per 1000 population are almost three times the world average, even higher for the developing world. Year after year, the Middle East places anywhere from six to eight states on the list of the world's top ten spenders, per capita, on the military.

The Middle East has one nuclear power. Others may follow soon. Chemical weapons have already been used. What the world has learned concerning Iraqi developments in both nuclear and biological research that escaped outside monitoring gives added urgency to the old nightmare about Power "X" that goes nuclear or develops biological weapons.

As long ago as October 1973 the second largest tank battle in world history (the first was between the Nazis and the Soviets during World War II) was fought between Egypt and Israel in the empty sands of Sinai, the two armies having been largely provisioned by the two rival superpower blocs. The sheer quantitative dimensions of Operation Desert Shield are too well known to require comment. Yet another sandy waste provided a battleground for over one million combatants.

Exacerbating these problems are the radical changes in the political climate of the Middle East as contrasted with 1945. The great mass of the Middle Eastern population are no longer politically quiescent and are, with limited exceptions, unsatisfied with their governments, their lack of liberty and their feeling of being hemmed in. Moreover, the oil boon is unevenly divided to an extraordinary degree. Kuwait before August 2 had a per capita income more than 25 times that of Egypt. Other things being equal, a reconstructed Kuwait will rapidly reach that level again. Only slightly different proportions hold for the other oil states of the Arabian peninsula. That Saddam Hussein put himself forward as champion of the Arab have-nots was yet another bitter irony. Iraq would be numbered among the haves, if only its leadership had not squandered so much in military expenditures and futile warfare.

As for the United States, there can be little doubt that Operation Desert Storm was largely an American venture. It is so viewed by both friend and foe, within the Middle East and beyond. US officials, supported by public opinion, act as if the United States has most of the high cards, as if only the United States can broker the agreements needed to reach a peaceful resolution of the region's problems, as if the United States must act in this preemptive way to protect its own interests. Is this the case?

The Cold War is over. The major problem now for Russia and for the western alliance is to guard against an overly traumatic aftermath to the breakdown of the Soviet Empire. If the Middle East ever needed protection against Russian incursions, as the US once assumed, such will not be the case for the foreseeable future.

The truly intractable problems are native to the region, even though exacerbated by outside intervention (such as the shameful record of arms sales by both superpowers and a large number of other states).

The entire western world, and for that matter much of the Third World too, has a pressing need for access to Middle Eastern oil at prices that do not fluctuate so violently as to set off economic dislocations. Protecting free world access to Middle Eastern oil has been a stated American goal since President Truman's days, but the overall geopolitical setting has changed. The United States in the years since 1945 has moved from being a net oil exporter to a significant reliance on Middle Eastern oil. That would argue for even greater American concern with the Middle East than in earlier decades.

On the other hand, the United States in the early post-World War II years produced a whopping 40 percent of the total Gross World Product. There was in those years a certain justification for the United States to take on a well-nigh exclusive role of supporting its infinitely weaker allies. Whether the United States undertook too much and for too long can be debated by historians, but this question has limited bearing on the present-day situation.

Economically, the United States is now matched by Japan and the Pacific Rim states on the one hand, by the emerging European Community on the other. To hold its own in this competition the United States will be well advised to find the often demanded "level playing field" by bringing non-productive military and political commitments abroad more in line with those of our competitors. One good way to start in the Middle East might well be to work toward a diplomatic burden-sharing roughly in line with the need of each outside player for Middle Eastern oil. This would result in a significantly increased contribution by Japan and Europe.

Moreover, the United States, simply because of its very assertive policies and presence in past years is not now, and cannot soon become, everyone's choice in the Middle East to play honest broker. The United States has been shown to lack the political will to tackle some Middle Eastern problems, and to lack the political access to tackle others. For the United States to stand back and let Europe, Japan and Russia participate in addressing the problems faced by the Middle East after the Gulf war can not only reduce American diplomatic costs. It may well even increase American leverage, for Middle Eastern players in the Eastern Question game have long been conditioned to mind with special care outside powers that are not fully committed.

Will such a gaggle of outside states matched in number by as many from within the Middle East be able to perform better than American unilateralism? There is reason for pessimism, considering historical precedent, not to mention the basic logic of "belling the cat" diplomacy. Who will come forward to take the risks that, if successful, will produce results shared by all? On the other hand, there are ways to lead by indirection and behind the scenes, ways also to get all or most parties to so time their moves that risks and reward are more nearly equalized.

Voices will be heard insisting that the United States, which took the lead and made the most sacrifices in the Gulf crisis, should not throw away the fruits of victory. Many will claim that, now more than ever, only the United States can produce positive political results. Not so. The fruits of this victory, if it can be so labelled, are the bitter grapes of costly developmental efforts to repair the damage of war plus an imposing political agenda: Creating a more secure Middle East with freedom from domestic or foreign oppression and a more equitable distribution of the region's resources. The United States cannot afford to go it alone. Many who must be brought along are most resistant to American leadership. Many more, even today's allies, fear American hegemony and will work to avoid it. If American hegemony is not a paying proposition in terms of the rigorous diplomatic cost accounting evoked at the beginning of this chapter then why not get out ahead of those Middle Eastern states concerned about the overly stifling American embrace?

Thus, it becomes a question of whether America's Middle Eastern policy is to be more of the same at higher costs and with reduced prospects of gain, or a policy more attuned to this country's true position in the world after the Gulf war. The United States has come a long way since 1945. The results are not all bad and not all good, but it is time to change.

There are those who suggest that, since Operation Desert Storm was basically an American victory (which it was, of course) Americans deserve the trophy. We would respond, as Lord Castlereagh insisted in 1815, " . . . it is not our business to collect trophies, but to try, if we can, to bring the world back to peaceful habits."[8]

Notes

1. L. Carl Brown, *International Politics and the Middle East: Old Rules, Dangerous Game* (Princeton: Princeton University Press, 1984).

2. Daniel Yergin, *Shattered Peace: The Origins of the Cold War and the National Security State* (Boston, 1977).

3. From the *Egyptian Gazette,* May 9, 1966, cited in Adeed and Karen Dawisha (eds.), *The Soviet Union and the Middle East* (New York, 1982), p. 13.

4. There are numerous works by both scholars and participants on one or another facet of these several early mediating efforts. An interesting general study is Saadia Touval, *The Peace Brokers: Mediators in the Arab-Israeli Conflict, 1948-1979* (Princeton: Princeton University Press, 1982).

5. See L. Carl Brown, "The June War: A Turning Point?" in Yehuda Lukacs & Abdalla M. Battah (eds.), *The Arab-Israeli Conflict: Two Decades of Change* (Boulder: Westview Press, 1988), pp. 133-46.

6. Joseph Sisco, "Middle East: Progress or Lost Opportunity?" *Foreign Affairs,* Vol. 61, No. 3 (1982), p. 638.

7. Robert O. Keohane, "Lilliputians' Dilemmas: Small States in International Politics," *International Organization,* Spring 1969, p. 306.

8. Castlereagh's maxim is cited in Henry Kissinger, *A World Restored: Metternich, Castlereagh and the Problem of Peace, 1812-1822, Boston, 1957* (paperback edition 1973), p. 183. Kissinger's early study has much of value concerning what we prefer to call the Eastern Question system. It deserves the attention not just of old-fashioned Eastern Question scholars or for that matter of those seeking to take the measure of Kissinger the man and diplomat but of social scientists interested in the theory and practice of modern diplomacy.

3 OIL DIMENSIONS OF THE GULF CRISIS

Abbas Alnasrawi

The deterioration of relations between Iraq and Kuwait that led to the invasion of Kuwait by Iraq had roots in the drastic changes that took place in the international oil industry in 1973. The sharp increases in the price of oil and the expanded importance of the oil sector transformed Arab economies, leaving them with both new opportunities and new vulnerabilities. Economic and social development plans on an unprecedented scale were launched by oil-producing countries. The future became dependent on continued high oil revenues and a favorable oil market. Decisions on oil pricing acquired an urgency and intensity that had not previously been known, and were treated as matters affecting the destiny of nations. The stage was set for disagreements among oil-producing countries to become sources of conflict.

Some analysts have interpreted the Iraqi invasion as the reassertion of a long-standing Iraqi claim to Kuwait. Yet the invasion of Kuwait took place more than a quarter of a century after an Iraqi government had recognized Kuwait for the first time and established an embassy there. During the 1980s, relations between the two countries had been good on a number of occasions. The invasion of Kuwait and the resurrection of Iraq's territorial claim were precipitated by a bitter dispute over oil issues.

Introduction

Any analysis of the oil dimensions of the Iraqi invasion of Kuwait must start with the oil measures taken by Arab oil-producing countries in October 1973, during the Arab-Israeli war. These measures included the quadrupling of the prices of oil, a cutback in oil production and the imposition of an embargo on oil exports to the United States and the Netherlands. The measures were taken in support of the Egyptian and Syrian war effort, and aimed at obtaining Israel's evacuation of the occupied territories and a resolution of the Palestine problem.

The political objectives of the embargo were short-lived. Only a few weeks after the imposition of the measures, oil-producing countries started to relax them, and by March 1974 all oil restrictions were removed, although their stated political objectives had not been achieved.

In contrast to the failure of the political objectives of the embargo, the quadrupling of oil prices created a new pattern of economic ties between oil-producing countries and the industrialized countries. It also established new relationships between the Arab oil-producing countries and those which did not produce oil.

Consequences of the Oil Price Revolution

For the oil-producing countries, the quadrupling of the prices meant much more than the quadrupling of the revenue per barrel that they received. Net revenue per barrel in the 1950s and 1960s—which had ranged between 75 cents and 85 cents—represented one half of the difference between the cost of production and the posted prices. In the post-1973 oil era, governments of the oil states began to receive the much higher difference between the cost of production and the posted prices, as multinational oil corporations surrendered their concessions to governments.

Suffice it to say that as a result of these changes the oil revenue of Saudi Arabia jumped from $5 billion in 1972, the last full year before the October War, to $35 billion in 1974, the first full year of the new oil prices. In Kuwait, oil income increased from $2 billion to $10 billion and in the United Arab Emirates (UAE) the increase was from $1 billion to $7 billion. Since oil revenue constitutes by far the major source of national income, the sharp and sudden increase in oil prices altered drastically the distribution of income among the Arab states, greatly increasing the gap between the "haves" and the "have nots."

A measure of the new pattern of relations between Arab economies may be seen in the distribution of the GNP of all Arab countries combined. In 1972, the total Arab GNP amounted to $55 billion. By 1975 it jumped to $145 billion—an increase of $90 billion. Of this additional $90 billion, more than one half or 54 percent went to Saudi Arabia, Kuwait and the UAE, which have less than 8 percent of the total Arab population. Another 26 percent went to Iraq, Algeria and Libya, with 21 percent of the Arab population. By contrast, the rest of the Arab world, with 70 percent of the population, received only $15 billion or 17 percent of the increase in Arab GNP.

Another way of looking at the changes between the haves and the have nots is to compare the economies of Egypt, which has 26 percent of the Arab population, and Saudi Arabia, with 5.5 percent. In 1972, Saudi Arabia's total GNP was $6.8 billion, or 86 percent of Egypt's GNP of $7.9 billion. By 1975, the relative importance of the two economies had changed so drastically that Egypt's GNP of $9.3 billion had become a fraction of Saudi Arabia's $40.4 billion. Malcolm Kerr's observation that Egypt had fallen in the shadow of the Gulf is not without its economic basis.[1]

If we consider the relative changes in the income obtained by the Gulf states—Saudi Arabia, Kuwait, the UAE, Qatar, Oman and Bahrain—which are organized in the Gulf Cooperation Council (GCC), we find the following: in 1972 these countries received 26 percent of Arab GNP. By 1975 the ratio increased to 46 percent. The non-oil-producing states saw their share of Arab GNP decline from 44 percent to 26 percent during the same period.

In their attempt to develop and run their economies, the oil-producing states, which had small population bases and a limited labor force, resorted to the importation of workers from other Arab and non-Arab countries. In the 1970s, millions of such workers found employment in the Gulf states. While the workers found such gainful employment to be an important source of income to themselves as individuals, their governments found their remittances to be an important source of income and foreign exchange. In some cases, income from this particular source surpassed export earnings and invariably helped finance a major portion or all of the imports of a country.

It should be stressed that while such benefits are obvious, they were not without their economic and social costs to the labor-exporting countries. One such consequence was the unavoidable shrinkage in the supply of skilled and professional workers, which in turn increased inflation and distorted economic development. Another was the impact remittances had on consumption patterns, since the availability of foreign exchange made it easier to import consumer goods, both durable and non-durable.

The combination of remittance flows, together with economic assistance, gave rise to a new phenomenon of dependency, which might be called derivative or secondary dependency. One group of developing countries became dependent for a considerable part of their foreign exchange earnings on another group of oil-producing developing countries.

The rise in oil income resulted in the transfer by the Gulf of considerable amounts of financial assistance to Arab countries through multilateral organizations such as the Arab Fund for Economic and Social Development (AFESD) or through bilateral arrangements between governments. It should be noted that the bulk of economic aid was provided bilaterally through newly created national funds for external development. Thus data compiled by Mohammad Imady, former director general of AFESD, show that for the period 1974-81 multilateral official development assistance (ODA) amounted to $600 million per year. Bilateral ODA, on the other hand, was $3 billion per year. This in turn gave the donor states the option to slow down or suspend the aid for whatever consideration.[2]

Despite the importance of this assistance to the Arab world by oil-producing countries, the principal new capital relationships established by the rich oil-producing states were with the West. While the Arab region received $30 billion in various forms of economic assistance and loans during the period 1974-81, the accumulated petrodollar surpluses invested in western economies amounted to $350 billion by the end of 1981.

The level of oil production, its prices, and therefore oil revenue were all dependent in the final analysis on the level of demand for Arab oil. This in turn was determined by the economic conditions in and the policies of the industrial countries, as well as the level of supply from non-Arab oil-producing countries. While the dependency status of oil-producing countries is not a new phenomenon, the sharp increase in the size of the oil sector and its share in the national economy had the effect of accentuating and deepening such dependency. Since most oil-producing countries, especially the Gulf states, lacked goods-producing sectors, they found themselves increasingly dependent on foreign imports, which could not be reduced easily in the face of declining oil income. The non oil-producing Arab countries—such as Yemen, Egypt, Jordan, Syria, Sudan and the Palestinians—grew increasingly dependent on remittances and other forms of financial flows coming to them from the Gulf states. As the demand for and/or the price of oil declined so did the oil income and the level of economic activity. This in turn had the effect of reducing financial flows to countries that had already become increasingly dependent on these forms of income. To fill the gap in foreign exchange earnings these countries found themselves resorting increasingly to foreign indebtedness and reducing the scope of social services provided by governments.

Oil prices remained stable for most of the 1970s, but took a sharp upward turn due to developments associated with the Iranian Revolution and the oil policies of the newly established Islamic Republic, and the Iran-Iraq war.

In 1974 the oil income of the OPEC countries was $121 billion and by 1978 it was $136 billion. The Iranian Revolution of 1979 pushed OPEC's income to $203 billion, as a decline in the supply of Iranian oil led to a major price rise. The Iran-Iraq war, which broke out in 1980, pushed prices up again, causing OPEC oil revenues to reach $285 billion in that year and $263 billion in 1981. The price of oil jumped from $13.03 per barrel in 1978 to $34.32 in 1981. Saudi Arabia's oil income increased from $40 billion in 1978 to $116 billion in 1981. Similarly, the UAE's income increased from $9 billion to $19 billion and Kuwait's from $9 billion to $14 billion during the same period.

OPEC Policy and Oil Prices

The Iran-Iraq war also brought to the fore differences within OPEC about the price and supply of oil. Since its founding in 1960, OPEC had traditionally focused on the issue of the price rather than the supply of oil. The immediate reason for its creation had been the unilateral decision by multinational oil companies to lower prices, which automatically lowered government revenue from oil, because government income was fixed at one half of the difference between cost of production and price. Given the rising dependence of the state on its income from oil, any price cut would have an immediate impact on development and the ordinary budgets of oil-producing countries.

Although OPEC failed to persuade the companies to restore prices, its attention remained focused on the price issue to the exclusion of nearly all other issues such as oil development, production regulation, downstream operations, and oil policy coordination. Moreover, because it was founded as a group of sovereign states, OPEC as it evolved did not have powers that were independent from those of member countries. The prerogatives of the sovereign state, and the paramount importance of the state's independence to make decisions, constricted OPEC's scope of action. This meant at first that member countries preferred to make their arrangements with the companies to the exclusion of other countries and OPEC. It was not until 1971 that OPEC member countries negotiated collectively with the oil companies over prices.

This first exercise in collective bargaining resulted in the February 1971 Tehran price agreement.

The Tehran price accord was followed in 1973 by an OPEC-wide decision to fix prices but not output. At that time there was no need to agree on output, since capacity output was in equilibrium with demand. But the quadrupling of oil prices and the conservation measures consequently taken by oil-consuming countries, as well as the emergence of new producing areas outside OPEC, made the task of selling all the oil available at the OPEC fixed price increasingly difficult.

Two Distinct Approaches

Two distinct approaches emerged within OPEC toward the issue of price and supply. One group of countries led by Saudi Arabia favored maintaining stable or relatively low prices, and keeping output at the levels required to sustain these prices. These states were characterized by small populations, large reserves of oil and large capital surpluses, which were primarily invested in the West. Because of their large reserves of oil, they were able to adhere to a strategy of obtaining revenues by pumping oil at relatively low prices, without feeling that they were significantly depleting the value of their oil reserves.

Typically, these countries did not suffer from the burdens of foreign debt and were able to generate balance of payments surpluses. They were politically pro-western, and were clearly interested in maintaining good relations with western countries. They argued that it was in the interests of oil-producing countries to maintain oil prices at levels acceptable to the West, since this would lessen the incentives for western countries to seek alternative forms of energy or to implement more radical conservation policies. Because of their investments in the West, they were also sensitive to the health of the western economies and financial markets, which were adversely affected by rapid oil price rises. Of the OPEC countries, the most dependent on investments in the West was Kuwait, which possessed refining and marketing outlets abroad, in addition to major investments in the western financial markets. From Kuwait's perspective it made little sense to have an integrated international operation and at the same time to restrict its own spare capacity, and supply overseas outlets with expensive crude bought on the international market.[3]

A contrasting position was usually taken by oil-producing countries with smaller reserves and/or large populations and extensive development commitments that consumed oil revenues rapidly. On average, the population size of these countries was larger than in those countries advocating moderate prices, and the level of *per capita* income was smaller. In general, they favored high prices to implement their ambitious development plans and to ensure that the oil revenues on which their plans depended were not eroded by price inflation. Their *per capita* capital surpluses were smaller than the average of those oil-producing countries that favored cautious pricing policies. Countries adopting this approach included Iraq, Iran, Algeria, Libya and Nigeria. The fundamental argument of these countries for higher prices was driven by their short term need for cash and their desire to stretch their reserves by regulating output. The countries in this group were politically heterogeneous, though generally non-aligned, and their ideological range was broad.

An outstanding feature of Arab oil production between the 1973 price changes and the events of the Iranian revolution was the ability of the Saudi government to force its policy of relative price freeze on its reluctant fellow members of OPEC. Whenever other OPEC members advocated an increase in the price, the Saudi government warned that it would raise its oil output (thus increasing its market share and lessening that of other countries) and force prices down. Given the paramount importance of market shares and oil income for each oil-producing country, this tactic proved to be successful. In this respect, the Saudi government was engaged with the United States in an understanding to provide adequate oil supplies at moderate prices—a long-standing objective of United States Middle East oil policy. This situation was described by the General Accounting Office as follows:

> To achieve the U.S. objective of access to adequate supplies at "reasonable prices," the United States uses its bilateral relation-ships with friendly producers in attempts to influence their pricing and production decisions. This is especially apparent with Saudi Arabia with which . . . the United States has a "very active" bilateral policy. Frequent visits by cabinet-level officials, including the Secretaries of State, Treasury, Defense, and Energy, during the past several years illustrate this bilateralism.[4]

Oil Policy in the 1980s

In the course of the Iranian revolution and the Iran-Iraq war, Saudi policy continued to increase output to dampen the unprecedented rise in oil prices and to offset the decline in output caused by the conditions of revolution and war. But the high level of output was subsequently continued at a time when the world market was no longer deprived of all of Iraq's and Iran's oil. This policy of overproduction, which was intended to create an oil glut, was acknowledged publicly in April 1981 by Saudi oil minister Ahmad Zaki Yamani in an interview with the NBC news program *Meet the Press:*

> Q. As a result of conservation, a stagnant economy, and other factors, there is now an oil glut on the international market . . . Would your country have any plans to lower production or to lower prices?

> A: Well, as a matter of fact, this glut was anticipated by Saudi Arabia and almost done by Saudi Arabia. If we were to reduce our production to the level it was at before we started raising it, there would be no glut at all. We engineered the glut and want to see it in order to stabilize the price of oil.[5]

This policy of glut creation prompted Saddam Hussein in 1981 to make the following criticism:

> We direct our friendly but also serious criticism toward some Arab brothers whose production and marketing policies have led to the creation of a glut in the oil market. We cannot possibly find convincing arguments in favor of this policy and its goals. Its harmful effect upon the Arab oil-producing states and others is very clear. If some oil-producing states have financial surpluses, we do not all possess such an accumulation of wealth. We also do not see any wisdom in production that leads to a glut in the oil market.[6]

While the Iraqi president's remarks may be considered as an appeal to the Saudi government to reconsider its production policy, Tayeh Abdel Karim, Iraq's minister of oil and a member of the Revolutionary Command Council, accused the Saudi government of using its oil to prolong the Iran-Iraq war:

> That country's policy of continuing its high output beyond its needs is suicidal and cannot be explained in any terms other than the desire to harm others . . . were it not for the oil glut, which

may have been inspired and planned to prolong the Gulf war and wear down Iraq, the Gulf war would now be over . . .[7]

Taken together, these three statements contain major elements of friction between Iraq and other major oil-producing countries. It was in the context of such perceptions that Kuwait's production policies were later accused by Iraq of threatening its viability.

It is important to stress in this connection that Saudi Arabia has always maintained as a matter of principle that it alone had the sole right to decide on the level of its output. It was not until the second half of the 1980s and mainly in the aftermath of the 1986 price collapse that the Saudi government finally agreed to the adoption of a formal system of quotas, as will be seen later.

The day to face the task of production regulation was postponed by the Iranian revolution and the outbreak of the Iran-Iraq war. But once the initial surge in panic demand was met, the demand for oil and consequently OPEC oil production and revenue resumed their downward trend.

Member countries began to consider the adoption of some form of output regulation or quotas. The changes in the international energy market that OPEC was facing were too structural to be solved by a simple quota system. Moreover, OPEC was caught in a fundamental contradiction of its own in that it wanted to sell its oil at the price it chose to fix. A seller can control either the quantity to be sold, leaving the price to be set by the market, or the price, leaving the determination of the quantity to be sold to be decided by the market. In addition, OPEC had no control over the price or the quantity other producers were bringing to the market. The combination of these conditions forced OPEC to reduce its output from 30.9 million barrels per day in 1979 to 15.4 million barrels per day in 1985, lowering its share of the world total from 47.8 percent to 29.8 percent during the same period. This sharp decline in output resulted in a drastic decline in oil income from $203.2 billion to $127.2 billion between 1979 and 1985.

This sharp decline in output and revenue prompted OPEC to abandon all restraints on output and adopt a new policy to defend and expand its share of the market in order to generate the necessary income for its countries' development. This drastic change in policy was put into effect in early 1986. The new policy proved to be disastrous and had to be discarded as the price of OPEC oil collapsed to less than $10 per barrel (at one point $7 per barrel), causing OPEC oil revenue to decline from $127 billion in 1985 to $77 billion in 1986, although its oil output increased by 20 percent. It should be noted in this context that President Reagan claimed credit for this price collapse when he said that his administration's policies had been responsible for OPEC being dramatically undercut and for the decline in oil prices.[8] But this policy resulted in considerable losses not only to OPEC but to all sectors of the energy industry throughout the world, including the United States.

By October 1986 OPEC had no choice but to abandon its policy of maximizing market share, re-introduce the quota system of production, and return to a fixed pricing system at a level of $18 per barrel for OPEC's reference price. The selection of this particular price was deemed necessary for member countries' social and economic development.[9]

The core point of the policy was that member countries linked their social and economic development to the oil income that was going to be generated by a certain level of output associated with a given price. Hence any attempt by any one member country to produce more than its assigned quota in circumstances where demand remained stable would mean a lower price and lower revenues for members adhering to their quotas, with serious implications for their economic development. The problem would exacerbate the losses already being caused by the decline in the real value of the agreed price of $18 per barrel as a result of inflation and the weakness of the dollar, the currency in which oil is traded internationally.

In the aftermath of the Iran-Iraq war, which came to an end in 1988, there arose a special need for both Iran and Iraq to see their oil income as not only stable but also rising. The economic losses of the war, foreign indebtedness, the requirements of reconstruction, and the need for development tended to narrow the options of these two governments in pursuing their national policies. Before dealing with the implications of this situation for Iraq-Kuwait relations, it will be useful to review some features of the Iraqi economy in the aftermath of the Iran-Iraq war.

The Iran-Iraq War and the Iraqi Economy

In the years following the nationalization of the Iraq Petroleum Company in 1972 and the 1973 oil price explosion, Iraq focused its attention on the development of its infrastructure, its oil sector, and its goods producing sector. It also invested in modernizing and expanding its military. The outbreak of the war found Iraq, due to the availability of foreign exchange, increasing spending on both military and civilian programs. One indicator of such spending may be found in the phenomenal rise in imports from $4.2 billion in 1978 to $20.5 billion in 1981. Military imports rose by 131 percent, while non-military imports rose by 546 percent. Similarly, the value of contracts with foreign enterprises for non-military projects increased from $14.8 billion in 1980 to $24.3 billion in 1981.[10]

This pattern of spending could not be sustained once Iraq's oil-exporting capacity was damaged, which resulted in a sharp decline in oil exports. This and the decline in the price of oil caused Iraq's oil income to fall from a peak of $26.3 billion in 1980 to $7.8 billion in 1983. Such a decline in conjunction with inflation, a rise in import prices, the depletion of foreign reserves, the increase in the size of armed forces, the closure of the Iraq pipeline by Syria, and the shift of the war front to Iraqi soil forced the government to adopt policies of austerity and economic retrenchment.

These policies were reflected in the decision not to start new projects, a drastic reduction in non-defence related spending and reductions in agricultural and industrial investment and imports, restrictions on foreign travel to conserve foreign exchange, and the curtailment of foreign aid. One measure of Iraq's financial difficulties in this period may be seen in the decline in its share of the combined value of projects contracted by members of the Organization of Arab Petroleum Exporting Countries (OAPEC). This share amounted to 17 percent in 1979 and rose to 30 percent in 1980 and 31 percent in 1981. In 1982 it fell to 9 percent and in 1983 it declined further to 2 percent.[11]

One of the significant economic changes in this period was the transformation of Iraq from a creditor country to a debtor country, as it was forced to enter the international financial markets as a borrower in order to meet its foreign exchange requirements to prosecute the war. Iraq was also compelled to devalue the dinar, enlarge the scope of private sector activity, reschedule debts to foreign contractors, and increase its borrowing from Gulf states, mainly Kuwait and Saudi Arabia. By the end of 1982, the extent of this borrowing is estimated to have reached $35 billion.[12]

Changes in imports and debt status do not give a full picture of the destructive effects of the war on the Iraqi economy. In order to arrive at a fuller understanding of the cost of the war, at least three elements have to be taken into consideration: military expenditure, lost oil revenue, and lost gross national product. For the period 1980-1985, military expenditures amounted to $94 billion; lost oil revenue was estimated to be $55.5 billion; and lost GNP was estimated to be $26.2 billion. To the combined cost of these three elements, which amounted to $175.7 billion, should be added the value of the damage to physical assets which has not been made public. Relating the cost of the war to Iraq's GNP during the period, it was found that the annual cost of the war amounted to 87 percent of Iraq's GNP. To put the total cost of the war in another perspective, suffice it to say that it exceeded Iraq's cumulative oil revenue from the time it became an oil exporter in 1931 to 1985.[13]

In short, Iraq emerged from its war with Iran with a devastated economy. Its infrastructure was extensively damaged; oil-exporting facilities were out of commission; its basic industries were destroyed; its goods-producing sectors were heavily damaged; whatever success along the road of economic diversification was achieved prior to 1980 had been stopped and reversed by the long war. Iraq's reliance on food imports increased; its planning policy was disorganized and lacking in investment funds; its reliance on the oil sector increased; the large number of workers imported during the war had become a burden on a smaller economic base; inflation was rampant; privatization was not proceeding according to declared plans and intentions; Arab and foreign capital was not flowing for investment in the economy according to expectations; foreign debt service was constituting a major portion of a declining level of oil income; and multinational capital for the development of already discovered oil fields was not being made available.

Moreover, soon after the war with Iran ended, Iraq opted to focus on the development of its domestic arms industry and an extensive rearmament program which was given a priority claim over the country's limited economic resources. But this claim on resources was in conflict with government promises made during the war that more civilian goods would be made available and higher living standards would be made possible in the postwar period.

In addition to these difficulties, policy makers had to face a number of other problems. One such vexing problem was the ever rising inflation rate. War shortages, the low postwar level of oil income and, therefore, imports, privatization's lack of success, and a stagnant non-military domestic industry were among the factors which contributed to the high postwar inflation rates.

Another and more vexing problem was the problem of foreign debt. The foreign debt was owed to three groups of countries. First, there was the debt to the Arab states. Estimates of this debt vary but they seem to revolve around $40-50 billion, most of which was owed to Saudi Arabia and Kuwait. Second, there was the debt owed to the West, which was estimated at $35 billion by the end of 1989. Another $11 billion was owed to the Soviet Union and Eastern Europe.[14] Given Iraq's low level of oil income and the multiplicity of claims on this income, the question of trying to make arrangements for low service payments became an important one because of the implications of debt payments for the economy as a whole. Any decline in oil revenue would affect Iraq's ability to meet its debt obligations, and its ability to reschedule debts and raise new credits.

It was this problem of how to stabilize and/or raise its oil income which led Iraq to its economic confrontation with Kuwait.

The Oil Dimension of the Iraq-Kuwait Dispute

The oil factor as a source of the dispute between Iraq and Kuwait centered on two issues: the Rumaila oil field which straddles the border between the two countries, and Kuwait's production policies. In the dispute over the Rumaila oil field, Iraq accused Kuwait of taking advantage of Iraq's preoccupation with its war with Iran to use diagonal drilling to extract oil from that part of the oil field which is located in Iraq. This issue was basically a technical one that was transformed into a political dispute. It would almost certainly not have been difficult to make a technical formulation of what belonged to each country.

The second and far more serious dispute between the two countries centered on the production policy of Kuwait and the UAE. It will be recalled that the 1986 OPEC experiment with unrestrained production ended up in price and financial disaster for all countries. To put an end to that policy it was decided to re-establish a reference price of $18 per barrel. In order to stabilize this price the system of quotas was re-introduced. Yet member countries failed to adhere to their quotas and produced above their assigned shares, causing prices to remain well below the agreed-upon reference level—averaging $16.92 per barrel in 1987; $13.22 in 1988; and $15.69 in 1989.

The evolution of crude oil prices in 1989 and the first half of 1990 brought the conflict between price maximizers and output maximizers into sharp relief, with Iraq and Kuwait becoming self-appointed advocates of their preferred approach.

The year 1988 closed with OPEC's oil price hovering around $14 per barrel. This was a significant improvement over its lowest level of less than $12 per barrel, which was reached in October of that year, but considerably below the reference price of $18 per barrel. The upward trend of the price which began in December 1988 continued throughout 1989 when the price rose above the reference to reach $18.84 per barrel in December 1989. This trend continued in the first month of 1990, when the price peaked at $19.98 per barrel. Between January and June 1990, the price fell sharply to $14.02 per barrel—a decline of nearly 30 percent, wiping out a major portion of the oil income of many producing countries.

One of the most significant expressions of the fundamental difference between the two approaches came in the form of a policy statement enunciated by Kuwait's oil minister Ali Khalifa Al-Sabah in February 1990 in which he said:

> First of all, I will tell you that we are producing above quota at the moment. Let us not beat about the bush on that. And I think that our obligation to stay within the quota applies when the price of the OPEC basket is below $18 per barrel and if the price is above $18 per barrel, I think everyone should be producing above quota.[15]

The minister went on to say that he hoped that the current range of $18 per barrel for the OPEC basket would remain in nominal terms for a considerable period of time—at least three or four years. And when asked when he would like to see the OPEC quotas scrapped, his answer was categorical:

> As soon as possible. From a practical standpoint they are already irrelevant, so all that is needed is a recognition of that fact.[16]

Taken together these statements constituted a policy for Kuwait and OPEC based on the following elements: (1) that the price should remain stable in nominal terms at $18 per barrel; (2) that whenever market forces pushed the price above this level, countries with spare capacity should expand their production to bring the price down; and (3) that the quota system should be scrapped. From Kuwait's perspective this policy made eminent sense, given the fact that

Kuwait's production capacity was about 2.5 million barrels per day or 1 million barrels per day above its quota; that its reserves were considerable relative to the size of its population; that it had downstream outlets for its own oil; and that its income from its portfolio investment was considerable. On all these points, Iraq was, so to speak, on the other side of the track in that it had no spare capacity, it wanted to adhere to the quotas, and it had no portfolio income.[17]

Because of the interdependence among oil-producing countries, unilateral action by any country or countries risked reducing the revenues of others by lowering prices. In a downward slide, the price of oil declined by 33 percent between January and June 1990, from nearly $20 per barrel to $13.67 per barrel. This decline triggered a series of reactions by Iraq. In early May 1990, the Ba'th party organ *al-Thawra* carried a statement by Iraq's foreign minister attacking the production policy of Kuwait and the United Arab Emirates.

More important was a statement made on May 30 by Saddam Hussein at the Arab Emergency Summit Conference in Baghdad in which he spoke of the damage inflicted upon the Iraqi economy as a result of lower oil prices. He asserted that for Iraq a drop in the price of oil of $1 per barrel translated into a loss of oil revenue of $1 billion per year. Given the Iraqi government's belief that the market was prepared to pay up to $25 per barrel within two years, this was perceived as causing an enormous loss of potential oil income to Iraq. Particularly significant was the kind of language which he used when he argued that the kind of economic damage experienced by Iraq was similar to that inflicted by conventional wars, in that wars are sometimes carried out by soldiers and sometimes as a result of economic measures. He went on to issue this warning:

> I wish to tell those of our brothers who do not seek war, and those who do not intend to wage war on Iraq, that we cannot tolerate this type of economic warfare which is being waged against Iraq. I believe that all our brothers know our situation and are informed about it and that, God willing, the situation will turn out well. But I say that we have reached a state of affairs where we cannot take the pressure. I believe we will all benefit and the Arab nation will benefit from the principle of adherence to OPEC resolutions on production and prices.[18]

A few weeks later, Iraq's deputy prime minister Saadoun Hamadi announced in Kuwait that the price would go up to $18 per barrel if

Kuwait and the United Arab Emirates refrained from overproducing. Iraq was not the only OPEC member country at this time advocating adherence to OPEC quotas. Indeed, there was a broader effort to pressure these two states to lower their production.[19]

During July, the dispute between Iraq and Kuwait took a decisive turn, escalating as Iraq expanded its list of grievances against Kuwait. In addition to the subjects of levels of production and oil pricing, Iraq raised the issue of the burden of repaying its debts arising from loans made to it by Kuwait during the Iran-Iraq war. Iraq also accused Kuwait of establishing military and police establishments on the Iraqi side of the border.

The levels of oil production were the focus of a meeting in the first part of the month between Iraq, Saudi Arabia, Kuwait, the UAE and Qatar. An agreement was made on July 10 on a Saudi-sponsored proposal for Kuwait and the UAE to reduce their oil output to 1.5 million barrels a day.

Other issues were thrust into center stage in the middle of July, when Iraq stepped up its campaign against Kuwait and the United Arab Emirates and widened its scope against Kuwait. In a memorandum to the League of Arab States Iraq repeated its accusation that Kuwait and the UAE were violating the principle of production quotas, and accused the government of the UAE of participating with the Kuwaiti government in what was described as "a planned operation to flood the oil market with excess production." The Iraqi memorandum accused Kuwait of far more serious acts than mere overproduction. In short:

> As far as the Kuwaiti Government is concerned, its attack on Iraq is a double one. On the one hand Kuwait is attacking Iraq and encroaching on our territory, oil fields and stealing our national wealth. Such action is tantamount to military aggression. On the other hand the Government of Kuwait is determined to cause a collapse of the Iraqi economy during this period when it is confronting the vicious imperialist Zionist threat, which is an aggression no less than military aggression.[20]

In addition to the issues of oil and borders, Iraq also complained of the burden of repaying the Gulf countries for the assistance it received in the early stages of the war with Iran. From the Iraqi perspective, such loans or debts should have been canceled for at least three reasons. First, Iraq maintained that the objective of its war with Iran was not only to defend its own sovereignty but also to defend the eastern flank of the Arab world, and particularly the Gulf region. According to Iraq, this view had been confirmed by the leaders of the Gulf themselves in the strongest of terms. Second, Iraq maintained that Kuwait had benefitted financially from the war because it was able to sell oil at higher prices. Third, the length of the war and therefore its cost had not been foreseen. The military hardware which Iraq had purchased and used in the war had amounted to $102 billion in addition to other enormous military and civilian expenditures.[21]

On July 17 Saddam Hussein spoke of an international campaign waged by imperialists and Zionists to halt Iraq's scientific and technological progress in both the civilian and military fields, and to impoverish Iraq by methods implemented by Arab states in the region:

> By that I mean the new oil policy being followed by some of the rulers of the Gulf states based on the fall in the price of oil . . . against the wishes of the majority of OPEC producers, as well as against the interests of the Arab nation.[22]

As to Iraq's losses, he reiterated the Iraqi argument that a drop of one dollar in the price of a barrel of oil would lead to a fall of $1 billion in Iraq's annual oil revenues. Reflecting Iraq's economic plight as a result of the war with Iran, he said that a few billion dollars could solve much that had been at a standstill or postponed in the life of the Iraqi population. He went on to say that the new policy of lower oil prices was intended to benefit the United States, which had been increasing its imports of Arab oil, and help it to control the destiny of oil producers.

In a memorandum to the Arab League dated July 18, Kuwait rejected Iraq's assertions. The memorandum maintained that Kuwait had a good record in offering aid to Arab states, and that the aid which it had already offered to Iraq was indisputable.

> Perhaps the effective and powerful role played by the various Kuwaiti financial institutions since Kuwait's independence is the best proof that Kuwait has been eager to push the development process forward to meet the legitimate ambitions and interests of the Arab nation. It is known in this respect that Kuwait is at the top of world nations whose aid constitutes the largest percentage

of its national revenues. The lion's share of this aid goes to the fraternal Arab states . . . . Everyone is aware of Kuwait's support for sisterly Iraq.[23]

The memorandum also added that Kuwait had suffered substantial material damage during the Iran-Iraq war, "when it was exposed to direct aggressions that were targeted against its sons, territory, oil installations, oil tankers and trade interests." It rejected responsibility for the decline in oil prices, which the memorandum stated "was caused by a world problem, to which producers, consumers, OPEC and non-OPEC members are parties."

The Kuwaiti government also rejected Iraq's accusations that it had established military and economic installations on Iraqi territory, asserting instead that Iraq had violated Kuwaiti territory. On the Iraqi claim that Kuwait had extracted oil from the southern part of the Iraqi Rumaila oilfield, the Kuwaiti memorandum asserted that Kuwait drilling had been in the "part of the field [which] exists inside the Kuwaiti territories."

Regarding the issues arising from the lack of a border agreement between Kuwait and Iraq, the memorandum proposed that the matter should be referred to "an Arab arbitration committee whose members will agree to decide on the issue of border demarcation on the basis of the charters and documents between Kuwait and Iraq."[24]

On July 25, an OPEC meeting was held in Geneva, in the shadow of the movement of Iraqi troops along the Iraqi-Kuwaiti border. At the meeting, Iraq demanded an oil price of $25 per barrel. Eventually, on July 27, the Kuwaiti government and the rest of OPEC agreed to set a higher reference price of $21 per barrel and adopt new quotas without allowing any member country to exceed its allocated share for any reason whatsoever.[25]

It was arranged that Kuwait and Iraq should have talks in Jeddah to discuss the further unresolved issues, including both the debt owed by Iraq to Kuwait and border disputes. By now, however, the tensions between them had reached a critical point, where further agreements would be difficult. Iraq was interested in using the talks as a means of achieving Kuwaiti concessions on the remaining Iraqi demands, while Kuwait considered the demands unjustified. The talks in Jeddah collapsed on August 1. The Deputy Prime Minister of Iraq, Saadoun Hammadi, made an announcement maintaining that Kuwait was not serious about "redressing the grave damage" inflicted on Iraq.

A Kuwaiti official was reported as saying that the reason for the collapse of the talks was that Kuwait had rejected Iraq's financial and geographic demands.[26]

On August 2, Iraq invaded Kuwait, and its annexation was announced in Baghdad on August 8. Despite Iraq's advancement of a territorial claim to Kuwait, the evidence suggests that the invasion would never have happened had it not been for the bitter dispute over oil pricing and production. Prior to the invasion, Iraq's publicly expressed positions focused on oil, debt and border disputes, not on historical claims to Kuwait. More clearly than most, this was a war with economic origins.

Notes

1. See Malcolm H. Kerr and El Sayed Yassin (eds.), *Rich and Poor Countries in the Middle East: Egypt and the New Arab Order.* Boulder: Westview Press, 1982, p. 1

2. For a discussion of Arab aid flows see Mohammed Imady, "Patterns of Arab Economic Aid to Third World Countries," *Arab Studies Quarterly,* Vol. 6, Nos. 1 & 2 (Winter/Spring), 1984, pp. 75-123.

3. On this point see Nadim Jaber,"What Could Come Out of Jeddah," *Middle East International,* August 3, 1990, p. 5.

4. See General Accounting Office, *The Changing Structure of the International Oil Market,* Washington, 1982, pp. 49-50.

5. See *Middle East Economic Survey,* (MEES), April 27, 1981 (Supplement), p. 1

6. See *MEES,* July 27, 1981, pp. 1-2.

7. *MEES,* September 7, 1981, p. 2

8. See *MEES,* April 21, 1986, p. A7

9. See OPEC, *OPEC Official Resolutions and Press Releases,* 1984-1989, Vienna, 1990, p. 254. Henceforth *OPEC Resolutions.*

10. For a detailed analysis of these issues see Abbas Alnasrawi, "Economic Consequences of the Iraq-Iran War," *Third World Quarterly,* Vol.8, No. 3 (July 1986), pp. 869-895.

11. See OAPEC, *Secretary General's Annual Report,* Kuwait.

12. See The Economist Intelligence Unit, *Quarterly Economic Review of Iraq,* No. 2, 1983, p. 7. See also *Middle East Economic Survey* (MEES), March 14, April 4, May 23, and July 11, 1983.

13. For a more detailed analysis of these cost elements see Alnasrawi, "Economic Consequences." See also Karman Mofid, *The Economic Consequences of the Gulf War,* London: Routledge, 1990.

14. See Keith Bradsher, "War Damages and Old Debts Could Exhaust Iraq's Assets," *The New York Times,* March 1, 1991.

15. *MEES,* February 12, 1990, pp. 1-5.

16. *Ibid.*

17. For an articulation of Iraq's policy see Ramzi Salman, "Iraq's Oil Policy," *MEES,* March 12, 1990, pp. D1-6.

18. See "Documentation on Iraq-Kuwait Crisis," *MEES,* pp. D1-9.

19. See "OPEC lobbies overproducers," *Middle east Economic Digest* (MEED), July 6, 1990, p.9.

20. See "Documentation," p. D5.

21. See "Documentation," p. D6.

22. See "Documentation on Iraq-Kuwait Crisis," *MEES,* July 23, 1990, pp. D1-9.

23. Foreign Broadcast Information Series, *Daily Report—Near East and South Asia,* July 25, 1990.

24. *Ibid*.

25. See *OPEC Bulletin,* September 1990, p. 7.

26. Radio Monte Carlo in Arabic, reported in Foreign Broadcast Information Service, *Daily Report—Near East and South Asia,* August 2, 1990.

PART 2: THE GULF CRISIS AND THE WORLD

4 WASHINGTON'S INTERVENTION IN THE GULF: TOWARD A NEW MIDDLE EAST ORDER?

Michael C. Hudson

Excluding Thomas Jefferson's campaign against the Barbary pirates, the war against Iraq in 1991 was the first American war against an Arab country. That the US was joined by an international coalition including three major Arab countries does not obscure the fact that this was very much an American-led and American-fought war that reduced one of the most developed Arab states, in the words of a UN report, to a "pre-industrial" condition.

How can we explain this extraordinary and uncharacteristically violent American intervention? Traditionally, the US government had based its Middle East policy on three major interests: oil, Israel, and denial of the region to Soviet domination. By August 1990 the third element in this trinity of security concerns was no longer a major worry. But Iraq's occupation of Kuwait rang the alarm bells over oil and Israeli security. By seizing a country that supplied a significant portion of the world's oil supply and that was friendly to the United States, Saddam Hussein crossed a line that had never been crossed previously. Since World War II, the US has regarded the continued production and supply of oil at prices considered reasonable in the West as vital for sustaining economic growth in the industrialized societies. The American need for oil from the Middle East, more-over, is expected to increase as production in the US and Russia continues to decline and as the possibility of major new finds outside the Middle East decreases.[1] American officials were convinced that a failure to evict Iraq from Kuwait, or an outcome in which Iraq might have achieved even a minor advantage from having invaded that country, would have created a situation in which Saudi Arabia and the lesser oil-exporting states of the Gulf would have felt compelled to accommodate Iraqi policies on issues ranging from the production levels and pricing of oil to the settlement of the Arab-Israeli dispute. With Kuwait as its "nineteenth province" Iraq would have controlled some 30 percent of Middle East and 19 percent of world oil reserves.[2]

Iraq's growing challenge to Israel was perhaps most sharply brought home to Washington policymakers by Saddam Hussein's speech of

April 2, 1990, in which he declared that if the US and Britain thought that their criticism of Iraq would provide political cover for another Israeli strike against Iraq (the first having been the Israeli air raid against an Iraqi nuclear facility in 1981) they were mistaken. "Because, by God, we will make the fire eat up half of Israel if it tries to do anything against Iraq," he said.[3] The fire he referred to was not just nuclear but chemical. Coming upon press reports of Iraqi development of various weapons of "mass destruction," and the execution of an Iranian-born British freelance journalist for spying, Iraqi policy appeared to be seeking—at the minimum—a degree of strategic parity with Israel that would give the Arabs the power necessary to bring Israel to accept a just solution of the Palestine problem. The leader of the Palestine Liberation Organization, Yasser Arafat, welcomed Iraq's tough stand at a time when an accommodating Palestinian diplomatic initiative directed toward the US seemed to have come to nought.[4]

These examples of Iraqi capabilities and intentions raised anxieties in Washington, particularly in Congressional circles and among the partisans of Israel. But the Bush Administration sought to avoid a showdown with Iraq. The United States had provided discreet but important support for Iraq during its long war with Iran during the 1980s and appears to have been persuaded by Saddam Hussein's arguments after the war was won that his country was prepared to behave constructively and pragmatically in the region. By July 1990, however, the combination of Iraq's belligerence toward Israel and its sudden bitter quarrel with Kuwait and the United Arab Emirates over their oil export levels began to raise questions among Administration policymakers about an Iraqi threat to oil and to Israel. On July 24 the US dispatched two aerial refueling planes to the UAE and six combat vessels to the Persian Gulf, while issuing a warning to Iraq against "coercion and intimidation."[5] The following day Saddam Hussein summoned without warning US Ambassador April Glaspie for a meeting in which he complained about the deployment of American forces in the Gulf. In response Glaspie reiterated the standing US policy, which was to take no position on Arab-Arab conflicts and to avoid a confrontational relationship with Iraq.[6] "US policy was muddled," writes *Washington Post* reporter Bob Woodward: at the same time some US officials had been "talking tough" about Saddam's threats against Israel, other US officials were trying to block Congressional attempts to impose economic sanctions against Iraq.[7] As Arab efforts to avert an Iraqi move against Kuwait failed and

Saddam Hussein's army overran the tiny emirate, the Administration's policy of trying to accommodate Saddam Hussein was suddenly overwhelmed by the perception that Saddam now had to be stopped and Iraq, if possible, had to be reduced as a regional threat.[8]

1. Effects of the Gulf War on the Region

Eight months later, the crisis was over, the Iraqi invasion repulsed, the war won. The question now became whether the overwhelming military response to that threat had essentially restored the status quo or whether it had set in motion changes in the structure of the Middle East regional system itself. If so, would these changes redound positively or negatively for American security and other interests in the Middle East?

It seems paradoxical that the first application of the New World Order in the Middle East may have resulted in reestablishing and strengthening an old regional order. But the paradox is more apparent than real. The "minimalist" goal of the sanctions and war was to protect Saudi Arabia and the small Arab emirates. But President Bush almost immediately decided to go farther and roll back Iraq's annexation of Kuwait. Of crucial importance from the beginning was the protection of GCC oil reserves from an independent and less-than-friendly Arab state. Most far-reaching was the decision to crush decisively the increasing Iraqi challenge to Israeli military superiority and security. If these were the only results of the Gulf war, one might well conclude that what occurred between August and March was less a historical turning point than a major repair operation, requiring some military surgery, on the Middle East regional system.

Historical turning point or not, the US-led intervention against Iraq's aggression is likely to have broader ramifications, some of which are only beginning to be clear. The United States has learned that a massive intervention can produce unexpected consequences, some of them awkward, even painful. It seems increasingly evident that the structure of the regional state system has been altered well beyond the effects of "normal" interactions. The war has also significantly affected the domestic political environment within the states of the region. And it is at this sociological level that the political outcomes for the US are likely to be problematic. The military campaign produced what is euphemistically called collateral damage; but what kind of collateral damage has been done on the political level?

International relations theory suggests two broad approaches to analyzing this sort of question. One derives from what one might call the classical paradigm, which conceives of states as primary, unitary, and rational actors seeking security through power in an environment marked by anarchy. This is what is commonly known as the realist approach, and it focuses on strategic relationships. The other approach is sometimes dubbed "behavioral" or "sociological," and it takes individuals rather than states as the unit of analysis. It seeks to explain the foreign policy behavior of leaders by examining the social, economic, and psychological factors bearing on their decision-making. Here the focus of analytic attention is the domestic environment. Classical analysts are often called "tough" or "hard" because they deal with concepts such as military capacity, the balance of power, threats, and interests. Behavioral theorists are sometimes called "soft" because they deal with amorphous factors like values, ideology, public opinion, perceptions, images, attitudes, social tensions, inequalities, the psychology of leadership, and the like. Let us try to calculate, first, whether the Gulf war has significantly altered Middle Eastern realities in these two domains; and second, the prospects for the New World Order in the Middle East proclaimed by the Bush Administration.

A. *The State System Level*

The Iraq-Kuwait crisis created a moment of opportunity for the United States to deepen western hegemony over the Gulf in particular and the Middle East in general. Unchallenged militarily or strategically in the world since the collapse of the Soviet empire, Washington aimed at the construction of a stable New Middle East Order anchored in Riyadh, Cairo, and Damascus. Perhaps even more important than the Arab partners are the non-Arab members: Turkey and—at one remove—Israel. This is a formidable set of allies, possessing as they do oil, water, money, manpower, and military capacity quite in excess of any combination of the Arab countries outside the coalition. The governments outside the coalition are not as cohesive or united as the coalition members: all they share is the distinction of having not been on the winning side, as well as poverty and a host of socio-economic problems. They depend on the industrialized powers for financial and material resources, so they are not in a very good position to press their political disagreements. In terms of conventional realist perspective in international relations, it thus seems likely that Washington's New Middle East Order will indeed succeed in keeping order.

Analysts with a sense of history, however, might have reservations. Secretaries of State from Acheson to Haig tried repeatedly to establish or encourage NATO-style regional security organizations—MEDO, the Baghdad Pact, the Eisenhower Doctrine, the Islamic Group, the strategic consensus. All came to nought. Popular ideological resistance accounted for much of the failure but there were also factors arising out of the regional and international system. In the region, owing to the workings of the balance of power, a counter-coalition with a strong leader—Egypt—arose to challenge the western scheme. On the international level, again owing to the workings of the balance of power, a strong competitor—the Soviet Union—supported the regional competitor. The fact that in the aftermath of the Gulf war, there was no strong leader for a counter-coalition of "have not" countries, since Iraq was destroyed and Egypt and Syria coopted, clearly gave hope to the proponents of Washington's new strategy. Even more important was the non-existence any longer of a serious counterweight (militarily and strategically) to the United States on the world stage.

Nevertheless, it is far from clear that peace and quiet will now set in on the turbulent Middle East. The crippling of Iraq as a regional power for the immediate future may reduce an overt threat from that quarter to the Arab oil-exporting monarchies, but it also leaves Iran as the dominant state in the Gulf. In addition, inter-Arab state quarrels could become more intense. The regional winners may attempt to punish the losers in a way that leads to local conflicts: the Saudi-Yemeni relationship, for example, may well deteriorate to the point where it endangers regional security. For their part, regimes or elements in the "losing" countries may resort to subversion and internal destabilization toward some of the winning countries. The Gulf war has caused, or revealed, for the first time, a serious conflict among different Arab peoples, and not just between governments or leaders. The possibility of messy regional strife, within and between countries on both sides of the new divide, may challenge the new Pax Americana.

B. *The Popular Level*

In addition to inflamed interstate rivalries, the new Middle East order could also be marked by internal unrest fueled ironically by its very instrument of "order"—Washington's higher profile and expanded presence. The internal political arenas are likely to be more volatile in the post-Gulf war period than before; and populations will be more mobilizable in radical causes. Some of the factors creating this new volatility were evident before August 2, 1990. Economic indicators show a general downturn that dates from the collapse of oil prices in the mid-1980s. Growth in GNP, GNP per capita, and direct investment has slowed, while inflation, unemployment, and debt have increased.[9] The Gulf crisis has delivered a devastating body blow to growth, prosperity, and the quality of life, not just in Iraq and Kuwait but throughout the region. In December 1990, four months into the crisis and before the war itself, a World Bank official was estimating a loss of $40 billion to Middle East and affected Third World countries in terms of displacement of persons, lost employment income and remittances, and secondary effects such as the collapse of tourism.[10] The costs of the war itself obviously far exceeded even those catastrophic indicators. Estimates of the number of Iraqi military deaths ranged between 30,000 and 100,000.[11] Iraqi civilian deaths during the war might have been as low as 3,000, but tens of thousands may have died in the Shi'ite and Kurdish uprisings after the war. The UN Secretary-General's special representative for humanitarian efforts in Iraq warned in September 1991 that, without an unfreezing of Iraqi assets, the country would face "massive malnutrition and hunger," and "epidemics of staggering proportions."[12] The cost of cleaning up the oil fires in Kuwait was estimated at $1.2 billion. Saudi Arabia agreed to pay the United States nearly $20 billion as its share of the costs of Operation Desert Storm.[13] At the end of March 1991, according to the UN, twenty-one particularly severely affected countries had reported a loss of more than $30 billion as a result of complying with the UN-imposed sanctions against Iraq.[14] According to the World Bank, the cumulative negative impact of the crisis through June 1991 on Turkey, Egypt and Jordan was thought to be between $12 billion and $15 billion.[15] The Jordanian losses alone were estimated at $1 billion in 1990 and $2.5 billion for 1991.[16] The International Labor Organization reported that some two million migrant workers and their families fled Iraq and Kuwait during the war.[17] Hundreds of thousands of Yemenis were expelled from Saudi Arabia.

One likely result of such socioeconomic reverses is frustration, anger, and even political unrest on the part of affected populations. For their part, Middle Eastern governments are deeply concerned about possible instability. Intelligence services across the Middle East have gone on higher alert as regimes calculate the possibilities of new social and political turmoil. During the war demonstrations occurred in Morocco, Algeria, Tunisia, Libya, Sudan, Yemen, Jordan, and the Israeli-occupied Palestinian territories. According to western as well as local observers, anti-American sentiment was evident even in the capitals of Arab members of the coalition—Egypt and Syria—whose security services were trying to discourage public expressions of dissent. Islamic radical movements sided against Washington and gained strength. American policymakers presumably hoped that postwar socioeconomic distress in Iraq would bring down the regime of Saddam Hussein without leading to chaos and fragmentation in Iraq itself; but in the immediate postwar period, it was the opposite that occurred. The government in liberated Kuwait, where Washington wanted stability, appeared to have suffered a significant political setback. The State Department may well have had mixed feelings about the postwar strains on governments in traditionally friendly countries like Jordan, Yemen, and Tunisia, even though they had criticized the US-led military intervention.

Notwithstanding all the damage, there has been speculation that the New World Order at the popular level could help bring forth a new era of political participation. Some liberal Arab intellectuals argue that democratization is the only way for the Arab world to heal the wounds of the war and resume the slow march toward a better quality of life. Before August 2, 1990, one could almost sense the onset of "an Arab spring," with significant political openings having occurred in Egypt, Algeria, Yemen, Jordan, and Tunisia.[18] But in countries where some freedom of expression was possible, public opinion was largely against the use of western troops in the Gulf war. Even in Egypt, despite the acrimony involving Egyptian migrant workers in Iraq, the substantial rewards offered for membership in the coalition, and the official discouragement of opposition voices, there was significant criticism. Several months after the fighting ended such criticism appeared to be growing in many parts of the Arab and Islamic world as the messy results of the war became better-understood: Iraq appeared to be less of a threat to the Gulf states, yet the suffering of the Iraqi people was increasing because of the international sanctions; and America's prestige was becoming more dependent on its ability to resolve the Arab-Israeli conflict.

It would be plausible, therefore, to expect that governments which find continuing criticism of the New World Order embarrassing for one reason or another may not be encouraged to open the doors of public discussion further. So rather than promoting democracy in places like Saudi Arabia or Egypt, the Gulf war may come to have the opposite effect. In Kuwait, longstanding discontent with the government's autocratic ways intensified immediately after the war, but the government (after agreeing under pressure to hold parliamentary elections in 1992) appeared determined to maintain a traditional system of rule. Even Jordan, which has gone farther than others in allowing public expression, may find that the sentiments expressed complicate its desperate need to restore working relations with the US and Arab coalition members. As incumbent regimes, elites, and *mukhabarats* (intelligence services) strive to maintain control (in most cases with US encouragement), Arab politics may sink back into the vicious circle of repression, tension, and instability. That is the bad news. The good news is that it is a *sine qua non* of official US policy (in theory at least) to encourage democracy everywhere — including, one would suppose, in the Middle East.

2. Challenges for US Policy in the "New Middle East Order"

Reflecting on the victory over Iraq, President Bush declared that a New World Order in the Middle East required the US to assume "a responsibility imposed by our successes."[19] Its four tenets, he asserted, were "peaceful settlements of disputes, solidarity against aggression, reduced and controlled arsenals, and just treatment of all peoples."

If the Gulf war itself was one of the first manifestations of the New World Order, it was hardly an example of a "peaceful settlement" of the dispute between Iraq and Kuwait. Nor was there wall-to-wall solidarity behind Mr. Bush's response to Iraq's aggression: despite the active participation of Saudi Arabia (and its ministate neighbors), Egypt, and Syria, nearly half the member states of the Arab League opposed the military campaign. Countries in which there were significant popular protests against the war accounted for over half the population of the Arab world. As for "reduced and controlled arsenals," it seemed clear that the new era of US-Soviet cooperation had not induced Iraq to reduce or control *its* arsenal, which therefore necessitated a massive use of the American arsenal to cut Iraq's military power down to size. Mr. Bush's last tenet, "the just treatment of all peoples," was decisively demonstrated, and rightly so, in the liberation of Kuwait; let us not minimize President Bush's success in restoring the sovereignty and rights of the 700,000 Kuwaitis. Just treatment was also accorded to the Israeli people. But let us not minimize either the "collateral damage" suffered by other peoples in the process: Kurds, Palestinians, North Africans, Yemenis, Jordanians, and innocent Iraqis (Sunni, Shi'ite, and Kurdish).

But, recalling the adage that a few eggs have to be broken to make an omelet, perhaps we should ask if the war in the Gulf will make it easier to achieve these goals in the future? And will the United States in fact shoulder these new responsibilities? Let us look first at the "peaceful settlement of disputes." Certainly there is no shortage of disputes in the Middle East for which a settlement—especially a peaceful settlement—might earnestly be hoped. At the top of the list is the Arab-Israeli dispute. Peaceful resolution of this festering problem will be the necessary—and perhaps sufficient—test of the proposed New World Order in the Middle East. According to New World Order proponents, the United States reaped from the Gulf war a bountiful harvest of influence, leverage, and clout. With Saudi Arabia, Egypt, and Syria lined up on the Arab side in Washington's coalition, it should be possible to offer Israel, eventually, formal recognition and normalization of relations with these countries; and that should be an inducement to Israel to make concessions toward the Palestinians under occupation. According to this analysis, there is no significant Arab militant opposition left.

Washington's track record on the Palestine problem provides no grounds for optimism. Despite numerous initiatives dating back to the very establishment of Israel, US partisanship in favor of the Jewish state has ultimately crippled American diplomacy. America's failure to address fairly the grievances and rights of the Palestinian people has, on the one hand, emboldened Israeli governments (especially during the ascendancy of the right-wing Likud bloc) to take rigid and extravagant positions while, on the other, it has sowed deep anger and distrust on the part of the Arabs. Reflecting their despair, the Palestinians in the occupied territories launched their uprising—the *intifada*—in 1987, employing the only weapon at hand—stones—against one of the world's most formidable military establishments. Even the best-intentioned, best-informed American President, Jimmy Carter, whose Camp David initiative was the most successful of all American efforts, failed in his effort to bring the Palestinian issue to a just and acceptable conclusion.

Carter's Palestinian project was undermined by an intransigent Israeli government. Would the project launched after the Gulf war meet the same fate? Confounding the skeptics, Bush wasted little time after the Gulf war victory in pushing ahead with the same vigor that characterized his prosecution of the war. Through the diligent efforts of Secretary of State James Baker, significant progress was made in convening an Arab-Israeli peace conference featuring both international participation and direct Arab-Israeli negotiations. Unlike his more timid predecessors and advisors, the President and the Secretary appeared to be committed to the idea of a comprehensive solution. The project gained wide support from most of the key Arab governments—not just the Gulf war coalition partners, but also Jordan and others that had opposed the US military intervention. The Palestinians, weakened even further by Palestine Liberation Organization Chairman Yasser Arafat's handling of the Gulf crisis, were willing—albeit reluctantly—to join in a process that was likely to yield results far short of their aspirations. Unprecedented pressure by the Bush Administration on the Israeli government made it at least thinkable that a peaceful settlement might eventually be achieved, despite the historical record and the power of Israel's lobby in the US Congress.

Important as it is, the Arab-Israeli problem is not the only dispute racking the Middle East. There is also the ongoing matter of Gulf security. If the Gulf war had any rationale, it was surely to settle this problem. The Gulf leaders presumably have been able to sleep easier, knowing that the New World Order, in the form of a far more institutionalized American political and military presence, will protect them from external dangers. Iraq, it would seem, no longer represents much of a danger, at least in terms of an overt military threat. Yet the expectations held in Washington and elsewhere that the Gulf security problem had been "solved" were being scaled down only months after the end of the war. Although badly bloodied, the Iraqi government had survived the defeat, and officials in the Gulf Cooperation Council states—especially Kuwait—could not be insensible to the possibility of Iraqi-inspired conspiracies, internal unrest and even terrorism. Paradoxically, however, the possibility remained that Iraq itself could disintegrate politically, something that the neighboring states did not appear to want, yet might be prepared to exploit. Iran, by default, had emerged as the strongest power in the Gulf, and even though President Hashemi Rafsanjani appeared to be less threatening than the late Ayatollah Khomeini, the Arab Gulf states were not entirely sanguine about Teheran's future intentions. The re-establishment of diplomatic relations between Riyadh and Teheran, according to a Saudi diplomat, was less a sign of trust than one of prudence on Saudi Arabia's part.[20] At the same time, the postwar security formula endorsed by the US under which Egypt and Syria would provide a limited military presence in the GCC countries was received so coolly by those countries that Egypt and Syria decided to withdraw their forces, leaving them without any formalized regional support. In addition, the rift between Saudi Arabia and neighboring Yemen was greatly aggravated by the Gulf war, increasing the possibility of overt border conflict between the two largest states in the Arabian peninsula.

A second tenet of Washington's New World Order—"solidarity against aggression"—is intended to deter these kinds of tensions from erupting into open conflict. The principle of collective security, rarely effective in the Middle East in the past, commits the states of the region to unite against aggression against any one of them. But can such solidarity be achieved in the Gulf and the Arabian peninsula? What if either Saudi Arabia or Yemen occupied border zones of the other? The beauty of *the theory* of collective security, of course, is that because all actors are so utterly certain that their aggression will be met with military punishment, they never commit aggression in the first place. Utter certainty, however, is a scarce commodity in Middle East regional politics.

A third tenet in President Bush's exposition of a New World Order was "reduced and controlled arsenals." In recent years, the Middle East was perhaps the most arms-rich region on the globe, with the possible exception of Central Europe during the Cold War. Middle East countries regularly dominated the top ten countries in terms of military expenditures per capita and as a percentage of GNP or government budgets. Qualitatively, Israel's army is rated as one of the best in the world. Quantitatively, the military machines in Egypt, Syria, Turkey, Iran, and (until recently) Iraq were counted in the hundreds of thousands of troops, tens of thousands of tanks and armored personnel carriers, and thousands of fighter and bomber aircraft (some quite modern). Worrisome to western strategists in recent years was the appearance of medium and long-range missiles, chemical warfare capabilities, and nuclear weapons potentialities. Worrisome to regional development specialists was the vast proportion of public spending on military hardware when there were so many pressing social and economic needs.

Operation Desert Storm was, among other things, an exercise in selective disarmament. With Iraq's present and future military capabilities significantly limited, attention has turned to region-wide arms control efforts. Analysts including William B. Quandt have proposed an ongoing regional conference, modeled on the Conference on Security and Cooperation in Europe, that would tackle arms control along with other key issues, such as the Palestine problem.[21] The record on Middle East arms control goes back at least to the

1950 Tripartite Agreement between the US, Britain, and France, and success—to say the least—has been limited. Better prospects for arms limitations would require at least three new developments. First, the major world powers would need to agree to no longer underwrite arms acquisitions in furtherance of their respective clients in the region. Second, in addition to the elimination of a regional bully (Iraq), the successful institutionalization of the regional security system based on the anti-Iraq coalition would be necessary in order to reduce the security fears of states in the region, removing the main incentive for heavy military spending and buildup. Third, governments would need to be convinced that the economic and financial damage to the region as a whole resulting from the Gulf crisis and war should bring about the diversion of expenditures from military to social development purposes.

After the war finished, however, Saudi Arabia and other Gulf states advanced vast new military purchase plans. Israel was demanding increases in military assistance from the US. Egypt and Syria are not planning to reduce their military establishments. Why is the arms race continuing? Let us not be so cynical as to consider that government officials as well as arms sellers might be driven by the desire to make a great deal of money. Nor let us speculate that it might have something to do with the continued availability of military hardware. Absurd as it seems, countries manufacturing advanced arms—even the United States—will continue to sell them, even when they are calling for arms reduction. Perhaps the most important reason is that Middle East governments continue to feel insecure even though one major threat has been much reduced.

For example, the government of Kuwait, the chief beneficiary of the war, still fears Iraq and requests the indefinite stationing of American military forces. A major expansion of the Kuwaiti armed forces seems likely. Countries that did not join the coalition appear apprehensive about the intentions of the victorious countries that did; thus, it would not be surprising if Yemen, impoverished as it is, might try to strengthen its armed forces because Saudi Arabia is expanding its own. By all accounts, Jordan feels less secure now than it did before August 2, 1990; will it reduce its arms if its increasingly unfriendly neighbors are increasing theirs? Will Sudan, which has a military government, feel that it is more secure now *vis à vis* Egypt and thus be amenable to an arms control regime? The PLO, a very big loser in the war, presumably can ill afford to maintain such military capacity as it possesses, but there is no sign that it is willing to reduce what is left of its capability for armed struggle. Some militant Palestinians under occupation seem actually to be escalating the use of the rudimentary arms available to them—moving from stones to knives and the occasional handgun. Egyptian officials may well feel that their role as a regional policeman in the new Middle East order requires a qualitative and perhaps quantitative buildup. Syria presumably feels that the threat from the Iraqi army has receded, but do Syrians feel sanguine enough about their relations with other neighbors to reduce their military budget? Perhaps the longstanding Israeli strategic threat is lower now, but are Syrians confident enough that this is the case for them to contemplate a "reduced arsenal" and a drawdown of their forces in Lebanon?

Finally, in calculating the prospects for "reduced and controlled arsenals," we must at least raise the question of *internal* as well as external security. A major function of Arab military establishments is, of course, internal security. In light of all that has happened because of the Gulf war in the domestic arena of countries across the area—economic hardship, social dislocation, political tension—there is probably not a regime from the Atlantic to the Gulf that does not worry more about internal instability now than it did before August 2.

The fourth tenet of the New World Order, as described by President Bush, was the "just treatment of all peoples." As has already been noted, the war itself meted out just treatment to some people but not to others. But let us recognize that the rights of different people may conflict, and that we cannot hold the New World Order to perfect standards of justice. Moreover, the record of two of President Bush's illustrious predecessors, Woodrow Wilson and Franklin Roosevelt, who expounded their own new world order projects, was less than sterling when it came to providing justice to the peoples of the Middle East. This said, has the groundwork finally been laid for more just treatment of peoples in the Middle East? More specifically, what grounds are there to expect that the new hegemonic coalition (the US plus its key Arab and other partners) is going to deal effectively with some of the major cases of unjust treatment of peoples in the area? One compelling issue involves assisting or compensating the peoples who have suffered significantly because of the war. What will be done to alleviate the suffering and restore the previous quality of life for Kurds, Iraqi Arabs, Palestinians, Yemenis, Sudanese, and North Africans? Perhaps it is too early to expect much, but so far there has been rather little sign of movement—except in the case of the Kurds—on Washington's part.

The main issue involving the just treatment of peoples in this region is, of course, the Palestinian case. Because it is so fundamental, the US hope for a New World Order in the Middle East will stand or fall depending on whether it can lead to some "just treatment" for Palestinians—treatment which they have long been denied. The most optimistic scenario for this problem rests on the proposition that the US Administration is prepared to make an extraordinary effort to alleviate the injustice perpetrated on the Palestinians in a manner consistent with Israel's security. At a moment of maximum leverage with key Arab governments from the coalition—plus Jordan and the PLO—the Arab side presents fewer problems than the Israeli does. But the Israeli government, under pressure from the political right wing, is not likely to be easily amenable to the kind of concessions that would be necessary to achieve peace with the Arab world. And with the afterglow of military success fading following the Kurdish and Shi'ite uprisings and Iraqi government resistance to UN-mandated inspections, the window of opportunity may close sooner than one would wish.

Finally, and paradoxically, the very fact of an American military victory over a major Arab country may contribute to the loss of one key element in the "just treatment of peoples": their independence and sense of dignity. Whether in Saudi Arabia, Iraq, Egypt, or Algeria, Arabs realize that they have fallen under the hegemony of a western power to an extent comparable to the era of Pax Britannica. Under the new Pax Americana, Washington already thinks of itself as the dispenser of "just treatment." Arabs have lost a great deal of control over their own destinies; if they want just treatment they will have to petition for it. As the Gulf war fades into the past the key question will be how the Arab governments and peoples will react to the increased influence of the US in the area.

Notes

1. For geologic reasons among others, the dominant position of the Middle East as a world oil supplier is likely to continue. See C.D. Masters, D.H. Root, and E.D. Attanasi, "Resource Constraints in Petroleum Production Potential," *Science,* 253, July 19, 1991, pp. 146-52.

2. Michael C. Hudson and Bernard J. Picchi, *Crisis in the Persian Gulf: Political Causes and Oil Market Effects* (New York: Salomon Brothers, 1990), p.14.

3. Alan Cowell, "Iraq Chief, Boasting of Poison Gas, Warns of Disaster if Israelis Strike," *The New York Times,* April 3, 1990, p.1.

4. Interview by the author with Yasser Arafat, Baghdad, June 14, 1990.

5. *The Washington Post,* July 25, 1991.

6. See *The Washington Post,* July 26, 1990. The Glaspie meeting with Saddam became the focus of controversy between the opponents and supporters of the pre-August 2 US policy toward Iraq. In her testimony to Congress in March 1991, Glaspie defended her statements as representative of US policy, insisted that she made it clear to Saddam Hussein that disputes must be settled peacefully, and charged that the Iraqi government's transcript of the meeting distorted her role. *The New York Times,* March 19, 1991.

7. Bob Woodward, *The Commanders* (New York: Simon and Schuster, 1991), p.211.

8. According to Woodward, *op. cit.,* pp. 260-61, 318-26, and *passim,* President Bush from the outset was more "hawkish" than some of his advisors about the need not only to defend Saudi Arabia but to reverse Saddam's seizure of Kuwait.

9. See, e.g., the statistics drawn from World Bank, UNESCO, UN, and CIA publications presented in Hudson and Picchi, pp. 10-13.

10. Presentation by Mr. Ram Chopra of The World Bank to the Carter Center Consultation on Economic Development in the Middle East, Atlanta, Georgia, November 29, 1990.

11. "How Many Iraqi Soldiers Died?" *Time,* June 17, 1991, p.26.

12. Sadruddin Aga Khan, "Help Iraq Help Its People," *The New York Times,* September 14, 1991.

13. Thomas W. Lippman, "Lawmakers Want Saudi IOU Paid in Oil," *The Washington Post,* September 26, 1991.

14. "The Spoils of War," *UN Chronicle,* June 1991, pp. 16-18. The countries were Bangladesh, Bulgaria, Czechoslovakia, Djibouti, India, Jordan, Lebanon, Mauritania, Pakistan, Philippines, Poland, Romania, Seychelles, Sri Lanka, Sudan, Syria, Tunisia, Uruguay, Viet Nam, Yemen, and Yugoslavia.

15. The World Bank, *Annual Report, 1991,* as cited in *World Bank News,* September 19, 1991, p. 7.

16. According to The World Bank and the International Monetary Fund, as reported by the Jordan Information Office in Washington, September 1991.

17. *UN Chronicle, op. cit.,* p.18.

18. See Michael C. Hudson, "After the Gulf War: Prospects for Democratization in the Arab World," *Middle East Journal,* 45 (Summer 1991), pp. 407-26; and Louis J. Cantori *et al.,* "Democratization in the Middle East," *American-Arab Affairs,* 36 (Spring 1991), pp. 1-30.

19. President George Bush in a speech in Alabama on April 12, 1991, cited in *The New York Times,* April 13, 1991.

20. Conversation with an official of the Saudi Arabian Embassy in Washington, DC on September 23, 1991.

21. For an elaboration of this idea see the "Statement of Purpose" by the Initiative for Peace and Cooperation in the Middle East, a project of the non-profit organization Search for Common Ground, Washington, DC, September 1991.

5 SOVIET POLICY AND THE GULF CRISIS*

Yelena S. Melkumyan

The Gulf crisis of 1990 demonstrated the dramatic reversal that had taken place in the international policies of the Soviet Union since the time of the Cold War. During the 1961 Iraqi-Kuwaiti crisis, the Soviet Union had taken the side of Iraq when its leader, Abdul-Karim Qasim, advanced an Iraqi claim to Kuwait, claiming it to be an integral part of Iraqi territory. On two occasions the Soviet Union used its veto power as a permanent member of the UN Security Council to block the admission of the newly independent Kuwait to the ranks of the UN General Assembly.

In 1990, the policy of the Soviet Union was completely different. It cooperated with the United States in establishing an international boycott of Iraq after its invasion of Kuwait. In the United Nations, it supported American-initiated resolutions condemning Iraq and legitimating the use of force against the occupying Iraqi army if it did not leave Kuwait.

The Gulf crisis of 1990–91 crystallized the changes that had taken place in the international system since the end of the Cold War. It can be seen as a turning point marking a shift in the pattern of global confrontation from an East-West to a North-South direction. East-West relations had advanced from a stage of political confrontation and military rivalry to one of mutual understanding and interaction.

The changes in Soviet policy were driven by the political transformation of the Soviet Union. By 1990, cooperation with the West was a major aim of the Soviet leadership, which was concerned with ending the arms race, obtaining western understanding for Soviet policies toward republics seeking independence, and seeking economic and technical assistance for the crucial goal of the economic restructuring of the Soviet Union. With the end of the Cold War, the Soviet Union was reconsidering its relations with militant Arab states, especially where these had required substantial Soviet aid. It had increased its interest in developing relations with Middle Eastern oil-producing states. More than ever before, the Middle East was a region where the Soviet Union was prepared to cooperate with, not compete with, the United States.

---

* Translated and edited by Garay Menicucci

76

1. The Background

At the time of the Gulf crisis, the Soviet Union was at a historical turning point. The need for domestic transformation was an all-encompassing priority. The chief concerns of the Soviet leadership were the implementation of fundamental reforms of the political and legal systems, the democratization of social life, the introduction of a multiparty system, and the establishment of the freedom of the press.

With the help of the United States, the Soviet Union hoped to become a full-fledged member of the world community and to be included in the system of global economic links. It was in the midst of a deep economic crisis from which there was no possible exit without outside help. The Soviet Union considered that the United States and other leading governments in the world could render it necessary financial support, as well as scientific and technical cooperation in carrying out structural changes in the economy, with accompanying assistance in training the labor force with the necessary skills. It also sought most favored trading status and the lifting of existing restrictions on its participation in various international economic organizations. The Soviet leaders hoped that with assistance from the West, they could succeed in preserving a single economic framework within a renovated union established on the basis of the mutual interests of all of the republics in drawing up policies to deal with the economic problems facing them.

There were important political differences between the old and the new political forces, and these influenced the evolution of Soviet policy toward the Gulf crisis. The Communist Party still retained full power, and the President of the USSR was still simultaneously the General Secretary of the Communist Party. Party members filled practically all the seats in the Supreme Soviet and commanded majorities in the parliaments in the republics. The implementation of reforms was being dragged out as the *nomenklatura* (high party officials) and the party apparatus continued to retain political and economic power.

Political polarization was occurring on different levels and in different spheres. Soviet society was divided into a multitude of political splinter groups ranging from the extreme radicals to the extreme conservatives. While the new political parties were weak, a similar process of division was occurring inside the Communist Party.

Three blocs of forces reflected the existing political directions—
the center, led by Gorbachev; the democratic opposition, which was
associated in the Russian Republic with Boris Yeltsin; and the
conservative forces, which were grouped together in a number of
neo-Bolshevik associations.

The central leadership considered it necessary to introduce economic
reforms in stages directed toward creating a mixed economy combining
a market with government regulation. It stood for preserving the
union government with expanded rights for the republics, but also
for guaranteeing the political unity of society. It characteristically
oscillated back and forth from the side of the democratic opposition
to the side of the conservatives.

The democratic opposition called for the liquidation of the Communist Party's monopoly on power and for the accelerated development
of a market economy, including limits on state interference in the
nation's agriculture. It strongly supported the attempt of the Soviet
Union to strengthen cooperation with the United States and other
western governments, and called for radical reductions in the size of
the armed forces and a reduction in military spending. Representatives
from the democratic bloc considered that Soviet national security
would be best guaranteed by organizing fruitful cooperation with
western countries which, they believed, did not pose any threat to the
Soviet Union.

The conservative forces, unwilling to reconcile themselves with
the "capitalization" of social and economic relations, declared the
necessity of returning to the principles which governed Soviet domestic
policies and foreign policy before *perestroika*. They considered that
the Soviet Union was betraying its own state interests by reducing its
military forces and armaments and thereby weakening its own armed
potential. Their view was that the Soviet Union's new foreign policy
line served the interests of the West, which they believed sought the
disintegration of the Soviet state. Conservative forces accused the
Soviet leadership of obliging the US in a way that facilitated the
dissolution of the Warsaw Pact, and threatened further inroads into
socialism.

Another internal factor influencing the Soviet leadership at the
time of the Gulf crisis was the national question, which stood at the
center of political struggles in the republics. Regardless of which of
the political forces were currently dominant in one or another of the
allied republics, all of them—both the communists and the national

movements—were calling for political sovereignty and greater economic independence from the center.

The reopening of the national question had brought new attention to the Muslim population of the Soviet Union, totalling about 70 million persons. Soviet Muslims resided in a number of republics with predominantly Muslim populations—the republics of Central Asia, Kazakhstan, and Azerbaijan—and also in a number of autonomous regions within the territory of the Russian Republic. These republics represented the regions of the country with the least social and economic development. Their population was mixed, and included both Muslims and other groups that had immigrated from other parts of the Soviet Union. The natural resources of the republics, in particular Baku's oil or Kazakhstan's fossil fuels, were controlled by the Soviet state and the budgets of the republics were only allotted an insignificant portion of the profits from the exploitation of their resources. Industrial zones in the Muslim republics posed problems in terms of relations between nationalities. The multi-ethnic population provided most middle-level qualified workers and specialists in various fields. The overwhelming majority of the Muslim population was involved in agriculture and the service sector. At the same time, the party-state apparatus in these regions basically represented the interests of ethnic groups that could claim a Russian ancestry or background.

Within the heart of the Muslim population, a kind of kin-based social structure had contributed to the preservation of a way of life based on tradition and the norms of Islam. Islam in its most simplified shape had become a form of national identification that withstood the Soviet system of devaluing nationality which was applied to Central Asia. The nationalist movement in the Muslim regions was, however, weak, and this allowed the party-state apparatus to evolve in the direction of national communism. In spite of that, the different movements in these regions which appealed to Islam had grown and represented the most serious alternative to the communist leadership. Representatives of these movements considered the Muslim regions of the Soviet Union as a part of the broader world of Muslim civilization. This constituted a source of pressure on the Soviet leadership to maintain a policy toward the Muslim world that allowed for the future development of closer relationships between these republics and most Muslim countries. While at the elite level in the Muslim regions, there was a special interest in Muslim countries that could help the economic development of the republics, there were also politically active groups that identified with a view that was widespread in the Islamic world, which saw western imperialism as the principal historical threat to Muslims. Soviet policy was sensitive to the concerns of both groups.

2. The Priorities of Soviet Foreign Policy

The Middle East had traditionally been of interest to the Soviet Union by force of its geo-strategic position. During the Cold War, Soviet relations with countries in the Middle East were premised on the principle of struggle between the two centers of the developed world and were based on the division of the countries in the region into reliable allies of the Soviet Union or allies of the West.

Characterizing the Middle East as a zone for national liberation movements, the Soviet Union had traditionally considered its own foremost task in the region as assisting governments which were disposed to the path of noncapitalist development. The Soviet Union gave its Middle Eastern allies economic assistance and military and political aid on a significantly greater scale than other governments with which it had relations, calculating that such aid would strengthen the allied regimes.

This policy did not take into account the fact that the declaration by the Soviet Union's Middle East allies of a socialist orientation had its own nationalistic basis, that these regimes would gradually depart from their earlier declared socialist goals, and that the result would be a contraction of spheres of relations with the Soviet Union. This process characterized Soviet relations with Egypt, Algeria, and a number of other countries. Even when relations were formally preserved on the previous level, the Soviet Union was forced to adjust to a kind of behavior on the part of its allies which contradicted their own avowed principles. Soviet relations with local allies were nevertheless uncritical, as evidenced by the blind eye turned to a number of the activities of Syria, the People's Democratic Republic of Yemen, and the PLO. From the Soviet viewpoint, the PLO was a basic element of the Arab national liberation movement objectively possessing an anti-imperialist and progressive character. Its operations were never realistically evaluated by the Soviet leadership.

Since its revolution in 1958, Iraq had been one of the Middle Eastern countries that played an important role in Soviet strategic planning. The Soviet Union had supported the anti-monarchist revolution and established friendly relations with General Qasim's regime. The two countries signed an economic and technical cooperation agreement under which the Soviet Union began to aid Iraq in the construction of a number of industrial enterprises, irrigation projects, transportation facilities, and communications.

No change in Soviet-Iraqi relations was marked by the evolution of the Qasim regime into an authoritarian, dictatorial form of government. The Soviet Union continued to regard Iraq as a pillar of the national liberation movement destined to assist in the development of the revolutionary process in the region. Both countries established a strategic alliance with an ideological basis. The Soviet Union regarded Iraq as a country with a "socialist orientation." During the 1961 Kuwait crisis, it offered Iraq diplomatic support.

In April 1972, the Soviet Union and Iraq (now governed by the Ba'th Party) concluded a Friendship and Cooperation Treaty strengthening their mutual relations. The Soviet Union offered assistance in the development of the Iraqi economy and trained Iraqi experts, including military cadres.

In the 1980s, Iraq became one of the most important Soviet partners in the Third World. In 1989, Soviet trade with Iraq amounted to 1.2 billion rubles, surpassing Soviet trade with other developing countries, with the exception of India.[1]

The main emphasis of Soviet-Iraqi relations was the development of military collaboration. During the mid-1970s, the Soviet Union mainly supplied Iraq with obsolete military hardware. In the subsequent period, modern Soviet weaponry was supplied on a commercial basis. Iraq paid for Soviet military supplies in hard currency. During the 1980s, the Soviet Union received a total of $13 billion in payments from Iraq for military exports.[2] The Soviet Union supplied Iraq with 53 percent of its military deliveries in the 1980s.[3] According to official Soviet Foreign Ministry data, about one thousand Soviet military experts were assigned to the Iraqi armed forces.[4]

The Soviet Union encouraged Iraq's military build-up and was instrumental in supporting the socio-political development imposed on the country by Saddam Hussein's government. The Soviet interest in maintaining Iraq as an ally in its global confrontation with the US in the region meant that the Soviet leadership did not react to such Iraqi actions as the liquidation of the Iraqi Communist Party, operations against the population of Kurdistan, or Iraq's support for terrorist organizations in the region.

The one-sided orientation of the Soviet Union toward Iraq exerted a negative influence on the development of Soviet relations with the conservative Arab Gulf states. With time, however, the Soviet Union sought to improve these relations, and this process accelerated, with Kuwaiti assistance, between 1985 and 1990.

After the establishment of Soviet-Kuwaiti diplomatic relations in 1963, ties between the two countries increased gradually, and were based primarily on the proximity of their approaches toward settling the Middle East conflict. In 1986, Kuwaiti imports from the Soviet Union amounted to 1.6 million dinars, but its exports to the Soviet Union amounted to only 21 thousand dinars.[5] Kuwait purchased Soviet weapons in a limited quantity. By August 1990, about 50 Soviet military experts were working in Kuwait assisting in the mastery of military technology.[6]

Kuwait favored the development of relations with the Soviet Union, considering them a counter-balance to its own close ties with the West. When the Iran-Iraq war escalated in the spring of 1987, Kuwait appealed to all permanent members of the UN Security Council to help it ensure the safe transport of its oil. The Soviet Union supplied three chartered tankers.

Kuwait also initiated an expansion of contacts between the Soviet Union and its Arab Gulf partners in the Gulf Cooperation Council (GCC). In 1986, Qatar was added to the number of GCC members having diplomatic relations with the Soviet Union. However, Soviet relations with Saudi Arabia, which had been established as early as 1926, remained suspended.

The negative attitude of Saudi Arabia toward establishing relations with the Soviet Union was directly related to a number of factors, including the Soviet intervention in Afghanistan. After the decision was taken to withdraw Soviet troops from Afghanistan, Saudi representatives acted as intermediaries in talks between Soviet officials and the Afghan opposition. The unqualified Soviet condemnation of Iraq's aggression against Kuwait was highly appreciated by GCC member countries. During the Gulf crisis, relations between the Soviet Union and Saudi Arabia were fully resumed. Diplomatic relations were also established between the Soviet Union and Bahrain.

Trade and economic relations between the Soviet Union and GCC member countries remained limited. Besides Kuwait, only Saudi Arabia maintained trade relations with the Soviet Union. Soviet exports to Saudi Arabia amounted to 10.5 million rubles in 1989. Imports from Saudi Arabia amounted to 12.6 million rubles.[7] Soviet exports to Saudi Arabia consisted of piping, electrical equipment, and lumber. Soviet imports mainly consisted of wheat.

Another important consideration in Soviet policy was its role as one of the largest oil-producing and exporting countries in the world. In the past, it had on occasion purchased oil from the Gulf countries with the sole purpose of re-exporting it. However, since 1989 there had been a falling rate of oil extraction in the Soviet Union. In 1989, oil extraction fell by 2.8 percent and oil exports fell by 12 percent. In 1990, extraction dropped by 5.6 percent and exports fell by 10 to 11 percent.[8] There were predictions that the progressive exhaustion of the principal oil fields in the Soviet Union would cause the country to face the problem of importing oil for domestic needs in the near future. The Soviet Union was thus concerned that it would be increasing its oil imports from the Gulf region not only for reexport, but also for its own domestic needs.

The Soviet attempts to develop mutually advantageous relations with Middle Eastern countries that were not traditionally friendly had often been restrained by the prospect of a negative reaction from pro-Soviet political forces in the Arab World. Leftist and radical movements viewed any such policy as a betrayal of the interests of the Arab national liberation movements and beneficial to imperialism. When the new Soviet policy included the increased emigration of Soviet Jews to Israel and moves toward normalization of relations with Israel, it was widely condemned in the Arab world.

Despite this, socio-economic and political processes in Arab countries in the late 1980s were leading traditional allies in the region to part ways with the Soviet Union. Syria and Iraq were practicing economic liberalization. Even the People's Democratic Republic of Yemen changed its militant Marxist stand and unified with the Yemeni Arab Republic. The loss of the Soviet Union's former standing in these Arab countries was one of the factors influencing Soviet policy during the Gulf crisis.

3. Soviet Positions during the Gulf Crisis

During the Gulf crisis, representatives of the higher echelons of Soviet power were not fully united on the path which Soviet Middle East policy should take, and this division was reflected in an attempt by the leadership to balance between two approaches to the crisis. A number of leaders were proponents of preserving close ties with Soviet allies in the interests of conducting a policy which was independent of the US in the Middle East region. Others wished to avoid an active Soviet role in the region and to subordinate Soviet regional policy to the greater global interest of developing ties with the West.

The political arena was also divided. Conservatives called for a return to the former principles of Soviet policy. However, the democratic opposition was calling for a full revision of Soviet Middle East policy. Democratic parties held the widespread view that it was necessary to pursue a pragmatic approach to relations with countries of the region. They considered it necessary to raise relations with Israel to full status, since they regarded Israel as a country of major interest for the Soviet economy. They were against any policy of significant Soviet participation in a political settlement of the problems of the region, including the Arab-Israeli conflict. In the first phase of the Gulf crisis, the Soviet Union refrained from issuing any statement contradicting those of the United States. This represented a marked contrast with the former Soviet positions on conflict situations in the Middle East. The Soviet government's first statement on the crisis on August 2, 1990 denounced Iraq's invasion as an aggression and stressed unequivocally that it was unacceptable and contradicted the positive trends taking place in international affairs. The Soviet government advocated the "immediate and unconditional withdrawal of Iraqi forces from Kuwaiti territory" and "the re-establishment of the sovereignty, national independence, and territorial integrity of the State of Kuwait."[9]

In the initial phases of the crisis, Soviet and American actions were coordinated. In the first US-Soviet joint statement on August 3rd issued by Soviet Foreign Minister Edward Shevardnadze and Secretary of State Baker (who had been visiting the Soviet Union when the invasion took place), the Iraqi invasion was sharply condemned and an appeal was addressed to Iraq to withdraw its troops unconditionally from Kuwait. The statement also declared that it was indispensable as a matter of principle for the UN Security Council resolution on the invasion to be fully and immediately implemented.[10] The coordination of Soviet and American positions was demonstrated not only by joint actions in the UN Security Council, but also by parallel moves outside of it. The Soviet Union stopped its arms deliveries to Iraq and the US froze Iraqi bank assets.

Soviet-American joint action was further developed at the Helsinki summit on September 9, 1990. The joint statement of the two presidents envisioned the possibility of employing all means to obtain an Iraqi withdrawal, although it stressed the priority of finding a peaceful political settlement. The declaration stated: "We are determined to see this aggression end, and if the current steps fail to end it, we are prepared to consider additional ones consistent with the United Nations Charter. We must demonstrate beyond any doubt that aggression cannot and will not pay."[11] The Helsinki summit sought to emphasize that it was not only the US that opposed the Iraqi attempt to swallow up a sovereign state, but the entire world community.

From the very beginning, the accent in the Soviet position was on the necessity of resolving the crisis by political means through the United Nations. Although the US was ready to take upon itself full responsibility for ending the crisis, there were no insurmountable contradictions in the approaches of the two sides. They both showed willingness to reach reasonable compromises. For instance, in the Helsinki joint statement, a sentence was incorporated into the text on the necessity to "work actively to resolve all remaining conflicts in the Middle East and Persian Gulf."[12] Yevgeny Primakov, who acted as Soviet President Gorbachev's special representative in dealing with the Gulf crisis, has pointed out that it was the Soviet side that insisted on the inclusion of that sentence, believing that such an approach was a necessary step to reach a political settlement of the crisis.[13]

The Soviet leadership did not make any serious objections to the concentration of American forces in the Gulf, as a result of President Bush's representations at the Helsinki Summit that the American military presence would be of a temporary nature.[14]

The Soviet Union meanwhile encouraged the Arab countries themselves to find a solution to the conflict. This approach was considered preferable since it precluded Soviet participation in the actions of the anti-Iraq coalition, which held out the threat of striking an irreparable blow to Soviet prestige in some parts of the Arab world where its position had been strong. The Soviet Union would also have had to face the extremely painful problem of the "Afghan syndrome," had it taken part in military operations against Iraq.

Another feature of Soviet policy was the desire to retain an open channel of diplomatic pressure on Iraq by continuing a dialogue with it. The Soviet Union had long-standing bilateral relations with Iraq, and needed to take into consideration the fact that thousands of Soviet citizens were resident in the country at the start of the crisis. Acting for a speedy cessation of the crisis, the Soviet Union believed that it was possible to make certain compromises that would give Iraq an opportunity to retreat without losing face. As a means of resolving the crisis, the Soviet Union suggested discussing the

Palestinian issue and a general Middle East settlement if Iraq agreed to pull its forces out of Kuwait.[15] President Gorbachev sent his personal representative Yevgeny Primakov to hold talks with Saddam Hussein to attempt to find a peaceful means of resolving the crisis.

Iraq tried to make use of its close contacts with the Soviet Union for its own purposes of weakening the anti-Iraq coalition. Iraqi diplomatic activity was directed toward preventing the UN Security Council from passing a number of harsh resolutions against Iraq. In conjunction with this, an Iraqi official, Saadoun Hammadi, paid a visit to Moscow to meet with Soviet leaders to seek assistance in blocking the UN Security Council resolution on the economic blockade of Iraq. Similar moves were taken in regards to Security Council resolution 678 of November 1990, which allowed for the employment of any means necessary to restrain the aggressor. The Soviet vote in favor of the resolution was significant. The Soviet Union proposed the incorporation of a clause providing for a "goodwill pause" until January 15, 1991 in the hope that Iraq would be able to realistically assess the situation and pull its forces out of Kuwait.[16]

When the Gulf war began, the lack of Soviet participation in military operations put the Soviet Union in a special position compared with other members of the anti-Iraq coalition. As hostilities expanded and the impending rout of the Iraqi army became obvious, the Soviet leadership showed more concern for the role that the country would play in the region after the end of the crisis. The Soviet Union began to differentiate its stand from that of the West to strengthen its influence on the course of events in the Gulf, hoping to ensure its participation in resolving the fate of the region in the post-crisis period.

The Soviet leadership came out against the complete devastation of Iraq and the possibility arising in this context of the dismemberment of Iraq. The Soviet Union emphasized the need to preserve the pre-crisis balance of forces in the region and to ensure Iraq's active participation in setting up a regional security system after the end of military operations. The Soviet Union criticized those actions of the US-led multi-national force which seemed to aim at the complete destruction of Iraq's military-industrial potential.

At this time, tension between the Soviet Union and the United States was increasing as a result of the Soviet crackdown in the Baltic republics. Early in February, Washington responded negatively to Soviet army actions in the Baltic republics, and announced that it intended to substantially increase political and material support for the Baltic republics. President Gorbachev responded by criticizing

US actions in the Gulf war. On February 11, 1991, he stated that a possibility existed for the use of weapons of mass destruction by both sides and that such a threat exceeded the mandate formulated by UN Security Council resolutions. He also condemned the tremendous number of victims among the civilian population.[17]

In stressing the negative aspects of continuing hostilities, the Soviet leadership was preparing the ground for a new round of its own diplomatic activity aimed at an immediate end to the war. This new initiative, however, showed that the Soviet Union lacked the ability to exert an independent influence on the Gulf situation. On February 17, Soviet President Gorbachev met with Iraqi Foreign Minister Tariq Aziz in Moscow, and presented a plan calling for the full withdrawal of Iraqi forces from Kuwait, and a number of other proposals, including the lifting of UN economic sanctions against Iraq after most Iraqi troops had withdrawn from Kuwait, and the monitoring of the withdrawal by non-combatant forces. Two days later, however, President Bush stated that the Soviet proposal "falls well short of what would be required." Facing the prospect of a major US ground offensive, Iraq accepted the Soviet proposal on February 21. After an American ultimatum to Iraq on February 22 to withdraw unconditionally from Kuwait by noon the following day or face a ground attack, the Soviet Union submitted a revised proposal modifying some of the points about the Iraqi withdrawal and its supervision that the United States had found objectionable. The revised proposal was accepted by Iraq on February 23, on the same day that it rejected the American ultimatum. The US offensive was then launched. In response, the Soviet Union issued a critical statement, asserting that the US had lost a "very real chance for peace."

4. Domestic Reactions to the Soviet Gulf Policy

The absence of a true national consensus in the Soviet Union on policy toward the Gulf crisis allowed decision-making to be carried out by a narrow circle of representatives in the highest echelon of power. Domestic pressures, however, were both a direct and indirect concern for the decision-makers. A key factor influencing Soviet decision-making in the crisis was the reaction of the Soviet Union's Muslim population to events in a region adjacent to the southern borders of the Soviet Union. Even in the Muslim republics, however, there was a lack of consensus. Some sectors of the population viewed the actions of the anti-Iraq coalition headed by the US as being anti-Muslim and held the belief that Muslims themselves should settle conflicts that arise among them. The emphasis here was not on Iraq's aggression against Kuwait, but on the West's conspiracy against Islamic countries. Other groups in Muslim areas of the Soviet Union held contrary views. The attitudes of the parliaments of Soviet republics with Muslim populations did not differ from those of the central authorities in Moscow, and discontent with official government policy was only demonstrated by individual Muslim religious leaders.

In the Supreme Soviet, representatives of two groups of deputies voiced particularly strong opposition to any idea of sending Soviet troops to the Gulf. One was a group of deputies representing Afghan war veterans. These representatives were of the opinion that the Soviet Union had no right to send citizens to die in the Gulf after the recent war in Afghanistan, which they regarded as criminal. Speaking at the Fourth Congress of Soviet People's Deputies, a representative of this group stated: "While categorically condemning aggression, we are convinced that the world community will bear in mind the decision of the legislative authorities in our country that it will be impossible for our soldiers to participate in a war in the Gulf region."[18]

The second group opposed to any Soviet intervention against Iraq was the Soyuz group, which represented certain members of the Soviet army, groups associated with the Soviet military-industrial complex, and ethnic Russians residing in minority republics. This group took an extremely negative stand in the Supreme Soviet against the policy pursued by the Soviet leadership on the Gulf crisis. It criticized the government for subordinating itself to the US, for refusing to support its traditional allies, and for sanctioning the rout of the Iraqi army by voting for UN Security Council resolution 678. One of the main causes of the resignation of Foreign Minister Edward Shevardnadze in December was the attacks made against him by members of the Soyuz group in the Supreme Soviet.

The stand of representatives of new democratic groups in Soviet politics, like Boris Yeltsin, was decidedly isolationist. Their position was that under the existing difficult economic and political conditions, the Soviet Union should not strive to play the role of a great power, and could not play this role in any event. Some deputies in the Supreme Soviet from the democratic groupings, however, gave their full support to the actions of the anti-Iraq coalition. For example, in the independent newspaper "Megapolis Ekspress" [Metropolis Express], Supreme Soviet member and corresponding member of the

Soviet Academy of Sciences Yablokov expressed the opinion that "the world does not have the right to give in to Iraq" since if it did, the result of the "insane policy of the Iraqi leadership could kill many more times the number of people than would be killed during the war."[19]

In the Russian Federal Parliament, which had more deputies from the democratic bloc than the Supreme Soviet, the majority of deputies supported the demand that the Soviet Union not participate in military actions against Iraq. On December 11, deputies adopted an appeal to President Gorbachev not to involve the Soviet Union in a military conflict.[20] The vote on the resolution was 683 in favor to 161 against. Most of those voting against were representatives of the bloc calling itself "Democratic Russia," which argued that the Soviet Union as a member of the world community had the same obligation as other civilized states to make a contribution to curbing aggression.[21]

5. Moscow's Middle East Policy after the Gulf Crisis

The Gulf crisis was a turning point in Soviet Middle East policy. It demonstrated a departure from previous principles of Soviet foreign policy and at the same time showed the absence of a new conception of Soviet involvement in regional politics. The crisis showed the weakness of the Soviet position in the Middle East and its lack of active levers to exert an influence on the course of events in the region. Its position during the crisis evoked sharp criticism from many of its traditional allies. Its relations with Arab governments in the Gulf region had not, however, reached a level which allowed for advanced development in the future.

During the Gulf crisis, the Soviet Union established consular relations with Israel, representing official recognition of the contacts which had been made over the past several years by the Soviet and Israeli sides over the issue of the emigration of Soviet Jews. The visit of Soviet Foreign Minister Bessmertnik to Israel in May 1991 was the first official visit of a leading Soviet representative to that country. Although the visit was not marked by the establishment of Soviet-Israeli diplomatic relations, Soviet leaders repeatedly announced the necessity of supporting continuing contacts with all governments in the region for achieving a settlement of the Arab-Israeli conflict. The Soviet Union backed the convening of an international conference on the Middle East. However, it did not propose any kind of preconditions on its outcome and, after the Gulf war, dropped its insistence that the PLO was the sole legitimate representative of the Palestinian people. The pronouncements of Soviet leaders were moderate, and contained words to the effect that "a Middle East settlement ought to have an all-encompassing character and take into account the interests of all sides involved in the conflict."[22] In the period following the end of the Gulf crisis, there was more affinity between Soviet and American views than ever before regarding a Middle East settlement. Both sides affirmed their intention to undertake joint coordinated actions in this direction.

After the failure of the conservative coup d'etat in August 1991, the democratic forces came to power in the Soviet Union. The activities of the Communist Party of the Soviet Union were suspended, it was deprived of power and its property was nationalized. Relations among the republics were greatly influenced by these developments, and their search for independence gathered momentum. Soon after the democratic victory in August, the Soviet Union recognized the independence of the Baltic republics. In December, the creation of the Commonwealth of Independent States provided a new framework for independence and cooperation among the remaining republics, except for Georgia.

These developments meant that economic and social transformations would continue to dominate the politics of the different republics. By 1992, the development of trade and economic relations with the outside world had become a priority of their governments. It seemed clear that the different republics would take responsibility for their own separate relations with the Middle East. Muslim republics would certainly attempt to cooperate with Arab and other Muslim states, while Russia, Ukraine and Belarus would consider more prioritized relations with Israel, a significant part of whose population emanated from these republics. Armenia and Georgia would likely attempt to develop cooperation with both the Arab countries and Israel.

In Russia, the democratic forces which had come to power had been opposed to the idea of an active, independent role of their country in the Middle East, and favored recognition of the responsibility of the western powers for guaranteeing the stability and security of the region. The democrats supported Moscow's participation in Middle Eastern affairs in the form of carrying out the responsibilities of membership of the Security Council and other international organizations. They were in favor of a reduction in military expenditures in general, and the curtailing of military ties with Middle Eastern countries that had been promoted by the Soviet Union as a means of extending its global power. However, the need for hard currency meant that military exports by Russia and other former Soviet republics would continue on a commercial basis. Because of the isolationism prevalent among the democratic forces, and the limitations imposed by the economic crisis facing Russia, it could be predicted that Moscow's levers of political and ideological influence on Middle Eastern governments would continue to weaken.

Notes

1. "Soviet Foreign Economic Relations in 1989," *Statistical Yearbook,* Moscow, 1990, p. 5.

2. *Middle East International,* London, August 31, 1991, p. 21.

3. N. Gnevushev, "Military-Economic Activity of Developing Countries and its Consequences," *Actual Problems of International Life in Asia,* (Collection of Papers Presented at the Scientific Conference Convened in Moscow July 26, 1990), Institute of Oriental Studies under the Academy of Sciences of the USSR, Moscow, 1990, p. 100.

4. *Izvestiya,* Moscow, July 7, 1990.

5. State of Kuwait, *Annual Statistical Abstract 1988* (Kuwait, 1989), pp. 246-248.

6. *Middle East International,* London, August 31, 1991, p. 21.

7. *Soviet Foreign Economic Relations in 1989,* p. 248.

8. A. Kondakov, "Specter of a Crisis," *Novoye Vremya* [New Times], Moscow, October 12, 1990, p. 30.

9. *Pravda,* Moscow, August 3, 1990.

10. *Pravda,* Moscow, August 4, 1990.

11. *Pravda,* Moscow, September 10, 1990.

12. *Pravda,* Moscow, February 27, 1991.

13. *Ibid.*

14. See Yevgeny Primakov, "The War Which Might Not Have Been," *Pravda,* Moscow, February 27, 1991.

15. *Ibid.*

16. See interview with Edward Shevardnadze, *Moscow News,* Moscow, March 10, 1991.

17. *Izvestiya,* Moscow, February 11, 1991.

18. *Izvestiya,* Moscow, December 21, 1990.

19. *Megapolis Ekspress* [Metropolis Express], Moscow, February 14, 1991.

20. *Sovetskaya Rossiya* [Soviet Russia], Moscow, December 13, 1990.

21. *Ibid.*

22. *Izvestiya,* Moscow, May 15, 1991.

6 CHINA AND THE GULF CRISIS: A NEW PHASE OF SINO-ARAB RELATIONS

Xiaoxing Han

The Gulf crisis marked the first occasion on which China was forced to take sides among countries which were all friendly to China in a conflict without direct relevance to China's strategic interests. During the crisis, China openly condemned Iraq and committed itself to sanctions against the country. Its voting behavior in the United Nations was unprecedented: in 17 votes in nine months on Gulf crisis-related resolutions at the United Nation Security Council, China voted with the western powers on all occasions except three (Resolutions 678, 686 and 688) when it abstained, allowing the resolution to be passed.[1] In spite of these actions, however, China failed to satisfy Saudi Arabia and Kuwait fully. It was also unable to play a major role in diplomatic negotiations to resolve the problem. China's approach to intra-Arab rivalries along with China's strategy in dealing with the West was repeatedly modified in the course of the crisis.

1. Sino-Arab Relations in Perspective

Useful clues for understanding the new departure of Chinese diplomacy can be found in the school of realist interpretations. According to this school, the behavior of a nation-state is driven by its interests, which are in turn crystallized and substantiated by its relative position in the global system of power distribution. China's power projection capabilities in the Middle East in the late 1980s, especially at the bilateral level, were far from being negligible. China's ability to supply relatively sophisticated weapons, its permanent seat and right of veto on the Security Council, its advanced technological and industrial development among developing nations, and its nuclear arsenal were all "big power" attributes which boosted Chinese diplomacy. With the Soviet Union's collapse as a superpower, China's relative international preeminence was further enhanced. China preceded the Soviet Union in normalizing relations with Saudi Arabia in spite of a thorny problem over Saudi relations with Taiwan that impeded Sino-Saudi relations before Saudi Arabia established diplomatic relations with the People's Republic in 1990.

China's interests in the Arab world grew at an impressive rate. From an extremely low level in the late 1970s, the volume and scope of China's economic transactions with the region had expanded enormously. A Sino-Arab joint chamber of commerce was established in 1988, "the first of the kind to be established between China and other countries."[2] Before the Gulf crisis Iraq had become by far the largest market for China's overseas construction enterprises, while, ironically, Kuwait distinguished itself in the Third World by its large investment in and its unique lending practices toward China. Iraq and Iran were also principal importers of Chinese arms. Although its sales to Saudi Arabia were less in value than its sales to Iraq and Iran, China sold ballistic missiles to Saudi Arabia, the only country ever to conclude such a deal with China. Together, China's economic ties with the Arab world constituted a hard-currency and profit-generating source of tens of billions of dollars in the 1980s. Thus, China's stake in the region at the time of the Gulf crisis was very different from what it had been a decade earlier. A major change of a country's interest formation, as realist interpretations predict, will induce a corresponding shift in its policy position.

But China's interests and its policy had their peculiarities. Interpretations based on power status and economic interests alone cannot adequately account for China's timidity, if not passivity, toward intra-Arab rivalries prior to and even at the outset of the Gulf crisis. Theories that relate Chinese policy to its power projection capabilities alone also cannot address the fact that while China was much weaker than it is now more than one decade ago, it was nonetheless more assertive and defiant then to either or both superpowers on a wide range of issues, including those related to the Middle East.

Two factors that are crucial for an understanding of Chinese policy are the distinct character of China as a state and the normative framework of Chinese diplomacy. As a one-party state ruled by the Communist Party, China had an interest in ensuring that its foreign policies did not open it to relationships and influences that might weaken its political structure. Closely related to this was a set of norms of Chinese diplomacy. Although by the late 1980s, Chinese diplomacy no longer advocated world revolution, its normative framework still included ideas of Third World solidarity, of opposition to superpower intervention, and of a Chinese role as a model for and leader of Third World countries.

There was sometimes tension between these traditional norms and Chinese policy after Deng Xiaoping's Open Door policy triggered off a major commitment to external economic expansion, and neo-mercantilism consequently replaced a revolutionary mission. In the late 1970s, Yitzhak Shichor commented that the Sino-Middle Eastern relations "provide[d] one of the best examples of the use of economic policies for political ends."[3] Some ten years later, the relationship between political and economic factors had been almost completely reversed. A top priority of China's policy, especially toward Arab states, was to sell more in the form of goods and services and to gain more in the form of capital and profits. But China's economic offensive had over the years seriously challenged China's ideological role in the world, and had also compelled China to put up a semi-permanent defense against unapproved political influence from the outside.

China realized painfully that its economic and technical needs had to be satisfied largely in the West, but that western influence could be a source of destabilization of communist rule. China attempted to reduce its commercial and financial dependence on the West by promoting other relations, such as Sino-Arab relations. After Tiananman Square, it felt a critical need for international political allies. Thus under the battle cry of countering "foreign (western) interference" in domestic affairs, China attempted to rally like-minded states, among them Arab states. It was not coincidental that Yang Shangkun, the most crucial figure next to Deng in masterminding the Beijing crackdown, chose Arab states for the first post-massacre trip abroad by any top Chinese leader.[4] Other than combating the West as an enemy, China also worked to mitigate tensions in its relations with the West by yielding to it in less critical issue areas, including again those related to the Arab world. In this sense, the Gulf crisis provided China with a valuable indirect bargaining chip with the West.

In the 1970s and 1980s, China's policy on intra-Arab rivalries had been that they should be settled by Arabs themselves, without external intervention. Chinese policy had thus moved a long way from the 1960s, when it had been involved in an intra-Arab conflict, the Dhofar conflict. In the late 1960s, China even had combat personnel on the side of the Popular Front for the Liberation of Oman and the Arabian Gulf. But by the late 1980s, China had official representatives in all the member states of the GCC and Jordan, the most conservative cluster in the Arab world. For more than a decade before the Gulf crisis, China had refused to involve itself in intra-Arab conflicts beyond the expression of goodwill or even to differentiate between contending parties. China had not grown out of an East and South

Asian regional mold sufficiently for its influence to be strong enough to sway the outcome of a faraway conflict. But the weakness of Chinese influence accounted only for a part of its passivity. China's former policy toward intra-Arab rivalries was caused to a large extent by the inertia of China's outdated normative diplomatic framework. The Gulf crisis finally prepared China to confront the fact that universal Third World solidarity was unattainable. Even the Third World as a key concept has been largely taken out of China's diplomatic vocabulary. Under enormous pressure brought upon China by the Gulf crisis, and with the breakthrough in its foreign policy normative framework, China eventually started cautiously to take sides.

2. Taking Sides

China's immediate response to the Iraqi invasion was orthodox. Even China's vote for Resolution 660, which condemned the invasion and demanded Iraq's withdrawal, was tempered by China's attempt to reconcile Kuwait with Iraq "through friendly consultation."[5] China began to take sides definitively only three or four days after the invasion by voting for Security Council Resolution 661 and announcing its own arms embargo against Iraq. From this time onward, a new departure in Chinese diplomacy took shape. China unequivocally declared its opposition to the Iraqi invasion, and demanded Iraq's "immediate and unconditional withdrawal" from Kuwait.

This demand was declared to be the basis of China's approach to the solution of the crisis. There were, according to the official articulation of the Chinese policy, two additional elements: opposition to military deployment in the Gulf region by great powers, and insistence that the crisis should be solved by the Arabs themselves. However, if China's position is carefully examined, there was clearly a fourth element: strong advocacy of a peaceful resolution. But except for the demand for Iraqi withdrawal, none of the components was stated in an equally lucid and consistent manner. Chinese opposition to military deployment in the Gulf region was expressed early on, with the claim that China "all along opposed the military deployment by any country on the soil of another country . . . ."[6] By and large, however, China emphasized its objection to the deployment by "big powers," thus excluding Arab, Islamic, or Third World countries from its objections. Even China's objection to the "big powers" was measured; China's "disapproval" rather than opposition, as its top diplomats repeatedly stated, was "in principle"—namely, not absolute. Such qualifications were compatible with China's expression of "understand[ing for] the defensive measures taken by [countries of] the region," especially Saudi Arabia.[7] The stated Chinese policy was that the search for a peaceful solution should continue so long as a gleam of hope for such a solution existed. But China did not spell out circumstances or a time frame during which the hope for peace could still be viable.

It was not clear whether China viewed the military option as a viable way of solving the crisis, and Chinese statements were unclear as to whether the use of force might be a necessary auxiliary means for achieving a negotiated solution. China's vote for the revitalization of the long-dormant United Nations Security Council Military Staff Committee, as stipulated by Resolution 665 on the enforcement of trade sanctions against Iraq, and its full participation in the Committee's activities did not prevent China from interpreting the resolution as not endorsing "using force."[8] Ironically, however, in order to carry out, not to say strengthen, an embargo which was actually a comprehensive and massive blockade, force was intrinsic and essential. The Chinese position seemed to be in favor of giving teeth to United Nations resolutions, but reluctant to use those teeth.

A statement by Qian Qicheng, the Chinese Foreign Minister, before the vote on Resolution 678 on the use of "all necessary means . . . to restore international peace and security in the area" addressed the issue in the clearest terms used by any Chinese official. He asserted that "the wording 'use all necessary means' [in the proposed resolution] . . . runs counter to the consistent position of the Chinese government—namely, to try our utmost to seek a peaceful solution."[9] Even this statement can be read in two ways: one, using force is unacceptable; two, seeking a peaceful solution should be the absolute priority, connoting in the meantime that a not-so-peaceful alternative might exist. Nowhere did any Chinese official publicly and categorically rule out the military option.

3. China and the Split in the Arab World

China's call for an Arab solution seemed to suggest that Arab countries should take the primary initiative and have the final say in resolving the crisis, and that the Arab League should be the coordinating vehicle. Publicly, however, this conception was presented rather vaguely.[10] From a practical point of view, it was obvious that there was a serious flaw in calls for an Arab solution. The Arab League had been paralyzed by an acute split. Iraq stood alone, on one side, opposed by a coalition of Saudi Arabia and the rest of the GCC, Egypt, and a few other countries. In the middle was a group of slightly less than 40 percent of the Arab League members, who sought a peaceful solution through Arab mediation, and were at odds with both Iraq and the coalition arrayed against it.

The coalition members were united in staunch opposition to the Iraqi invasion. They supported military deployment by an outside power, thus breaking a long-time taboo in intra-Arab relations. Furthermore, they maintained that the military option was indispensable for the solution of the crisis.

The group advocating a peaceful "Arab solution" included eight members of the Arab League, with Jordan as a key member. Like the anti-Iraq coalition, this group opposed the Iraqi invasion of Kuwait, and demanded the withdrawal of the Iraqi forces. At the same time, its members were willing to give Iraq the benefit of the doubt on the issue of whether it would ever be willing to withdraw from Kuwait, and its members adopted a distinctly conciliatory attitude toward Iraq. The underlying common denominator of this group's position was its vocal opposition to any military deployment by non-Arabs and to any attempt to solve the crisis militarily. A major difficulty was that members of the group entered into an acrimonious dispute with members of the coalition. Some were even accused of complicity in deploying troops on the Iraqi side.[11]

One pillar of China's Arab policy had been a doctrine of Arab solidarity, i.e., that no conflict or little conflict existed among Arab states. Whenever that assumption was shattered by reality, China found itself in a difficult position. The case most comparable in the previous two decades to the Arab rift over the Kuwait crisis had been the dispute over Sadat's peace initiative in 1977-78. That strife also shook the entire Arab world and caused the removal of the Arab League headquarters from Cairo. Yet even that incident did not match the magnitude, pervasiveness, and bellicosity of inter-Arab tensions during the Gulf crisis.

In 1977-78, China had no diplomatic relations with several Gulf states, especially Saudi Arabia. China was also extremely concerned about the Soviet Union, so that its relations with "the Steadfastness Front" of Arab countries opposed to Sadat's initiative and supported by the Soviet Union were by no means as good as its relations were with Egypt. China showed clear sympathy and support for Egypt. Even so, China did not officially take a stance in favor of Egypt against the rest. Rather, the Chinese position was always expressed as backing Egypt's recovery through negotiation of its territory lost to Israel, thereby fending off the Soviet Union, which was seen as lying in wait to make a comeback. Regardless of the cogency of China's argument and of how the argument was received by the Arab states, Chinese diplomats could at least make such an argument, claim that China had a consistent position demanding Israeli withdrawal from the occupied territories, and avoid becoming embroiled in a dispute.

The Gulf crisis was different. Even though there was no option other than to condemn the Iraqi invasion, the dispute over the means of obtaining an Iraqi withdrawal left the Chinese leadership in an awkward position. On the one hand, the leadership was disgusted by the invasion. Although public attack was muted in the Chinese press, the leadership privately assailed Iraq as a "regional hegemonist power,"[12] a derogatory label reserved by the Chinese leadership for the worst kind of international villain below the rank of superpowers. On the other hand, China assiduously avoided any dispute with Iraq at the bilateral level. Its decision to stop arms sales to Iraq was presented by the Foreign Ministry spokesman as a matter of fact and as a corollary to China's vote for Resolution 660 condemning the invasion and calling on Iraq to withdraw its forces from Kuwait.[13] China said nothing when its embassy in Kuwait was the first embassy "forcibly entered" by Iraqi troops. It voted for Resolution 664 demanding that Iraq release all foreigners detained in Iraq and Kuwait, and for Resolution 667 regarding diplomatic immunity in Kuwait, but was perhaps the very first nation to evacuate its mission in Kuwait. China only belatedly and modestly admitted that Chinese laborers in Iraq were in "difficulties." Still, the Chinese leadership did not raise this issue with the Iraqi First Deputy Prime Minister, who was then on a visit to Beijing.

China's silence on bilateral frictions with Iraq and its self-portrayal as a "disinterested party" allowed the Sino-Iraqi relationship to remain largely untouched at the political level. When Qian Qicheng paid a visit to Baghdad in early November 1990, the only foreign minister of a permanent member of the Security Council to have done so since the crisis, Saddam Hussein received him and praised "the relations of friendship which bind Iraq and [the] People's Republic of China."[14] But China was cautious not to give the Beijing-Baghdad relationship a high profile. Thus Iraq was the only country in Qian's four-country tour whose visit was described in the Chinese press as a "working visit," a term subtly suggesting that the visit was meant only for a specific business, the Gulf crisis, and had nothing to do with the status of the bilateral relationship.

Before the visit, Qian's tour had begun in Egypt, and continued to Saudi Arabia and the Kuwaiti government in exile there, then on to Amman and Baghdad. The visit concluded with a return trip to Saudi Arabia. Judged by its traditional standards, China was extraordinarily active in crisis-related diplomacy at this time. Although Qian stated at the beginning of his tour that he would not be "a mediator," concealed expectations were certainly very high. On the day when Saddam Hussein received Qian, *Dagong Bao,* a China-controlled newspaper in Hong Kong, claimed that "China is the most appropriate one to perform the final round of the campaign for peace. If Iraq again misses this chance and waits . . . then it will be indeed too late!"[15]

Qian's tour included the principal actors in each of the three Arab groups. It also showed that China gave most importance to the coalition, which included both Egypt and Saudi Arabia. Egypt had maintained a rarely interrupted friendly relationship with the PRC for almost 35 years. Although Saudi Arabia was the very last Arab state to have established diplomatic relations with China, China had great hopes that it could be relied upon with Egypt to be twin pillars for China's own Arab policy. Saudi economic resources ranked very high in China's strategic thinking about the Middle East. Saudi Arabia's relative political stability, its moderate foreign policy, and its particularly good and seemingly lasting relationship with Egypt were all considered meritorious by China.

China nevertheless faced a dilemma arising from its opposition to the idea of military involvement by the great powers. Li Peng, China's Premier, reiterated China's accusation in public on August 28, 1990 that military involvement by "big powers" would "threaten the peace and stability of the entire region."[16] About the same time, Egyptian Foreign Minister Ismat Abdul-Maguid strongly stated: "Egypt does not accept mixing cards . . . the fundamental issue is the Iraqi invasion of Kuwait, and not foreign [military] presence . . . ."[17] The two leaders were not reproving each other but, rather, were addressing different audiences. Still, these statements show how far apart China and the coalition were in a crucial respect. China's continued championing of an Arab solution after an abortive emergency meeting of the Arab League at the end of August 1990 was certainly another position disagreeable to the coalition. Mahmoud Riyadh, the former Secretary

General of the Arab League, bluntly stated that the League "cannot play any role, given the current strife."[18]

The Arab states whose position fell between those of Iraq and the coalition of forces against it were in accord with Chinese policy. During his four-nation tour in November, Qian stated in Amman that "China and Jordan are of the same view and stance toward the Gulf crisis."[19] No similar statement was made by him in any other capital during his tour.

After the passage by the Security Council of Resolution 678, on which China abstained, calling for the use of "all necessary means" to obtain an Iraqi withdrawal, the Chinese leadership told the Kuwaiti government that the reason for China's abstention was that it wanted to be "an arbiter one day rather than being a party [in the conflict]."[20] And in order to appease the unhappy Kuwaitis, China gave an extraordinary reception to the visiting Emir of Kuwait in December 1990. At the end of the Emir's visit, Yang Shangkun, the Chinese President, was eager to claim the meetings as "very successful." However, the Emir stressed that "any initiative [for the peaceful solution] is too late and futile,"[21] which could be interpreted as a mild and oblique admonition to the wishful Chinese "arbiter."

China did not want to be seen as siding only with a minority of the Arab world, and it felt uncomfortable because of its difficulties in reaching full accord with a majority of more than 60 percent of the Arab League members on a major issue in the region. China labored hard to establish an inclusive position, accommodating all the parties, though in different degrees. China could not afford to be passive and withdrawn in the crisis, yet it could not afford to be caught in the dispute. This was not an easy position from which to maneuver, and the outbreak of the war made it even harder.

4. China and the Gulf War

When war inaugurated the second stage of the crisis, China's diplomacy took another turn. New proposals were put forward replacing the idea of an Arab solution with one negotiated within a UN framework. This stage in particular was characterized by a significant softening of China's rhetoric as well as a less active involvement in the crisis-related diplomacy.

China's negative reaction to the war was rather subdued. It expressed "deep concern" about the outbreak of the war and the later launching of the ground offensive, but did not condemn the war. Even more striking was that, as the war intensified, and despite the urging of several nations that China should become involved in mediation, no public statement was ever made by China calling for a cease-fire. Throughout the war, China's standard appeal was for "the maximum restraint by both combatants" and for the prevention of "the escalation and spread of the war."

China was certainly greatly disturbed by the war. It went on record as commending the USSR and France and registering its support for their proposed peaceful solutions. Nonetheless, it reduced its own involvement. It launched only one mission after the war began that was comparable to Qian's four-nation tour in the pre-war stage. The second mission, also a four-nation tour, was conducted only by Yang Fuchang, one of Qian's deputies. The nations chosen for Yang's mission also reflected the low-key tenor of Chinese diplomacy at this stage: they were Syria, Turkey, Yugoslavia, and Iran. Excluding Syria, none of the four was in the strict sense a direct party to the crisis. Even Syria was not the leading member in the Arab coalition. By staying away from the direct parties, China tacitly abandoned its once coveted role as a leading peace broker.

Yang advanced a six-point proposal. The first three points were basically demands for Iraqi withdrawal and for all the parties to accept a peaceful solution. The fourth and fifth points called for placing "the Middle East problem" on the international agenda, and allowing the countries in the region to take charge of post-war arrangements, while the "foreign forces" were to pull out. The most interesting element in Yang's proposal was point six, stating that no linkage should be made between the preceding points, and yet that "all issues" presented by those points "should be given equal consideration and attention."[22] China had formerly accused Iraq through the media of attempting to "gain time" through the "linkage" issue, but had also showed a certain sympathy for the Iraqi position. The Arab-Israeli conflict, in China's view, was correlated with the Gulf crisis, and China called for the negotiation of that conflict to be arranged "as soon as possible."[23]

Overall, the change in Chinese diplomacy tilted against Iraq. Having abstained from Resolution 678 calling for the use of "all necessary means" to obtain an Iraqi withdrawal from Kuwait, China avoided criticizing the attacking coalition forces after the war had broken out, as the Soviet Union and India did.[24] China also abstained from Resolution 686, which dictated the terms of a cease-fire, objecting that it extended the validity of Resolution 678.[25] But finally, after a series of behind-the-door meetings with the other four permanent Security Council members, China went along with Resolution 687, which confirmed virtually all the major points of 686 and imposed further and tougher conditions on Iraq.

5. Repercussions of the Crisis

No longer attempting to gain the leadership in the Third World, China now labors to be identified not so much as a member of the Third World but as a sympathizer. It cherishes its permanent seat in the Security Council, and it has begun to use the designation "five big powers" quite freely in a semi-official way.

The Gulf crisis was widely viewed as a golden opportunity for China to gain diplomatic ground. A western diplomat stationed in Beijing was quoted as saying: "It's the best of all worlds for them [the Chinese leadership], because they've been able to reintegrate themselves with the West without sacrificing any Third World credentials to do it."[26] That assessment, however, was overstated. The overall balance for China in the Gulf crisis was in its favor. The crisis gave strong impetus to the West to accelerate the relaxation of the sanctions it had imposed against China after June 1989, and thus greatly helped China's diplomacy toward the West. But as a result of the crisis, the costs for China in terms of its relations with a number of developing and Arab nations were by no means negligible.

China must face a new reality in the Arab world. While Arab support and sympathy for Iraq went well beyond the Iraqi borders, the Arab coalition, especially the GCC countries, were occasionally no less belligerent toward Iraq than was the West. For instance, Jordan's foreboding that the continued fighting would "drag [Jordan] into the Gulf war" was met by the GCC's stern rejection of any mediation effort prior to the Iraqi withdrawal.[27] This division between friendly countries placed China in a predicament.

The high-profile approach adopted by China in the first stage of the crisis allowed its leadership to state for domestic consumption that "all parties involved in the Gulf crisis looked to China. This is a diplomatic status that other big powers do not enjoy."[28] Despite China's condemnation of the Iraqi invasion, problems remained in its relations with the Gulf states. The discontent felt by the Gulf states with China's approach to the crisis was manifested even before the vote on Resolution 678 calling for "all necessary means" to be employed to obtain an Iraqi withdrawal.[29] The Gulf states ignored China's claim that it had suffered more than $2 billion in "direct economic losses" as a result of having "seriously carried out" the embargo, about three times the figure of the Soviet "trade losses" given in the same month. Indeed, in the autumn of 1990, the Gulf states signed a huge loan agreement with the Soviet Union after it had given its "qualified approval" to the use of force to compel Iraq from Kuwait.[30] This strongly indicated the discriminating assessment made by the Gulf states of the roles of the two socialist powers at that stage of the crisis. The failure of Chinese diplomacy in the first stage led to a marked softening of diplomatic efforts in the second.

One set of problems that arose during the crisis concerned relations between the Gulf states and Taiwan. The normalization of Sino-Saudi relations was the apex of the PRC's diplomacy in the Middle East almost two decades after China's diplomatic breakthrough with Iran. Nevertheless, rivalry continued in the region between Beijing and Taipei. Taipei's Vice Foreign Minister visited Saudi Arabia in February 1991, a practice normally strongly protested by China, and was received by the Saudi Foreign Minister. It was also reported that Kuwait, the first state in the Arabian Peninsula after the two Yemens to establish diplomatic relations with Beijing, had agreed to allow Taiwan to open "the Representative Office of the Republic of China."[31] There was no public reaction to these developments from Beijing, which suggests that it was attempting to handle an awkward situation delicately.

The setback to Beijing's diplomacy against Taipei was partly due to Taipei's more forceful position against Iraq. But Taipei's deep pocket was another weighty cause for its diplomatic success in the Arab world. While Beijing was building up a foreign debt of some $50 billion, by the end of 1990 Taipei had accumulated a foreign reserve of $72.4 billion, one of the largest in the world. China's ambassador to Saudi Arabia stated to the Saudi press that China was not in a position to contribute financially to the coalition. Five months after Taipei had announced its aid to Jordan, Egypt and Turkey, none of which had diplomatic relations with Taipei, China decided to donate goods worth less than one percent of what Taipei had provided (in dollar terms). By that time, Taiwan had already become one of the sources sought after by Saudi Arabia for billions of dollars in loans.[32]

Seen more broadly, the Gulf crisis will have substantial effects on China's plans for massive and multi-faceted economic cooperation with Arab Gulf states. Capital flight, war costs, reconstruction spending, and the focus on intra-regional aid will dry up the Gulf states' funds for long-distance investment, let alone for aid, if there are no overwhelming political and strategic incentives. Many Arab investment projects in China will be adversely affected as a result of such changes. China's role in construction and labor service contract business in the Arab world is similarly vulnerable. China's performance during the crisis will certainly be a factor taken into consideration by the Gulf states. The Kuwaiti Ambassador to the United Nations said in almost plain language that India did not stand much chance to win contracts in the reconstruction of Kuwait because of India's "neutrality."[33] He might well also have had China in mind, although given the weight of the two nations and the traditional ties they have had with Kuwait, they probably will not be treated too severely, even though they will not be favored.

6. China's Role in the Middle East

China has been probing for a new role in the Middle East. It has no stomach any longer for being the only challenger to the superpowers or the West as it used to be so often and so proudly. It is pleased with its identity as one of the "five big powers," though it has not shifted its international outlook completely, because its interests still require a close relationship with developing nations. The contradiction between being a rebellious Third World advocate and a law-abiding big power will be settled in a way exemplified by China's handling of the Gulf crisis. China may lean more toward a big power model if the West does not try to corner the Chinese leadership on the issue of human rights. Depending on how far China may lean, its friendly image in the Arab world, especially at the popular level, could suffer correspondingly as a result.

Overall, China chose during the crisis to be on the side of the big-five club, on the side of international legitimacy, on the side of the winner, and on the side of the best economic prospects. The decision was perhaps not difficult because of the unique features of the Gulf crisis that are unlikely to be repeated in future conflicts in the Middle East. The issues of international legitimacy were resolved by a unanimous world condemnation of the Iraqi invasion. The war fought by the coalition resulted in a decisive Iraqi defeat. Hardly anything remained to be mediated, so that there was little chance of China playing a more active role. Finally, Iraq was reduced to a destitute status, in sharp contrast with the GCC, the richest bloc in the Third World. Even if the uniqueness of the Gulf crisis is acknowledged, however, China's newly-fashioned position was not a one-time shot, but is·more likely to be a rule of thumb for China's future policy making, especially in the Middle East.

A process of pragmatizing China's diplomacy has been drastically accelerated by the Gulf crisis. But intra-Arab and intra-regional (Arab-Iran) tensions will still require China to be more selective in its approach than before. No matter how much China may dislike it, taking sides, cautiously yet definitively, will become a conventional feature of China's Arab policy. But China will likely not approach such conflicts alone. When facing an intra-Third World conflict, China is likely to join the side whose most assertive or dynamic members are likely to be well-connected to the North.

Notes

1. Resolution 678 was the "war resolution," Resolution 686 set the preliminary conditions for the cease-fire, and Resolution 688 was devoted to the protection of the human rights of Kurds.

2. *Xinhua,* April 14, 1988, in Foreign Broadcast Information Service, *Daily Report— China* (henceforth referred to as *FBIS-CHI*), April 14, 1988, p. 26.

3. Yitzhak Shichor, *The Middle East in China's Foreign Policy: 1949-77* (Cambridge: Cambridge University Press, 1979), p. 203.

4. For the absence of political problems in Sino-Arab relations, Yang's tour, and the problems in China's relations in the Asian-Pacific region, see Xiaoxing Han, "China's Arab Policy: Present Policy and Prospective Direction," in *The Arab World in the New International Order,* ed. Ibrahim Ibrahim (Washington, DC: Georgetown University, Center for Contemporary Arab Studies, forthcoming).

5. *Renmin Ribao (Haiwaiban),* [People's Daily (Overseas Edition)] (Beijing), August 6, 1990, p. 1.

6. *Renmin Ribao (Haiwaiban),* September 7, 1990, p. 1.

7. *Renmin Ribao (Haiwaiban),* September 6, 1990, p. 6; *Xinhua,* September 26, 1990 in *FBIS-CHI,* September 26, 1990, p. 1.

8. *Renmin Ribao (Haiwaiban),* August 27, 1990, p. 6.

9. *New York Times,* November 9, 1990, p. A10.

10. The ambiguity was compounded by China's juxtaposing the words "Gulf states" or "states" with the Arab states from time to time. That phrasing was probably intended to accommodate Iran's desire to play a major role.

11. *Sawt Al-Kuwait al-Duwali* [The Voice of Kuwait International] (London), December 1, 1990, p. 1.

12. *Zheng Ming* [Contention] (Hong Kong), September 1990, p. 15.

13. *Renmin Ribao (Haiwaiban),* August 6, 1990, p. 1.

14. Iraq News Agency, November 14, 1990, in Foreign Broadcast Information Service, *Daily Report—Near East and South Asia* (henceforth referred to as *FBIS-NES*), November 14, 1990, p. 21.

15. *Dagong Bao* [Dagong Daily] (Hong Kong), November 13, 1990, "Political Talk" column.

16. *Renmin Ribao (Haiwaiban)*, August 29, 1990, p. 1.

17. *Al-Ahram* [The Pyramids] (Cairo), August 27, 1990, p. 1.

18. *Riyadh* (Riyadh), October 23, 1990, p. 19.

19. *Renmin Ribao (Haiwaiban)*, November 12, 1990, p. 6.

20. *Sawt al-Kuwait al-Duwali*, December 28, 1990, p. 2.

21. *Sawt al-Kuwait al-Duwali*, December 28, 1990, p. 1.

22. *Beijing Review*, March 4-10, 1991, p. 7.

23. Statement by the Chinese Foreign Ministry Spokesman. *FBIS-CHI*, March 14, 1991, p. 2.

24. India's criticism was centered on "overstepping the United Nation's mandate" by bombing "industrial and technical infrastructures." It insisted on "taking up the issue" at the United Nations Security Council (*FBIS-NES*, February 14, 1991), p. 48. In addition to similar charges, the Soviet Union made an even harsher rebuke as Yevgeny Primakov, Gorbachev's personal envoy to the Middle East, called for "stopping the slaughter" (*Washington Post*, February 20, 1991, p. 1).

25. *Renmin Ribao (Haiwaiban)*, March 4, 1991, p. 6; February 22, 1991, p. 1.

26. *New York Times*, November 11, 1990, p. A1.

27. *Al-Safir* [The Messenger] (Beirut), January 23, 1991, p. 7; January 28, 1991, p. 7.

28. "China as seen from the Gulf Crisis: Who Can Belittle this Giant?" was the title of the headline article in *Zi Jing*, a newly instituted mouthpiece for the leadership in Hong Kong, October 1, 1990, pp. 15-16, quoted in *FBIS-CHI*, October 1, 1990, pp. 8-10.

29. A senior Arab diplomat from a Gulf state acknowledged "disappointment" by the Gulf states at China's abstention on Resolution 678 (personal interview).

30. *Xinhua*, October 3, 1990, in *FBIS-CHI*, October 3, 1990, p. 1; *Xinhua*, November 1, 1990, in *FBIS-CHI*, November 1, 1990, p. 1; *Riyadh*, October 11, 1990, p. 23. Kuwait was also a big partner in the loan package (*Sawt al-Kuwait al-Duwali*, November 29, 1990, p. 1; *Washington Post*, November 29, 1990, p. A37).

31. *Zhongyang Ribao (Guojiban)* [Central News (International Edition)] (Taipei), March 7, 1991, p. 1.

32. *Al-Safir*, February 7, 1991, p. 7. *Renmin Ribao (Haiwaiban)* February 22, 1991, p. 4; *Zhongyang Ribao (Guojiban)*, February 4, 1991, p. 1; *Zhongyang Ribao (Guojiban)*, March 7, 1991, p. 1.

33. *FBIS-NES-91-050*, March 14, 1991, pp. 48-49.

7 THE UNITED NATIONS AND THE GULF CRISIS

Augustus Richard Norton

Even in Washington, D.C., where the United Nations (UN) was a popular target for derision not so long ago, it is fairly common to hear laudatory remarks about the role which the international organization played in the Gulf crisis. Sometimes the compliments are even coupled with optimistic assessments about the role which the United Nations may play in a post-Cold War world which many observers, including this one, anticipate will be marked by increasing violence and unrest within the borders of states.[1] This turnaround is startling, especially considering that the more strident critics of the UN even questioned whether membership served the interests of the United States. The rehabilitation of the UN marks the dividing line between the relative rigidity of a familiar and predictable bi-polar world, and a world—yet to be fully defined—which lies beyond. In this essay some conclusions about the significance of the UN role in the crisis are offered, followed by some hopeful musings about roles to which the UN may be called.

No event more dramatically symbolized the end of the Cold War than the meeting of the United Nations Security Council on November 29, 1990, when the Soviet Union joined the United States, Britain, France and eight other Council members in approving Resolution 678, which authorized the use of "all necessary means" to bring an end to the Iraqi seizure of Kuwait.[2] The unprecedented coupling, in a Security Council resolution, of those three words—"all necessary means"—marked a seminal moment in the history of the United Nations. Despite the use of an elliptical diplomatic vocabulary, the resolution put the stamp of international legality on a sweeping use of military power to reverse a transparent act of aggression. Thus, when the United States and its allies launched their offensive against Iraq and Iraqi forces in and around Kuwait, the figurative imprimatur of the international community, however imperfectly expressed in the Security Council, was emblazoned on every bomb. Wars, justifiable or not, persistently put the lie to notions that warfare can be clean or targets may be hit "surgically," and the fact that many people and governments got more war than was bargained for when "all necessary means" were sanctioned only increases the signal quality of the resolution.[3] One can only hope and presume that the extensive damage inflicted upon both Kuwait and Iraq will provoke a continuing search for means short of the blunt instruments of war with which to exercise claims and enact international standards of order.

Four factors were essential to the passage of the historic resolution: the nature of the Iraqi action, namely undisguised aggression; sweeping international changes, in particular the end of the Cold War; the absence of a unified Arab response to the crisis; and the resolve, indeed obduracy, of the United States, and Britain as well, to deny Iraq any gain from its aggression.[4] (On the last point, an unanswered question, which lies beyond the scope of this brief treatment, is whether an "Arab solution" was short-circuited intentionally by the United States.)[5] The absence of any of these four factors would have made Resolution 678 improbable, if not impossible. Thus, it is not merely difficult to conceive of a plausible scenario in the Middle East or elsewhere where one state would act with the arrogant blatancy of Iraq, but it may also be hard to duplicate the special circumstances which enabled an international response.

It may also be hard to find a leader who will make consistently foolish decisions like Saddam. Not to minimize the diplomatic energy which was mobilized in Washington, New York and in capitals around the world, Saddam made it all a lot easier than it might have been. In effect, he stood by passively while the United States and its allies accumulated an unprecedented force in the Gulf, never interdicting the deployment, but waiting cooperatively for his forces to be destroyed and much of his military infrastructure to be crushed. For good measure, he deployed his forces with neither sophistication nor imagination. So, while a precedent has obviously been set, the relevance of the precedent is, unfortunately, relatively limited, both in terms of the types of leaders involved, and in terms of the nature of the threat to the peace. Iraq's invasion of Kuwait marked the limiting case. In the Gulf, as in the larger Middle East, the underlying problems will come in shades of gray, not with the black and white clarity of the recent crisis.

Looking forward from August 2, 1990, when Iraq's army crashed into Kuwait, it was not possible to foresee the many twists and turns which the crisis would take, but it was clear from the very onset of the crisis that a successful counter to Iraqi aggression would involve the United Nations. Even for the United States, the political and economic costs of going it alone were too high, and the benefits of working through the United Nations were too obvious, for the crisis to have played out differently. This is not to claim that the Bush Administration was of one mind regarding the importance of the UN. There were moments when the go-it-alone voices might have carried the day, were it not for the pressures of outside powers, particularly the Soviet Union. Thus, in August when the United States was moving unilaterally toward the creation of a naval blockade, it was, in part at least, a Soviet demurral which convinced the US Administration to win the blessing of the United Nations in Security Council Resolution 665.[6]

Changes at the United Nations

The Soviet Union played a significant role in fostering a new mood of cooperation and activism at the United Nations. Throughout the course of the crisis, the Soviet Union voted with the Charter and against its erstwhile ally, Iraq. Soviet diplomacy sometimes reflected mixed voices, some of which, like the military and the area specialists within the Foreign Ministry, were intent on preserving the relationship with Iraq as a valued ally. There were relatively open policy debates in the Soviet Union.[7] Western analysts, still finding their own feet in the post-Cold War world, were sometimes inclined to interpret the internal debates in the Soviet Union too malevolently. In the process, they understated the consistency which Soviet policy had shown vis-a-vis the UN for several years. One respected scholar even wrote that "Moscow was too closely following its own perceived national interests to be a genuine partner for the United States," a strange judgment when compared to the views expressed by leading US participants in the process.[8] For instance, Ambassador Thomas R. Pickering reflected frequently on the "shift in Soviet behavior" and a "greater willingness to condemn acts of aggression, even when perpetrated by a longtime friend, such as Iraq," as well as on the striking cohesion of the five permanent members of the Security Council.[9] Thus, when then-Deputy Prime Minister Saadoun Hammadi visited Moscow in August 1990 with the transparent goal of winning a Soviet veto in the Security Council, where enforcement measures for the UN-ordered embargo were being debated, he failed. Moscow voted with the alliance, as it did throughout the crisis. Moreover, when the Soviet Union had opportunities to scuttle US diplomacy, as it might have done in the past, it did not exploit the opportunities. Rather than insist on a public session of the Security Council to deal with the Temple Mount incident in October 1990, when Israeli police unjustifiably killed demonstrating Palestinians, the USSR went along with private sessions.

None of this is to suggest that, in retrospective assessments of the crisis, policy analysts will deduce that the Soviet policy was "successful," but the consistency of the policy is hard to fault. At the UN, there is widespread grumbling on the "hijacking" of the UN by the United States, and, given the extent to which the United States did have its way during the crisis, the complaining is not hard to understand. In fact, one result of the crisis is likely to be a concerted effort—in the next crisis—to circumscribe US options more actively, perhaps even to the point of insisting that any forces deployed should be explicitly under the UN flag and a UN command.

The end of the Cold War has been reflected very clearly in the Security Council, the UN body with the clear mandate to oversee the maintenance of international peace and security. The changes at the UN passed largely unnoticed, except by a small band of specialists and UN-based diplomats.[10] The sea change was authenticated by the impressive performance of the Security Council during the crisis.

A significant dividend of the recent dramatic improvement of relations between Moscow and Washington is that the Security Council has been functioning since mid-1987 as the collegial body anticipated in the United Nations (UN) Charter, rather than as a rhetorical battleground for great and not-so-great powers. Even cynical diplomats are speculating about collective security, a concept long thought buried with the idealism of the post-war era.

Coming so soon after the years of the Reagan Administration, the rejuvenation of the UN has been breathtaking.[11] One of Ronald Reagan's favorite campaign themes, in his 1980 victory over Jimmy Carter, was that America had gone "soft" in the post-Vietnam era. A decade of unchecked Soviet activism had increased Moscow's Third World clientele and influence. US policy had to change, and a most viscerally gratifying place in which to attack was the United Nations, where anti-US tirades were taken to be symptomatic of American anemia induced by the Carter presidency.

During the Reagan presidency, official US support for the United Nations plummeted. Unilateralism—intervening in Grenada, bombing in Libya and arming guerrillas in Afghanistan, Cambodia, Nicaragua and Angola—systematically supplanted American consideration of multilateral approaches to regional security. In addition to withdrawing or threatening to withdraw from a number of UN agencies, the US began to use the veto with unaccustomed regularity. The administration's hostility lent encouragement to congressional opponents of the UN, who voted to withhold some assessments, including those for peacekeeping.

While Washington was spurning the United Nations, the Soviet Union was discovering that the UN could help contain regional crises.[12] With the Red Army being bogged down in Afghanistan, and Soviet military assistance around the globe draining the treasury, Moscow came to the conclusion that UN conflict management was not so bad after all. At a time of straitened resources, when many influential Soviets were questioning the value of expensive efforts to prop-up "friendly" Third World regimes, a heightened role for the UN made good economic sense. The Kremlin, traditionally skeptical towards UN peacekeeping, began to give prominence to the work of its own diplomats and scholars who viewed the world organization positively. Concrete proof of a changing position came in 1986, when the Soviets announced that they would pay their assessment for the UN Interim Force in Lebanon (UNIFIL). Even more surprising was the 1987 commitment to reimburse what was then over $200 million of hard-currency peacekeeping arrears. Moreover, the Kremlin's acceptance of UN participation in monitoring the withdrawal of Soviet troops from Afghanistan, and behind-the-scenes cajoling of Cuba and Vietnam, lent additional authenticity to Moscow's new policy.

The renovation of Soviet Third World doctrine had begun subtly under Yuri Andropov and Konstantin U. Chernenko, but significant policy shifts coincided with Mikhail Gorbachev's tenure. At the 27th Party Congress in February 1986, Moscow began to call for a "comprehensive system of international security." Over the next four years, lofty platitudes were replaced with more specific proposals for the prevention and containment of regional conflicts.

In 1987 Gorbachev began to emphasize the potential role of the UN in conflict resolution. Moscow embraced the UN across-the-map as the most effective actor to stem and solve Third World conflicts. Perhaps more than any other single event, Gorbachev's December 1988 speech before the General Assembly reflects the sea change in Soviet diplomatic efforts; it stands in sharp contrast to his September 1987 *Pravda* article, a sweeping and vague "shopping list." Under the guidance of Deputy Minister of Foreign Affairs Vladimir F. Petrovsky, a UN veteran and skilled technician of multilateral affairs, the Soviets sought to make the peacekeeping regime more solvent, active, and effective.[13]

To the irritation of some of the UN's more trenchant American critics, marked policy shifts, first by the Soviet Union and then by the United States, brought the world body back to center stage. Washington's response to the Soviet overtures was generally cautious. But the mistrust and distaste for the UN, which was so evident from 1981-88, was displaced by a pragmatic willingness to exploit UN instruments for mitigating regional conflicts. After prolonged episodes of ideological axe-grinding by US ambassadors at the UN, the US returned to the motif of quiet diplomacy with an emphasis on the UN's positive peacekeeping and peacemaking roles. Early in his presidency George Bush took steps to symbolize his commitment to the institution, where he represented the United States as ambassador in the early 1970s.

Pinpointing Saddam Hussein's most egregious miscalculation is a real challenge. But one of his most serious blunders was the failure to understand the dramatic shift which had occurred at the UN.

Building on the Gulf Victory

When attempting to weigh the significance of what was actually accomplished in the Gulf, a due sense of modesty is justified. Certainly, in narrow terms, the war was a success. Iraq was expelled from Kuwait and Kuwaiti independence was restored, but whether the means chosen to accomplish this goal reflected a decision that was right and wise remains to be seen. The geo-political equilibrium of the Gulf—not to mention the Middle East—was shaken, and it will be some time before a new balance is reached; that will probably not happen until the final outcome of the postwar turmoil within Iraq reaches a conclusion. All that is sure, for the moment, is that the crisis and war in the Gulf have rudely shaken the ground, and that, truly, the Middle East may never again be the same.[14]

Ironically, the most significant impact of the event may have been, as one Arab scholar noted recently, that the "wall of fear" separating citizens from autocratic rulers has been broken. If this is so, George Bush and his leader-colleagues may have unleashed whirlwinds of change which will engender profound instability in the Arab world.[15] The irony, of course, is that while the great powers applaud participation and exalt democracy, they loathe instability, yet the achievement of greater participation and democratization without accompanying instability is difficult to imagine. To embroider the irony, there is, of course, no necessary affinity between popular (often populist) political voices and western governments, and the contrary is often the case. These "inconveniences" notwithstanding, there can be little doubt that the long-term outcome, namely more open government, is in the enlightened self-interest of the United States and the West.

Respected observers have emphasized the significance of the war for its demonstration effect—its message to tyrants, as it were. For instance, Georgi I. Mirski, the Russian scholar, observes: "The UN recently was able to overcome differences of opinion, mobilize dozens of nations and mount a large-scale campaign in order to liberate one of its member countries which had fallen victim to aggression. [The] vast potential of this international body has been demonstrated to the whole world."[16] But the crisis also demonstrated that the United Nations enjoys little autonomy and that it can accomplish very little—in terms of insuring international peace and security, the mandate of the Security Council—unless the Council, and the five permanent members in particular, permit it to do so. Even so, it was encouraging to witness a rediscovery of the United Nations, even if the actions carried out under its mandate often were ad hoc.

But as a model for action, the response to Iraqi aggression was so consumptive of time, resources and the world's attention that it is obvious that it will not soon be replicated. As Stanley Hoffman observes, "If, in a world of shaky regimes, contested borders, ethnic upheavals and religious revivals, every act of aggression requires the mobilization of three-quarters of a million troops, many sent across the seas to face well-armed troublemakers and obtain their unconditional surrender, there will be very few cases of collective security."[17]

Was the Gulf crisis a flash in the pan? In other words, can we expect the UN to play a larger role in the solution of other regional conflicts? Has a new urgency arisen?

An important question, really the crucial one, is whether it will be possible to build on the success in the Gulf by institutionalizing instruments of collective security which will enable the international body to react in order to pre-empt aggression, rather than simply respond to it. If there is hope to be drawn from the Gulf crisis, it is that despite all of its tragic aspects, it is no longer naively idealistic to talk about the establishment of a standing United Nations force as envisaged in the Charter, specifically in Chapter Seven. Especially with great power participation, such a force might represent a credible deterrent. As Lawrence Freedman notes correctly, "The sweeping victory in the Gulf undermined any notion that the Third World can now compete with the West in the military sphere."[18] Had a UN force been deployed to the Iraq-Kuwait border in July 1990, it is just possible that Saddam Hussein would not have launched his star-crossed invasion.[19] Even without the creation of a standing United Nations force, the resolve shown in the Security Council can go a long way toward impeding aggression. Imagine that the Security Council had acted with concerted resolve in 1982 to prevent an Israeli invasion of Lebanon and had given clear orders to the UN force to stand its ground rather than ignominiously watch while Israeli tanks rolled by. A series of tragedies precipitated by that ill-fated invasion might have been prevented or at least lessened in their extent.

The point would be for the Security Council, in cooperation with the regional organizations, like the Arab League or a more inclusive regional grouping, to guarantee credibly the territorial integrity of member states. However, the guarantees would not be credible unless positive steps were taken to create procedures, forces and means to implement the guarantees. Bluntly, significant steps—well beyond allusions to the new systems of international order—are necessary. For instance, some of the states which have traditionally supported UN peacekeeping, Canada and the Scandinavian countries, have earmarked forces for deployment under UN command. This is in the spirit of Article 43 of the Charter, in which all members of the UN agree to make forces available to the Security Council to contribute to the maintenance of international peace and security. It would be a major step forward if the permanent members of the Security Council also earmarked forces to be deployed under the control of the Security Council in coordination with states threatened with imminent attack. A reliable system of international guarantees, coupled with the ability to deploy international forces to preempt aggression, would enhance the confidence of governments otherwise plagued by insecurity and routinely dominated by militarized policy making. To offer two hypothetical cases, the Security Council might direct pre-emptive deployments along the Jordan river valley or on the Saudi-Yemeni border in order to forestall military attacks. Especially in the Middle East, where expenditures for weapons routinely rival expenditures for education, this type of initiative offers some hope for putting the brakes on, if not stopping, the enormously wasteful acquisition of weapons, notably by Egypt, Iraq (until recently), Israel, Saudi Arabia and Syria.[20] To underline the point in another way, about 60 percent of all Third World arms imports occur in the Middle East.

In monitoring compliance with Security Council Resolution 687, the omnibus resolution which defined the terms of Iraq's capitulation, the United States has demonstrated an impressive surveillance capacity. Given state-of-the-art technology, it is completely feasible for the international community to anticipate menacing movements of troops, the fabrication of worrisome facilities for the construction of mass destruction weapons, and general compliance with a range of international agreements. The coupling of an early warning system with a standing force capable of prompt deployment would be a major step forward. However, many threats to international peace and security originate within the borders of states, and, as an institution, the UN persists in its reluctance to intervene in the "internal affairs" of member states; that reluctance will impede the capacity of the UN to forestall, if not quell, violence. There is a tension between the rights of individuals and the prerogatives of states. This tension is inherent in the Charter, and is also symbolized by the juxtaposition of the Universal Declaration on Human Rights to the state-centric empirical reality of the UN. In recent years, however, there has been increasing debate over circumstances which might justify, if not demand, intervention by the UN.[21] The active, albeit reluctant, role accepted by the UN in northern Iraq may prove to be a harbinger for future humanitarian intervention.

The UN's involvement in Iraq has, in point of fact, had a schizoid quality about it. On the one hand, the basic twelve resolutions were prompted by a principled upholding of the sovereign independence of a state, namely Kuwait. On the other, subsequent intervention by the UN within Iraq underlined that sovereignty was not absolute. With the weight of time, the second norm may prove to be the most momentous one, if the hardest to apply impartially.

Part of the problem in the humanitarian area has been the innate and explicable conservatism of the Secretary-General and his staff which also needs to be overcome. The status quo bias of the Secretary-General reflects the continuing—albeit waning—influence of the state system,[22] but it is also a function of practical dollar and cents questions. After the resolutions are passed, the speeches made and delegates leave for home, the professional leadership and staff of the organization must see to implementation, which necessarily means financing as well. In recent years there has been an unfortunate tendency for members (the United States has been a notable case, but is by no means the only example) to withhold part of their assessments, or simply to pay late.[23] This means that member-states not only must commit themselves to implementing collective security, but perforce must pay for collective security. The costs would not, however, be exorbitant. By way of illustration, the complex UN operation in Namibia, which oversaw elections and shepherded Namibia to independence, cost well under a billion dollars.

The crisis marked the emergence of an assertive Security Council, emboldened by the vanquishing of Iraq. The example of UN Resolution 687 is illustrative.

The solidarity of the permanent five members is noteworthy, though the Chinese abstained rather than cast a positive vote for the key resolution, number 678. The smooth coordination among the permanent five was not a simple product of an improved international climate, but was the result of active coordination, which began during the Iran-Iraq war. That war ended in a ceasefire within the framework of Security Council Resolution 598. During the course of the Gulf crisis, scores of meetings of the five were held, most of them at the French mission to the UN.

The Security Council succeeded in tying the hands of the Secretary-General throughout the Gulf crisis. Participants in the Security Council deliberations emphasize that the Secretary-General was pliant. When allied commanders met their Iraqi counterparts in Safwan, the Secretary-General and the UN were not even represented, an extraordinary symbolic omission. The pattern continued. In 1991 the United States Secretary of State, James Baker, made repeated visits to the Middle East in a dogged effort to launch negotiations in the Arab-Israeli peace process. When the envisaged negotiations actually began, the sponsors were the US and Soviet Union, and the role of arranging subsequent rounds of negotiations was assumed by the US.

A Double Standard?

The charge of a double standard is usually intended to mean that the United Nations acted forcefully against Iraq, while it has not acted with equal force to apply resolutions passed earlier which have gone unenforced. There are two counters to the charge: one is that in most regional conflicts it is by no means so obvious as it was in the Gulf crisis who the victim is and who is the aggressor. Second, no progress will ever be made in establishing an international order based on non-aggression, if no action may be taken until every wrong in the world is righted.[24]

The integrity of the newly activist Security Council will not go

untested. Of course, the test for the United States and the other permanent members of the Security Council will come when the implementation of collective measures contradicts rather than complements
the interests of one or more of the permanent members or, for that
matter, fails to win widespread support in the Third World. (On the
latter point, with half a dozen votes in the Security Council, Third
World states wield what amounts to a sixth veto. The importance of
the Third World ballots is buttressed by the fact that the Chinese
identify with the Third World group. One senior diplomat with intimate
exposure to the Security Council notes that China was deeply influenced
in its voting during the crisis by the pro-alliance tilt reflected in Third
World votes.)

Future crises in the Middle East, or in other regions where the
strategic and economic interests of the major world powers are
less salient, will provide the test. As Bernard Wood notes, "If,
at that stage, this new international consensus and the new international security structure fails to respond with equal vigor and
even-handedness, the cynics will have been vindicated, and more
importantly, the world will be plunged backward."[25]

Lingering disputes and old complaints are now resurfacing, borne
by the rejuvenation of hope which has been one effect of the
international response to the crisis in the Gulf. The United Nations
will continue to be enmeshed with the situation created by the Gulf
war. In addition, the United Nations will be challenged also to prove
its good faith in Cyprus, Lebanon, and even in Palestine. One test
will be in Lebanon, where the government is pushing, with surprising
vitality and growing credibility, for the application of UN Resolution
425, which calls for the withdrawal of Israeli forces from the south
and the restoration of government authority. The successful disarming of
the PLO in the South during early July 1991 undermined Israel's
argument for its "security zone."

Given the unipolar moment through which the world is now passing,
some critics argue that the United Nations has become a mere surrogate
for the United States. Certainly, the US performed throughout the
crisis as the primus inter pares. One well-placed secretariat veteran
characterized US diplomacy during the crisis as one of the most
outstanding performances he had ever witnessed. Perhaps the key to
the US success was that it was a product of give and take, as when the
US supported a fairly tough treatment of Israel for its role in the
Temple Mount shootings in October. Retrospective assessments of
the crisis are likely to lead prospective diplomatic partners of the US
to insist on taking more and giving a little less.

Meanwhile, the influence the US enjoys with its friends may be used constructively to move Middle East friends to compliance with UN resolutions or to request a more active UN role in some realms. Notably, the continuing Israeli occupation of a portion of Lebanon would seem to qualify for an expenditure of US diplomatic energy to implement Resolution 425.

As noted here, it is unlikely that there will be a close analogue to the Iraq-Kuwait case. If, however, there is reason to be hopeful about what has happened, it is that there may now be a chance for the United Nations, with the support of its key members, to live up to the promise of the Charter as agreed to by some 150 states, including every state in the Middle East.

To maintain international peace and security, and to that end: to take effective collective security measures for the prevention and removal of threats to the peace, and for the suppression of acts of aggression or other breaches of the peace, and to bring about by peaceful means, and in conformity with the principles of justice and international law, adjustment or settlement of international disputes or situations which might lead to a breach of the peace. (Article 1, Chapter I of the Charter)

Notes

1. Observers from disparate backgrounds have reached this conclusion. Brian Urquhart, for example, notes that: "We are entering a period of great instability, characterized by longstanding international rivalries and resentments, intense ethnic and religious turmoil, a vast flow of arms and military technology, domestic disintegration, poverty and deep economic inequities, instantaneous communications throughout the world, population pressures, natural and ecological disasters, the scarcity of vital resources, and huge movements of population" (*New York Review of Books,* March 7, 1991), pp. 34-37. See also James Rosenau, *Turbulence in World Politics: A Theory of Change and Continuity* (Princeton: Princeton University Press, 1990); Augustus Richard Norton, "The Security Legacy of the 1980s in the Third World," in Thomas G. Weiss and Meryl A. Kessler, eds., *Third World Security in the Post-Cold War Era* (Boulder: Lynne Rienner, 1991); Bernard Wood, *World Order and Double Standards: Peace and Security 1990-91* (Ottawa: Canadian Institute for International Peace and Security, 1991), pp. 22-26.

2. Yemen and Cuba voted against the resolution, and China, consistently the most reticent permanent member, abstained. Canada, Finland, Colombia, Ethiopia, Finland, Ivory Coast, Malaysia and Romania joined Britain, France, the Soviet Union and the United States in voting in favor of the resolution. Of the twelve resolutions passed from August 2, 1990, when the Security Council condemned the Iraqi invasion, until the approval of Resolution 678, there were six unanimous ballots, one with fourteen positive votes, and five with thirteen positive votes. There were twelve affirmative votes for Resolution 678.

3. For an authoritative assessment of the damage in Iraq see the report by Under-Secretary-General Martti Ahtissari, S/22366, March 20, 1991, and the companion report for Kuwait, S/22409, March 28, 1991. Given the restrained quality of the diplomatic vernacular, the Ahtissari reports are unusually explicit. He refers to "cataclysmic" conditions in Iraq, and vividly describes the damage wrought by Iraq in Kuwait.

4. George Bush met the British Prime Minister Margaret Thatcher at a meeting at the Aspen Institute in August. Several reports indicate that Mrs. Thatcher urged Bush to take the firmest possible stand and to mobilize the world under the auspices of the United Nations, but other accounts imply that the Prime Minister was preaching to a choir. For instance, see Pierre Salinger and Eric Laurent, *Secret Dossier: The Hidden Agenda behind the Gulf War* (Harmondsworth, England: Penguin, 1991), p. 106.

5. See Pierre Salinger and Eric Laurent, *Secret Dossier: The Hidden Agenda behind the Gulf War* (Harmondsworth, England: Penguin, 1991); and Milton Viorst, "A Reporter at Large: The House of Hashem," *New Yorker,* January 7, 1991, pp. 32-52. In both accounts, inconclusive evidence is offered to raise the possibility that the United States aborted an Arab solution by applying pressure on Egyptian President Hosni Mubarak in particular. According to these accounts, Mubarak, in turn, roundly condemned the Iraqi invasion (privately citing "tremendous pressure"). The Egyptian condemnation thereby made it impossible for Iraq to withdraw gracefully from Kuwait. In Viorst's account, Saddam Hussein reputedly reached early agreement with Saudi King Fahd to withdraw from Kuwait, retaining the Rumaila oil field and the islands of Bubiyan and Warbah.

6. See Robert Legvold's incisive analysis, "The Gulf Crisis," *The Harriman Institute Forum* 3, No. 10 (October 1990), especially p. 42.

7. For a timely discussion see Graham Fuller, "Moscow and the Gulf War," *Foreign Affairs* 70, No. 3 (Summer 1991), pp. 55-76.

8. Robert O. Freedman, "Moscow and the Invasion of Kuwait: A Preliminary Analysis," unpublished paper, May 8, 1991.

9. As an example, see Pickering's speech before the Veterans of Foreign Wars, March 4, 1991.

10. For a readable overview, see George L. Sherry, *The United Nations Reborn: Conflict Control in the Post-Cold War World* (New York: Council on Foreign Relations, Critical Issues, no. 2, 1990).

11. For a more detailed treatment, the interested reader is referred to Augustus Richard Norton and Thomas G. Weiss, *UN Peacekeepers: Soldiers With a Difference* (New York: Foreign Policy Association, 1990). Some of the material in the remainder of this section is adapted from Augustus Richard Norton and Thomas G. Weiss, "Superpowers and Peacekeepers," *Survival* 32, no. 3 (May/June 1990), pp. 212-20.

12. For a discussion of the changes, see Mark Katz, *Gorbachev's Military Policy in the Third World* (New York: Praeger, 1989); and Thomas G. Weiss, ed., *American, Soviet, and Third World Perceptions of Regional Conflicts* (New York: International Peace Academy, 1989) and idem., *UN Conflict Management: American, Soviet, and Third World Views* (New York: International Peace Academy, 1990).

13. Mikhail S. Gorbachev, "Reality and Guarantees of a Secure World," *Pravda,* September 17, 1987, pp. 1-2; see also "Comprehensive Review of the Whole Question of Peacekeeping Operations in All Their Aspects," letter from the Deputy Head of the Delegation of the USSR, document A/43/629, September 22, 1988 and "Statement by V.F.Petrovsky," mimeograph, Soviet Permanent Mission to the United Nations, October 17, 1988.

14. For one attempt to come to grips with the significance of the events in the Gulf, see Muhammad Muslih and Augustus Richard Norton, *The Middle East after Desert Storm* (tentative) (New York: Foreign Policy Association, forthcoming).

15. For a discussion of the Arab malaise which underlies the phenomenon of Saddam Hussein, see Muhammad Muslih and Augustus Richard Norton, "The Need for Arab Democracy," *Foreign Policy,* no. 83 (Summer 1991), pp. 3-19.

16. "The Middle East after the Gulf War," a paper presented in Vienna at the International Peace Academy conference on "Middle East Challenges after the Gulf War," May 27-29, 1991.

17. "Avoiding New World Disorder," *New York Times,* February 25, 1991.

18. Lawrence Freedman, "The Gulf War and the New World Order," *Survival* 33, no. 3 (May/June 1991), pp. 195-209. Quotation from p. 202.

19. See Bruce Russett and James S. Sutterlin, "The UN in a New World Order," *Foreign Affairs* 70, no. 2 (Spring 1991), pp. 69-83.

20. A former US Secretary of Defense and World Bank President, Robert S. McNamara, has developed this argument persuasively. "The Post-Cold War World and Its Implications for Military Expenditures in Developing Countries," in *Toward Collective Security: Two Views,* Occasional Paper No. 5 (Providence: Thomas J. Watson Jr. Institute for International Studies, Brown University, 1991).

21. See Leon Gordenker and Thomas G. Weiss, eds., *Soldiers, Peacekeepers, and Disasters* (London: Macmillan, 1990); and Thomas G. Weiss and Larry Minear, "Do International Ethics Matter?: Humanitarian Politics in the Sudan," *Ethics & International Affairs* 5 (1991), pp. 197-214.

22. James Rosenau tackles the ramifications, for the United Nations, of global turbulence and the resultant challenges to the state system in *The United Nations in a Turbulent World* (Boulder: Lynne Rienner, International Peace Academy Occasional Paper series, 1992).

23. On financing and management, see Susan R. Mills, *The Financing of United Nations Peacekeeping Operations: The Need for a Sound Financial Basis* (New York: International Peace Academy, Occasional Papers on Peacekeeping, No. 3, 1989).

24. Wood, "World Order and Double Standards," pp. 12-13.

25. Wood, "World Order and Double Standards," p. 13.

8 AFTER THE GULF WAR: THE GCC AND THE WORLD

John Duke Anthony

The defense policies of the countries of the Gulf Cooperation Council (GCC) face severe constraints posed by the vast territory of the GCC, its exposed infrastructure, and the small size of its population and armed forces in comparison to Iraq and Iran. The main implication of these constraints is that the GCC will, for the foreseeable future, pursue a strategy that combines enhanced deterrence with a reliance on the geopolitical and, *in extremis,* military components of the allied coalition that confronted the Iraqi invasion of Kuwait.

The strong moral, political, diplomatic, and military support that the GCC received from regional and global powers during the Kuwait crisis convinced it of the necessity to ensure that such support will be as readily forthcoming in the future, if necessary, as it was in 1990. In the aftermath of Kuwait's liberation, more than a dozen countries could be envisaged as playing possible roles in the new, more credible deterrence and defense mechanism that the GCC sought to construct.

These countries are a diverse group, whose ties with the Gulf countries differ in nature. Some have strong economic interests in the flow of oil; others are linked by a common Arab or Islamic historical and cultural background. In the Gulf crisis, they were bound by a common interest in preventing the annexation of Kuwait by Iraq and the resulting Iraqi dominance over the world oil market, the Gulf and the eastern Arab world. This interest serves as a basis for their incorporation in future GCC strategies. GCC planners are also aware that the policies of their potential regional partners may be variable. The overall GCC strategy will aim to consolidate ties with a large number of countries to reduce problems that might arise from volatility in the behavior of any one country.

1. The Role of Middle Eastern States in GCC Strategic Planning

In its planning for a more effective defense in the postwar period, the Gulf Cooperation Council (GCC) has concentrated on both short-term and longer-term challenges from three countries: Iraq, Iran, and

Yemen. Among the three, Iraq is considered the foremost real threat, followed by a potential threat from Iran and, to a much lesser extent (if at all), Yemen.

The predominant belief among GCC governments is that the blame for the breakdown in regional order in 1990 lay with the government of Saddam Hussein, not with the Iraqi people. The GCC is also united in its view that Iraq must remain a unitary state. It is opposed to supporting either Kurdish or Shi'a separatism in Iraq and is not willing, under any circumstances, to accept the establishment of an independent state by either group. In this regard, the GCC's policy remains unchanged from the days of the Iran-Iraq war when it repeatedly stated that the regional status quo, particularly the territorial inviolability of the Gulf's existing eight riparian countries, must be upheld at all costs.

At the same time, the GCC is keen to see Iraq's future potential for military adventurism or revenge severely circumscribed. Further, the GCC wants to ensure that international arrangements are undertaken which will result in future Iraqi governments being held much more effectively to international law than was the case with Saddam Hussein's regime.

The GCC is also a vocal advocate of the unanimously passed Article Eight of UN Security Council Resolution 598 of July 1987 pertaining to the Iran-Iraq war. Article Eight voiced the international community's consensus (with Iraq adhering immediately and Iran agreeing a year later) that all eight of the Gulf countries should work to achieve a comprehensive regional security agreement for the Gulf as a whole. Implicit was the understanding among the signatories that the achievement of a tripolarity among Iraq, Iran, and the GCC would be the cornerstone of any such agreement.

As the GCC has been unable to be a credible "third pillar," either militarily or demographically, it has had to seek exceptional support to attain a level of overall parity vis a vis Iraq and Iran in terms of power and influence. It can become a credible third pillar in any regional defense arrangement only if it can succeed in enlisting the support of a sufficient number of powerful partners. As shown below, however, the regional components of what might constitute a successful arrangement are by no means certain.

In the broadly defined Middle East region, six countries are of major interest to GCC strategic planners. Egypt and Syria, as members of the coalition that liberated Kuwait, are prominent potential Arab partners in future GCC strategic planning. One other Arab country,

Morocco, has also traditionally played a role in the defense and security policies of a number of GCC states, although a number of factors limit the extent of the role it may be able to play in future GCC plans.

Among the leading non-Arab Muslim countries, Turkey played an important role in the Gulf crisis and continued close ties with Turkey are desired by the GCC countries. One country that is considered a possible threat by the GCC, Iran, is also viewed as sharing some common interests that would make it a possible partner under certain circumstances. A more distant country that has offered military advice and assistance to the Gulf countries in the past has been Pakistan, but its failure to offer wholehearted support to the GCC countries during the Gulf crisis has meant that its role in Gulf planning is not a primary one.

Egypt

When the guns fell silent in the aftermath of Kuwait's liberation, Egypt was the major Arab country that seemed likely to be accorded a prominent role in any new Gulf defense arrangement. From the GCC leaders' perspective, such a role would have followed naturally on Egypt's quick support for the GCC, the deployment of crack elite Egyptian troops, and Cairo's critical role in hosting the two Arab League summits that condemned Iraq's invasion and provided important Arab and Islamic geopolitical legitimacy to the allied coalition.

Soon after Kuwait was liberated, an important military role was envisaged for Egypt in the context of the Damascus Declaration, a communique issued following the meeting of the GCC's Ministerial Council plus the foreign ministers of Egypt and Syria in Damascus on March 6, 1991.[1] An important feature of discussions accompanying the Declaration was the eight countries' intention to establish a permanent peacekeeping force in the Gulf; however, within a few months after the announcement, the idea was scrapped.

One major reason was the objection of Iran, which balked at the concept of non-Gulf countries being invited into the Gulf to play a military role.[2] A second reason was that several GCC countries began to have second thoughts about the wisdom of the arrangement. In some, religious leaders and other conservative elements, reluctant in any case to endorse the concept of foreign troops on their soil, expressed displeasure at the thought of troops from Egypt and Syria, since in recent decades governments of these foreign countries had supported efforts to subvert what later became the GCC governments.

In the midst of Iran's highly vocal recriminations and the GCC's second thoughts, Egyptian President Mubarak, whose troops were to have been the backbone of the peacekeeping force, declared that he was having more than second thoughts. Insinuating that Egypt had been insulted, inadequately consulted, and insufficiently appreciated for its contributions to the liberation of Kuwait, Mubarak announced that Egypt would not participate at all in a peace-keeping force. Underlying the rhetoric was Egyptian disappointment that the GCC countries, and Kuwait in particular, had not been as forthcoming on the number of postwar reconstruction and related contracts offered to Egyptian firms and workers as Cairo had expected.

Weeks later, there were candid admissions by both the GCC and Egypt that they had expressed their doubts and criticisms in haste and should continue to meet with a view to agreeing on as many areas of potential cooperation as possible. In this spirit, the eight foreign ministers met again in Kuwait in July. At the Kuwait meeting, the ministers agreed to forego the idea of external Arab military involvement in any GCC regional defense arrangement, but indicated that they would not oppose a GCC member country entering into bilateral arrangements, with Egypt, Syria, or anybody else, which it felt necessary to enhance its defense. The ministers agreed that a role for Egypt, Syria, or any other Arab non-Gulf country should be confined solely to meeting the defense needs of Kuwait and such other GCC members as might wish to enter into separate bilateral arrangements for that purpose. While many Egyptians and Syrians viewed this development as a setback, the GCC saw it differently, as a policy sensitive to strategic considerations raised by Iran and opposition voiced by important domestic constituencies.

Syria

The Syrian potential for playing a significant role in postwar GCC defense or geopolitical arrangements was, in GCC eyes, at least as mixed as Egypt's. Apart from the fact that Syria, like Egypt, is not a Gulf country, there was opposition by the religious establishments, and the politically conservative constituencies in the GCC countries in general, to anything more than nominal Syrian involvement in any matter pertaining to defense. One reason given was that recent pro-Gulf changes in Syria's foreign policies notwithstanding, the Damascus regime had for a long time been considered a close copy of Iraq in its governmental structure, domestic political dynamics, and alleged hegemonic ambitions vis-a-vis its neighbors.

As such, in GCC eyes, Syria did not yet warrant the kind of trust and confidence that GCC members had extended to one another and, to a lesser degree, to Egypt. Other reservations were rooted in concern for operational details. Among such concerns were the perceived potential security risks that could ensue from Syrian involvement in the early stages of the GCC's planning for a postwar defense structure, in GCC command, control, and communications systems, and in intelligence-sharing activities. In addition, the GCC countries were reluctant to enter into arrangements with Syria that might involve them in Syria's disputes with its neighbors or its uneasy relationships with the United States, Great Britain, and others. The Gulf states were also wary of the possibility that a future Syrian government might be less willing than that of Hafiz al-Assad to enter into Gulf security arrangements.

For all these reasons, the GCC is likely to want any potential post-war role for Syria in the Gulf to focus on the following GCC goals: (1) enlisting Damascus' assistance in the GCC's objective of providing an important geostrategic and political counter-weight to Iraq; (2) engaging Iran in a multifaceted network of constructive relations; (3) achieving a semblance of political balance within the Arab League; and (4) working with Egypt, Lebanon, Djibouti, and as many other non-Gulf Arab countries as possible to form a moderate bloc within an eventually revived Arab order.

Nevertheless, a more extensive role for Syria may be agreed upon in the foreseeable future. In return, Syria, with de facto GCC political and diplomatic support, could stand a greater chance of regaining sooner rather than later the Golan Province lands that it lost to Israel in the June 1967 War and which Israel formally annexed in November 1981. Apart from the potential that close GCC-Syria cooperation offers prospects for securing a Middle East peace beyond the Gulf, there is also a potential for mutual benefit in the area of economic cooperation. For example, any financial assistance from the GCC countries to the Damascus government could be designated in such a way as to further facilitate the increasing transformation of Syria's economy into a market economy. Beyond encouraging trade and investment with Syria, this development might also help facilitate yet another GCC objective: the phased withdrawal of Syrian forces from Lebanon in accordance with the Taif Accord of 1989.

Morocco

Another potential but far less likely claimant for special consideration by the GCC in terms of regional defense cooperation is Morocco. Had it sought such a role, which it did not, Morocco would likely have received favorable consideration for reasons that went beyond those pertaining to Egypt and Syria. Morocco, like Egypt and Syria, voted with the GCC on both of the critical Arab League resolutions in August 1990 and contributed troops very early in the Kuwait crisis. Moreover, unlike Egypt or Syria, it had provided special training and other security assistance to Saudi Arabia and the United Arab Emirates for much of the past decade.

Despite its favorable standing in the eyes of the GCC countries, Morocco was compelled, primarily for domestic reasons, to adopt a low profile on matters pertaining to Gulf defense arrangements during the Desert Storm phase of the Kuwait crisis. Little has changed in this regard in the postwar period. As the internationally concerted action to liberate Kuwait got underway in the autumn of 1990, the same anti-western religious currents that were manifested in Jordan, Mauritania, Pakistan, Sudan, Yemen, and several other countries in opposition to the allied coalition made themselves felt in Morocco. Had the Arab League met two months later to reconsider its August 10, 1990, vote in support of the member countries' contributing troops to the Multi-National Force, the need to maintain domestic stability would have compelled Morocco either to reverse its vote or to abstain.

Aside from the opposition to a regional defense role by Egypt, Syria, Morocco, or any other non-Gulf country, by Iran and elements within the GCC and its member countries, the potential for rapid progress in reaching the GCC's postwar defense goals in partnership with its regional allies remains problematic for another reason as well. It remains unclear whether the GCC would be able to pay for the costs of such an arrangement.

Egypt, Syria, Morocco and numerous other Arab countries have a legitimate need for capital—and certainly one way to obtain it would be to obtain major financial support from the Gulf states. Most of the GCC countries, however, continue to have pressing needs for increased revenues to address a range of domestic needs and prior obligations. All six GCC countries, moreover, have been in budgetary deficit each year since 1983. The boom has long since passed.

What this means insofar as non-Gulf potential regional partners in a postwar Gulf defense scheme are concerned is that such hopes and expectations as were raised in the immediate aftermath of the war have had to be trimmed back. Initial talk of a $15 billion GCC fund to assist Egypt and Syria that was initiated at the time of the GCC's heads of state summit in Qatar in December 1990 has been reduced to $10 billion.

As a result of these developments and, more directly, the GCC's decision to engage Tehran constructively, Iran has moved to a more prominent place in the GCC's postwar planning. Even so, the prospects for Iran playing a role of any significance in either the short term or the long run are quite problematic.

Iran

Dating from before the August 1988 ceasefire in the Iran-Iraq war, the GCC has been communicating with Iran on a range of common concerns. Among the more important of these has been the extent to which Iran is willing to work with the GCC on a range of issues in which not only they but Iraq, too, share an interest. The issues include trade and investment, quotas for the Islamic pilgrimage, and the rationale for a western military presence in the Gulf. In the event that these topics are addressed to their mutual satisfaction (and only then), a role of some kind for Iran may well be welcomed by the GCC, and possibly also by others, in whatever regional defense arrangements are devised.

Iranian and GCC leaders indicate that neither of them has yet developed specific ideas and details with respect to defense cooperation in the post-crisis period. However, both are in agreement that Iranian views on any postwar regional defense arrangements will not be dismissed out of hand.

In the postwar period, diplomatic movement between Tehran and most GCC capitals, which was on a slow ascent prior to the Kuwait crisis, accelerated on the whole. Most of the GCC countries have encouraged their ministries of commerce and their private sectors to increase trade and related links with Iran, a development particularly welcomed by the highly influential GCC business communities. Building on the robust Iran-UAE trade that continued throughout the Iran-Iraq war, this informal governmental green light has spurred a flurry of new and renewed contacts between Iranians and Arabs on both sides of the Gulf.

Nowhere was this flurry more obvious than in Bahrain and Kuwait, with the latter conducting a brisk trade in fruits and vegetables with Iranian merchants who, by mid-summer 1991, were arriving at Kuwait's dhow harbor almost hourly unencumbered by the previous requirement of visas and with customs duties waived.

One of the intended consequences was that Baghdad and, by extension, Amman, Sana'a, and other Arab capitals, should receive a clear GCC message: that the GCC's future cooperation with non-GCC countries would be reciprocal and based on mutually beneficial needs, concerns, and interests. Foremost among the latter, the GCC insists, must be its partners' strict adherence to the principle of non-interference in one another's domestic affairs. Another criterion, definitionally imprecise but intuitively understood throughout the Gulf, is "good neighborliness."

Although most GCC leaders are pleased with their accelerated dialogue with Iran, there are major items of unfinished business on the GCC-Iran agenda. Iran frightened all the GCC leaders in 1992 when it challenged UAE sovereignty to a UAE island it had occupied since 1971 and, in response to the ensuing reaction by the UAE, refused to discuss the issue in dispute. And it deepened pan-GCC causes for concern when it purchased not only long distance SU-27 fighter-bombers and additional SCUD missiles from China and Korea but, also, advanced Russian submarines equipped with amphibious landing capabilities, which altered the strategic military balance of the Gulf countries overnight. As Iraq's coast is very short and in numerous places quite shallow, this suggests, in GCC eyes, that the submarines' intended use could be against one or more of the GCC states.

Among other outstanding issues are the GCC's questions of whether Iran will defer to the Organization of the Islamic Conference's policy of limiting the number of pilgrims from any country who can go on the Hajj to one pilgrim per thousand Muslim inhabitants in the mother country. This formula was accepted by all other Muslim countries, but in Iran's case would limit the number of Iranian pilgrims to 46,000 instead of the minimum 150,000 that Tehran has been demanding or the 1991 special dispensation allowing it to send 110,000 pilgrims. In 1992, although the official Organization of the Islamic Conference (OIC) quota remained the same, Saudi Arabia interpreted the numbers liberally. This helped accommodate the many Iranian pilgrims who were unable to participate in the Hajj during the 1988-90 period when, owing to the rupture in diplomatic relations between Riyadh and Tehran, most Iranians were unable to obtain visas to Saudi Arabia.

Additional GCC concerns are whether Tehran will reverse its opposition to the Middle East peace process which began in 1991 in Madrid and, for the first time, brought Israel, on one hand, into face-to-face talks with Palestinians, Jordanians, Syrians, and Lebanese, on the other; whether it will cease the stridency of its media's denunciation of GCC-Western defense cooperation; whether it will do all within its power to curb the militancy in Lebanon of Hizballah (the Party of God), which is guided, inspired, financed, and armed by Iran, and the Iranian Revolutionary Guards who, by remaining in Lebanon, delay the prospects for more rapid implementation of the aforementioned Taif Accord; whether it will cease its insistence on being accorded the predominant role in any Gulf-related defense agreement; and whether its avowed intent to cease seeking ways to expand its radicalism to the GCC countries is strategic and permanent or merely tactical and, for the present, expedient.

GCC leaders have not forgotten Tehran's partial support for the GCC's political, economic, and military approach to solving the Kuwait crisis. They appreciated Tehran's support for the UN Security Council resolutions against Iraq; its refusal to countenance Iraq's attempts to avoid withdrawing from Kuwait completely and unconditionally; and its refusal to succumb to Baghdad's offer of material reward had Iran agreed to help Iraq evade the UN-mandated economic sanctions.

At the same time, however, the GCC resented Tehran's strident denunciation of its reliance on Western and other support to reverse the Iraqi invasion. It also resented the transparent hope of some Iranian leaders, during the Gulf crisis, that the crisis would continue indefinitely, if only to further benefit Iranian short-term strategic, economic, political, and military interests. The GCC, moreover, has continued to express concern about the uncertainty of who speaks for whom in Iran's many official pronouncements, both during and subsequent to the Kuwait crisis, including those that criticize, deride, and chastise the GCC governments in tones reminiscent of the Khomeini era. All of this is considered to be evidence that Iran has much further to go before it is likely to inspire sufficient confidence in GCC eyes to be a serious actor in regional geopolitical frameworks, let alone defense arrangements.

Other Islamic States

There are two remaining potential regional players in a postwar defense arrangement or geopolitical entente: Turkey and Pakistan. However, the passage of time since the war has resulted in a diminution of the likelihood of either country playing an important role. The reasons have been GCC endorsement of the aforementioned UN Security

Council Resolution 598 of 1987 and, of related significance, Iran's insistence that only the Gulf countries themselves should be afforded a role in any postwar regional defense arrangement. Even so, both Turkey and Pakistan have been associated with Iran and Iraq in previous regional defense arrangements, and each, in different ways, enjoys a close relationship with almost all of the GCC countries.

Turkey

Unlike Pakistan, Turkey has no soldiers in any of the GCC countries, and has never been party to a formal agreement or undertaking with any of the GCC countries in the area of defense cooperation. The extraordinary decisiveness of the Turkish leadership in the early days of the Kuwait crisis provoked an admiration among GCC leaders which, at the time, was arguably greater than that for any other Islamic country, with the exceptions of Egypt and Syria.

Notwithstanding this, the GCC does not presently foresee a significant role for Turkey. Were this to change, Turkey could be a formidable partner in any defense arrangement. Turkey has a status within NATO and a reputation for having one of the most admired armed forces in the non-Western world. It is also unique in being the only country that borders — and borders on the far side — both of the GCC's eastern neighbors, Iran and Iraq.

Turkey's continuing geopolitical support for the GCC countries will continue to be critical in the short term. In the longer term, the GCC will need to revaluate continually the potential role that can be played by Turkey, not least because of Ankara's ongoing close relationship with Israel, but also because of the web of contentious issues between Turkey and Syria. As for Iran, with the breakup of the Soviet Union and consequent growing Turkish interest and involvement in the Turkish-speaking communities adjacent to Iran, there is an added incentive for Tehran, also, to engage Ankara constructively on the range of issues between them.

Pakistan

Pakistan has played a long-standing role in the secondment of specific units to individual GCC countries and in training their armed forces. Pakistan has also played a consistent role of support over the years on a range of Arab and Islamic issues of great concern to the GCC. In times and circumstances other than those which occurred during the Kuwait crisis, such considerations would likely have placed Islamabad near the head of any queue of Muslim non-Arab countries seeking a participatory role in whatever regional defense system may emerge in the Gulf.

Despite this, opposition to a Western military presence in the region by large numbers of religious militants in Pakistan is sufficiently strong to render unlikely any scenario in which the Islamabad government could formally pursue a significant Gulf defense role. Domestic constraints within Pakistan are likely to continue to limit the nature and extent of Pakistan's involvement to the current kind of bilateral defense assistance agreements which Pakistan enjoys with most of the GCC countries.

In the early days of the Gulf crisis, Saudi Arabia requested that Pakistan render practical assistance to reverse the Iraqi invasion of Kuwait. Specifically, Pakistan was asked to contribute to the allied coalition tanks and other armored vehicles, especially those that Saudi Arabia had purchased on Islamabad's behalf with the clear understanding that Pakistan would come to the Kingdom's defense if it should ever come under threat of attack.

Pakistan, however, offered instead to send drivers and troops to defend the Islamic holy places, although neither of the shrines was even remotely under threat of attack. Its refusal to send tanks and armored personnel carriers came as a major affront to the GCC. The constraints on the Pakistani government were partly domestic; they were also fueled in part by Pakistani resentment at the US inconsistency in applying long-standing UN Security Council resolutions against Israel's occupation of Palestinian lands, on one hand, and against Iraq's occupation of Kuwait, on the other.

Uniquely compounding the Islamabad government's resentment against the US in the Kuwait crisis was Washington's 1990 decision to suspend US economic assistance to Pakistan. Pakistanis took special umbrage at the reason given for the curtailment: continuation of their country's nuclear weapons development program. In the eyes of many Pakistanis, Washington's development and application of the criterion by which Pakistan—but neither Israel nor Pakistan's arch-adversary, India, which also have nuclear weapons development programs—was, in effect, to be punished, were examples of US short-sightedness and application of a double standard.

The Pakistani example illustrates the significant role that public opinion can play in the prospects for specific countries contributing meaningfully to any regional defense arrangement that turns on

US-Arab or Western-Islamic cooperation. For many countries in the area, public opinion continues to be directly affected by the credibility of US efforts to bring about a just and lasting settlement of the Israeli-Palestinian conflict. In this context, Pakistan was a non-Arabian mirror of the lack of support for the international coalition that was also seen in Algeria, Jordan, Libya, Mauritania, the PLO, Sudan, Tunisia, and Yemen.

2. Global Powers in GCC Strategic Planning

The United States

The US is aware that both Iraq and Iran will remain major Gulf powers and recognizes, accordingly, that any hope the GCC countries have of deterring either of these countries in the future turns heavily on the establishment of the tripolarity of power discussed earlier. There is little doubt that the United States and other countries are in a position to augment substantially the defense equipment and systems of the GCC countries and, if necessary, to defend them in the event of a future breakdown in regional order. Strategists within the allied coalition and the GCC alike agree that only thus can the GCC hope to provide a sufficiently credible deterrent to a threat from either Iraq or Iran or, in a worse-case scenario, from both.

Implicit in such an approach, however, is an unprecedented degree of intimacy and cooperation between the GCC countries, the US, and other sources of defense assistance. Also implicit is a much greater degree of standardization of GCC and allied forces' defense equipment than has hitherto been the case, plus joint procurement, combined maneuvers and training, regular meetings among force commanders of all three military services, and effective command, control, and communications systems linking the six countries' respective military establishments.

The goal of maintaining regional peace, security, and stability through this arrangement would stand a good chance of success with such a system, provided the politics were favorable. If there is a flaw, it lies in the proviso that the politics, while not completely disabling, are less than favorable.

Several political obstacles remain toward realizing this scenario. The biggest one, which by its nature has a pervasive influence on most of the others, is that US supporters of the Israeli government are opposed to a major military build-up by GCC countries. Their reasoning, repeated in conjunction with their opposition to previous US arms sales to these countries, is that such sales significantly augment the armed forces of countries which, as yet, have no formal peace arrangement with Israel.

Israel's lobby accepts only carefully calibrated increases in prepositioned equipment for use primarily by American and other Allied forces. Anything else, Israel's supporters argue, should be approved or denied on the basis of whether they upset the military balance between the Arab world and Israel. If deliveries are likely to alter the balance, the lobby insists that Israel receive an equivalent compensating arms package.

Israeli opposition is a powerful factor. The Israel lobby forced a 60 percent reduction in the original US defense package intended for GCC countries in the fall of 1990. A $7.2 billion sale was allowed to proceed; however, the remaining $13.5 billion component was still on hold a year later. Not until the fall of 1992 was the Bush Administration able to gain authorization for the US to sell Saudi Arabia additional fighter aircraft and tanks to augment the Kingdom's Gulf defense capabilities.

One objective of the lobby is clearly to link any approval of sales to GCC countries with substantial increases in the level of economic and military assistance to Israel.

Also in the background are the Israeli government's wish for US gifts of replacement planes for Israel's aging Kfir fighter aircraft, cancellation of Israeli debts to the US in an amount comparable to the $7 billion debt forgiveness to Egypt during the Gulf crisis, Israeli achievement of NATO "associate status," a US commitment not to try to force any Israeli diplomatic team to deal with anyone associated with the PLO in the Middle East peace talks, a US promise not to renew its dialogue with the PLO, and additional technology benefits in the form of greater privileged Israeli participation in research and development contracts for the US defense industry.

In addition to the Israel lobby, there is strong opposition in Congress, much of it influenced by the lobby, toward arms sales to the GCC in general. Quite apart from the lobby, for some, the issue is emotional; for others, the issue is partisan politics, with most Democrats pitted against Republicans. Leading members of the Democratic Party have traditionally opposed any effort to sell significant amounts of additional armaments and weapons systems to the GCC countries. An additional argument of these Democratic Party leaders in support of their rationale for opposing these scenarios posits that in the course of the allied coalition's successful efforts in liberating Kuwait, the nature and extent of the threat to the GCC countries was so diminished that this, in itself, obviated the need for substantial new arms sales to these countries.

This argument, however, is oriented exclusively to short-run considerations. Those within the GCC and the allied coalition who are seeking to prevent a recurrence of the breakdown in regional order that occurred in 1990 are in agreement that the short term is but one among other considerations. The medium term and the longer term can be just as, if not more, important, especially given the uncertain long-term prospects regarding Iraq and the constants and trends noted earlier with respect to Iran.

GCC, US, and other allied coalition planners argue further that the building of a credible defense structure requires long lead times. Like those of the US and other well-defended countries, it cannot be achieved overnight. Nor is the goal of building credibility into such a structure well served if the focus of planning is only on the here and now, on the constellation of one's friends and adversaries at a given moment. Today's friends may become tomorrow's enemies—as history has shown, often with striking swiftness.

From the aftermath of the Iran-Iraq ceasefire in August 1988, less than 24 months separated GCC and Iraqi friendship from enmity in the conflict that ensued in 1990. While GCC relations with Iran have improved in some areas, Iran still occupies three UAE islands which it took by force in 1971 and, as noted earlier, shows every sign of preparing the islands for a future military role in its quest to become the dominant power in the Gulf. Unlike Iraq, Iran has close to a quarter of a million of its citizens living and working inside the GCC countries. A number of its religious kinfolk, Shia minority elements within the GCC citizenry, were trained in guerrilla warfare, sabotage, subversion, and related techniques in the 1980s so as to serve Iranian interests when and if the need arose.

It is only four years since the Iranian government belatedly accepted the UN ceasefire resolution on the Iran-Iraq war which effectively ended its threat at the time to the GCC. Many in the GCC still believe that an Iranian government of some kind will seek revenge against the GCC for its extensive, and in many ways vital, support for Iraq during the Iran-Iraq war. With armed forces more than three times the size of the combined forces of all six GCC countries, and with an intent to pursue an aggressive foreign policy in support of political and religious radicals both regionally and in the Islamic world as a whole, Iran, in GCC eyes, will remain a major strategic adversary.

If the degree of potential US support is rendered problematic by the uncertain variable of American domestic politics and Congressional constraints, such reservations, in GCC eyes, do not apply to the second most important power in the allied coalition: Great Britain.

Great Britain

The relative ease of logistics and administrative roles in operations Desert Shield and Desert Storm can be attributed in substantial measure to the legacy of Great Britain in the GCC region. Britain administered the defense and foreign relations of most of the GCC countries from the early 19th century until as recently as two decades ago. The result was a multi-faceted foundation—language, standards, strategic and tactical doctrine, educational and administrative systems—that greatly facilitated not only the level of US participation in the multi-national force, but the participation of Egypt's, Pakistan's, and numerous other countries' armed forces as well.

Prior to the Gulf crisis, Britain had replaced the US as the leading supplier of defense equipment to Saudi Arabia. The effectiveness of the Israel lobby in the US in blocking American arms sales to the country allowed the British to take advantage of the opportunity, as evidenced by Great Britain's multi-billion dollar sale of Tornado fighter planes and other defense equipment to Saudi Arabia in increasing amounts after 1985.

The sale of British military equipment to the GCC countries is not subject to the kind of severe Israeli-stipulated restrictions that have been routinely placed on the sales of American aircraft and other defense equipment to the Arab world. The resultant strategic and tactical strength that Great Britain continues to be able to provide the GCC countries can probably be counted on as a constant and, as such, a valued asset in GCC deterrence and defense planning.

Great Britain can likely be counted on to continue providing such assistance to virtually all the GCC countries. In the event of heightened regional tensions, Britain would likely be willing to resume some version of the naval protection role, with its Armilla Patrol, which it assumed during the oil tanker war phase of the Iran-Iraq conflict. The British intelligence and institutional memory regarding the dramatis personae in most of the GCC countries, and the large number of GCC officers who have been trained in Britain, will remain important to training and inter-force communications, command, and control.

France

France will also remain an important player in GCC postwar regional defense planning. There are several reasons. French officials know leading decisionmakers in Iran and Iraq as a result of French involvement in the region over the years.[3] This knowledge includes a familiarity with significant segments of the leadership of Iraq's air force.

France has a close relationship with the naval forces of Saudi Arabia and the air forces of Kuwait, Qatar, and especially the UAE. There is, moreover, a shared concern between France and the GCC about the forces of Islamic militancy that target Arab governments and their Western partners, especially France, on whose soil these problems tend to be played out more than any other European country. France has the strategic advantage of continued privileged access to and use of valuable Red Sea naval and telecommunications facilities in Djibouti and other facilities at Reunion and Mayotte in the Indian Ocean. The French government demonstrated its commitment to peacemaking and peacekeeping efforts during the Iraq-Iran war, and won the confidence of GCC countries through its role in the Multi-National Force during the Gulf crisis.

Russia and the Former Soviet Republics

Russia is likely to offer far less than either the US, Great Britain, or France to GCC postwar defense planning needs. The reasons are rooted both in the uncertain governmental structure and political stability of the country, and in the lack of Russian involvement in such matters historically.

Despite the severe domestic restraints on Russian capabilities, there are, however, two areas in which the GCC states are interested in cooperating with Russia. One is the UN Security Council, where Russia holds a position as a permanent member with veto power over the Council's resolutions. The GCC is appreciative of the unprecedented role that the Soviet Union played in this regard throughout the Kuwait crisis.

The second area is the realm of state-of-the-art defense equipment and defense systems. Any Russian contribution in either of these areas would add credibility to both the deterrence and defense dimensions of the GCC's postwar planning. With the obvious need to earn vitally important hard currency, Russia is certainly prepared to play as contributive a role as possible in meeting GCC defense needs.

One focus of GCC attention will be the newly-independent Black Sea and Central Asian Republics that were formerly part of the Soviet Union. Owing to their status as neighbors or nearby countries, both Turkey and Iran are actively engaged in expanding their ties with the new Republics. Because of ethnic, linguistic and historical ties, and the largely secular cast to their political structures, Turkey sees the Republics as a natural focus of Turkish influence; the rebuff to its quest to join the EEC is likely to propel Turkey all the more strongly toward acting as an important force in the Black Sea area and establishing strong ties with them. Of greater concern to the GCC countries, however, is the nature of Iranian involvement in the former Soviet Republics. All the GCC countries are keen to moderate Iranian influence of the kind that would spread Iranian radicalism, or augment Iran's role among Islamic states with the backing of the new Republics. The GCC's member states are thus likely to use their financial and diplomatic leverage in an attempt to influence the new Republics toward non-revolutionary, non-militant expressions of Islam.

The People's Republic of China

If the past and present are any guide, China seems less likely to feature in GCC defense planning than any of the four other global powers discussed above. Yet China, much like Russia, can potentially play an international role of great significance to the GCC. One area in which it may be influential, like the other four countries mentioned, is in the UN Security Council where it has veto power. That it did not veto any of the dozen Security Council resolutions calling for Iraq to withdraw from Kuwait unconditionally was a significant contribution to the outcome of the crisis.

Secondly, China can play both a positive and a negative role with regard to the GCC's hopes for a peaceful and stable Gulf. On the positive side, it added immensely to Saudi Arabia's deterrence credibility, and potentially its defense capabilities, by providing the Kingdom versions of its long-range CSS II missiles during the latter stages of the Iran-Iraq war when the so-called war between the cities (Baghdad and Tehran) threatened to spread to Riyadh and possibly other GCC capitals. The Reagan Administration had been unable to meet that particular GCC defense need owing to the Israeli lobby's pressures and despite repeated Saudi requests for such assistance.

3. Potential Roles for International and Other Regional Organizations

The United Nations

On matters pertaining to international law and diplomacy and the important geopolitical component of deterrence and defense, some of the GCC's most important international links with institutions outside the Gulf are those it has formed with the UN. No regional organization worked with other countries more effectively than the GCC to help ensure the successful passage of three key UN Security Council resolutions during the Iran-Iraq war. GCC countries were among the first, moreover, to render material assistance to the UN in the days immediately following the August 1988 ceasefire. All GCC leaders were impressed by the display of an unprecedented degree of unity of purpose among the UN Security Council's five permanent members in the Council's 12 resolutions aimed at repelling Iraq's invasion of Kuwait. Building on this foundation, the GCC is actively engaged in seeking ways to strengthen and expand the UN's effectiveness in conflict resolution.

Although mindful of the need to combine the geopolitical efficacy of the UN with additional means of deterrence and defense—of the need, as Secretary-General Abdulla Bishara has frequently stated, "to combine power with political persuasion"—the GCC can be counted on to enhance the role of the UN in regional and international affairs in general. In the aftermath of the Kuwaiti-Iraqi ceasefire, the role of the UN in Iraq, on one hand, and in Kuwait and along the Kuwait-Iraq border, on the other, has continued to demonstrate, as it did throughout the crisis itself, its multifaceted and far-ranging utility in the arena of conflict resolution.

If the UN, a truly ecumenical organization, can help to fashion a new Gulf order on matters pertaining to diplomacy, deterrence, and defense, thereby minimizing notions of a "pax Americana," the GCC and other Arab countries could reap important dividends.

Europe-GCC Relations: A Multifaceted Partnership

The centerpiece of the GCC's web of cooperative relationships with Europe is the European Economic Community, or the European Community (EC). On a day-to-day basis the emphasis has long been on issues of trade, investment, and technology transfer, not deterrence or defense as such.

The EC presently accounts for nearly 40 percent of the GCC's lucrative import market. The United States, by contrast, accounts for less than 20 percent. This state of affairs may in time work to the further advantage of Europe for the following reasons: (1) the size of the EC market, which has a population of 325 million as compared to the US market of 248 million; and (2) time and distance and their bearing on costs. The EC's closer proximity to the GCC countries — three time zones as compared to a minimum of seven and, in many cases ten, for the US — gives Europe a competitive advantage in land, sea, and air transportation. This edge also has potential deterrence and defense dimensions, in GCC eyes, as the efforts to deploy troops to the region during the Kuwait crisis underscored in force.

Other Organizations

The prospects for any fundamental change in the GCC's relationship with the 12-member NATO, the nine-member Western European Union (WEU), or the 34-member Conference of Security and Cooperation in Europe (CSCE) are far more uncertain. This uncertainty exists despite the profound interest and involvement by some NATO, WEU, and CSCE member countries in the Kuwait crisis and their hopes for a more credible defense system for the Gulf region in the postwar period.

In the case of the Brussels-based NATO, a major reason for the uncertainty is NATO's long-standing policy of non-involvement in theaters of operation outside its member countries' territory. Indeed, in recognition of such constraints, the GCC pursued the 1987-89 Gulf naval protection scheme and the mobilization and deployment of European forces to the Multi-National Force with the Paris-based Western European Union (WEU) instead. For this reason, within GCC planning circles, the WEU, having performed effectively in two test cases, is likely to remain first among equals on the list of potentially helpful European defense organizations.

The CSCE, which emerged from the much more recent Helsinki Accords, looks at many of the same issues as the WEU, plus additional ones, such as human rights. Given the international concern for human rights violations in Iraq and the Arab areas under Israeli occupation, in particular, the CSCE may bear watching as a model of potentially greater relevance for the GCC's postwar efforts to secure peace, security, and stability in at least parts of the Gulf. However, critics of the CSCE's almost totally ineffective role in dealing with the crisis in Yugoslavia argue that any likelihood of GCC and other strategic planners' being able to derive much inspiration or relevance for the CSCE in the case of the Gulf is, at best, minimal.

4. Forging the Postwar Peace: A Strategic Appraisal

After the Gulf crisis, the GCC's interests included the establishment of a more credible mechanism that would effectively deter acts of aggression, threats, or intimidation, from within or outside the Gulf, while upholding each of the Gulf states' sovereignty, independence, and territorial integrity. For outsiders, the stake was regional peace and stability, linked as these are to the world's interest in continued access to and uninterrupted production of the GCC's prodigious supplies of energy, a commodity upon which all countries are dependent for their survival. Two additional international interests remain the perpetuation of the generally moderate and conventional orientations of the GCC member countries' foreign policies and the preservation of their record of making substantial philanthropic contributions to many of the world's lesser developed countries.

Notwithstanding the unprecedented threats and considerable damage to the above interests occasioned by Iraq's invasion of Kuwait, and all that occurred in the process of repelling the invasion, the bulk of these interests remain intact. Within the GCC and the allied coalition there is a pervasive sentiment that the important question is not *whether* to establish a means for greater protection of these interests but *how*.

A number of uncertainties remain regarding the policy of the leader of the allied coalition, the United States. Here a question asked by GCC and Coalition planners alike is to what extent the US can realistically expect to be able to consolidate the gains from its unprecedented cooperation with the GCC countries in the deterrence and defense areas if it fails to stay the course in helping to settle the Israeli-Palestinian conflict and its ancillary Arab-Israeli components. From Kuwait to Salalah, from Aden to Aleppo, and from Mauritania to Muscat, virtually all Arabs long to see the US demonstrate leadership in solving this conflict comparable to that which it displayed in helping Kuwait regain its freedom and security.

Not until the US exhibits such leadership and sees the peace talks through to a broadly acceptable solution will the GCC countries, not to mention any group of other Arab countries, have any realistic hope of being able to strengthen and expand significantly their long-term interests with the US. The GCC-wide accolades and approbation for US leadership, courage, and commitment in bringing the Coalition into being and then directing the successful effort to repel Iraq's invasion will be short-lived if there is not sustained and major progress toward a just and peaceful settlement of the Israeli-Palestinian dispute. Certainly, the potential for significantly enhanced GCC-US cooperation in a matter so sensitive and vital as regional defense will be lessened substantially if the US allows Israel to veto or effectively paralyze American and other efforts in this regard.

The rewards for the world as a whole in settling the unresolved Israeli-Palestinian, Arab-Israeli conflict cannot be underestimated. Quite apart from ending one of this century's greatest tragedies, it would remove the one issue from which radical groups have long derived one of the greatest sources of their support, moral fervor, and legitimacy in challenging individual Arab governments, in attacking the rationale for Western-Arab relations generally, and in opposing regional security arrangements with Western components specifically.

A settlement deemed satisfactory to the broadest number of Palestinians and Israelis, as well as Lebanese and Syrians, would likely thereby improve the atmosphere for increasing the level of popular participation in the region's national development processes. With the greatly lessened need for sustained high levels of expenditure on defense resulting from a settlement, funds that could be used to help alleviate the misery of the region's poor would be available. A settlement would help ensure more reliable access to and export of the region's energy resources. Most significantly, it would contribute, like no other single factor, to the preservation of regional peace, security, and stability.

Notes

1. For reports on the Declaration itself, see Carol Berger, "Arab Ministers Discuss Regional Pact for Security, Economic Cooperation," *Christian Science Monitor,* March 6, 1991; William E. Schmidt, "Arab Nations Propose a Peacekeeping Force," *New York Times,* March 7, 1991; and Andrew Borowiec, "8 Arab Nations Agree to Become Gulf Watchdogs," *Washington Times,* March 7, 1991.

2. John Duke Anthony, "The 12th GCC Summit: Betwixt War and Peace," *Middle East International,* Vol. 8, No. 6 (July-October, 1992), pp. 57-58.

3. For background on France's relations with Iraq, see William Drozdiak, "Gulf Crisis Ends 15 Years of French-Iraqi Closeness," *Washington Post,* October 12, 1990.

PART 3: THE GULF WAR AND THE MIDDLE EAST

9 IRAQ'S FUTURE
PLUS ÇA CHANGE ... OR SOMETHING BETTER?

*Phebe Marr**

The end of the Gulf war revealed an apparent paradox in Iraq. Despite substantial losses to its human, physical and economic resources, the political upheaval resulting from a rebellion in the north and south of the country, a massive Kurdish exodus and the loss by the central government of control over parts of Iraqi territory, there was little political change in Iraq. Saddam Hussein and his Ba'th apparatus remained in power, and neither his methods of rule nor the direction of his policies had changed substantially. These circumstances raised a fundamental question. Had the war, the rebellion and the sanctions delivered a sufficient shock to the political system to effect a change over time? Or was the edifice created by the Ba'th, repressive though it might be, sufficiently strong and resilient to resist all but cosmetic change?

This study is designed to explore Iraq's future and the regional role it might play in the aftermath of the war. In order to examine the parameters of change and continuity in Iraq, four questions will be addressed. First, how much damage was inflicted on Iraq as a result of the war and the sanctions, and with what impact on Iraq's role in the regional power equation? Second, what can be learned from the 1991 rebellion about the forces at work in Iraqi society and the direction they may take Iraq in the future? Third, what plausible scenarios can be envisioned for Iraq's political structure based on the configuration of these forces? And lastly, what would these scenarios portend for Iraq's regional role? All conclusions must be tentative, given Iraq's isolation and the impenetrability of its political system to outside inquiry. On the whole, the best that can be said about Iraq's future is that it is uncertain and difficult to predict, with or without Saddam Hussein. The Gulf war left the country economically and militarily weakened, and unlikely to play an active role in the international arena for a number of years. Under certain circumstances, it might be more "acted upon" by its neighbors than the reverse, and its state structures might be further weakened. The war probably

---

* The author is Senior Fellow at the Institute for National Strategic Studies, National Defense University. The views expressed in this article are those of the author and should not be construed as reflecting the policy or positions of the National Defense University, the Department of Defense or the United States government.

145

hastened events that would have occurred without it. Even if Saddam Hussein had withdrawn peaceably from Kuwait, sanctions, combined with the effects of the Iran-Iraq war, would have meant a long recovery period for Iraq as well as a weakened political position for Saddam Hussein. However, Iraq's military would have survived intact and the postwar rebellion, together with the Kurdish exodus and the loss of control over parts of Iraq's northern territory, would not have occurred. Given Iraq's debt and its poor credit rating, its economic situation might not improve dramatically in any circumstances, even though the chances for improvement would be better if a change of regime brought about a government more acceptable to Iraq's neighbors and the international community.

1. Iraq's War Damage

Before assessing Iraq's position in the aftermath of the war, it is necessary to have some understanding of the war's impact on Iraq's power base, on its recuperative capacity and on its population. Unfortunately, our knowledge of postwar Iraq, although improving, is still sketchy. Despite numerous reports on Iraq's war damage,[1] there is little hard data on which to make conclusive statements. Nevertheless, the broad outlines of the damage can be depicted.

A close reading of UN reports and observations of Western correspondents who travelled to Iraq after the war leads to the conclusion that severe, but not irreparable, damage was done to Iraq's economic infrastructure. More serious damage may have been inflicted on its human resources, not only by the war but by the rebellion and by sanctions. The political-military apparatus, though weakened, remained intact.

The Economic Toll

War estimates indicate extensive damage to Iraq's economy in some areas; much less in others. This issue has been clouded by controversy and exaggeration.[2] The most extensive damage was done to the telecommunications system, the electricity grid, the overland transportation sector and some parts of the petroleum industries. Naturally, defense-related industries sustained extensive damage, but possibly less than originally estimated.

The telecommunications network, including the international and domestic telephone system, received the most damage with almost half of Iraq's original telephone lines destroyed, and additional damage to the microwave links connecting cities to the international network.[3] However, by the end of 1992 much of the system had been repaired. Also seriously damaged was the electricity grid. By mid-1991, electricity production was still only 40 percent of the 1990 level, and much of that was due to cannibalization of spare parts from damaged units.[4] Damage to the electricity system caused collateral problems, particularly in the delivery of uncontaminated drinking water to the population, in sewage disposal, both of which rely on electrically driven pumps, and in the health care system. In Basra, where damage to these systems was extensive, sewage and drinking water were still problems late in 1992. However, by the end of 1992, much of Iraq's electricity supply had been restored.

Iraq's ground transportation system, particularly roads and bridges, received extensive damage. At the war's end, over 35 bridges were reportedly unusable, including three key arteries across the Tigris in Baghdad. Roads and bridges could, for the most part, be repaired domestically with local resources, even if not to previous standards. By the end of 1992, most of Iraq's road network was functioning again, and two of the three arteries in Baghdad had been restored. In the petroleum sector, there was little or no damage to oil wells — in contrast to Kuwait. The main destruction was to production, refining and pipeline facilities, such as pumping stations and storage facilities. By the end of 1992, Iraq's production capacity was estimated at 2.1 million b/d, but according to the Iraq government itself, this could be raised to over 3 million b/d if it could receive financing for repairs and the import of spare parts and equipment. This requirement was unlikely to be met, however, until sanctions were removed. The cost of full repair of oil production facilities, pipelines and refineries could reach $6 billion.[5]

The damage to Iraq's productive sectors — agriculture, light industry and construction — was relatively light. The agricultural sector needed to replenish used-up stocks of seed and livestock, repair irrigation pumps and acquire spare parts for machinery.[6] The Baghdad government proceeded with a large-scale irrigation and drainage scheme ("The Third River") in the south of Iraq, which was completed late in 1992, to drain marshland, mainly for military purposes, but partly for agriculture. Light industry and construction required improvements in electricity, water supply and spare parts. By late 1992, many factories were back in operation, except those in need of spare parts, and construction was in full swing, especially in Baghdad. Iraqis, with typical energy and organizational ability, showed considerable enterprise in undertaking repairs. Late in 1992, the majority of essential refineries, factories and power plants were functioning, although by itself Iraq would be unable to restore its high technology capacity.

Despite the clear damage to Iraq's economy, there may be a few long-term benefits from the war. The Coalition's forcible reduction of Iraq's defense industries, together with probable future restrictions limiting Iraq's military imports, will mean a future reduction in Iraq's military expenditures. Prior to the Gulf crisis, these expenditures were consuming 35 to 40 percent of Iraq's export earnings.[7] If these sums were shifted to the civilian sector, they could go some way toward addressing Iraq's revenue needs once sanctions were removed. Whether they would be so diverted depended on the political leadership. A second consequence of the war was the departure of over one million Egyptian workers from Iraq, freeing up future jobs for Iraqis.

The chief difficulty Iraq faced in reconstruction was finance. A continuation of the sanctions regime would make revenue to finance reconstruction difficult to find; indeed, without a removal of sanctions, Iraq's economic infrastructure would continue to deteriorate. In addition to sanctions, Iraq faced previously accumulated debt from the Iran-Iraq war and a poor credit position. Even if the sanctions were lifted, Iraq's potential oil revenues were likely to fall well short of its reconstruction requirements. If Iraq could export 3 million b/d (roughly its prewar figure) at about $15 a barrel, it could earn about $16.5 billion a year.[8] If 30 percent of this went toward reparations (at least initially) that would leave less than $11.5 billion a year. Even if higher oil prices are assumed, this would not give Iraq more than marginal economic leeway. Civilian imports were likely to total between $7 to 10 billion, leaving little, after debt servicing, for reconstruction and for badly needed public sector pay raises. Serious problems would exist even under much more favorable oil pricing conditions; for example, the export of 2.75 million b/d at $22 a barrel would leave Iraq with a net of about $16 billion after the deduction of 30 percent for reparations. If a tough sanctions regime remained for a considerable length of time, if Iraq's reserves and other outside revenues, especially those in the hands of the middle class, dried up, the shortfall would be high and the time for economic recuperation longer.

The key to economic recovery will be political management and availability of credit. To a lesser extent, Iraq will need materials and technical assistance from abroad. A replacement of Saddam Hussein's government in Baghdad would improve the prospect of reconstruction efforts, but perhaps not dramatically, at least in the short term. In the longer term, however, a change at the political helm will be essential for Iraq to restore its economy to a position similar to that occupied before the Iran-Iraq war, at which point it began a long, slow decline. If Saddam Hussein remains, slow growth—or more likely economic stagnation or disintegration—is to be expected.

The Human and Social Costs

The long-term human and social costs of the war could be higher than the damage to Iraq's physical infrastructure, particularly if the social costs of the rebellion and the sanctions are added.

Estimates of the number of Iraqis killed in the eight-year Iran-Iraq war range around 135,000 to 150,000, roughly 4 to 5 percent of the military age population.[9] There are no reliable figures on the casualties of the Gulf war. The US military has used a rough estimate of 100,000, but some think this is too high (40,000 to 50,000 has been cited as more realistic), while others think it is too low.[10] How many Iraqis died in the rebellion can only be guessed at, but it seems likely to have been in the tens of thousands at a minimum.[11] These tentative estimates could add up to a possible total of 6 to 8 percent of the military age population in the 1980s. This toll includes all classes, educated and uneducated, although it undoubtedly fell heaviest on the poor and unskilled. In addition to the obvious trauma inflicted on the population, the reduction of such a high percentage of the work force, along with needed skill levels, can only affect Iraq's productivity adversely.

Nevertheless, one should not overestimate Iraq's population loss or the depletion of its skill levels. The war estimates could prove to be on the high side; there is as yet no way to know how many soldiers simply deserted or went home on leave and never returned. Iraq has a high birth rate—3.5 percent—which should help replenish losses. Moreover, Iraq followed a conscious policy of preserving its skilled population all during the Iran-Iraq war, allowing its students to finish high school and college before the draft. Iraq has a large, educated middle class compared to many other developing nations; much of its skill level was probably preserved through its wars, and with it the capacity to organize and to work for reconstruction. Indeed, Iraq's capacity to patch up its transport, electricity and communications network following the war and the uprising is a testimony to its human resources. So, too, is the evidence of Iraq's capacity to develop an indigenous nuclear program and its assiduousness in preserving what is left of its military industrial complex.

Notwithstanding these factors, the population is war weary and unlikely to bear up well under further military adventures. More significant, the widespread rebellion, affecting virtually all of the Kurdish areas, and much of the Shi'ite south, provided ample testimony of the extent to which the Iraqi population was alienated from the regime. The destruction of homes and damage to religious shrines in the south will leave a legacy unlikely to be erased in a long time among people with long memories. Many key professionals, seeing no hope for the future, left the country when the regime began to issue visas, an indication of disillusion among Iraq's educated middle class. This exodus could reach major proportions if foreign countries become willing to take Iraqis in.

The imposition of sanctions took a social toll on key segments of the population. First, they created nutrition and health problems not experienced in Iraq in decades—lack of food, medicines and malnutrition—even death—among infants.[12] Second, they created rampant inflation. By the end of 1992, the Iraqi dinar, worth thirty cents at the official rate on international markets in July 1990, was fluctuating between three and five cents in the free market.[13] The government, short of cash, flooded the market with cheap dinars, sometimes printed on only one side of the bill. Visiting journalists noted the toll on the poor, often pressed into selling jewelry or family possessions to buy food.[14] The toll on middle-class bureaucrats, teachers and employees on fixed salaries, though less severe, was equally significant. Their savings, standard of living and hopes for the future were gradually being depleted, leaving growing feelings of frustration, even despair. Third, the government's priorities in preserving its support meant that family, military and party loyalists were getting a disproportionate share of the benefits available. (Military salaries were raised several times following the end of the war.) Meanwhile, entrepreneurs and some officials in high places were profiting from scarcity, selling goods brought in from Jordan at high prices. As a result of the inflation, the gap between the privileged and the poor was widening. The effects of such discrepancies could have long-term consequences for governmental stability, if not corrected.

A third social consequence of the war, or, to be more exact, of the rebellion, brutally repressed by the regime, was a severe exacerbation of ethnic and sectarian tensions in Iraq, a factor that did not bode well for its future. The uprising in the south, which spread widely in Shi'ite areas, resulted in such fierce fighting in the holy cities of Najaf and Karbala that a legacy of bitterness was bound to be left in the Shi'ite community. Shi'ite atrocities against Ba'thist leaders in southern cities (often Shi'ah themselves) and the damage and destruction visited by government forces on the holy Shi'ite shrines, including the venerated tomb of Hussein, left lasting stains on a regime which claimed to be non-sectarian.[15] The rebellion unquestionably rekindled

Shi'ite consciousness and greatly enhanced Shi'ite alienation from the regime. This alienation would make it difficult for the Ba'th, or any Sunni-dominated regime in Baghdad, to return to "business as usual" in the south.

A similar situation emerged in the north, where some two million Kurds (at least half of the entire Kurdish population in Iraq) fled to the mountains or across the borders into Turkey and Iran rather than face the Iraqi army or the restoration of Iraqi government control in the north. While the bulk of these Kurds had returned home by the fall of 1991 under the protection of foreign troops, these events and the new internationally "protected" status of the Kurds north of the 36th parallel gave Kurdish separatism a new lease on life. The subsequent election of a democratic Kurdish government on Iraqi soil and the strong support Kurds received from key segments of the international community meant that it would be difficult to put the genie of Kurdish nationalism back in the bottle of Iraqi sovereignty.

Meanwhile, back in Baghdad, the immediate impact of the war was to narrow regime support more obviously to a base in the Arab Sunni minority. In the wake of the war, Saddam Hussein placed more power in the hands of his clansmen from Tikrit, in Sunni loyalists in the Republican Guard, and, in the rural areas, on Arab tribal chiefs, in a return to policies harking back to the days of the monarchy. The result was an erosion of the Iraqi nationalist sentiment that emerged among the Arab population in the wake of the Iran-Iraq war and was one of its chief benefits.

The Military Impact

While Iraq's military machine was weakened, it was by no means destroyed. A number of Republican Guard and Regular Army units survived the war intact. Other units, though damaged and disrupted in the war, managed to reconstitute the remnants of their forces. On the other hand, the military also saw some unit defections during the rebellion, particularly in the north, although they were insufficient to turn the tide in favor of the rebels.

In the aftermath of the rebellion, Saddam undertook purges of suspect military leadership and began the process of military reorganization. The so-called Popular Army, an ineffective militia, was disbanded, while much of the Regular Army infantry, which had taken the brunt of the losses at the front, was demobilized. The Republican Guards, the best trained and presumably the most loyal of Saddam's armed forces, were retained as the probable core of a new "leaner, meaner" army, which would include the best units of the Regular Army.

Tentative estimates put the size of this restructured army at somewhere between 300,000 and 400,000, a force slightly larger in size than Iraq's regular army prior to the Iran-Iraq war.[16] Rough estimates of Iraq's remaining equipment (tanks, armored personnel carriers, artillery) indicate that it lost about half of its prewar equipment, but would have sufficient material to supply the army, even though this equipment might not be top of the line. Iraq has no navy. Its air defense system suffered severe damage and its airforce was greatly depleted, but not entirely eliminated. As is well known, over 100 of its best planes were flown to Iran, but about 300 planes probably remained. A substantial force of helicopter gunships remained virtually intact after the war and was on display during the crushing defeat of the rebellion.[17]

Iraq's remaining forces, especially its ground force, are fully sufficient to keep order in Iraq and to protect its borders from its neighbors, although it would undoubtedly have difficulty in repelling a concerted air and ground attack from Syria or Turkey, both highly unlikely. If there were no foreign presence in the Gulf, Iraq's forces would be sufficiently large and well armed to constitute a threat to its Arab neighbors to the south, and even to Iran, which has not yet fully rearmed in the wake of its defeat in the Iran-Iraq war, although it is doing so. However, the weakness of Iraq's air force and its air defense system, as well as the destruction of its logistical support, will make it difficult, if not impossible, for Iraq to undertake major aggression on its neighbors to the east, west or north until these deficiencies are repaired.

Iraq's defense industry suffered severe damage but was not totally destroyed. Iraq retained the capacity to manufacture small arms and some artillery, but the cease-fire provisions mandating the destruction of weapons of mass destruction and longer range delivery systems made it difficult, though probably not impossible, for Iraq to start up these industries in the future. It is not yet clear whether Iraq has sufficient knowledge of the processes involved in manufacturing nuclear weapons, or missile systems to complete any of these programs indigenously. Whether Iraq will be able to manufacture such weapons in the future will depend on the kind of controls the international community is willing and able to enforce on Iraq. If, with the passage of time, sanctions on weapons and high technology imports were to weaken, and if Iraq's oil revenues were again to make it an attractive arms market, Iraq would probably be able, gradually, to revive its conventional—and even its unconventional—arms industry. If a Ba'th regime or a strong nationalist government remained in power through the decade, the military would be likely to constitute an important part of the political structure. Military leadership that required benefits in return for loyalty would cause the continued diversion of scarce economic resources from the civilian to the military sector.

The Political Costs

Politically, the war weakened the regime, but not enough to unseat it. The instruments of coercion—the military and the secret police—were sufficiently disrupted during the coalition's air attack and the ground war to permit a widespread rebellion in the wake of the defeat. After the rebellion, the pervasive Ba'th party apparatus remained in existence, and all instruments of control were partially rebuilt, although the security resources were still weak in some areas, such as the marshes of the south, where a low-level rebellion continued.

The war and the resounding military defeat also dissipated much of the regime's support, and reports from Iraq after the rebellion indicated a widespread crisis of confidence in the government, even among those who served it in high places.[18] However, had the crisis of confidence in the leadership, the dramatic erosion of regime legitimacy, gone far enough to cause a collapse of the regime or a change of leaders? Much depended on continued pressure on the economy and society from outside. If international pressures continued, and if there was mounting discontent inside Iraq (both big "ifs"), over time it was possible that the balance of fear and alienation would shift against the regime.

The Iraqi government also had to contend with another political liability, a derogation of Iraq's sovereignty. First, it had lost control over portions of Iraqi territory. Iraq's southern borders with Kuwait constituted a demilitarized zone, a belt of territory 10 kms (6 miles) wide, in which a UN observer force monitored violations of the cease-fire provisions. Iraqi bureaucrats, however, administered their portion of the DMZ. In addition, in 1992 in order to monitor human rights abuses in the south, the US, Britain, and France under UN authorization instituted a no-fly zone over all Iraqi territory south of the 32nd parallel, an area that included Najaf, but not Karbala. However, the Iraqi government remained in control on the ground. A more serious infringement of Iraq's sovereignty occurred in the north, where UN resolutions forbade the operation of Iraqi aircraft north of the 36th parallel, a wide swath of territory that included the Kurdish cities of Dahuk and Irbil, and Iraq's third largest city, Mosul. Within the Kurdish portion of this territory, Kurdish leaders and their forces were in control; the same was true even in the Kurdish city of Sulaimaniyya south of the 36th parallel. In this territory, an elected Kurdish government gradually took root.

Second, the Iraqi government was denied revenue from its key resource, oil, through a continuation of sanctions on oil exports, and it had to submit to intrusive inspection of its military industries by UN observers preparatory to destruction of production facilities for weapons of mass destruction. For a regime that had been fiercely anti-imperialist and for which independence from foreign control had been a cardinal aim, this erosion of sovereignty signified a humiliating loss of legitimacy, which could not be lost on a population that had recently been told it could lead the Arab world. This humiliation and the Iraqi sense of national pride could, however, result in Iraqi sentiment turning against the West and, thus, in some blame being deflected from the Iraqi government.

2. The Rebellion and Its Consequences

The second factor to be considered in assessing Iraq's future is the significance of the 1991 rebellion and what it revealed about the political forces at work in Iraqi society. Solid information on the *intifada*—its leadership, aims and the extent of its domestic support—is still scant, but enough has emerged to allow for some tentative conclusions.[19]

The Revolt in the Shi'ite South

First, the rebellion that erupted in Basra on March 1, 1991, began as a spontaneous reaction to an overwhelming military defeat.[20] Angry and disillusioned soldiers returning from the front attacked a statue of Saddam, hated symbol of the regime, and, like a prairie brushfire at summer's end, the rebellion quickly spread through the cities and towns of the Shi'ite south. It was significant that the revolt ignited in Basra, where the instruments of the regime's coercion were weakest. Initially, the revolt was an act of rage against Saddam and the regime which had caused so much unnecessary death and destruction. Not surprisingly, outraged soldiers and citizens had no particular vision of an alternative future.

Second, however the revolt started, its spread through the Shi'ite south revealed a pattern with potential significance for the future. The fighting was fiercest in the heartland of Shi'ism—the holy cities of Najaf and Karbala, and in towns like Nasiriyya, near the marshes where dissident Shi'ites and army deserters were hiding. It may also have been strong in areas more distant from the capital, like Basra, which saw sustained fighting. While almost all southern Shi'ite towns put up some resistance, it died out sooner in areas closer to the capital and more accessible to Saddam's forces, although significant unrest occurred in the main Shi'ite quarter of Baghdad. It should be noted that this area, containing a million inhabitants, is the poorest and least developed area of the capital.

Third was the role played by Iraqi exiles who entered Iraq from across the Iranian border. This large Shi'ite exile community in Iran (estimated at several hundred thousand) was more committed to the regime's overthrow, and at the same time more reliant on Iran for support, than the indigenous Shi'ite community in Iraq. The most influential leader of this group was the Iraqi cleric, Muhammad Baqir al-Hakim, the head of the Supreme Assembly of the Islamic Republic of Iraq (SAIRI), who favored an Islamic regime, although he called for elections.

A substantial number of these Iraqi exiles had been formed into a military unit, the Badr Brigade, numbering at least 8,000.[21] Thousands of members of this brigade crossed the frontier to help their coreligionists in the south. So, too, did some Iranian *pasdaran* (revolutionary guards) units, although these probably focused on attacking armed Iranian opposition forces located on Iraqi soil. These cross-border elements provided the "spontaneous" revolt with some leadership, an element of organization, a sense of direction and a boost in morale, although they were too few in number to affect the outcome appreciably. On the negative side, they gave the revolt in the south a coloring it did not originally have and one that may have alienated Arab Sunnis and even educated Shi'ah in Baghdad. Throughout the south, they raised the slogan of Jaafari (Shi'ite) rule, and hoisted pictures of al-Hakim and Khomeini. What originated as a distinctly Iraqi revolt against a discredited government was perceived in Baghdad as a political-religious movement with a distinctly sectarian base, supported by a feared former adversary, Iran. In the end, it is not clear how much of the uprising in the south was driven by anti-Saddam sentiments and how much by rising Shi'ite consciousness; nor is it yet clear how many residents in the south actively participated in the revolt, despite its territorial spread, and how many merely waited to see its outcome. In any event, the revolt finished by being more Shi'ite than it began.

The Kurdish Revolt

In the north, too, the initial act of revolt was probably more spontaneous than organized.[22] Although there were unofficial hints by Kurdish leaders before the war began that Kurds might rise if the central government was weakened in the war, the decisive action appears to have been taken on the ground in northern Iraq. In Raniyya, a town near Sulaimanaiyya, tensions erupted between the populace and the security forces a few days after the Basra uprising, and armed masses took control of the city. From there, rebellion spread to Koi Sanjaq, Sulaimaniyya, Irbil, Dahuk and other cities. The Fursan (Cavaliers), Kurdish forces paid to hold the northern areas for the central government, played a critical supporting role by deserting the government in droves. Mas'ud Barzani, leader of the Kurdish Democratic Party (KDP), who had returned to northern Iraq to test the waters for revolt, and had been in contact with the Fursan, may have ended up leading a groundswell he could not have contained, even if he so desired.[23]

Much of the denouement of the Kurdish revolt is well known. From the start, Kurds took over cities and towns in the north, including the oil center of Kirkuk, rather than confine their operations to the hills and mountains as had usually been the case in previous revolts. By the time the Iraqi military finally turned their attention to the north—after quelling the revolt in the south—the Kurdish opposition was in control of most Kurdish territory in the north. But the Kurdish fighters were defenseless against Iraqi armor and helicopter gunships. Only in a few cities, notably Kirkuk, did the Kurdish fighting forces put up armed resistance. Most Kurds, possibly fearing attacks with chemical weapons, deserted the cities and towns en masse, taking refuge in the mountains of northern Iraq, Turkey and Iran, and creating, overnight, a massive refugee problem and an international crisis of the first order. Eventually, the international community mounted, first, a humanitarian aid effort and then, under the leadership of British Prime Minister John Major, the creation of a "safe haven" for Kurds in northern Iraq. Under this program, Kurds, especially those in Turkey, were encouraged to return to their towns and villages under the military protection of the Coalition. By the fall of 1991, virtually all of those in Turkey and most of those in Iran had returned to the northern region of Iraq. The protective military umbrella continued to be extended to the Kurdish population north of the 36th parallel in Iraq at that time.

On April 19, before the safe haven concept could be put into effect, leaders of the Kurdish opposition front began negotiations with the central government in Baghdad for a permanent autonomy agreement. These negotiations, like others before them, foundered on the shoals of conflicting interests: the degree of control Kurds would be allowed in their region; the geographic extent of the Kurdish autonomous zone; jurisdiction over Kirkuk; and a sharing of revenues from the northern oil fields. This time, a new issue was injected into negotiations—a request for genuine democracy, not only in the north but in the remainder of the country as well.

After the failure of the negotiations, the Kurds turned their attention to creating a new administration in the north. In the spring of 1992, the Kurdish National Front, consisting of the major Kurdish parties under the leadership of the KDP and the Patriotic Union of Kurdistan (PUK) held internationally supervised elections for a Kurdish assembly. This was followed by the appointment of a Kurdish cabinet, which assumed administrative functions in the north. Meanwhile, early in 1992, Saddam Hussein pulled his forces back from Kurdish territory, and established a military perimeter around the protected Kurdish area. At the same time, he instituted an internal embargo on the passage of goods north of this line, further isolating the Kurds. These events deepened a sense of Kurdish national identity in the north.

The Center

The third important outcome of the rebellion was that the country's geographic and political center did not join the revolt. This "center" is best understood as a geographic concept, but it also includes a political and social component. Geographically, it includes Baghdad, containing some four million Iraqis, about a quarter of the country's population, and the territory to the north as far as Mosul, east as far as Ba'quba and west to the borders of Syria. This Sunni-dominated triangle contains the traditional core of Ba'thist support and a population more sympathetic than the Shi'ah and the Kurds to Arab nationalist causes, primarily through long-standing commercial and intellectual links with fellow Arab Sunnis in Syria and Jordan. But the triangle also includes substantial components of Arab Shi'ah and Kurds, as well as minorities such as Christians and Turcomen. Baghdad itself probably has a Shi'ite majority, although no Shi'ite-Sunni census has ever been published. The "center" is also characterized by its higher standard of living. The benefits of modernization, as measured by education, housing, health care and relative sophistication of the population, are concentrated in Baghdad and its environs. As a rule, the further the distance from Baghdad, the greater the attenuation of these benefits, regardless of the ethnic or sectarian composition of the population. Not surprisingly, Iraq's substantial middle class is concentrated in this "center." And it is from this area, particularly, though not exclusively, its provincial Sunni towns, that the Ba'th leadership has recruited its supporters in the military, the security services and the party.

It is significant that the military—notably the Republican Guard—

did not collapse or turn against the regime during the rebellion. While there were some defections and instances of intermilitary fighting, these were not sufficient to cause a breakdown of military discipline. Indeed, the military put the rebellion down with extreme brutality.

Nor was there much hint of rebellion in the "center." A brief, but sharp, spate of unrest in Shi'ite quarters in Baghdad was brought under control. Compared with the Shi'ite south and the Kurdish north, the Sunni-dominated middle class in the "center" was quiet. This behavior, in marked contrast with that of the rest of the country, requires some explanation.

Several tentative reasons can be suggested. The first may well have been fear. The "center" was the area in which the regime's security control was strongest and where its retribution would be swift and decisive. Enough secret police and military remained in Baghdad and its environs to enforce law and order. Second may have been indecision. Like most civilians caught up in civil strife, much of the population probably preferred to wait and see who won before taking sides. Third may have been fear of retribution by the rebels. In Najaf, Karbala and other rebel centers in the south, atrocities were committed by rebels against Ba'th officials. These acts provided little incentive for defections from the military or the party.

But these explanations do not go far enough to account for the fact that the "center" did not revolt against a government in which most have admitted losing faith. Some have claimed that lack of support for the rebellion by the UN coalition—particularly the failure of the coalition to provide military protection in the form of air cover— allowed Saddam's forces to put down the revolt and turned the tide against his overthrow.[24] Had such support been given, in this view, the army might have revolted. This may be the case, but it cannot now be determined. Such support might, equally, have led to prolonged conflict and a collapse of authority at the "center." It is impossible to tell what the outcome might have been in the event of varying degrees of outside support for the rebellion. Without such help, the uprising failed.

This suggests that forces other than mere acquiescence may have been at work. One such element may lie in the self-conscious identity of the middle-class elements composing this "center," who can be said to constitute a bureaucratic and technological establishment. This identity predated the Ba'th and will probably outlast it. While the leadership of the party, the military and the security services have been drawn from provincial towns north of Baghdad—mainly Tikrit—the cadre of the central government has been drawn from middle-class professionals—lawyers, teachers, army officers and officials. Their loyalty to the regime had been secured over time by a network of privileges, from education for their children to health benefits, housing in new and affluent districts, travel privileges and a life style that placed them squarely in the middle and upper-middle class. While these privileges may be monopolized by Sunnis, they also extend to many Shi'ah and Kurds. Like established classes the world over, they are reluctant to lose their status and privileges to unknown forces. Moreover, this urbanized establishment has considered itself the "glue" that holds the state of Iraq together; indeed, consolidation of state power over an ethnically diverse country has become its main vocation. As the rebellion gathered momentum in the south, as it took on a more sectarian coloring, as the Iranian leanings of some of its leaders became more evident, this establishment recoiled. In addition to dislike of sectarianism, the "center" may also have feared the disintegration of the state through the collapse of the army and the authority of the government. Such an outcome was inimical to the "center's" middle class, whether Sunni or Shi'ah, regardless of their dislike of Saddam and his repressive apparatus. While these sentiments were probably felt more strongly in the Sunni community, they may have been shared in some measure by educated Shi'ah as well. What the rebellion could not answer was how much the "center" acquiesced in the status quo for fear of losing its privileged status, and how much because it shared a strong Iraqi nationalist sentiment that feared a collapse of the state along with the regime, and disliked foreign interference more than it abhorred repression. Was there within the "center" a non-sectarian core committed to an Iraqi identity from which an alternative leadership could be drawn? Or would the regime, and specifically Saddam Hussein, be able to play successfully on fears of collapse and anti-imperialist sentiment to stay in power?

While the rebellion left more questions than answers, some tentative conclusions can be drawn about the forces at work in Iraq in its aftermath. First, the brutality with which the uprising was quelled left Iraq with greater ethnic and sectarian divisions and eroded the sense of nationhood that emerged from the Iran-Iraq war. Second, the war and the sanctions sharpened divisions between rich and poor and depleted the economic benefits of the middle class in Iraq, and thus weakened the group which must underpin any future stability. Despite these difficulties, however, the establishment was still under Saddam's control, and his security apparatus still had sufficient tentacles throughout the country to control the population. Except in Kurdish areas of the north, supported by the coalition umbrella, no alternative structures or organizations were permitted. Iraqi society was politically atomized. Creating a civic culture in Iraq, to say nothing of alternative leadership groups, would be extremely difficult. At the same time, the old social contract between the regime and society had broken down. Under that "contract," the population acquiesced in repressive rule it did not like in return for economic benefits and upward social mobility. Without the revenues to provide these benefits, the threads which tied the establishment to the regime in the past were at risk of shredding and finally snapping.

3. Potential Political Scenarios in Iraq

Once the effects of the war became clear, it was possible to envisage four potential long-term scenarios, broadly defined, for the political future of Iraq.

A Continuation of Saddam Hussein's Rule

The continuation of Saddam Hussein's rule seemed the most likely scenario in the near term, although Saddam's span of interest had shrunk to personal survival. Whether Saddam and his entourage of Tikritis could remain to the end of the decade was more doubtful. If Saddam did remain, there seemed likely to be little change in direction or policy in Iraq. Such a regime would necessarily remain Sunni-dominated and heavily reliant on the Tikriti loyalists in the security services and the Republican Guard. Attempts at political reform would be likely to remain cosmetic and to benefit mainly the "center," rather than the Shi'ite south or the Kurdish north. The longevity of Saddam's government would depend on how long the sanctions regime prevailed, and after they were lifted,on how much help Iraq could get from abroad for development. If Iraq failed to receive economic and technical help from the industrial democracies (by no means a cer-tainty), it would probably turn to Third World countries for tech-nology, spare parts and what credit it could get. China, India, North Korea, Brazil and possibly Eastern European and former Soviet republics come to mind.

A relaxation of sanctions could provide some economic respite and buy time for Saddam to renew the social contract among elements of his population. If he could convince them of his staying power and the alleged dire consequences that would attend his political departure, it might be possible for him to prolong his rule for a number of years. To do so he would have to rely heavily on a regime of repression to keep disgruntled Shi'ah and alienated middle-class Iraqis in line. The military would be an essential element in this structure and therefore likely to absorb scarce economic resources. After the war, Saddam appeared unrepentant for the damage caused Iraq and Iraqis, and still desirous of resuming his role as a future Arab world leader. Under these circumstances, Iraq's economic recovery was likely to be slow, its full integration into the Arab world delayed, and its social regeneration stunted. However, as long as Saddam Hussein remained in power, protection of the Kurdish area in the north was likely to remain, making that area increasingly independent of Iraqi government control.

A Change of Leadership but not of Regime

It was possible that new leadership might emerge from within the regime or the establishment. Such leadership could include members of the Tikriti clan, military leaders, Ba'th party officials or combinations of all three. While the mechanism by which Saddam might be replaced was difficult to envision after the end of the war, given the tight security that surrounded him, his removal by members of the establishment remained the most plausible replacement scenario. Indeed, numerous earlier failed military coups indicated the most likely quarter from which his overthrow could be accomplished. The difficulty of gaining access to Saddam or of organizing alternative leadership groups made it difficult to see when or how such an eventuality could occur. His continued survival after war, rebellion, and sanctions, with little evidence of internal regime instability, indicated the obstacles to any such change. Nevertheless, the hardships created by the war, the intense alienation produced by the rebellion, and the continued economic erosion caused by the sanctions were certain to make Iraq increasingly difficult to rule. Iraq's problems would be exacerbated if a tight sanctions regime remained, but even if sanctions were removed, Iraq's recovery would be slow and its stability uncertain. A change of leadership some time in the 1990s seemed more likely than not.

Iraq's policy under such a replacement group would depend on whether its composition was mainly military or civilian, Ba'thist or non-Ba'thist, and on whether a younger generation of reformers existed within the establishment. But any such group would probably continue to represent the Sunni-dominated middle class, at least initially. Reliance on the military, or key portions of it, would be essential to consolidate power. Younger technocrats or Ba'th party members were more likely to be pragmatic, rather than ideological, and more inclined to concentrate on development rather than foreign adventures. New leaders might be forced to undertake a more conciliatory policy toward Kurds and Shiʻah in an effort to consolidate power and turn over a new leaf. And such leaders would most likely attempt, with more success than Saddam, to mend fences with Arab neighbors, such as Kuwait, Saudi Arabia, Egypt and possibly even Syria. They might even have improved, though wary, relations with Iran. Aside from these steps, a change more of method than direction, such a regime would probably continue to emphasize the cohesion of the state and its independence of foreign influences to the detriment of liberalizing policies. They would also be likely to continue the modernizing, secular policies of the Baʻth at home. A change of this kind would be likely to meet with acceptance in the Gulf, with ensuing economic benefits.

This outcome would represent the optimistic side of this scenario, but a change of this kind would also be likely to have a risky downside. Any new leadership, even within the Baʻth, would likely be weaker than Saddam and subject to challenges from all the repressed elements in Iraq seeking total, not partial, change. At a minimum, Kurdish separa- tists and Shiʻite opposition elements would be likely to assert demands that the central government would not be willing to meet. Even within the regime, the new leaders might be challenged by ambitious contend- ers. Any severe struggle for power from within could lead to chronic instability, an unravelling of state power, or more likely, the inauguration of the regime by a brutal repression of dissent. Any ruthless reassertion of control would make modest reforms or a change of methods difficult.

An Alternative Regime: the Radical Scenario

It is also plausible that the Iraqi Baʻth could be replaced by an entirely different regime, composed of some of the elements that participated in the 1991 rebellion. For Iraq, this would be a radical change. The most likely components of such a regime would be a loose amalgam of the Kurdish leadership, already ensconced in the north, elements of the Shiʻite population, who constitute at least 55 percent of the inhabitants of Iraq, and Sunnis unaffiliated with the Baʻth. An array of political groups, comprising parties ranging from the Communists on the Left to Shiʻite religious groups on the Right, and including ex-Baʻthists and Liberal Democrats, constitute an Iraqi opposition that sees itself as an alternative government. In the autumn of 1992, this group met in the north of Iraq, outside government control, to elect a National Assembly and an Executive Committee, and to draw up a program for the government of Iraq. This National Assembly is illustrative of the range of political orientations available in an alternative government.

Any group that wished to replace the regime would have to deal with the Sunni-dominated establishment, however, especially its military component. Replacing the regime without incorporating at least some of the establishment at the "center" would be very difficult, and it is hard to envision a mechanism by which this could occur peaceably.[25] Uprooting the regime and the establishment that acquiesced in its rule would probably require a major social upheaval. Rioting, perhaps due to food shortages or other privations which might cause a collapse of authority, would be one possible scenario. Another would be long-term political instability at the center that caused a dissolution of the military. A collapse of this order, unless it were sudden, would be likely to invoke some action on the part of Iraq's neighbors, who might take preventative action as the situation unravelled.

Should a new regime displace the traditional Sunni Arab leaders in Baghdad, its policies would probably differ substantially from those of most past regimes in Iraq. Such a government could take several potential directions. It might have a leftist or, more likely, a populist thrust, in which case it would be likely to focus on domestic restructuring. It is worth noting that Iraq has had such a government several times in the past—once in 1936-37, after a military coup brought to power a group of liberal reformers (mainly Kurds and Shi'ah), and again in the early years of the Qasim era (1958-1960), when political parties were licensed.[26] Both experiments failed because reformers had too shallow a base in society. Alternatively, a new regime of this kind could have a religious orientation if it contained a substantial Shi'ite element with a strong component from among the Iraqi exiles in Iran. In any event, any such movement would have to come to terms with the traditional Sunni-dominated establishment that leads the armed forces and the bureaucracy, on which any new regime would have to rely for a transitional administration, at least until new institutions could be formed. It is precisely because this establishment has become so deeply entrenched that such a scenario is difficult to imagine without substantial upheaval.

A Diminution of Authority

Lastly, a variety of pressures could cause a serious diminution of authority in Baghdad, resulting in a long period of turmoil. While such a drastic denouement might not seem likely, it remained within the realm of possibility. Such an outcome could emerge in a number of ways. A worsening economic situation over time could cause social upheaval and rioting, and the military might eventually refuse to fire on the population to keep order. A change of leadership within the Ba'th, or even the continuation of Saddam's rule with severe pressures on the regime from the international community, might gradually erode the ability of the central government to control an unruly population in the north and the south. Or a widespread rebellion that unseated the regime could produce a government unable to establish law and order. A long period of turmoil and decentralization of authority could destroy what remains of Iraq's national identity. Although in the period following the Gulf war, this was the least likely scenario, it was also the most dangerous for Iraq, for the region and for Western interests in the Gulf.

4. Iraq's Regional Role

Iraq's future regional role will, in large measure, be determined by which of the above-mentioned scenarios prevails.

Under the first scenario, that of the survival of Saddam Hussein, sanctions would be likely to remain for a longer period of time than if he were displaced. Even if they were lifted, many economic constraints would probably continue. Coalition members, in varying degrees, might prove reluctant to do business with Iraq; reparations would undoubtedly have to be paid, and credit would not be readily forthcoming. Restrictions on arms sales would be enforced with as much muscle as the coalition could muster. Some effort would be made to keep Iraq isolated.

While Saddam and his entourage might be successful in restoring stability by ruling with an iron hand, the stability would be more apparent than real, especially if economic conditions failed to improve. Under such a regime, Iraq could be expected to follow much the same strategy in the region as it did during the build-up to the war. On the one hand, it would probably turn to Arab states for help in reintegrating the country into the Arab community and as a means of facilitating commercial ties with Europe, from which it would need assistance. On the other hand, Iraq would probably play on anti-Western sentiments in the Arab world, exacerbated by the war, and would likely appeal to Arab populations and governments for Arab solidarity in the face of foreign pressure, strike anti-imperialist themes in the Third World, and play on humanitarian and other sentiments to weaken the Western alliance arrayed against it. Iraq could be expected to play the role of "spoiler" in the Arab-Israeli arena if the opportunity presented itself. Saddam and his followers did not appear to have abandoned a long-term vision of Iraq's (and his) leadership of the Arab world even if his own population no longer believed this to be possible, at least within the 1990s.

If Saddam were to be replaced by some combination of leaders within the current ruling group, Iraq's economic recovery could be speeded up, although much would depend on the quality of leadership, the thrust of their policy and the rapidity with which they could consolidate power. Such a regime would be likely to be more pragmatic and to place more emphasis on economic development than Saddam. Rather than defy the West, it might attempt to mend fences with its neighbors, gain Arab cooperation in its reintegration into the Arab world, and present a "moderate" front to the West in an effort to obtain the loans and credits it needed. While focusing on the Arab world, such a regime would almost certainly improve relations with Turkey and Gulf Arabs, and might even patch up relations with Iran. Like Iran under Rafsanjani, new, more pragmatic leadership might turn first to Europe or the new republics of the former Soviet Union for help, rather than the US. The main problems faced by such a government would be domestic—consolidation of power and an improved economy, both of which could prove overwhelming if not managed properly. If such a regime did not moderate its foreign policy in a more cooperative direction, and if it felt it necessary to pander to radical sentiments in the Arab world, reactions in the West, and among Iraq's neighbors, would make its future less certain.

In the event of a totally new regime, one dominated by Shi'ah and Kurds, with a large dose of Iraqi populists, or religious elements, Iraq's foreign policy could change substantially. Such a regime would be much more likely to be dominated by "Iraqi Firsters." By inclination and by necessity, such a regime would probably be inward looking and highly unlikely to pursue an Arab nationalist policy. Indeed, it could look more toward Turkey and Iran. Should Shi'ite religious elements come to the fore, a leaning toward Iran could become much more pronounced, although no Iraqi regime, Shi'ite or otherwise, is likely to become a satrapy of Iran. Suspicions of Iraq's larger neighbor are too deeply ingrained in all Iraqis to permit such an outcome, and, in addition, a pro-Iranian policy would encounter too much hostility from Saudi Arabia and Kuwait for comfort. Nevertheless, Iranian influence over Iraqi policy, as well as Iraqi sensitivity to Iranian interests, would be likely to increase.

A government representing such a radical change would not be likely to achieve rapid economic development—at least not in the short term. Questions about its stability could delay help from outside, although a new regime could improve Iraq's chances for development in the long term, if it stabilized itself, soothed the fears of its neighbors and concentrated on the home front. Iraq's regional role would, under such a government, be dramatically reduced for some time to come as it struggled to create a new and different socio-political structure in Iraq.

Under the last scenario, the erosion of Iraq's "center," the Iraqi polity, as it is now constituted, could disintegrate. Iraq would be able to play no regional role. Rather, its neighbors would probably seek to carve out spheres of influence. Turkey would, at a minimum, insist on some means of control over Kurdish areas adjacent to its own Kurdish population and might even attempt an agreement with Kurdish leaders that gave it a degree of access to Iraq's northern oil fields. Iran would naturally seek a measure of influence over the Shi'ite population, especially in the holy cities, and, to some extent, over Kurds in the north as well. It might take coveted border areas, such as territory on the Shatt al-Arab. In this, Iran's interests would clash with those of Saudi Arabia and Kuwait; both would seek to protect their borders and their society from Iranian Shi'ite influence. Syria, too, would probably assert its influence with the Arab Sunni population. Such a scenario would be potentially destabilizing for the region, and for Western interests in the Gulf, as Iraq's neighbors struggled for spheres of influence at the head of the Gulf. Before Iraq could reach this state, powerful pressures would probably be exerted to prevent its collapse.

5. Conclusions

Regardless of the leadership of Iraq or the scenario that unfolds, Iraq's regional role is likely to be limited, at least until the mid- or late 1990s. Its economic recuperation will take time, even under favorable circumstances. The debt accumulated from the Iran-Iraq war as well as the costs of the Kuwait crisis will take years to pay off. Without more cooperative leadership, better credit arrangements are unlikely to be forthcoming from international institutions. Iraq also faces choices on how much of its scarce resources to invest in the military and its military industrial complex. Under unfavorable scenarios, Iraq could face a long period of instability that could hamper its development.

Whatever scenario unfolds in Iraq, the key issue is not how much economic, military or political power the country will have to bring to bear—it will have far less than in the past. It is the vision of Iraq's regional role that prevails in Baghdad that will be decisive. If Iraq clings to Saddam's vision of Iraqi preeminence and if it continues to pose as a champion of Arab nationalism and anti-Western imperialism, it will gain some support among the disaffected. But the price—a foreign policy at odds with its domestic needs—will keep Iraq weak and delay its reconstruction. If Iraq does turn inward, if it cultivates a more pragmatic stance and a pluralistic political culture, it will sooner achieve its economic potential and the stronger regional role that is its corollary.

Notes

1. While numerous reports have been issued by the UN and other international organizations, they sometimes disagree in their findings. Most are drawn from short visits to Iraq by experts who have relied on information from the Iraqi government as well as on independent observation and interviews. It will be some time before a complete picture of the damage can emerge. The information here has been drawn from the following: "Report to the Secretary General on Humanitarian Needs in Iraq" by a UN Mission led by Sadruddin Aga Khan, Executive Delegate of the Secretary General, July 15, 1991; "Report on Public Health in Iraq after the Gulf War," by a Harvard Study Team, May 1991; "Nutrition Mission to Iraq: Report to UNICEF" by Tufts University, July 8, 1991; "FAO Report on Food and Agricultural Requirements," July 18, 1991; and the "Report of the United Nations Mission to Assess Humanitarian Needs in Iraq," led by Martti Ahtisaari, Undersecretary General for Administration and Management, March 27, 1991. The most extensive report to date has been that of Sadruddin Aga Khan, whose mission included teams investigating food and agriculture, water and sanitation, health care, and the energy sector. The report also drew on the findings of a separate team from the International Telecommunications Union.

2. For example, the UN report by Ahtisaari characterized war damage as bringing "near apocalyptic results" and relegating Iraq "to the pre-industrial age" for some time to come, an assessment generally regarded as too severe by later missions which observed Iraq after its attempts to repair its infrastructure. The UNICEF Fact Finding Mission disputed other UN reports charging immediate famine in southern Iraq or severe malnutrition caused by the war. See the Ahtisaari Report and the "Nutrition Mission to Iraq," cited above.

3. Sadruddin Aga Khan, "Report to the Secretary-General on Humanitarian Needs in Iraq," (New York: United Nations, July 15, 1991), p. 7, hereinafter referred to as Sadruddin Aga Khan Report.

4. Sadruddin Aga Khan Report, p. 6.

5. Sadruddin Aga Khan Report, pp. 31-32.

6. Sadruddin Aga Khan Report, pp. 24-25; FAO Report, p. 4.

7. Phebe Marr, "Iraq's Uncertain Future," *Current History,* January 1991, p. 2.

8. Sadruddin Aga Khan Report, p. 31. For a slightly different estimate, see Economist Intelligence Unit, "Iraq Country Report," No. 2, 1991 (London), p. 6. This estimate assumes exports of 2.75 million b/d at $22 a barrel giving Iraq $22 billion, from which 30 percent would have to be extracted for reparations, leaving about $16 billion.

9. Phebe Marr, "The Iran-Iraq War: the View from Iraq," in Chistopher C. Joyner, *The Persian Gulf War: Lessons for Strategy, Law and Diplomacy* (New York: Greenwood Press, 1990), pp. 40ff., 70.

10. The 100,000 figure is cited in Peter Galbraith, "Civil War in Iraq," a Staff Report to the Committee on Foreign Relations, US Senate, May 1991 (Washington, DC: US Government Printing Office, 1991), p. 1. The lower estimate was suggested in a speech by Zbigniew Brzezinski at a Middle East Institute Conference on "The Future of the Persian Gulf: Political and Economic Issues," Washington, DC, June 13, 1991.

11. The numbers given by Tehran claim 12,000 to 16,000 killed in Najaf and Karbala

alone, but these are probably high. (Pierre Martin, *Monde Arabe, Magreb-Machrek* (Paris: La Documentation Francaise), No. 132, April-June, 1991, p. 27.

12. Several UN reports in mid-1991 pointed to widespread malnutrition in Iraq, particularly among children below the age of six, possibly reaching 10 percent of this age group. (Sadruddin Aga Khan Report, p. 20). Food rationing is providing only one third of the food consumption levels of recent years, although these were high for a Third World country. The prices of imported food were beyond the reach of most Iraqis. The health sector was affected by Iraq's inability to import medicines and to repair medical facilities dependent on water, electricity and other spare parts (*ibid.,* pp. 16-22). Rice and wheat were estimated to cost 22 and 45 times their prewar price (FAO Report, p. 2). Meanwhile, child mortality rates have doubled (Harvard Medical School Report, p. 1). However, at least one other report has questioned the extent of deprivation, claiming that these estimates may be exaggerated. According to the UNICEF Report, some child malnutrition is a long-term — not a short-term — problem which predates the war (UNICEF Report, p. 1).

13. Trevor Rowe, "Desperate Times in Iraq," *Washington Post,* November 7, 1992, p. A1.

14. For example, Michael Massing, "Can Saddam Survive?," *The New York Review,* August 15, 1991, pp. 59-63; Tony Horowitz, "Casualties of War," *The Wall Street Journal,* July 15, 1991; Trudy Rubin, "The Economic Embargo on Iraq Won't Hurt Hussein and Company," *The Philadelphia Inquirer,* May 19, 1991.

15. For an eye-witness report, see Trudy Rubin, "The Shiite Rebels Paid Dearly for Resisting Saddam Hussein," *The Philadelphia Inquirer,* May 9, 1991.

16. Iraq's regular army was estimated at about 250,000 in 1980. For the afterwar estimates of Iraq's army, see Ahmed Hashim, "Iraq, the Pariah State," *Current History,* January 1992 and Ehud Ya'ari, "Iraq's New Order of Battle," *Jerusalem Report* (Jerusalem), July 4, 1991, p. 36. Estimates of how many tanks and APCs remain vary and hence are less reliable.

17. *Military Aviation News* (Stansted Airport, UK) No.Al-355, May, 1991.

18. See, for example, Milton Viorst,"Report from Baghdad," *The New Yorker,* June 24, 1991, p. 60; Trudy Rubin, "Saddam's own Actions Plant the Seeds of his Downfall," *The Philadelphia Inquirer,* July 5, 1991; Tony Horowitz, "Triple Devil," *The Wall Street Journal,* July 25, 1991.

19. For accounts of the rebellion from those sympathetic to its aims, see Laurie Mylroie, *The Future of Iraq,* The Washington Institute Policy Papers, No. 24. (Washington, D.C., The Washington Institute for Near East Policy, 1991), and Peter Galbraith, *op. cit.* Both rely heavily on exile opposition sources for their information. For the view from Baghdad, see Milton Viorst, *op. cit.,* who interviewed many officials and members of the middle class in the capital.

20. For a good account of the Shi'ite rebellion see Pierre Martin, *op. cit.,* and Faleh Abd al-Jabbar, "Why the Uprisings Failed," The *Middle East* (May-June 1992), pp. 2-14. According to Abd al-Jabbar, the rebellion began in the southern Sunni towns of Abu'l-Khasib and Zubair at the end of February, and then spread to Basra.

21. Mylroie, *op. cit.,* p. 34.

22. The fact that there was no coordination between the revolt in the south and that in the north was a contributory factor to its failure, and made it easier for the central government to deal with the rebellion in stages.

23. According to Kurdish sources, Barzani was cautious about starting a revolt which could cause a calamity for Kurds in the face of superior Iraqi armor and the potential for use of chemical weapons (interview with members of the Kurdish Front, London, June 1991).

24. For this view see Laurie Mylroie, "Led Astray by the Saudis in Iraq," *The Wall Street Journal,* April 10, 1991, and Peter Galbraith, *op. cit.,* pp. 15-17.

25. UN-sponsored elections have been mentioned, but it is hard to see how these could be carried out before a collapse of the regime, since the regime is not likely to permit them peaceably.

26. For these episodes, see Marr, *The Modern History of Iraq,* pp. 72-76 and 159-176.

10 THE POLITICAL CONSEQUENCES OF THE CRISIS FOR KUWAIT

Shamlan Y. Al Essa

During the three decades between 1960 and 1990, the principal objective of governments in the Gulf was to bring about the rapid economic transformation of their countries. This was an undertaking with which they coped successfully.

The Gulf crisis of 1990-91 raised new political challenges that were much more complex than those of economic management. The crisis had implications for the defense and security of Gulf countries, their international relations, and their internal politics. Some of the most important questions posed were the future relations of the conservative governments of the region with their peoples, and, more broadly, of the states of the Gulf with Gulf societies.

This paper will focus on some major political consequences of the Gulf crisis, dealing principally with Kuwait, but comparing Kuwait's situation with that of other Gulf Cooperation Council (GCC) states. It will review the traditional relationship between government and society, and identify changes in this relationship. Particular emphasis will be placed on the role of a number of non-governmental institutions as agents of political change. The key postwar issues facing the Gulf will be identified, and the factors working for and against greater participation by populations in the political systems of their countries will be discussed.

1. Background

The political leadership of the Gulf region is traditional in nature and has a long history. The ruling families of the Gulf—Al-Sabah (Kuwait), Al-Khalifa (Bahrain), Al-Thani (Qatar), Al-Nuhayyan (United Arab Emirates), Al-Saud (Saudi Arabia), and Al-Said (Oman)—ruled the area for a long time before the discovery of oil. Three of these families—Al-Sabah, Al-Saud and Al-Khalifa—belong to the same tribe, Anaza.

Prior to the discovery of oil in the Gulf States, the economy of the region was based on trade, pearl diving, shipbuilding, seafaring and some cultivation in a few small oases.[1] All of the ruling families obtained their income from two sources: taxes on goods and income tax from the merchant class. Gulf society was dominated by a mixture of tribal leaders and prominent merchant families, whose importance was magnified because trade was the main source of income and the backbone of the Gulf's economy.

British colonial rule in the area during the nineteenth and early twentieth centuries maintained the status quo, and this helped to prevent any attempt to make changes in the Gulf. The British rule gave the conservative autocratic regimes in the area protection from any external or internal disturbances.[2]

Despite the fact that the merchant class had close tribal relations with the ruling families, it played a leading role in moves for reform and opposition to the ruling families of the Gulf. This was especially evident during the early twenties and thirties, mainly during the period of reform movements in Kuwait in 1921 and 1938, in Bahrain in 1934, and in Dubai in 1938.[3] These attempts to establish political participation in the Gulf failed because the traditional ruling elites refused to co-operate with the merchant classes. The British colonial rulers did not encourage the reform movements. Moreover, public support for the reform movements failed to gain momentum because the elections advocated by the democratic movements were limited to the merchant class. Only 150 families were allowed to vote in Kuwait.[4]

After the discovery of oil in the Gulf, the social and economic structures changed drastically. The ruling families became wealthier and more powerful because they controlled the oil revenues and consequently controlled the entire economy. J.E. Peterson writes, "The traditional leadership not only retained the power of distribution, but also determined the criteria of allocation."[5] The merchant elites were the main beneficiaries of the various plans to redistribute oil revenues, after the ruling class, but in the process they surrendered a major political role.[6]

Although demands for political participation in the Gulf were voiced as early as the 1920s and 1930s, the implementation of these demands did not begin until 1963, when Kuwait had its first elected National Assembly. Bahrain followed in 1973. A Consultative Council was established in Qatar in 1964, while the UAE National Federation Council was established in 1971. These attempts to achieve political participation failed, except in Kuwait. Even here, the National Assembly was dissolved twice, in 1976, and then again in 1986 (on the grounds that it was too unruly during the Iran-Iraq war).[7]

The question arises: what were the bases of the political power of the governments of the Gulf?

Professor K. al-Naqib argues that the Gulf States have ruled through unofficial corporations or institutions, such as:

1. The *tribal institution,* which includes the heads of various Arab tribes in the country;

2. The *elite merchant families,* which are represented by the Chambers of Commerce;

3. *Sectarian institutions,* which include the heads of various religious sects such as the Sunni, Shiite, Zaidi and Ibadi;

4. *Religious institutions,* which include religious leaders who represent Islamic movements;

5. The *middle class,* which deals with the government through family affiliations or connections, because Gulf governments have prohibited any formal organization for these groups;

6. *Labor movements,* which deal with the government in the countries which allow the formation of trade unions.[8]

The institutions described by Professor al-Naqib vary in power from country to country in the Gulf. However, they were all well represented in Kuwait. After the 1981 elections, the Kuwaiti National Assembly included about 27 tribal members from various tribes (Ajman, Owazem, Mutran, Rashidi, Anaza, Ottabi, and Fadli); 4 members from the merchant class; 5 members from the religious sects (Shiites); and 4 members from the religious organizations (2 from the Muslim Brotherhood and 2 from the Salafi movement).[9]

2. The Increasing Role of Non-Governmental Organizations

One of the forces making for major change in some of the Gulf States has been the increasing role of non-governmental organizations. Little has been written in the West about the role of these organizations in the region, as they have not played a major political role until recently. It is not the intention of this chapter to review the rise and the increasing role of non-governmental organizations or their activities in the Gulf region as a whole. However, it is important to note the increasing role of these organizations in Kuwait after the Iraqi invasion of the country on August 2, 1990, when various popular committees were organized.

Non-governmental organizations in Kuwait are not a new phenomenon. Some cultural and literary organizations were founded as early as 1923, prior to the discovery of oil. After Kuwait's independence, the Kuwaiti government aided all non-governmental organizations inside Kuwait by providing them with locations from which to operate and with financial assistance. The government's financial aid to these organizations in 1987 alone amounted to K.D. 1,405,219, or $4,289,000, distributed among 53 non-governmental organizations.[10] The main reason for the Gulf States' assistance to non-governmental organizations was to legitimize government authority by maintaining good relations with them in a situation where political parties and organizations were not legal.

Despite the fact that the principal functions of the non-governmental organizations were not political, but were rather social, educational, cultural, and religious, these organizations came gradually under the influence of four major political groups—Islamic fundamentalists, liberals, Arab nationalists and conservative merchants. The various non-governmental organizations included medical associations, and organizations of teachers, lawyers, economists, students, graduates, women, and labor.

The political groups operated through well-known non-governmental organizations. Some of the best-known were the following:

A. *Jamiyat Al-Islah Al-Ijtima'i,* or the Social Reform Society. This organization was officially formed in 1961 after Kuwait's independence. However, prior to independence, it operated under the name of *Jamiyat Al-Irshad Al-Ijtima'i,* or the Social Guidance Society. It was formed in the early 1950s, with the principal objective of spreading Islamic morals and teachings. The Social Reform Society is controlled by the Muslim Brotherhood Movement, which publishes a weekly magazine called *Al-Mujtama'* or *The Society.* At the present time, the Society controls the student movement and some women's groups.

B. Another political group with institutional representation has been *Al-Nadi Al-Thaqafi Al-Qawmi,* or the National Cultural Club through which the Arab Nationalist Movement (ANM) operated in the early 1950s. The founders of this movement were Kuwaiti graduates from the American University of Beirut and Cairo University, whose main goal was to establish Arab unity. This club was especially active during the time of Egypt's President Nasser. The club was closed in 1956 when its members protested against the British, French and Israeli attacks on Egypt. After Kuwait's independence, ANM operated through *Nadi Al-Istiqlal,* or the Independence Club. When the movement protested against the government during National

Assembly elections, the government closed the club in 1976. Now the group operates through *Al-Tali'a* or *The Vanguard,* a weekly magazine published in Kuwait. ANM influenced some labor trade unions after losing its student stronghold to the Reform Society in the seventies. ANM won 4 seats in the 1985 National Assembly elections.

C. *Al-Jamiya Al-Thaqafiya Al-Ijtima'iya,* or the Social and Cultural Society, was founded in 1963, with the main objective of educating and enlightening young Muslims about their religious duties. Controlled by young Kuwaiti Shiites, this society's influence increased among the Shiite community after the 1979 Iranian Revolution. Its members were very active in defending the Shiite community in Kuwait during the Iran-Iraq war, especially after some terrorist acts that had resulted in the arrest of some Shiites in Kuwait.

D. *Jamiyat Ihya al-Turath al-Islami,* or the Islamic Heritage Society, was formed in the late 1970s with the objective of reviving Islamic fundamentalism in Kuwait. The Salafi movement members of this group won some seats in the 1975 and 1981 National Assembly elections.

3. Non-governmental Organizations After the Iraqi Invasion

The Iraqi invasion of Kuwait and the departure of the Kuwaiti government for Saudi Arabia left the Kuwaiti communities inside Kuwait facing the ruthless and brutal occupation forces without the guidance of a government. How did the Kuwaiti communities inside Kuwait manage themselves? How did they organize their daily lives under occupation? Most importantly, how did they manage to operate as a resistance force fighting against the occupation forces?

After the invasion, the mosque became the center of Kuwaiti gatherings, the place where the men met after prayers to discuss the situation in the country during and after the occupation. The Kuwaiti communities used the various mosques in Kuwait to organize themselves into various committees.

The first committee to be organized was the medical committee. Members of Kuwait's Medical Society were the first volunteers, and opened 24-hour health clinics inside the mosques to treat sick and injured people.

Every day after the Maghreb prayer, young Kuwaitis met at various mosques throughout Kuwait to gather volunteers for new committees. Examples included the following:

A. An information and communications committee was formed. It gathered news about the occupation forces and published an underground magazine asking the people to continue their civil disobedience and their resistance against the occupation.

B. The food distribution committee was in charge of the distribution of food to the residents of Kuwait through each district's food co-op. Every district in Kuwait has a food co-op owned and run by the people in each district. Every two years the people of each area elect their co-op's board of management. Thus, elected people played a major role in providing food and other essential goods to the people in each district during the occupation.

C. The cleaning committee was in charge of gathering garbage and burning it in order to prevent the spread of disease. Thus, the mosques and the food co-ops became the centers of activity for over a month. When the Iraqi occupation forces noticed their activities and prevented Kuwaiti doctors from treating patients in the mosques, the medical committee members began visiting patients in their homes.

When the United Nations food embargo against Iraq began, the Iraqi occupation forces started to take food from the co-ops. In order to prevent this, young Kuwaitis took the food from storage and hid it inside people's basements for subsequent distribution.

The Kuwaiti merchants who remained in the country and the government in exile used to smuggle K.D. 200 million or $700 million into Kuwait each month to be distributed among Kuwaitis to support their civil disobedience. The risky task of distributing the money was left to the Kuwaiti women, a number of whom were caught and then killed as they refused to reveal the source of the money.[11]

Prior experience in the organization of non-governmental institutions helped Kuwaitis to recruit and organize others, including many young Kuwaitis who only became active because of the presence of the Iraqi occupation forces.

The political groups behind the working committees emanated from the Islamic fundamentalist movement. They included its two Sunni organizations—the Muslim Brotherhood and the Salafi movement—and one Shiite organization—"Al-Jamiya Al-Thaqafiya Al-Ijtima'iya." Each organization operated in a district independently of the others. The various committees helped each other when they needed certain items, such as food or medical care.[12]

4. Popular Committees Outside Kuwait

The Kuwaiti people who were outside Kuwait during the Iraqi invasion and occupation of Kuwait quickly formed popular committees in various Arab and European countries, as well as in the United States of America. The main objectives of these popular committees were to work for the liberation of Kuwait and to help the Kuwaiti communities abroad.[13] For purposes of illustration, this paper will describe the committees in one country, the United Arab Emirates (UAE).

In the UAE, there were more than nine Kuwaiti popular committees, serving more than 50,000 Kuwaitis. These committees were spread out though the Emirates. There were two in the emirate of Abu Dhabi, two in Dubai and five in Sharjah. The reasons why the emirate of Sharjah had the largest number of these popular committees are that: (a) The majority of Kuwaiti refugees in the UAE lived in Sharjah; (b) The government of the emirate of Sharjah is very liberal in its political outlook, and Kuwaitis were therefore allowed to form as many popular committees as they wanted; (c) Many Kuwaiti National Assembly members resided in Sharjah, and helped to establish popular committees in the hope that they would be recognized in the next political election in Kuwait; and (d) The concentration of Kuwaiti Shiites in Sharjah undoubtedly helped in the creation of many popular committees because Kuwaiti Shiites were more organized and more politically active.

While the other popular committees in the UAE accepted Kuwaiti government financial assistance, the popular committees in Sharjah refused any assistance from the government because of a desire for independence from government control.

The popular committees outside Kuwait were not like those inside. While the committees inside were assisted and directed by Islamic movements, the majority of the committees outside were not politically committed to any group. The exception was Solidarity International for Kuwait, which was founded in Washington, DC and published *Al-Murabitoon,* a newspaper in London. This committee was controlled by the Muslim Brotherhood in Kuwait.

In general, the organizers of the popular committees were young and western-educated. The board of one of the Abu Dhabi popular committees included two university professors with Ph.D.'s, two lawyers, three engineers, one businessman and one female social scientist. All of these people were elected by the Kuwaiti community in Abu Dhabi. None of the people whom I interviewed in popular committees in the UAE were affiliated with any of the political organizations inside Kuwait. However, many of them had had experience working with non-governmental organizations in Kuwait. The experience of young people working with others for the liberation of their country had a profound effect on their future political life, as they started to realize the importance of political participation and involvement.

5. The Postwar Political Challenges

After the war to liberate the country, new issues faced the Kuwaiti population. The collective experience of suffering as a result of the Iraqi occupation created a strong bond between Kuwaitis. Patriotism, concern about the future destiny of Kuwait, and aspirations to be involved in the future of the country were widespread.

On its return to Kuwait at the end of February 1991, the Kuwaiti government attempted to dissolve the existing committees inside Kuwait. The committees were to be replaced by government employees who would manage the food co-ops and distribute food to the populations. This attempt by the government failed because it led the committees inside Kuwait to boycott the government employees. The Crown Prince and Prime Minister intervened to solve the dispute between the groups and a compromise was reached. However, when the Prime Minister attempted to form a new cabinet in Kuwait after its liberation, all the political organizational groups which had remained in Kuwait refused to participate in the government unless it declared the date for the restoration of democracy.[14]

After suffering the Iraqi occupation, the people inside Kuwait were not willing to renounce their growing sense of power. By attempting to dissolve the existing committees inside Kuwait and replace them with others from outside, the government may have been demonstrating a realization that the power of the non-governmental organizations was growing and should be curtailed. However, from the reaction to its efforts, it was clear that Kuwaitis expected to participate in the politics of postwar Kuwait. While the gradual return of a normal situation meant that the committees established during the occupation no longer needed to function, the non-governmental institutions that had helped to organize the committees had been strengthened as a result. They had obtained increased social prestige, and had extended their organizational networks, which put them in a good position for effective participation in politics.

After liberation, the sentiments of Kuwaitis were inward-looking. The country had suffered enormous war damage, and the principal concerns of the population were reconstruction and the building of a better future.

The Changing Labor Force

Apart from the war damage, the character of Kuwait was changing. Prior to the war, Kuwait and other Gulf states had been dependent on labor from other countries. (See Table 1.) One of the major outcomes of the crisis in the Gulf was a change in the character of this labor force.

TABLE 1
GCC Population in 1985

Country	Nationals (thousands)	Non-Nationals (thousands)	Total (thousands)	% of Non-Nationals
Bahrain	276.1	158.6	434.7	36.5
Qatar	95.2	251.7	346.9	72.6
Kuwait	686.1	1,025.7	1,711.8	59.9
Oman	973.0	447.8	1,420.8	31.5
Saudi Arabia	8,764.2	3,878.0	12,642.2	30.7
UAE	378.4	1,145.1	1,533.5	74.7

Source: George al-Qasafi, *al-Mustaqbal al-Arabi,* August 1988.

As can be seen from Table 1, the native population of the Gulf countries constituted a minority in their own countries. Prior to the crisis, the Gulf countries had resolved on a number of occasions to change this imbalance. As one Kuwaiti official stated, "Kuwait's next Five Year Plan (1991–1995) may contain stricter labor controls designed to promote the contribution of Kuwaiti nationals to the economy"[15]

The Iraqi invasion of Kuwait increased the suspicions held by Gulf governments and peoples of their foreign labor forces. There was a major reduction in workers from countries whose governments had opposed Operations Desert Shield and Desert Storm, such as Jordan, Yemen, Sudan and the Palestine Liberation Organization. These suspicions led the Gulf States to take drastic measures to deport or reduce the presence of these workers. In Kuwait, the Palestinian community had been estimated at 400,000, making them the second largest community in Kuwait after the native population. Many

Kuwaitis believed, as the *Economist* reported, that "The Palestinians should be expelled from Kuwait en masse because of the pro-Iraqi views of their political leaders. Many Palestinians acted, or are believed to have acted, as informers for the Iraqi Intelligence Service."[16] Many Palestinians left during the occupation, and were not issued re-entry visas; others were denied the renewal of their work permits or deported, leaving only a fraction of the former Palestinian population in Kuwait. Saudi Arabia deported more than more than half a million Yemeni laborers.[17] Elsewhere in the Gulf, Palestinians, Jordanians, Yemenis and Sudanese faced major problems.

The dilemma of the Gulf States has been that they want to reduce the number of foreign workers in their countries, while they depend on them in every sector of the economy (see Table 2).

TABLE 3
Labor Force in GCC Countries by Nationality, 1985

Country	Nationals (thousands)	Non-Nationals (thousands)	Total (thousands)	% of Foreign Labor Force
Bahrain	88.6	114.7	203.3	56.4
Qatar	17.7	155.6	173.3	89.8
Kuwait	127.2	551.7	678.9	81.3
Oman	178.0	300.0	478.0	62.8
Saudi Arabia	1,621.1	2,721.0	432.1	62.7
UAE	71.8	746.6	818.4	91.2

Source: George al-Qasafi, *al-Mustaqbal al-Arabi,* August 1988.

The Gulf states' dependency on the foreign and Arab labor force has been so extensive that it has been impossible to manage or run the states without their help and assistance. Expatriate labor has constituted the majority of the labor force in the following sectors: professional and technical workers, sales workers, agriculturists, animal husbandry workers, fishermen and hunters, and production workers and laborers. The foreign labor force occupied and controlled the productive sector of the Gulf economies. The Gulf nationals in most cases were concentrated in the service sectors and in clerical and related jobs.

There was some concern in Kuwait that too rapid a change would lead either to an excessive replacement of Arab by non-Arab Asian workers, and that favoring workers from a few Arab countries over others would create a new dependency on those few countries. Some

Kuwaitis advocated a quota system that would allow workers from a wide variety of Arab countries to work in Kuwait. However, the reduction of the foreign labor force was not a major issue in Kuwaiti politics, as the process blended with the tendency of Kuwaitis to be more inward-looking and concerned with Kuwaitization after the Gulf crisis.

The Security Issue

The future security of Kuwait and the Gulf region was an omnipresent issue after the Gulf war. The invasion of Kuwait by Iraq exposed the military weakness of the Gulf Cooperation Council countries. This weakness was not due to a lack of expenditure on the military. The Gulf states, where the illiteracy rate is still very high, spend more money on defense and security than on social services (see Table 3). For example, in the late 1980s, Oman, a country whose economic and social development started only in 1970, allocated 43.7 percent of its budget to military and security and only 8.8 percent to social services.

The Gulf states allocate a greater proportion of their budget to military expenses than the rest of the Arab world, except Syria, which spends 55 percent of its budget on security and military, while only 3 percent is spent on social services.[18] The military expenditure of the Gulf states is best described by Michael Jansen:

> Before the Gulf War, Saudi defense expenditure amounted to $281,632 for every soldier, including the National Guard and the small Frontier Force, while Iraq spent $11,000 on each one of its men. The US per soldier expenditure at this time was $69,609.[19]

TABLE 3
Percent of Budget Expenditures on Social Services and Military/Security Needs

Country	Social Services	Military & Security
Bahrain	17%	33%
Kuwait	47.6%	15%
Qatar	14.6%	23%
Oman	8.8%	43.7%
Saudi Arabia	39.5%	25%
UAE	32%	42%

Source: Arab Monetary Fund, *Al-Taqrir Al-Iqtisadi Al-'Arabi Al-Muwahhad, 1989* (Arab Unified Economic Report, 1989), p. 364.

Despite the high military spending, a number of factors resulted in the GCC weakness vis-à-vis Iraq. One important reason was that in their conception of national security, the Gulf countries concentrated mainly on internal security. As Liesl Graz has stated, "the notion became an obsession, a veritable fetish."[20] The concern with internal security prevented the Gulf from taking the external threat seriously.

The GCC countries also misconceived the consequences of the Iran-Iraq war. While Saudi Arabia, Bahrain and Kuwait strongly supported Iraq throughout the war, other Gulf states, mainly Oman, the UAE, and Qatar, maintained friendly relations with Iran. The failure to predict Iraq's behavior after the Iran-Iraq war was due mainly to the lack of serious analytical and academic studies in the Gulf concerning political developments in both Iran and Iraq.

Another factor was that the issues of security and national defense in the Gulf states were the concern of only the Ministers of the Interior and Defense, who in most cases were members of the ruling families of the Gulf. These important issues were not considered national issues involving academic institutions, the educated elite and businessmen. Important segments of the population were thus excluded from decision-making concerning national security. No real effort has been made to establish a Center for Strategic Studies in the Gulf, to advise the governments on the issue of security.

After the Gulf crisis, many questions remained about the ability of the Gulf states to deal with the security of the area. Are the GCC countries capable of forming a large national army? Will they continue their dependence on the West for defense, or will they replace the western forces with Arab ones? And finally, how are they going to deal with the growing regional power of Iran and Iraq in the future? These questions and others cannot remain unanswered.

There is a growing movement in the Gulf calling for the rebuilding of the armed forces and spending more money on defense and security. It can, however, be argued that it would probably be a mistake to spend more money on defense before carefully considering several factors:

1. It is necessary to evaluate the strengths and weaknesses of the performance of the Gulf armies during the war. Major obstacles in building modern and effective armies in the region arise from the traditional conservative political systems in the area. Governments find it difficult, if not impossible, to adapt to change and accept criticism from their own young army officers and technocrats, who want to build a modern and professional army. Furthermore, the

conservative nature of the Gulf patriarchal systems makes it more difficult to have modern and efficient armies. There is a tendency for the governments in the region to resist any change in the structure of the armies and national guards because the criteria of recruitment of military personnel in the Gulf continue to be tribal affiliation and loyalty to the state.

2. There is a growing danger of over-militarization in the area, which would lead to a strengthening of the military elites, and allow ruling elites to ignore and disregard the calls for political participation and equitable distribution of wealth.

3. Despite increasing pressure to have a strong army in the Gulf, the Gulf states cannot challenge Iran or Iraq in the future because of the small population size and the socio-political make-up of the Gulf states. For example, Iraq has a population larger than the national population of all the Gulf states, including Saudi Arabia.

A new Gulf security system will include the Arab forces that supported the Gulf countries in the crisis, mainly the Egyptians and the Syrians, and the West. The Gulf states will be expected to bear the cost of the Arab and western forces. Unless the price of oil is high, such a policy may drain the wealth of the Gulf states, and hinder their economic and social development plans. This would create the the eventual possibility of social and political unrest, as the new generation in the Gulf, which is used to the welfare system, will most likely not tolerate cutbacks.

There is clearly a strong connection between security issues and politics in the Gulf. Whether or not the Gulf Cooperation Council governments are able to cope successfully with the political, social and economic fallout of the Gulf war will depend on their ability to change and adapt to the new reality left after the war.

In Kuwait, the country most dramatically affected by the Gulf war, the attention of Kuwaitis became focused more than ever on the Kuwaiti political system. The organizations and individuals who played a role in resistance to the Iraqi occupation asserted their right to a political role in the liberated Kuwait. The Muslim organizations that had been prominent were able to take advantage of their increased prestige and extensive organizational networks to make a strong campaign in the 1992 elections. Individuals active in opposition to the Iraqi occupation continued to be interested in political involvement in postwar Kuwait, and many participated in political movements or associations.

When the postwar elections were finally held in October 1992, the new Kuwaiti Assembly was strikingly different from the old one. The majority of those elected represented a political platform, in contrast to earlier Assemblies consisting mainly of distinguished notables elected on the basis of family affiliations and prestige rather than ideology. The major issues in the election revolved around the future character of Kuwait's political and legal system, such as the demands of the Muslim movements that the *shari'a* be *the* source of Kuwaiti legislation (rather than *one* of the sources), the question of citizenship rights for naturalized Kuwaitis, and the issue of the status of women, including their right to vote. Of the 50 elected members, about 20 were members of religious or sectarian political groupings (mainly Muslim Brothers, but also Shiites and representatives of the Salafi movement). About 10 members (20 percent) were Constitutionalists, and three were members of the Democratic Platform. A number of tribal notables and members of leading merchant families who were elected had made arrangements with religious movements for their tacit support.

6. Future Political Participation in the Gulf

After the crisis in the Gulf, the idea of broadening political participation in the region remained a very sensitive issue for Gulf rulers. The drama in the Gulf both forced and allowed citizens to ask hard questions regarding the future role of the traditional form of government and of the people in politics. A widespread belief was that if the governments demanded that their nationals fight for their homelands, they would have to make concessions in the political arena.[21]

In the aftermath of the crisis, there were two schools of thought regarding the future of political participation and democracy in the Gulf. Some viewed the effects of the Gulf crisis as positive for democratization, while others viewed them as negative.

Those who regarded the chances of democratization as having improved argued that the political elites of the Gulf would become more democratic for the following reasons:

1. The Gulf governments had to call their citizens to mass in their support by participating in civil and military defense throughout the Gulf States. This participation, despite its limited role, could be expected to lead to more participation in the future. After the war, for example, Oman established a a Consultative Council. In 1992, King Fahd decreed the establishment of a ''Majlis al-Shura,'' or a Consultative Council, in Saudi Arabia.

2. The external pressures on the Gulf's autocratic regimes were likely to have a profound effect on the establishment of democracy in the Gulf. This point of view was stated in the *Economist:*

> Americans will find it hard to accept that they took so great a risk merely to give the antique politics of the Arabian Peninsula another generation or two of existence. . . . The handful of families that now run the Peninsula . . . freed from the ruder threat of Saddamization may be readier to experiment with democracy.[22]

3. After the eruption of the crisis in the Gulf, there was a strong demand by the intelligentsia of the Gulf for greater political participation by the people of the area. This view was well expressed by many newspapers in the Gulf, such as *al-Khalij* in the United Arab Emirates, which devoted daily articles to the issue of broader participation under the title "Hata Nastafid min al-Durus?" or "How Can We Learn From the Lessons?" during the first two weeks of March 1991.[23] Writers from Kuwait, Bahrain, and the United Arab Emirates wrote extensively during the Gulf crisis calling for more political participation and democracy in the Gulf.[24] Businessmen in Saudi Arabia have called for political participation. "The businessmen said with some trepidation, 'The people of Saudi Arabia must have a greater say in the affairs of the land.' "[25]

Others in the Gulf view the effects of the crisis as likely to be negative for prospects of democratization. They argue that the Arab rulers of the Gulf have long sought safety by avoiding change. According to this argument, the states in the Gulf will be stronger than before for the following reasons.

1. The traditional regimes will be more secure because of the removal of the external threat of Saddam Hussein. Furthermore, they have increased their security by agreements with the United States and other Arab governments, such as Egypt and Syria.

2. The political elites in the Gulf have not yet faced a great deal of pressure from the masses demanding more political participation. The principal exception to this has been Kuwait, both during the period of occupation, when the Popular Congress met in Jeddah in October 1990 to demand the restoration of the 1962 Constitution, and after liberation, when Kuwaitis continued to call for the holding of elections. So far, the demand for political participation and democracy in the Gulf has been limited to the educated elite, businessmen, young technocrats and students.

Two major factors will determine the future of the ideas of political participation and democracy in the Gulf. First, in the Gulf as a whole, there is a rising interest in Kuwaiti developments toward political participation and democracy. The success of the process of democratization in Kuwait would certainly be expected to have an effect on other Gulf States.

The second factor is the stand of the United States and the other western powers on the issue of democratization. If the American government stands strongly behind the principle of democracy and demands its implementation in the Gulf, then it is possible to envisage changes in the Gulf region toward political participation and democracy. On the other hand, if the American government focuses only on its economic interest in oil and puts aside its principle of democracy, then there will not be democracy in the Gulf or other Arab countries for a long time to come.

Notes

1. Joe Stork and Ann M. Lesch, "Background to the Crisis—Why War?" *Middle East Report* (November/December 1990), p. 13.

2. Muhammad G. al-Rumaihi, *Muwaqat al-Tanmiya al-Ijtima'iya wal-Iqtisadiya Fi al-Khalij* [Obstacles to Social and Economic Development in the Gulf], Kuwait: Dar al-Siyasa, p. 20.

3. Muhammad G. al-Rumaihi, *al-Judhur al-Ijtima'iya lil-Dimuqratiya fi Mujtam'at al-Khalij al-'Arabi* [The Social Roots of Democracy in the Societies of the Arab Gulf], Kuwait: Khadma, 1977.

4. Saad Eddin Ibrahim et al., *Azamat al-Dimuqratiya fi al-Watan al-Arabi* [The Crisis of Democracy in the Arab World], Beirut: Dar al-Mustaqbal al-Arabi, 1984, p. 646.

5. J.E. Peterson in *After the War: Iran, Iraq and the Arab Gulf States,* edited by Charles Davis (Chichester: Carden, 1990) p. 289.

6. Joe Stork and Ann M. Lesch, "Background to the Crisis—Why War?", *Middle East Report* (November/December 1990), p. 13.

7. "The Question of Democracy," *Middle East Business Weekly,* October 26, 1990, p. 9.

8. Khaldoun al-Naqib, *State and Society in the Gulf and the Arabian Peninsula* (Arabic text), p. 149.

9. Ibid., p. 150.

10. Kuwait, Ministry of Information, *Kuwait Yearbook* (1987, Arabic text).

11. Lecture by Jassim al-'Awn, member of the Salafi Movement in Kuwait, in Sharjah, UAE, March 1991.

12. Interview with Dr. Bader al-Houti, an active member of the Salafi Movement in Kuwait, in Al-Ain, UAE, March 28, 1991.

13. "Kuwait: Labor Imbalance Must Be Addressed," *Middle East Education and Training,* Vol. II, No. 4 (1989), p. 7.

14. *Al-Murabitoun* (Arabic), published in London, March 28, 1991.

15. *Al-Majalla,* a Saudi weekly magazine, October 17–23, 1990.

16. "The Vengeful One," *The Economist,* March 9, 1991, p. 53.

17. Nasra M. Shah and Sulaiman al-Qudsi, "The Changing Characteristics of Migrant

Workers in Kuwait," *International Journal of Middle East Studies,* Vol. 21 (1989), p. 37.

18. Arab Monetary Fund, *al-Taqrir al-Iqtisadi . . . , op. cit.,* p. 346.

19. Michael Jansen, "The Gulf States' Military Weakness," *Middle East International,* September 28, 1990, p. 21.

20. Liesl Graz, "The GCC as a Model? Sets and Subsets in the Arab Equation," in Charles Davies (ed.), *After the War . . . , op. cit.,* p. 5.

21. "The Question of Democracy," *Middle East Business Weekly,* October 26, 1990.

22. "The Old Arab Order Passes," *The Economist,* September 1, 1990.

23. This daily newspaper published in Sharjah, UAE, is widely read by the educated elite in the Gulf.

24. See the contributions of Ahmad al-Rubi of Kuwait, Muhammad Jaber al-Ansari of Bahrain, Muhammad al-Mani of Qatar, Baqer al-Nazar of Bahrain, and Hamdan of the UAE in *Al-Khalij* during this time.

25. *Time,* September 24, 1990.

11 THE ARAB STATE SUB-SYSTEM IN CRISIS

Jo-Anne Hart

The American sense of triumph in the Gulf war notwithstanding, the Middle East was hit by a devastating war and is worse off as a result. Furthermore, the crisis did not end with the war. The force and scope of human tragedy among civilians and refugees, and the economic losses caused by the war will maintain the trauma for years.

Two key consequences of the war are likely to affect politics in the Arab world and relations between the Arab states for a long time to come. One is that the economic costs of the war make it more difficult for oil wealth to play the same kind of role in the politics of the region as it did before. The Gulf states are likely to engage less in "oil diplomacy," especially toward Arab countries and political movements that did not adopt a position supportive of the Gulf during the war. The domestic policies of the Gulf states will also be affected. The costs of the war, and of the increased future military expenditures that are certain to be major parts of the budgets of Gulf countries, put unprecedented pressures on the ability of Gulf governments to maintain the growth of benefits for their populations that has been such a basic feature of their domestic policies.

A second crucial change has been in the strategic configuration in the region. Gulf security plans now focus on arrangements for balancing and containing Iraq. The new security system includes Egypt and Syria on the side of the Gulf states, but its power is derived mainly from the increased US military role in the region. The repercussions of the new US role are likely to be felt for a long time to come. There are strong historical misgivings in much of the region about the presence of Western military forces, and with the passage of time, the new United States role in the area is likely to be the target of criticism by Middle Eastern political movements.

1. The Costs of the War

The Arab world can be described as a regional subsystem in which there is an overlap of domestic and regional political-economic factors. Cantori and Spiegel define a subsystem as "proximate and interacting states which have some common ethnic, linguistic, cultural, social, and historical bonds, and whose sense of identity is sometimes increased by actions and attitudes of states external to the system."[1] This is the case in the Arab world, where the framework of these ties and interconnections is central to an understanding of inter-Arab relations. The overlap between domestic and regional factors exerts a dominant influence on political developments in Arab countries.

The Arab subsystem is itself intrinsically a part of, and reliant upon, a more dominant international system—as the Gulf war itself showed. Political developments within a single important Arab country often have major international implications, just as major international events such as the Gulf war have important implications for the domestic economies and politics of countries far removed from the front line of fighting. A set of concentric circles of interacting relations—the domestic, the regional, and the global—must thus direct our inquiry into changes of policy and behavior after the Gulf war.

The economic costs of the war include the costs of prosecuting the war and postwar reconstruction as well as lost income due to war damage and employment decline. For Saudi Arabia, estimated war and associated costs by August 1991 ranged from $64 to $80 billion.[2] Associated war costs included Saudi pledges to underwrite troop deployment expenses (and full in-country costs), funds to support allies upholding the sanctions against Iraq, and loans and grants to military partners Egypt and Syria. The economic strain on Saudi Arabia led to its borrowing billions of dollars from Western banks.

Reconstruction cost estimates vary by billions but could be at least $40 billion for Kuwait, an amount that is five times the expenditure of the Kuwait government on *all* items in the government budget in the last year before the Iraqi invasion.[3] Kuwait's ability to pay for reconstruction has also been diminished by the loss of oil income due to war damage.[4] The oil well fires resulted in enormous losses of oil and of tens of billions of dollars in potential revenues. Exacerbating the loss was the longer-term irreversible damage to reserves brought on by underground water seepage displacing oil. This affected Kuwait's reserves, pumping capacity, and the oil extraction process itself. Because of the geologic damage, production costs may triple and the lifetime of oil wells may have been cut by about one third.[5]

It needs to be emphasized in addition that an unprecedented regional ecological catastrophe was unleashed by the Gulf war. The massive oil spills in the Gulf, as well as the several hundred well fires indeterminately burning, created unforeseen environmental consequences which at this point can only be guessed at. The economic impact will be felt in the region and be reflected in the oil market. The collateral environmental damage will present new challenges to and constraints on the region's governments.

Finally, Gulf oil producers' income will be reduced if forecasts of falling oil prices are accurate. To make up the shortfall in the supply of oil after the cut in oil supplies that was caused by the embargo on Iraqi and Kuwaiti oil after the invasion of Kuwait by Iraq, Saudi Arabia greatly increased its production. The result was that world supply and demand became balanced *without* Iraqi or Kuwait oil. Any return of the oil production of these two countries to previous levels without a massive cut in Saudi production would thus depress prices substantially.

One of the problems leading to the Gulf war was an Iraqi complaint that Kuwait and the United Arab Emirates were producing at a level above their OPEC quotas, and that the result was diminished oil revenues for OPEC members in general. The costs of the war generated many pressures for Kuwait and Saudi Arabia to seek high oil revenues. Yet while both countries have an interest in a higher price of oil, between the mid-1970s and the Gulf crisis of 1990, both stood against the idea of sharp cuts in OPEC production to bring this about. Moreover, their new relationships with the oil-consuming countries of the West militate against strong positions in favor of OPEC oil price rises. If OPEC members maintain a high level of production, the price of oil will drop, leading to weak revenues and exacerbating the financial problems faced by the Gulf countries.

The invasion of Kuwait by Iraq in 1990 ensures that Iraq's smaller neighbors in the regional subsystem will seek to increase defense spending. Therefore, the intensive regional arms race and weapons proliferation which has characterized the Middle East for decades is now likely to be accelerated. The high-profile American use of advanced technology weaponry, and particularly the anti-missile defense systems, will drive future Gulf acquisition preferences. Meanwhile in the US, traditional political objections to Arab arms sales may be weakened in the light of support for the anti-Iraq coalition partners.

Since the oil boom, Saudi defense spending has been the highest per capita in the world—even despite falling oil prices. This pattern is likely to continue in the postwar period. Likewise, the Kuwaiti military sector has been a major focus of government spending, and lessons drawn from Iraq's invasion will increase defense spending even during times of economic strain.

One major feature of increased defense spending is that increased purchases of weaponry require outflows of capital to the West that do not stimulate the local economies of Gulf states. They will thus exacerbate a situation in which less of the wealth of the Gulf is likely to reach the non-oil-producing Arab world than before. The largest factor in the Arab world's economic interdependence is the migration of labor from countries without oil to oil-producing countries. The resulting worker remittances[6] have been a principal source of revenue for countries without oil reserves. Labor migration is directly correlated to the oil wealth of Gulf states: employment fell through the 1980s as the price of oil declined. In spite of this, in 1989, the number of foreign workers in the region was enormous, imperfectly estimated at 90 percent in the UAE; 85 percent in Qatar; near 80 percent in Kuwait; near 60 percent in Bahrain; and about 50 percent in Oman and Saudi Arabia.[7] At the time of the invasion of Kuwait, Arab workers comprised more than half of Gulf migrant labor. The Gulf states, especially Kuwait, have reduced their dependency on foreign workers, and shifted migration policies to replace workers whose states did not sympathize adequately with the anti-Iraq position. This will have a critical effect on countries such as Jordan and Yemen.

The diminished oil wealth is also likely to affect the inter-Arab foreign aid system. During the oil boom of 1974-1981, official aid given to other Arab states amounted to 15 percent of Arab oil states' cumulative current account surpluses.[8] Like migration, Arab aid levels fell consistently as oil income diminished. Once again, the countries that did not support the Gulf states are likely to bear the brunt of the decline in this kind of assistance.

2. The Political Repercussions of the War

The costs of the war, as well as the new system of relationships resulting from it, are likely to have a major effect on politics throughout the region. On the domestic front, the contraction of Gulf economies will directly affect the ability of Gulf governments to support the enormous welfare states which play a key role in the domestic policies of Gulf governments. Economic retrenchment should be expected to diminish Kuwait's standard of living, as imported labor will necessarily decline.

The Gulf war's economic impact may result in new pressures for wider participation by Gulf populations. So far, Gulf monarchies have used economic means to consolidate their political rule: even the unequal distribution of a very large pie among a small population creates a more or less privileged standard of living. The current and foreseeable economic constraints on the Gulf states may significantly jeopardize their remunerative cooptation strategies.

The security situation which the Gulf countries now face is also likely to encourage requests for greater political participation from their public, but may encourage resistance to the idea among their governments. Substantial resources had been invested in national defense for two decades prior to the crisis, and more will be in future. Clearly there is an opportunity cost to such defense spending (and because so much is procured abroad, it does not stimulate local development). In addition, there is likely to be heightened public concern about the manner in which these revenues are spent, and in particular whether they are used efficiently and effectively.

A call for increased participation became particularly evident in Kuwait. Eight months prior to Iraq's invasion, a Kuwaiti political movement to force the reinstatement of the National Assembly, a fledgling demand for increased and meaningful political participation, had begun with some tenacity. Dissidents were further emboldened by the Gulf crisis. Many Kuwaitis fled their country under Iraq's occupation, but many also remained: some resisted and nearly all were involved in a survival network. These conditions mobilized citizens and promoted political efficacy. Kuwaitis who struggled through the occupation felt entitled to political gains in addition to compensation. The holding of parliamentary elections in 1992 was a response to these sentiments, and showed that postwar Kuwaiti politics was starting on a different path from those of the prewar period.

In Gulf governments, however, there will be those who argue that there is a need to be more authoritarian and more repressive in order to cope with the various internal and external insecurities that have arisen from the war. These governments have long remained in power and may decide that familiar patterns of rule can be adapted to the new situation.

Political pressures on the domestic scene are considered consequential for regional dynamics. The attentive Saudi government is very sensitive to any prospect of opposition political activities and views negatively the kind of political freedom demanded by the opposition in Kuwait. Moreover, it is possible that there will be a "demonstration effect" throughout the Gulf from a major expansion of political participation in any one country.

The economic traumas brought on by the war also exacerbate fundamental regional problems. The constraints of reconstruction and changes in the oil industry can be expected to affect Gulf oil policy. This may promote more inter-OPEC conflict and decreased price discipline. In the Middle East, rich Gulf oil states have played a critical role in the region's economy through worker remittances and foreign aid. A tighter economic situation there will widen regional economic inequities.

Significant disparities between rich and poor Arab states represent a stress on the subsystem of relations among Arab states. When Iraq occupied Kuwait in August 1990, much animosity surfaced throughout the Arab world toward oil-rich Kuwait. This reflected an important tension between the respect for sovereignty expressed by the Arab League system and resentment by poorer Arabs at the wealth of oil-rich countries.

The conflict between Arab haves and have-nots has in the past been perceived by the Gulf states as a security issue. The Gulf monarchies, especially Saudi Arabia and Kuwait, have regarded foreign aid as mollifying what could otherwise be hostile and aggressive non-oil Arab attitudes. This form of regional insurance did not, however, prevent the invasion of Kuwait by Iraq, and is constrained by the postwar economic factors indicated. Gulf states will continue to provide some foreign aid but unavoidable retrenchment will affect their ability to purchase regional compliance with the status quo.

The effect is likely to be an increase in the gap between rich and poor in the Arab world as many of the poor become poorer. Social science literature identifies a significant relationship between deteriorating economic conditions and the tendency toward political radicalism. The oil-rich states are surrounded by large-scale poverty in the Arab world, yet their ability and inclination to redress it is increasingly limited. The region may, therefore, be characterized by a pattern of crisis and precarious relations rather than relative cooperation and lower levels of threats.

3. New Strategic Alliances

A key component of a regional system is the distribution of military power among its members. The Gulf war had a decisive effect on this dimension of regional politics. With one of the largest armies in the world, Iraq was a regional superpower before the war. It was militarily defeated, economically devastated and politically isolated — predominantly by Western force — in a war which witnessed the participation of other Arab states. Its postwar strength cannot as yet be determined but the devastating allied air campaign significantly reduced Iraq's ability to undertake major offensive efforts in the area for the foreseeable future.[9] This is an unparalleled event for the modern independent Middle East and its ramifications are uncharted.

By virtue of its resources and population size, Iraq will continue to be a major regional power despite its military defeat. Although during the war, US Commander Schwarzkopf publicly claimed that Iraq's chemical, biological and nuclear weapons potential was definitely eliminated for "a very long time," subsequent postwar reports cast doubt on this assessment. Clearly, a major aim of the diplomacy of Saudi Arabia and the Gulf Cooperation Council (GCC) will be to put into place a strategy of containment that would deter any future repetition of the Iraqi invasion of Kuwait.

Although the Gulf governments invest a great amount in arsenals, they are constrained in military manpower by small populations and need to rely on alliances with greater military powers. The strategy of containment works at three different levels: within the Arab world, within the wider Middle East region, and at the international level.

Within the Arab world, the strategy of Gulf countries is to consolidate political and military ties with Egypt and Syria, in a continuation of the coalition that fought the Gulf war. This creates a formidable alliance with two of the four Arab countries with sizable armies (Iraq and Jordan being the other two). At the same time, the coalition is an unusual one. A previous *entente* between Saudi Arabia, Syria and Egypt after the 1973 war was short-lived, largely because of a deep split between Egypt and Syria, who have traditionally been rivals for Arab leadership. Moreover, the priorities of Egypt and Syria are different from those of the Gulf countries, apart from a shared commitment to counterbalance Iraqi power. For Egypt and Syria, the alliance is a means of obtaining greater access to Gulf oil wealth. The Gulf countries are likely to be wary of getting into a situation that might open them to limitless claims from poorer countries, even if the latter are allies.

Iraq has two non-Arab neighbors, Turkey and Iran, who are both regional giants. Turkey's considerable military strength and NATO resources qualify it for regional military status. Yet it would require major changes in the direction of Turkish domestic and foreign policies to impute hegemonic ambitions to Turkey in the Gulf region. It seems more reasonable to expect a consistent Turkish position on issues affecting the Gulf, namely that its military force can in certain circumstances be used in support of pro-Western operations. If the Gulf war experience bears out, Turkey's support in the future will be forthcoming if the right combination of economic, political and military ties link Turkey with the Gulf states and the United States. On its own, Turkey has little motive to play a leading or independent military role in the Gulf.

Iran, unlike Turkey, raises more complicated issues for the Gulf states. It is not integrated into another regional system (such as Europe) but has been essentially isolated in the post-revolutionary decade. Even before Ayatollah Khomeini's death in mid-1989, a critical debate raged within the Iranian government over fundamental directions in domestic and foreign policies. President Rafsanjani successfully steered his pragmatic faction through the Gulf crisis, and his government's signals after the Gulf war indicated a coordinated attempt at re-integration into the regional and global political-economic system.

Iran was one of the clear beneficiaries of the Gulf crisis. Facing sanctions and international rancor following its invasion of Kuwait, Iraq quickly looked toward Iran. The unexpectedly favorable peace terms Iraq offered Iran to formally settle their border conflict were unimaginable prior to the Gulf crisis. While Iraq may have hoped for Iranian support in the conflict over Kuwait, Iran maintained neutrality, if a somewhat permeable border to Iraq. Indeed, Iran maneuvered skillfully through its most visible part in the crisis—when Iraq requested sanctuary for about a hundred fighter planes during the coalition's air campaign. Despite some initial uncertainty, coalition fears were allayed when Iran received the aircraft and provided no guarantees to Iraq on their release.

In its call after the Gulf war for wide international cooperation and ties to the West, Iran appeared guided by what Foreign Minister Velayati described as a new global order in which economic considerations overshadowed political priorities.[10] Iranian interests concentrated on stable oil prices and international investment in Iranian postwar and post-revolution reconstruction. It is possible that Iran could participate in an arms control regime (e.g., US proposals to ban chemical and nuclear weapons in the Middle East). Iran's relations with its Gulf neighbors improved substantially, and Iranian diplomacy sought to foster compliance with international norms.

Even so, Iran has a strong interest in preventing both the re-arming of Iraq and an American hegemonic military role in the Gulf. Its position on oil pricing issues in OPEC is hawkish, and has differed significantly from that of Saudi Arabia, Kuwait and the United Arab Emirates in the past. Furthermore, Iran's readiness to assist Iraqi Shi'ite and Kurdish refugees following their unsuccessful revolts against Saddam Hussein was well noted in the region and by the international community. Iran can be expected to continue to purchase arms, maintain its sizable military strength, and to some extent continue its support of regional Shiite opposition forces.[11] For this reason, Gulf states are likely to continue to be wary of Iranian intentions. It is likely that there will be an improvement in relations between Iran and the GCC states, but a cautious one.

Inextricably linked to the regional balance of power is the military weight brought to bear from outside the region. A crucial result of the war is the more explicitly close American military relationship with the Gulf states. Throughout the 1980s, regional states were hesitant to become associated with a large-scale American military presence in the region. A different postwar security regime is now in the making. Following Iraq's defeat, the US appears to be substantially expanding its operational base in the Gulf and preparing for a long-term presence. Plans now envisage substantial troop rotations and exercises "done with sufficient frequency that the US would have a regular military presence in the region without the permanent stationing of troops, which is politically unacceptable to many Arabs."[12]

This situation marks a major change in direction from the policy followed by most Arab states since World War II. In the Middle East, there has been a widespread perception of any Western military presence as a continuation of colonialism and a means by which the West can dominate the resources and attempt to determine the political character of the region by artificially dividing its communities from each other. Political independence in the Middle East is very recent — a post-World War II achievement. Economic independence, to the extent that it exists, which is through oil wealth, is even younger — two decades old. Both pan-Arab nationalist and Islamic movements have made independence from either the direct or indirect influence of the West a fundamental and essential basis of their ideology.

Pan-Arab nationalism was the most powerful basis of unifying political mobilization in the region in the 1950s and 1960s. Since then, disillusionment, disintegrative political events, and the rise of the price and importance of oil have brought state sovereignty and state interests to the forefront of regional political behavior. This has given a boost to the concept of individual sovereignty, a concept which has been regarded by adherents of regional ideologies—pan-Arabism or pan-Islam—as conceptually alien to the region. There are clear political tensions between the notion of state sovereignty and regional ideologies over many issues, ranging from relations with western countries that support Israel to the use of the resources of the region—i.e., whether oil revenues should be seen as a *regional* asset or subject only to the sovereignty of oil-producing countries, even if they do not intend to give priority to regional purposes in using their resources.

The new relationship between the United States and the countries that participated in the war is likely to bring divisions over these issues to the fore. A US military presence in Saudi Arabia, and the definition of regional security around a prominent American role, is widely seen by adherents of pan-Arab and pan-Islamic ideologies as being directly at odds with the core values of sovereignty and independence.

The influence of regional ideologies was apparent in the differences that emerged in the Arab world over the US response to the invasion of Kuwait. Arab leaders who spoke against the Western-led coalition found a large and attentive audience. During the air campaign against Iraq, King Hussein of Jordan asserted that "the true intention of the Western allies is to destroy Iraq and reorganize the area in a manner far more dangerous to our [Arab] people" than the British and French agreement to divide and rule the Middle East after World War I. "The war symbolizes dominance and manipulation by foreigners." These fears are tangible for many in the Arab world. Anti-American demonstrations occurred, despite the official government stance, even in countries whose governments were sympathetic to the position of the Gulf states. And the rejection of the American-led view of the Gulf conflict gained resonance beyond Western comprehension and beyond the expectations of the rich Gulf states. From reports of demonstrations, interviews and word-of-mouth, there is a clear sense that, outside the Gulf, much of the Arab street was galvanized behind Saddam Hussein's intransigence. Saddam appealed to "us vs. them" sentiments of the Arab world fighting against Western hegemony. His uncompromising stance against the US was regarded as a means of redeeming lost Arab pride. The much publicized "Scud-Mania" throughout the area reflected a sense of the power of being able to fight back—particularly the use of Arab power against the omnipotent Israel.

The movement of a half a million American soldiers into the Gulf area deeply intensified local fears. Saudi Arabia is the keeper of the Holy Places, which added another level of significance to the influx of foreigners—soldiers and entourage. Even among traditionally pro-Saudi religious circles there was a concern with the implications of reliance on American forces. In September 1990 the Saudi royal family invited a mission from the Muslim World League to visit and approve the foreign assistance the Saudis were receiving. The resulting Mecca Declaration placed the blame for the crisis on Iraq, proclaiming its actions to be un-Islamic felonies against other Muslims. The League preferred a pan-Islamic force to replace the international coalition. And though it upheld the Saudi decision to seek help, the ruling was unequivocal that it be temporary and must leave right after the crisis was resolved.[13] Any attempt by Saudi Arabia to make its close military relations with the US more formal, explicit and long-term would be difficult to reconcile with long-lasting Muslim sentiments against a Western military presence in the heartland of Islam.

Political ideologies in the Arab world are strongly tied to the sense of identity of the population. Some scholars have argued that pan-Arabism has played out its hand and the ascendance of state and religious identities has supplanted it.[14] In the responses to the Gulf crisis from countries outside the Gulf, however, there were strong elements of Arab nationalist consciousness.

Social science has not been able to adequately monitor self-identification in the Arab world. The empirical surveys of the subject focus on the attitudes of students, a population group that can be useful for the prediction of future political and social trends.[15] These surveys have so far shown that identification with the state—a form of commitment that might be expected to bolster states pursuing their particular interests rather than pan-Arab or pan-Islamic goals—has been much less strong than commitments to religion (in some parts of the Arab world) or Arab nationalism (in others).

The seminal work to investigate the hierarchy of affiliations was carried out in surveys of the attitudes of Lebanese and other Arab students at the American University of Beirut by Melikian and Diab in the 1950s and repeated in the 1970s. Their work found citizenship to be lower in the hierarchy of commitments than family, nationalistic orientations or religion. Ibrahim's work on students from a number of different Arab countries in the late 1970s suggests overwhelming Arab identification with the goal of Arab unity.[16] Faisal Al-Salem's study of over 1000 high-school students from five different Gulf countries in 1979-82 reports that, in answer to the question "how do you identify yourself?", the students responded: family, 19 percent; tribe, 14.4 percent; religion, 47 percent; and state, 19.5 percent.[17] More broadly, researchers have found evidence of a strong ascent of religious identification during the 1980s. It is reasonable to expect this to be reflected in the politics of the region in the 1990s.

In conclusion, the Gulf war created an unprecedented situation in which the United States has assumed a role in the Arab world whose magnitude has not been matched in the post-independence period in the Middle East. As the emergency situation caused by Iraq's invasion of Kuwait fades from memory, attention is likely to focus on US policies that deal with issues other than threats to the Gulf states. In the event of the exacerbation of tensions between oil-rich and oil-poor countries (e.g., over the distribution of wealth in the region), there may be pressure from the latter on the Gulf states to dismiss their American partners. Within Gulf countries, if there are pressures for increased participation and governments resist these, the United States may become identified as a force blocking political participation, with concomitant unpopularity. US attempts to broker an Arab-Israeli peace are also likely to be carefully watched. If the Israeli government were to initiate massive displacements of Palestinians on the West Bank or to pursue uncompromising policies on the future of the occupied territories, conditions could be created in which an identification with American policy, and especially a strong military relationship, would be a significant military liability for Arab governments. Alternatively, if the Arab-Israeli conflict were to become less conflictual and if Israel were to offer conciliatory moves in the context of a peace process, American influence might not be an obvious regional *bête noire*.

Notes

1. Louis J. Cantori and Steven L. Spiegel, *The International Politics of Regions* (Englewood Cliffs: Prentice-Hall, 1970), pp. 6-7.

2. For figures, see Yahya Sadowski, "Arab Economies After the Gulf War," Middle East Report, May-June 1991, pp. 4-6. Associated war costs include Saudi pledges to underwrite troop deployment expenses (and full in-country costs), funds to support allies upholding the sanctions against Iraq, and loans and grants to military partners Egypt and Syria.

3. *Wall Street Journal,* May 30, 1991.

4. The Saudis experienced a limited oil windfall when the early oil price spikes occurred in the late summer and fall of 1990. They earned $14-16 billion more than expected. However by the end of the same year the costs of the crisis had already exceeded that amount by more than $10 billion.

5. *Wall Street Journal,* April 26, 1991.

6. Giacomo Luciani and Ghassan Salame, "The Politics of Arab Integration," in *The Arab State,* edited by Giacomo Luciani (Berkeley: Univ. of California Press, 1989), p. 408.

7. *Ibid.*

8. R. Khalidi, "The Shape of Inter-Arab Politics in 1995," in *The Next Arab Decade,* ed. by Hisham Sharabi (Boulder: Westview Press, 1986).

9. Forms of threat or aggression using unconventional weapons nevertheless remain plausible other possibilities.

10. *New York Times,* May 28, 1991, pp. A1-11, as well as other reports throughout that week.

11. Beginning in the fall of 1990, Iran began to receive MIG fighter planes on order from the Soviet Union. To what extent these involved support personnel and training is unclear. After the collapse of the Soviet Union, Russian-Iranian trade relations were also likely to include significant arms sales.

12. Plans now envisage substantial troop rotations and exercises "done with sufficient frequency that the US would have a regular military presence in the region without the permanent stationing of troops, which is politically unacceptable to many Arabs." *New York Times,* May 5, 1991, pp. A1, 10.

13. *New York Times,* September 13, 1990.

14. See *Pan-Arabism and Arab Nationalism: The Continuing Debate,* ed. by Tawfic Farah (Boulder: Westview Press, 1987); *The Foundations of the Arab State,* ed. by Ghassan Salame (London: Croom Helm, 1987); and R. Khalidi, "The Shape of Inter-Arab Politics in 1995," *op. cit.*

15. Tawfic E. Farah has led several projects. See *Survey Research in the Middle East,* ed. by Monte Palmer, Mark Tessler and Tawfic E. Farah, (Boulder: Westview Press, 1987); *Political Socialization in the Arab States,* ed. by Tawfic E. Farah and Yasumasa Kuroda (Boulder:, Lynne Reinner Publishers, 1987).

16. Saad Eddin Ibrahim, *Trends of Arab Public Opinion Toward the Issue of Unity* (Beirut: Center for Arab Unity Studies, 1980), cited in his *The New Arab Social Order* (Boulder: Westview Press, 1982), Chapter six.

17. See Faisal Al-Salem, "The Issue of Identity in Selected Arab Gulf States," in Farah and Kuroda (eds.), *Political Socialization in the Arab States, op. cit.*

12 GULF SECURITY: PAST AND FUTURE

Michael Collins Dunn

Wars are invariably followed by efforts to understand the "lessons learned," and the war between the international coalition and Iraq has already generated a cottage industry dedicated to defining those lessons. Ironically, after the end of the war, many of the fundamental security problems which helped bring about the war remain in place. A Gulf security system which would prevent future wars seems as remote as ever. The fact that the Iraqi government did not crumble immediately after the war has helped drive the conservative rulers of the lower Gulf states back into their traditional cautiousness, which they seemed on the verge of transcending during the war itself.

Military forces are, or properly should be, instruments of government policy, not determinants. Clausewitz' famous, but often misunderstood, dictum that war is a continuation of policy, but by other means, demands an understanding that no war can be assessed purely in military terms, nor can its success or failure be judged purely by the results on the battlefield.

War is the ultimate instrument of policy—one not to be indulged in lightly, to be sure—but its lessons are meaningless unless understood in terms of the policy which the war sought to achieve. For this reason, an assessment of the implications of the war for Gulf security must go beyond the specifically military lessons obtained from the course of the war.

This paper does not seek to provide a comprehensive assessment of the highly complex policies which led to the war, or to fully analyze the arms race in the Gulf and the rest of the Middle East. It seeks, rather, to try to underscore certain points which are easily overlooked.

1. Lessons of the War

A. *The Military Course of the War*

From a purely military point of view, a few lessons already seem clear.

1. *In the right environment, air supremacy can very nearly win a ground war.* Air supremacy alone did not win the war for Kuwait,

but it so very nearly did that the ground war was extremely brief. While air power theorists for 70 years have been dreaming of such a victory, this war clearly had some special conditions which are not easily reproducible. Most puzzling of these, still, is the flight of the Iraqi Air Force to Iran. After the first day or two, the Iraqi Air Force simply did not challenge the coalition bombing attacks, and on only one occasion did Iraqi aircraft seek to reach and attack the allied fleet in the Gulf. Given the size and sophistication of Iraq's Air Force, the only explanation seems to be that, as in the war with Iran, Iraq's Air Force was never really intended to be put at risk in all-out combat with an external enemy, and, when challenged, the first instinct of the political and military leadership is to protect the expensive hardware rather than to use it to defend the nation's skies.

Secondly, Iraq's air defenses were outmatched by the countermeasures brought to bear against them. Some of Iraq's air defense missiles are *Crotale* and *Roland* missiles sold by France, which was a coalition partner. Others are older Soviet systems with which other coalition partners such as Syria were themselves familiar. And Iraq certainly lacked the sophisticated electronic counter-countermeasures (ECCM) to block the electronic countermeasures (ECM) being used by the coalition to deceive and confuse the Iraqi air defense radars. It is now known that the Iraqi national air defense shield was penetrated by a special operations helicopter raid at the moment the air war began; once that shield was down, the ability to detect and defend against air attacks was greatly reduced.

2. *Tactical defensive strategies which work in conventional, two-dimensional warfare are helpless against a three-dimensional "AirLand" Battle.* In the Iran-Iraq war, Iraq developed the tactical defensive to a new level of sophistication, developing dug-in positions with strategically-placed killing zones which Iranian troops were unable to breach. But Iran had virtually no tactical air power in that war, and its offensive doctrine was essentially that of massed troops thrown against an entrenched defensive line—a tactic which was outmoded well before this century, as Europe learned in 1914-1918.

By contrast, the US used a variant of the "AirLand Battle" doctrine of the US Army and its NATO relative, the Follow-On Forces Attack. In "AirLand" Battle, all aspects of the battlefield, including the enemy's deep rear, are seen as part of the whole, and all forces operate together with the objective of using speed and maneuver to isolate the enemy front lines by destroying his lines of resupply and reinforcement as well as by breaking up his lines. Speed and maneuver are vital; if necessary, enemy forces cut off from their own lines of supply are simply bypassed. Having broken through at some weak points in the Iraqi defense system, the coalition forces simply ignored the strong points and isolated them, leaving them well behind allied lines.

In a sense, the coalition did to the Iraqi defense lines a three-dimensional version of what the Wehrmacht did to the Maginot line in World War II, with air power and the ability to project heliborne air assault forces deep in the Iraqi rear providing an additional element the Germans lacked. But the basic principle was there: speed and maneuver simply isolated and went around the impregnable lines.

3. *The Advantage of Technology.* There has been much attention paid to the use of "smart" weapons and other high-tech items. Certainly in Baghdad itself, the use of Stealth and other delivery systems and precision-guided weapons kept civilian damage lower than in any previous air assault on a major city (though, of course, it did not eliminate it). But such smart weapons were not being used against military targets to the same degree. There, weapons of enormous force and penetrating power, such as fuel-air explosive weapons, were used to destroy fortifications and shatter morale. It was not merely the highly accurate weaponry such as laser-guided bombs and cruise missiles which marked the coalition's superior power, but also the enormous firepower of fuel-air explosives and other such weapons which helped destroy the Iraqi ground forces *well before* the ground war began.

Not all high-tech weapons worked as designed, but most worked far better than their Iraqi counterparts. Iraq did not use chemical weapons or its own alleged fuel-air explosives, perhaps because of lack of experience and fear of destruction of its own forces. Some coalition weapons were successful but at a cost: British ground attack Tornados in the first few days of the war were dropping British runway-destroying munitions at very low altitudes, with the result that in the first few days the British took unacceptable air losses from ground fire, and soon had to shift to higher approaches.

4. *Two Wrong "Lessons."* Popular commentary has drawn two mistaken lessons from the war. One is that the coalition really did not achieve that much, because it was fighting an army of poor quality. Anyone who has studied the Iran-Iraq war knows better than this. By late February, when the ground war was launched, Iraq's army *was*

probably an army of poor quality. But on January 16–17, when the air war began, it was a formidable fighting force. Forty days of bombing, of destruction of its command-and-control and communications nets, of deliberate targeting of its headquarters and of systematic destruction of its weaponry from the air, combined with morale-destroying efforts, had degraded a once powerful fighting force into a shell. But it had not been a shell to begin with.

The other mistaken lesson is the notion that the war showed that Soviet equipment was somehow innately inferior to Western equipment, and Soviet doctrine to Western doctrine. Iraq, however, was not the Soviet Union, and its equipment did not include some of the equipment (nor did its operators have the skills) of Soviet forces. In addition, Iraq's willingness to sit still for five months while the Western coalition built up its forces was a boon to the coalition: few other enemies would give their enemy time to put in place the weaponry to destroy them. An Iraqi thrust into Saudi Arabia in August or even September 1990 would have created a much more difficult situation for the US and coalition forces. Few potential enemies will behave in the same way in the future.

B. *The Political Objectives*

The military lessons cannot be understood without a brief look at the political objectives of the war. It is here that the irony of the Gulf war's results are most visible. Few military forces in modern times have as clearly, thoroughly, and decisively achieved the objectives set for them by their political leaders as did the coalition forces in the Gulf war. The expulsion of Iraqi forces from Kuwait was accomplished with relatively light losses to the coalition, and Iraq's ability to renew war in the near term was severely inhibited. Judged from the point of view of the stated objectives of the coalition—withdrawal of Iraqi forces from Kuwait, restoration of the Kuwaiti government, freeing of Westerners—the war was a major success.

Clearly, however, few of those who prosecuted the war were happy with the outcome. Once Kuwait was cleared of Iraqi troops, the coalition was (understandably) reluctant to pursue fleeing Iraqi forces into the cities of southern Iraq or to engage them in the Euphrates Valley proper. This avoided fighting in Basra and other southern cities and thus unquestionably avoided higher coalition ground force casualties. But it also left a substantial element of the Iraqi Republican Guard intact and able to suppress the insurrections which erupted soon after the war.

One of the reasons for this was a legacy of America's Vietnam experience. Vietnam was a classic instance of the poorly defined objective, of "moving the goal posts." The US entered the war seeing it as essentially a guerrilla conflict against the Viet Cong insurgency. By 1968 the Viet Cong had been destroyed as a coherent force, but the North Vietnamese Army had joined the battle, and the US found itself in a conventional war with severe political restraints imposed by the fear of Soviet or Chinese intervention. The war's objectives had subtly changed, and so had the war's nature. The US was ill-equipped to fight the sort of war which the North Vietnamese Army was prepared to fight, both for domestic political reasons and due to international political realities.

In a sense, this aspect of the "Vietnam syndrome" very much influenced the Gulf war. There was a determination to define achievable objectives and to apply sufficient force to achieve them quickly. This avoided the gradualist escalation of Vietnam, but in a case of a lesson *overlearned,* it included a strong determination not to change the objectives once they were set. Clausewitz said that no war is begun, or should be begun, without first determining what is to be achieved. The liberation of Kuwait was established, early on, as the objective, and there was a definite reluctance to "move the goal posts" — to change the objective after the war had begun.

It seems clear that the military plan for freeing Kuwait did not directly address the question of the results inside Iraq of the victory; certainly, coalition intelligence services were speculating about what might happen, but there was no contingency for coalition troops becoming involved in an internal Iraqi insurrection. This, too, is an obvious reflection of Vietnam: avoid getting drawn into a civil war; avoid having to fight in country where air and armor superiority cannot be brought to bear (the jungles of Vietnam, the swamps of southern Iraq), and avoid being drawn into any open-ended conflict where real victory is impossible. The coalition stopped when its stated objectives were accomplished: and then watched in horror as Iraqis north and south, Arab and Kurd, rose up against the regime and were crushed while Western forces still stood on Iraqi soil.

Certainly this was not part of the military planning. Certainly, too, there were political considerations involving coalition partners (Saudi concern about Shi'ite activism, Turkish and Syrian concern about the Kurds). But the enormity of the disaster was, I believe, a surprise.

In retrospect, one may ask whether, having already defeated the Iraqi Army, the coalition should then have "moved the goal posts" and prevented the carnage which followed inside Iraq. Knowing the scale of the tragedy as we do, it is easy to say so. When the decision for a ceasefire was made, the future was not yet clear. The tragedy was a reminder that, to paraphrase Eisenhower, war will always astound. All the planning and careful application of military force cannot control or predict the political and social repercussions of military action. Because of that very unpredictability, military force should never be resorted to unless no alternatives exist.

2. The Future Defense of the Gulf

In the period since the war, much rhetoric has been devoted to the need to remove weapons of mass destruction from the Middle East, or at least to forestall further proliferation; some have called for a ban on all weapons sales to the region. Certainly, a reduction in the level of armaments now found in the Middle East is desirable. But wars do not start merely because vast quantities of arms are present; nowhere in human history have such huge arsenals been assembled as those of NATO and the Warsaw Pact between the end of World War II and the loss of Soviet influence in Eastern Europe. Those large inventories of arms did not lead to war; arguably, they prevented it. The reason was that each side's arsenal provided a deterrent to the other side's use of its arms. Deterrence works when conditions are right.

In a sense, all wars are failures: failure to deter, failure of a credible defense policy to dissuade one's enemies from going to war. The failure inherent in the Gulf war was the fact that there was no deterrent to Iraq's invasion of Kuwait. That failure was itself a result of the lack of an adequate defense for the oil-rich states of the Arabian Peninsula, which in turn grew out of the enormous changes in the military balance in the Gulf region since the mid-1970s.

The strategic situation of the Gulf is, in some ways, a geopolitical nightmare. Two thirds of the world's proven oil reserves and some of the world's key sea lanes lie in a region in which some of the richest countries have tiny populations and armed forces, while their neighbors include some of the world's most powerful military forces. The temptation to occupy the weaker neighbor is obvious. The weaker states have historically relied upon foreign guarantors: the British until the 1970s, the US today.

So the first point to be made must be this one: *Despite the stunning success of coalition arms in Operation Desert Storm, war itself is always a failure: a failure of deterrence*. It is difficult to know precisely what was in Saddam Hussein's mind in the weeks before August 2, 1990. But the Iraqi leader's political history to that point had been that of a hardy and extremely shrewd survivor. He clearly calculated that he had a good chance of invading Kuwait successfully.

Now it is clear that Kuwait could never have built up a defense force capable of repelling an Iraqi invasion. But if two deterrent elements had been in place which were not in place, it is possible that Iraq would never have embarked on its fatal adventure. The first is a *genuine regional defense pact*. The six-nation Gulf Cooperation Council (GCC) had existed for a decade, and it possessed some elements of a defensive alliance: a small, combined force called *Peninsula Shield*, and periodic joint maneuvers, etc. But it remained basically a skeleton of an alliance, because of the divisions among the members and because of the reluctance of the smaller states to become excessively dependent on Saudi Arabia.

But what if, first, the GCC had already been a real alliance, and thus an attack on Kuwait would have automatically and certainly brought Saudi Arabia and the other states into conflict with Iraq? And, as a corollary to this, what if Saudi Arabia itself had possessed a credible ground force for its own self-defense? This force would not have needed to be capable of defeating an Iraqi army one-on-one, of course, but to assure at least that Iraq would not have an easy march into the oilfields; its purpose would have been to delay a decision until external help could arrive.

The other element in such a hypothetical system has to be an external guarantee of the Gulf states against attacks from their neighbors. For decades, the United States had regularly indicated that Saudi security was a crucial element in US policy, but it had never clearly included Kuwait within that umbrella, nor had it formalized a commitment to Saudi Arabia on which the Saudis—or a potential aggressor—could depend with certainty. If Saddam Hussein had known, first of all, that Saudi Arabia would definitely defend Kuwait (and if Saudi Arabia had had a more credible force than it now has), and if, secondly, he had known that the United States and other external powers would defend Saudi Arabia, would he have invaded Kuwait? It seems far less likely. Deterrence failed because, first, the Gulf states themselves had not created a credible collective defense for small states such as Kuwait, and secondly, because the US commitment to Kuwait was vague and uncertain.

Most of the scenarios for a postwar Gulf security system include a US guarantee. Since the Gulf states themselves could never hope to have an adequate defense against certain potential enemies, external guarantees will always be essential, just as Western Europe had to shelter under the US umbrella for decades. US guarantees alone, however, are not enough.

Some of the instant analysis after the war focused on the fact that Soviet equipment, Soviet-style doctrine, and Soviet training had not served Iraq well, which is true. At the same time, it would be foolish to base a future strategic policy in the Gulf on the assumption that a future Iraqi leader seeking hegemony would be deterred by this kind of problem alone. Any such leader might, on the contrary, believe that the principal reason for the Iraqi failure lay in the strategy adopted by Saddam Hussein. Suppose, for example, that, on August 6 or 7, Iraq had *simply kept on going?* It is not unlikely that Iraq could have occupied the Saudi Eastern Province, with the oilfields, in perhaps two or three days. Even if the US 82nd Airborne had begun arriving just as it did, and US air attacks from somewhere in the Indian Ocean had been possible, there would still have been little to stop an Iraqi occupation of the oilfields, and perhaps of both Qatar and the United Arab Emirates as well.

Undoubtedly, the United States would have responded massively, and ultimately the result would have been an Iraqi defeat. But the liberation of this huge area would have been far more difficult, and costly, than the liberation of Kuwait. And instead of controlling 20 percent of the world's oil, as he did after taking Kuwait, Saddam would have been sitting on half of it. A war through *those* oilfields would have devastated world oil production. Saudi and UAE production, instead of being increased to make up for the loss of Iraqi and Kuwaiti oil on the market, might itself have been removed from the market.

But Iraq did not keep going. In fact, Iraq did something for which US planners should be eternally grateful: it sat where it was, allowing the United States to take five months to build up its forces. It was this fact which led many to assume that Saddam intended to pull out: otherwise, why would he simply sit still and let the US assemble the forces with which to destroy his army?

If a future aggressor treated this policy as a mistake, and did not stop, but occupied all the Gulf oilfields quickly, the US would be placed in a difficult situation. It cannot currently insert forces quickly enough to block such a blitzkrieg, and even an increased sealift and airlift—surely needed—will not solve all the problems. Thus,

US guarantees alone are not enough: The Gulf must be given a credible "tripwire" deterrent capability which will at least slow down an invader. It is not enough to say that the US is there to protect the Gulf, and therefore the Gulf states need not build up their own forces. And the Gulf states must be persuaded to avoid the temptation to depend entirely on the United States.

A. *Assessing the Threat*

Two arguments can be anticipated against the building up of a credible Gulf self-defense and deterrent. One is that there is no imminent threat to the Gulf states. It is true that Iran's armed forces are far from what they were before 1988, and that it will be a long time before Iraq can ever be a threat again. But, given the long lead times involved in acquiring modern combat aircraft, main battle tanks, and other frontline equipment, a nation must defend not only against today's threat, but that of a decade hence. The following geostrategic concerns are clearly important to Saudi Arabia and other Gulf states.

1. *The Possibility of Another Iraqi Invasion.* The implementation of United Nations resolutions will strip Iraq of its chemical and ballistic missile arsenals and bar its nuclear program from further progress. But even assuming that this works perfectly, both chemical and *Scud*-style ballistic missile weapons have proven to be effective psychological weapons. Iraq's population will always give it the ability to build up significant ground forces, so long as the country remains unified. And a failure to remain unified would not offer much consolation to the Gulf: the lessons of Lebanon and Afghanistan remind us that a nation embroiled in civil war can draw in its neighbors inexorably.

2. *Iran.* Iran is a nation of 55 million people, three times as large as Iraq, and nearly twice as large as all the Arabian Peninsula states put together. In the first decade of the next century Iran may reach a population of 100 million. Its demographic growth, historical role in the Gulf—which has been called the Persian Gulf far more frequently than the Arab Gulf throughout its recent history—and pivotal geostrategic location guarantee that Iran will be an active player in the Gulf. This role need not depend on the kind of political leadership Iran enjoys: the Shah of Iran was also an interventionist.

3. *Yemen.* Newly united Yemen has a population larger than that of Saudi Arabia, probably about 12 to 13 million. Its armed forces are large in number, if weak in equipment and training. Its oil wealth is

just now becoming a factor: it is a long way from rich, but with luck may no longer be condemned to eternal poverty. And as recently as 1934, it surrendered the provinces of Jizan and Najran to Saudi Arabia. The Saudis have close links with the tribes of northern Yemen, and have pulled strings there when it suited them. There are potential grounds for conflict between Yemen and Saudi Arabia.

4. *Israel*. Saudi Arabia and Israel are on different sides of the Arab-Israeli conflict, and no rational Saudi planner could ignore the possibility of Israeli hostility.

5. *Instability Resulting from the Disintegration of the Soviet Union*. For decades, the Soviet Union was viewed as a threat to the Gulf from the North. After the disintegration of the Soviet Union, such views seem distant, even archaic. But Moscow's traditional geopolitical interest in the warm waters of the Gulf and the Indian Ocean will not necessarily vanish: this interest has never been a function of Communist control, but a historic trend dating from Czarist times.

The disintegration of the Soviet Union has brought about a whole new tier of Middle Eastern states whose future power and policies are hard to predict. Irredentism could be rampant, as the new state borders do not coincide with the national and ethnic concentrations of population. What will be the relations of the independent Republic of Azerbaijan with Iranian Azerbaijan, and with Azeris in Turkey? There are Tajiks in Tajikistan but also in Iran and Afghanistan; Kirghiz in Kirghizia but also in Afghanistan and Pakistan. The old northern tier might become something different indeed, and a new concern for the Gulf states.

B. *The Ground Force Problem*

The second argument against building a credible self-defense structure for the Gulf states is that their small populations make a credible defense impossible and only foreign troops or external guarantees can hope to dissuade aggressors. Traditionally, the Gulf states have had tiny armies (Oman being the exception) or relied heavily on foreign troops for their own protection. And certainly states as small as Bahrain or Qatar cannot be expected to be able to build up a significant ground force. In addition, the period of the 1950s and 1960s, in which groups of army officers launched military coups in a number of Arab countries, resulted in reservations in the Gulf about the creation of large standing armies.

The first reaction of the Gulf states in the recent crisis was to look for Arab troops: the so-called "GCC plus two" or "Damascus eight" formula announced in Damascus on March 6, 1991, under which Egyptian and Syrian troops would provide a defensive force for Saudi Arabia and Kuwait. But Egypt has since withdrawn its forces, and many in the GCC seem content to rely on the US rather than on Egypt and Syria, apparently believing that the Egyptian and Syrian governments have differing agendas from those of the Gulf countries. But the result is a vacuum which the US is not likely to be able to fill and which the Gulf states must accomplish themselves.

The largest Gulf country is Saudi Arabia, whose population is usually listed at between 8 and 12 million, though the former is closer to reality if the number is restricted to Saudi nationals. A country of eight million people can clearly support an army of more than 40,000 men. Eight million is a population the size of Switzerland's, and twice the size of Israel's Jewish population. Yet both of those countries can, within a few dozen hours of mobilization, field forces of more than 600,000.

There are constraints on an increase in Saudi forces. Saudi Arabia will never field a 600,000 man army, and the idea of women serving in the Army is unrealistic. But there seems to be little reason why a country the size of Saudi Arabia, with many potential threats, could not create a defense force capable of at least providing some sort of tripwire defense on its borders: an army of, say, 100,000-150,000.

It is sometimes said that there is no martial tradition in the Gulf states. While it is true that some merchant city-states have no martial traditions to speak of, this is not the case with populations with a recent bedouin background, who can be found throughout the area. Saudi Arabia itself was created in a series of wars fought only a little over a half century ago, and King Faisal, who ruled until his assassination in 1975, had personally led troops in battle. The tradition is there, though it is a tradition not of the conscript citizen-soldier, but of the warrior fighting for his tribe.

This tradition has been maintained in Saudi Arabia. The Saudi Arabian National Guard (SANG), the internal security force, has capitalized on the Bedouin tradition precisely to create a sort of martial heritage. It is separately commanded from the Army, is rooted in the tribes of the Najd (historical supporters of the House of Saud), and has a sense of continuity of heritage dating to the early wars of unification in the 1920s.

In contrast, the Army has been kept on the borders, far from major population centers, without any of the same sense of heritage. It has lacked the prestige of the other units of the armed forces. In the system that prevailed until the Gulf war, if a person came from the right tribes, the National Guard might appeal; and young members of key tribes, the Royal Family, or others with an interest in military matters would seek to join the Air Force, the elite service. Members of the merchant classes almost never thought of military service as an option.

The war in the Gulf *may* have changed this situation. There were signs, even before the war, that Saudi Arabia had finally realized that after years of building up the Air Force, creating the Navy, and modernizing the National Guard, it was the Army's turn. And the invasion of Kuwait certainly reinforced this need.

In the wake of the invasion of Kuwait, National Guard recruitment was opened up to the entire country, not just the selected Najdi tribes. If this approach is retained, it could change the National Guard from a tribally-based praetorian force to a genuine national force, and then its distinction from the Army would become more and more academic. Within the royal family, some of the younger princes have become advocates of a stronger ground force.

It is also important that there should be an extension of political participation in Saudi Arabia, resulting in the active involvement of the population in the process leading to decisions on issues of national importance, including the country's defense. It is important for Saudi Arabia to expand its own traditional consultative structures to include a greater dialogue between ruler and ruled. An ability to defend the country depends on a strong enough army to make deterrence credible. A strong bond between rulers and the ruled is essential to the defense of Saudi Arabia.

3. Arms Sales: A Means of Equalizing Imbalances

There is a genuine need to provide the Gulf countries with a credible deterrent, one which at least will hold the line until outside help can arrive. But providing a deterrent requires providing arms, which leads to charges that the US and the other Western suppliers are fueling the Middle Eastern arms race.

In the United States, two main groups, who otherwise would not often agree with each other, are opposed to major arms sales to the Gulf.

The first group includes those opposed to arms sales in general or to arms sales to "disturbed" areas of the world. One of its frequently voiced arguments is that sales of arms to the Middle East merely fuel regional arms races.

The second group consists of Israel's supporters in the US, particularly the American Israel Public Affairs Committee (AIPAC), which has a track record of opposing all significant arms sales to Arab states which are not at peace with Israel.

The "Arms Race" Argument. The argument that sales to countries like Saudi Arabia fuel a Middle Eastern arms race is fundamentally flawed because of its misinterpretation of actual Saudi capabilities. Until the decision to sell the M-1 tank, Saudi Arabia's tiny armored forces were so out of date that almost every neighboring state had tank forces which could easily penetrate the armor of Saudi tanks, particularly the outmoded AMX-30s. Saudi Arabia's lack of ground forces has already been mentioned.

The arms race in the Gulf began in the 1970s, but it was a race between Iran and Iraq. The smaller states of the Gulf have not even begun to rival their two rich and powerful neighbors. What resulted was an imbalance of power which has only been alleviated somewhat by the coalition's destruction of Iraq's military machine. Both Iran and Iraq rose to be among the world's ten largest military forces, and each had a million or so men under arms. By contrast, Saudi Arabia's ground forces were about 40,000 in 1990–91, and in tanks, fighter aircraft, and other mainline equipment, it was far outstripped by either of its northern neighbors. The principal race was not between Saudi Arabia and its neighbors, but between two potentially hostile neighbors, each of whom became progressively more powerful while Saudi Arabia could only modernize its relatively small forces.

Another variation of this argument is the belief that "Saudi Arabia spent tens of billions of dollars on arms in the 1980s, yet it was totally helpless when threatened by Iraq." This argument is particularly popular among op-ed columnists. In fact, Saudi Arabia's billions were spent on *infrastructure* and on building up its Air Force and Navy. Of non-Western countries, few have probably had as clearly defined a defense plan as Saudi Arabia. With rare exceptions, their arms acquisitions were not bought for "prestige" but for specific needs. What Saudi Arabia had *not* done was build up its ground forces. The 1989 order for M-1 Abrams tanks was the beginning of a long overdue process to upgrade the Army's equipment. But the war came long before Saudi Arabia's ground forces had benefited from the defense buildup of the 1980s.

The enormous investment by Saudi Arabia in the Air Force, and particularly in infrastructure, made winning the war much easier for coalition forces. The air bases from which they flew, and the communications, command and control, and logistical facilities available to them were, in large part, products of the Saudi arms buildup.

Finally, there are limitations to what any country can do against a much larger force. No single Western European country could have resisted a Soviet onslaught, nor could all combined have hoped to stand for long. Saudi Arabia, faced with the possibility of assault by one of the world's largest armies, needed outside help.

The AIPAC Argument. The AIPAC argument occasionally uses points derived from the anti-arms race argument (though never carries this to the logical extreme of arguing for a cutoff of all arms sales to the Middle East, since the massive defense relationship with Israel is an underpinning of AIPAC's *raison d'être*). In resisting the 1986 Saudi arms package, AIPAC argued that the threat to Saudi Arabia was not sufficient to demand such sophisticated weapons, that the weapons posed a threat to Israel's security, and that Saudi Arabia was not contributing to the peace process.

The argument that Saudi Arabia did not really face a major threat from the Gulf was answered decisively in the first week of August 1990.

The argument that Saudi Arabia's arms are a threat to Israel is only credible to those unfamiliar with the relative capabilities of the two forces. When the US Congress adopted this argument and blocked the sale of additional F-15s to Saudi Arabia, and Saudi Arabia then turned to Britain in the huge al-Yamama deal, the results were actually detrimental to Israel's security. The new Saudi fighters and bombers were not placed under the same restrictions which the (fighter only) F-15s had been. By blocking a highly restricted US sale, and forcing the Saudis to buy a far less restricted British system, AIPAC demonstrated its power on Capitol Hill once again, but it is highly questionable that it did Israel's security much good.

The most important reasons for American military assistance to Saudi Arabia are:

1. A credible deterrent on the ground in the Gulf will prevent future Desert Storms. If the Gulf states man the front lines of defense, American soldiers are less likely to be required.

2. Saudi Arabia is a weak state with a small population and a huge territory to defend; it is not a threat to any of its neighbors.

3. Saudi Arabia is not part of a Gulf arms race: its neighbors have been racing so far ahead of it that it is difficult for it to hope to defend itself.

4. US sales allow the US to place limitations on, and control deployment of, the equipment. If the US is unwilling to sell, Saudi Arabia may turn to other suppliers who do not place limitations on the weapons.

The United States should continue to oppose the proliferation of ballistic missiles and chemical weapons in the Middle East. Saudi adherence to the Nuclear Non-Proliferation Treaty was a step forward, and an open Saudi renunciation of chemical weapons and other weapons of mass destruction would be useful. A Saudi decision to remove its DF-3A (CSS-2) East Wind ballistic missiles would be welcome, but so long as neighboring states pursue advanced domestically-produced missile systems this is probably unachievable.

In addition, arms sales should be presented within the framework of a credible Gulf defense system. Therefore the US should encourage the Gulf states in the following endeavors:

1. Making the GCC a genuine alliance with cohesive and realistic joint defense planning. All the necessary decisions on paper are already in place; but *Peninsula Shield* should be made a real force, not a token. The GCC should be encouraged toward a genuine defensive alliance in partnership with the US, and whichever other Western/Pacific Rim states are prepared to participate.

2. Encouraging the GCC to adopt a joint procurement policy aimed at interoperability with (a) each other and (b) US and European intervention forces as required. When the Gulf crisis occurred, for example, even within the UAE, Abu Dhabi and Dubai were to some extent making separate procurement decisions. It is important to make the GCC think about interoperability. And it is equally important that these systems be interoperable with the likeliest foreign support: the US first, then Britain and France, to judge from the recent war.

3. Linking procurement and prepositioning decisions. The Saudi decision to acquire the M-1 has opened the door toward greater prepositioning of equipment as well. Prepositioning is obviously a key to US planning: it will facilitate the quicker insertion of intervention forces in the event of a crisis. Obviously it makes a great deal more sense to link these issues.

4. Greatly expanding joint exercises/training/contingency planning. Plans for these have already commenced.

5. Discouraging of unnecessary weapons acquired for "prestige," or impractical procurement. Weapons sold should directly reflect the threat (immediate or longterm) to the country.

6. Encouraging greater political pluralism. Encouraging Saudi Arabia to open up its society within the parameters of its own cultural and religious ideology is desirable for the reasons mentioned above.

4. Conclusions: Looking Forward

In the past, the refusal by Congress to provide to Saudi Arabia and its smaller neighbors the arms needed to defend themselves may have helped bring about the situation in which Iraq felt it could strike against a weak neighbor, believing that Saudi Arabia would do nothing, or would attempt to buy Iraq off. A price has been paid for a reluctance to build up Gulf defenses, in lives, expenditure of money and weaponry. The Iraqi people have paid a devastating price for the blunder their leaders made.

Saudi Arabia, exerting its influence over its smaller neighbors, will clearly be a leading force in creating a regional security system, based on the GCC and involving genuine mutual security, planning, intelligence, and procurement cooperation. A formula will have to be found for a genuine American guarantee of Saudi external security which is not seen in America as having a prime objective of defending a nondemocratic system domestically or dividing the Gulf region into blocs which do not reflect regional interests.

One view often expressed in the region is that foreign bases are anathema in the Gulf. The US, however, maintained an airbase at Dhahran into the early sixties. The reason British (Suez, Tobruk), American (Dhahran, Wheelus, Kuneitra) and French (Bizerte) bases were unacceptable in the 1950s and 1960s to Arab countries was not that they were foreign, so much as that they were unrelated to local defense issues; they were part of a broader, US-Soviet superpower confrontation, and had little to do with the immediate security of the host states. Any US presence after the Gulf war is something else: not directed at the Soviets, like the earlier military presence, or aimed at making the host country part of a broader geopolitical quarrel which is not its own, but protecting the host country at its own request against immediate neighbors who covet its wealth. There is a big difference. Assumptions that Saudi Arabia and other Gulf states do not understand this difference are yielding to conventional caution. Saudi Arabia will not leap blindly, however, and the first bases will not be on Saudi soil, but probably on the soil of its neighbors.

The Gulf states still look, I believe, for a solution which does not include long-term American ground forces in the region. The withdrawal of Egyptian and Syrian forces suggests that working out a system will not be easy. But a complete dependence on US forces, which are slow to deploy, would not guarantee the Gulf against an invader determined to seize all the oilfields before US intervention could occur. Thus the Gulf states must be encouraged to build up their own defenses, and to take the political and military measures necessary to create larger armies from among their citizenry.

13 THE ARAB POLITICAL ORDER AFTER THE GULF WAR

Hani A. Faris

Western political leaders have explained and defended their international policies since the collapse of the Eastern Bloc in terms of the concept of "The New World Order." Their counterparts in the Arab world resorted in the aftermath of the Gulf war to a concept of "The New Arab Order" to legitimize their regional policies. Both concepts have been lacking in definition. This paper will attempt to describe the effects of the Gulf war on the Arab political order and to analyze whether the same order has remained or a new order is emerging.

The Failure of the Arab Political Order

The Gulf war challenged the Arab political order in two significant ways. First, it challenged the ground rules that regulated the political behavior of the modern Arab state system since its inception following the Second World War. Second, it caused unprecedented divisions between the Arab countries and led to the emergence of an alliance among the Arab members of the US-led coalition against Iraq. This alliance has assumed the role of leadership of a new Arab order.

The ground rules in the pre-Gulf war era evolved over time. Admittedly, these rules were not always adhered to, but they were also seldom challenged or openly flaunted. Some of them were expressly recorded in bilateral and multilateral Arab pacts, treaties and agreements, and the others were political conventions endowed with sufficient authority as to force compliance. Combined, these rules provided the lowest common denominator required for co-existence among the various Arab regimes and amounted to a reciprocal undertaking by the ruling elites to conserve the existing order. Their observance allowed for a measure of stability in intra-Arab relations.

The first and most fundamental rule was the acceptance by Arab states of each other's independence and territorial integrity. The first concrete regional embodiment given to this rule was the founding of the League of Arab States. It is doubtful that the League would have been founded or survived were it not structured on this basis. During

216

the deliberations that preceded the founding of the League in 1945, the participants, without exception, rejected any notion of establishing a unitary or federated system.[1] The Pact of the League is replete with references to the predominant status of this rule, whose practical effect has been the preservation of the political map bequeathed to the Arab world by European colonial powers.[2] Since the Second World War, the interests of the major Western powers and the Arab state system have coalesced to preserve the status quo whenever it was challenged by an individual Arab state or an Arab political movement. The Arab political order, assisted by external forces, galvanized resources against any of its members that pursued an integrationist course and was able, in every instance, to either force a change of regimes or policies on the non-conforming member.

The invasion and subsequent annexation of Kuwait by Iraq set a precedent. The Iraqi leadership went beyond the limits of the tolerable norms of behavior of the Arab political order when it set out to wipe from the map the separate political existence and identity of Kuwait by force. Its decision to invade Kuwait undermined the very foundations of the Arab political order. Not surprisingly, all Arab states, without exception, rejected Iraq's claim to and annexation of Kuwait.[3] Similarly, when Iraq's own territorial integrity was in question following the insurrections in the north and south of the country, other Arab states, including Iraq's recent Arab enemies, defended the preservation of Iraq's independence and territorial integrity.[4] In other words, the Iraq-Kuwait crisis and the Gulf war indicate that the Arab political order will continue to uphold the principles of territorial integrity and independence of its composite units when challenged by the prospect of either forced mergers or internal rebellion. The lesson to learn from the Gulf episode is that regional political fragmentation is unlikely to be reversed through the use of force by one Arab state against another. The appearance of an Arab Bismarck is not a solution to Arab disunity.

The second rule in the Arab political order was the inadmissibility of Arab states forging open alliances with foreign powers against other Arab states. It was given its first expression in the June 1950 Joint Defense and Economic Cooperation Treaty.[5] It took a long and hard-fought struggle within Arab society to establish this rule. To a large measure, the turbulent politics of the Arab world in the 1950s and 1960s revolved around such issues as the presence in Arab lands of foreign military bases, foreign-inspired military blocs, military pacts with foreign powers and European colonial enclaves. The termination of the Suez Canal Treaty, the failure of the US-inspired Middle East Defense Organization, Baghdad Pact and the Eisenhower Doctrine, the Algerian war of liberation, the closing of US and British military bases in Libya and the collapse of Britain's East of Suez policy were all episodes in a process that culminated in the establishment of this second rule. By the 1970s and 1980s, all Arab governments were mindful of the consequences of violating its authority.

Iraq's invasion of Kuwait triggered a sequence of events that undermined and perhaps reversed the process described above. The invasion allowed the creation of a foreign and Arab multinational coalition against Iraq and re-introduced Western military forces into the Arabian Peninsula. Irrespective of whether it was driven by necessity or choice, the decision by Arab Gulf states to appeal to the US and other Western powers for military intervention caused very sharp divisions in the Arab state system.[6] Judging by past events, this decision by the Gulf states is likely to have serious repercussions in the post-Gulf war era. If the US decides to establish a visible or sizable military presence in the region on a permanent basis, its forces and interests, together with those of the Gulf states, will become a target for Arab nationalist and Islamic forces. The initial cause for bringing in foreign troops will be forgotten, the Western presence will be dubbed as imperialism and the call for confronting this presence could dominate Arab politics again.[7] Some Gulf and foreign nationals are urging the severing or weakening of the Gulf region's links with its Arab environment to pre-empt such an eventuality. It is clear, however, that a significant proportion of the Gulf populations are conscious that the policy of erecting walls between them and the rest of the Arab world is neither feasible nor acceptable, and that it will not provide them with security.[8]

The intervention of foreign armies may also have serious ramifications for Gulf states depending on how Iraq is dealt with in the post-war period. There already exists much animosity and bitterness among Arab countries because of the war. The more Western powers choose to humiliate Iraq and shackle it with future demands, the more the level of animosity is bound to increase, with implications that the future stability of the region will be jeopardized. The Iraqi leadership may change, but Iraq will continue to be located where it is and, given its resources and the size of its population, the country will ultimately resurface as a regional power. The policy of treating Iraq as an outcast nation has added to the suffering of the Iraqi population and could easily backfire. The long-term interests of the countries of the region are to begin a healing process.

A third guiding principle of the Arab political order was that Arab objectives were inextricably linked to two major aspects of the Palestinian issue, namely the plight of the Palestinians and the expansion of Israel. The dispossession and uprooting of the Palestinian people was perceived as a grave injustice that could only be remedied when the Palestinians exercised their rights to repatriation and political self-determination. A militant and expansionist state of Israel based on the principle of Jewish exclusiveness (and thus dispossession of the original Palestinian population) and occupying the most strategic juncture between countries of the Arab East and Arab West was perceived as a threat to the security and well-being of the whole Arab world.

There were three corollaries to this principle. The first was that the Palestinian cause was inseparable from the Arab-Israeli conflict. The second was that no Arab country should concede the rights of the Palestinian people through separate bilateral agreements with Israel. The third was that Arab relations with non-Arab countries should be based on the positions adopted by these countries on the issue of Palestinian rights. A fourth corollary was added when all Arab countries designated the Palestine Liberation Organization at the 1974 Rabat Summit Conference as the sole legitimate representative of the Palestinian people.

These principles assumed a certain level of sanctity in Arab diplomacy and politics. The discretion which surrounded most transgressions confirmed rather than denied the applicability of the rule. Arab leaders who violated the principle openly were assassinated by militant political opponents, as the examples of King Abdullah of Jordan, Anwar Sadat of Egypt and Bashir Jumayyel of Lebanon illustrate.

How will the commitment to the Palestine problem and its corollaries fare in the aftermath of the Gulf war? Iraq invaded Kuwait for its own reasons of state, which were primarily economic in nature, and not for any ideological or nationalist reasons. In an obvious attempt to regain Arab public support, the Iraqi leadership linked the solution of the Gulf crisis to Israel's withdrawal from occupied Arab territories and Syria's withdrawal from Lebanon. The approach was clearly opportunistic and damaged the Palestinian cause.[9]

The war left the Arab countries with deep divisions and sharp differences. The principles that guided the actions of the Arab political order vis-a-vis the Palestinian issue were questioned. Several Arab countries accepted the US-Israeli idea of a regional conference, two-track negotiations and the adoption of confidence-building measures as preludes to a settlement with Israel. In the process, they withdrew their support from the PLO and questioned its mandate. Such positions imply a separation between the Palestinian problem and the Arab-Israeli conflict, a willingness to drop out of collective Arab measures directed at Israel and the fragmentation and weakening of the Arab negotiating position. This approach is so drastically different from earlier positions that it may lead to serious tensions between Arab governments promoting the new approach and militant nationalist or Islamic movements opposing it.

In summary, the Arab political order in the aftermath of the Gulf war is in a state of flux. Of the three rules that defined the least common denominator among the members of the Arab League, one has been seriously violated and the other two have either been buried or suspended. An atmosphere exists in which Arab regional groupings now make their own rules.

The Saudi-Egyptian-Syrian Coalition: Basis for a New Order?

Saudi Arabia, Egypt and Syria are proclaiming the emergence of a new Arab order out of the ashes of the Gulf war. The three countries are also claiming the mantle of Arab leadership and, by virtue of the results of the war, have asserted that henceforth the Arab political agenda will be established by them and they expect other Arab countries to accept it.[10] Their joint declarations focus primarily on methods to regulate relations among Arab states with the objective of consecrating the principle of territorial integrity and national sovereignty.

Unlike the advocates of a new world order, the leading Arab states have not integrated individual freedoms, human rights or democratic participation into their proposed order. In view of the fact that their visions do not encompass a new value system, it would be more accurate to describe developments in the wake of the Gulf war in terms of shifting alliances and power relations among the Arab countries rather than as preludes to an evolving order. Accordingly, the success or failure of the three states in retaining their present control of the Arab political agenda will be a function of the strength of the relationship they have with each other, the nature of the relationship they develop with the US and, ultimately, the viability of their own state systems.

Events have invalidated the original rationale for the alliance, namely the reversal of the Iraqi occupation of Kuwait. As the Gulf war slowly fades from memory, members of the alliance will find it more difficult to maintain their solidarity. As it stands, their relationship can be jeopardized by two contentious issues: security arrangements in the Gulf and economic cooperation. Regarding the issue of security, Egypt and Syria aspire to replace Western forces with their own and be accepted as the custodians of the security of the Arab Gulf countries. They would like the forces they deployed in the Gulf Cooperation Council (GCC) countries to become the mainstay of an Arab peace force. Saudi Arabia and the other GCC countries approach this issue differently. Given their fragile social and political structures, limited manpower and military vulnerability, they prefer to rely on Western rather than Arab powers to satisfy their security requirements since arrangements with the former are not encumbered by ethnic, religious or ideological considerations. If other Arab countries are to be allowed a role in their security system, it can only be of a limited and complimentary nature. Contrary to current wisdom among Western journalists and academicians, Gulf governments are more wary of Arab than Western troops spreading new ideas among their citizens.

The differences in the two approaches to Gulf security are already public.[11] Initially, the GCC countries consented immediately after the war to the Egyptian-Syrian position. Shortly after, they promoted the stationing of an international force along the Iraqi-Kuwaiti border and entered into negotiations for joint and bilateral security arrangements with the US. Following this, both Egypt and Syria threatened to recall their forces, and actually withdrew troops. The disagreements over the issue of Gulf security have not been settled and could undermine the alliance in the future.

Economic cooperation is potentially another contentious issue. Although the three countries have called for "enhancing economic cooperation" and for "economic policies leading to balanced economic and social development," Saudi Arabia and the other GCC members demanded and received acknowledgements by Egypt and Syria that each Arab state has sovereign control "over its natural and economic resources," and that private sector establishments should "benefit from cooperation in a concrete way."[12] The recognition of the principle of sovereign control was meant to refute the Iraqi claim that its invasion was justified because of Kuwait's oil production and pricing policies, and to reject the view that all Arab societies have a right to share in Arab oil wealth. The acknowledgement of the principle of private-sector collaboration was meant to provide the GCC countries with a means of selecting private-sector establishments that might benefit from their assistance and, by implication, allow them to influence the course of economic and social development in the recipient countries.

Egyptian and Syrian recognition of the sovereign right of Gulf countries to control and dispense with their resources as they see fit was tempered by the expectation of both countries. Public disclaimers to the contrary notwithstanding, this recognition was induced by massive financial transfers and debt forgiveness, and would likely be withdrawn if Gulf countries were to withhold their assistance in the future, as evidenced by various incidents. For example, when Kuwait hesitated to allow Egyptian nationals to return to their former jobs and appeared to exclude Egyptian firms from participating in its reconstruction program, Egyptian officials and media launched a public campaign criticizing Kuwaiti policies. Saudi mediation and Kuwait's reversal of its policies helped to arrest the deterioration in their relationship. Meanwhile, Syria continued to insist that the Gulf countries were duty-bound to defray the cost of its defense program. Both Egypt and Syria expected the GCC countries to help finance their economic development programs. It was doubtful that Egyptian and Syrian officials would resign themselves to a process that channeled Gulf aid to the private sector and bypassed them. Public sector resistance, and the determination of public officials not to relinquish their authoritarian controls, as well as widespread practices of corruption in the civil service, will most likely frustrate Gulf aid policies aimed at influencing Egyptian and Syrian societies, and may develop into a point of contention in the alliance.

Essentially, then, the alliance was founded on the basis of a trade-off. GCC countries, led by Saudi Arabia, admitted Egypt and Syria into a new economic league, designating them the Arab beneficiaries of Gulf largesse. In return for financial rewards, Egypt and Syria gave the GCC countries a free hand to financially punish their Arab opponents, and extended their military and political support to the GCC. Clearly, the stability of the alliance depends, among other things, on the adherence of its members to their part of the trade-off.

The success or failure of the alliance in defining and controlling the Arab political agenda is also dependent on the type of relationship it maintains with the US. In the short term, the alliance stands to benefit from maintaining close working relationships. The disappearance of the Soviet Union as a balancing superpower, and the projection of a massive military force of its own into the region, have given the US unprecedented leverage to influence events in the Middle East. Arab allies of the US will draw strength from this new US presence. In the long term, however, the legitimacy of an Arab regime erodes and its stability is threatened when it becomes closely identified in the public mind with the policies of a foreign power. This explains the extensive security measures the Arab members of the coalition have put in place since the outbreak of the crisis,[13] and their eagerness to calm their public through repeated assurances that the coalition is a temporary arrangement forced by abnormal circumstances. The prospect of close ties with the US was the cause of the massive protest rallies against the Gulf War in Arab countries that allowed their public to express their sentiments.[14] The protestors were motivated by their concern about foreign interference more than anything else.

Each of the three countries in the alliance has particular circumstances that mold its relationship with the US. In the Saudi case, the country is heavily dependent on the US and its Western allies for security requirements and for management of the economy, although the legitimacy of the political system is anchored in an Islamic culture that is antagonistic to political and military alliances with Western powers. To satisfy these two contradictory demands, Saudi Arabia has traditionally kept its relations with the West under the lid and required Westerners in the country to maintain a low profile. The Gulf war upset this balance and left the government of Saudi Arabia feeling vulnerable in the face of aggressive regional powers. Meanwhile, the destruction of Iraq has created a power vacuum in the region that the country is incapable of filling and that may result in a resurrection of the Iranian role. The dominant sentiment in government circles is that the Gulf war saved the government, and the US will ensure its future security. The Saudi government has, therefore, become more emboldened and less discreet about its connections to the US. This, however, creates the possibility of alienating significant sectors of the population.

The relation of Egypt to the US is one of economic dependency. Guided by exaggerated hopes of development aid, the late President Sadat normalized relations with Israel and placed Egypt decisively in the US camp. An Arab boycott of Egypt ensued. His successor, President Mubarak, was able with the assistance of Iraq and the PLO to mend Egypt's Arab relations without departing from Sadat's policies. During the Gulf war, Mubarak was the most vocal Arab leader to back US measures against Iraq, and his commitment of Egyptian troops provided the coalition with an Arab face it desperately required. Mubarak was willing to risk being accused of political servitude to the US in the knowledge that Egypt would be guaranteed economic and political benefits after the war. Mubarak's gamble paid off when the war proved to be short and the domestic opposition to the government failed to mobilize the Egyptian people. Nevertheless, economic hardships and Islamic fundamentalist movements have the potential to upset the Egyptian-US relationship in the future if the image of political servitude persists.[15]

The Syrian-US relationship is the most complex of any relationship the US has with an Arab country. Successive Syrian governments have consistently sought to project an image of themselves and their society as the vanguard of Palestinian rights and the Arab national cause. They opposed Western interests in the Arab world, as well as political and military alliances with the West, and were at odds with US policies during most of the years following Syrian independence. Syrian collaboration with the US during and after the Gulf war was, therefore, a dramatic reversal of policy.

The Syrian policy of improving relations with the US was initiated before the Gulf crisis erupted. Several factors were responsible for this shift. First, the Syrian government felt that its security was threatened when the Soviet Union withdrew its support for the Syrian effort to build a strategic military parity with Israel. Feeling exposed, Syria hoped that better relations with the US would convince Israel's international benefactor to rein in the adventurism of Israel's Likud government.[16] Second, Syria was being progressively isolated in the Arab world. It failed to prevent other Arab countries from honoring their commitment not to resume relations with Egypt until Egypt severed relations with Israel. It was also left out of sub-regional groupings such as the Arab Cooperation Council and the Gulf Cooperation Council. Syrian support for Iran in the Iraq-Iran war had also increased Syria's isolation and made it unpopular with other Arab governments and the public. The government of President Assad calculated that improved relations with the US could be a conduit to rebuilding relations with the Arab allies of the US and allowing Syria to break out of its isolation. Third, the enmity between the Syrian and Iraqi governments reached new levels after Iraq began to supply General Aoun and the Lebanese Forces with military materiel to engage the Syrian army in Lebanon. It was thought that improved relations with the US would convince the US to support the implementation of the Ta'if Agreement on Lebanon and would strengthen

Syrian capabilities in facing Iraq.[17] Fourth and finally, Syria was experiencing serious hardships. Its economy was stagnant, the Gulf countries were not renewing their aid programs, and the US and Western Europe had increased boycott measures against Syria. It was thought that improved relations with the US would help to alleviate the Syrian problems.

The Iraqi invasion of Kuwait faced the Syrian government with difficult choices. Were Syria to side with Iraq, it would have likely become a military target for the US and Israel in an uneven match and without the benefit of support from the Soviet Union. If it had opposed the coalition and remained uncommitted, it stood to lose the expected benefits of its recently initiated policies without gaining domestic and Arab public support. Based on these pragmatic considerations, the Syrian regime committed itself to a policy of reserved collaboration with the US, hoping to benefit from the postwar situation. There was a possibility that the adoption of a policy unpopular at home would create political problems for the government.[18] This would most likely depend on how much development aid the government was able to obtain from the Gulf states and whether the US could bring about a settlement to the Palestinian problem and the Arab-Israeli conflict that was deemed sufficiently equitable in Syria to justify the government's policy of cooperation with the US.

The Arab order established following the Gulf war was based on an alliance of interests between states with different political characters and regional priorities. Two crucial issues affecting its stability were the future relationship between the United States and the region, and the responsiveness of the governments of the leading Arab powers to the increased demands of their publics for political participation.

Within the three countries, there were significant cultural, social, political and ideological forces—nationalist and Islamic—opposed to close ties with western powers. If the US-Arab relationship were to develop toward a situation where the leading Arab states were widely perceived as politically subservient to the US,[19] these forces would have the potential to destabilize the Arab state system. The objectives of the United States in the region were aimed at securing vital Western interests, namely control of the flow of oil, the destruction of Iraq's military and industrial capabilities and the security of Israel. This set of objectives was different from the priorities of the leading Arab states. As part of its newfound influence in the Middle East, the United States expected to be able to promote its own agenda for the region. Opposition movements throughout the region would clearly question whether Arab governments would be autonomous in formulating their policies or whether they had to play by American rules.

The second issue affecting the stability of the new Arab order was the increasing demand of Arab populations for the greater accountability of governments. The trend toward democracy and respect for human rights that was visible in other areas of the world could not be expected to leave the Arab world untouched. Decades of despotic leadership had not achieved the basic social, economic and political aspirations of Arabs: instead, they had culminated in the invasion of Kuwait, Arab divisions and the return to the area of the western military forces and political influence whose elimination had been the focal point of Arab and Islamic politics for decades. During the occupation of Kuwait, the occupying authorities had shown callous disregard for the lives and property of Kuwaitis, and had suffocated protests severely, drawing attention to the problems arising from disrespect for human rights. The stability of any future Arab order depended largely on the sensitivity of governments to the feeling of their populations that any "New Arab Order" would have to look appreciably different from the old one.

Notes

1. The deliberations of the Alexandria Conference are covered in Robert MacDonald, *The League of Arab States: A Study in the Dynamics of Regional Organization* (Princeton: Princeton University Press, 1965), pp. 37-41.

2. Article 8 of the Pact states: "Each member state shall respect the systems of government established in the other member states and regard them as exclusive concerns of these states. Each shall pledge to abstain from any action calculated to change established systems of government." For the text of the Pact, see MacDonald, pp. 319-326.

3. To illustrate, none of the Arab members other than Iraq cast an opposing vote against the resolution adopted by the Council of Arab Foreign Ministers at its Cairo meeting on August 3, 1990. The resolution "reject(ed) any consequences resulting from" the Iraqi aggression against Kuwait (Article 1), "ask(ed) for the immediate and unconditional withdrawal of the Iraqi forces" (Article 3) and "affirm(ed) the Council's firm commitment to preserving the sovereignty and territorial integrity of member states." (Article 5). The five members who expressed reservations explained that they were not opposed to the substance of the resolution but were concerned about the effect it would have on attempts to mediate a peaceful resolution to the crisis. For the text of the resolution, see *Journal of Palestine Studies,* Vol. 20, No. 2 (Winter 1991), p. 178.

4. In the preamble of the Damascus Declaration on Coordination and Cooperation Among Arab States of March 6, 1991, the foreign ministers of Egypt, Syria and the six Arab Gulf countries stated "that they are totally committed to the territorial integrity of Iraq and its regional safety." For the text of the Declaration, see *Journal of Palestine Studies,* Vol. 20, No. 4 (Summer 1991), pp. 162-163.

5. Article 10 of the Treaty states: "The contracting states undertake to conclude no international agreements which may be contradictory to this Treaty, nor to act in their

international relations in a way which may be contrary to the aims of this Treaty." For the text of the Treaty, see MacDonald, pp. 327-333.

6. For a penetrating analysis of the "moral and political dilemma posed by the invasion of Kuwait" at both the state and popular levels, see Walid Khalidi, "The Gulf Crisis: Origins and Consequences," *Journal of Palestine Studies,* Vol. 20, No. 2 (Winter 1991), pp. 5-28.

7. Some Western observers were quick to proclaim that the most profound change brought about by the Gulf war was the destruction of the pan-Arab idea "once and for all" *(The Economist,* September 28, 1991, p. 4). This is not the first time the death of Arab nationalism has been announced. The idea has proven itself very resilient and popular and has re-surfaced after every major setback. Although seriously impaired by developments attending the Gulf war, it would be presumptuous to conclude that the idea is no longer a force to reckon with. For an analysis of the Gulf crisis with a different viewpoint, see Rami Khoury "The Post-War Middle East," *Link,* 24, 1 (January-March 1991). For reactions to the war in non-Arab Muslim societies, see *Time,* February 18, 1991, p. 38.

8. For a sample of the controversy as expressed by Arab Gulf nationals, see Abdullah Bishara, Secretary General of the GCC, in *Sawt Al-Kuwait* (April 30, 1991), Jassem al-Sa'doun, former speaker of the Kuwaiti Parliament, in *Al-Hayat* (April 30, 1991), Saud Muhammad al-Osaimi, former Kuwaiti Minister of State for Foreign Affairs, in *Al-Sharq Al-Awsat* (May 1, 1991) and Yusuf bin al-Alawi, Minister of State for Foreign Affairs in Oman, in *Al-Hayat* (May 2, 1991).

9. Emile Habibi pointed out the damage when he described how the Iraqi proposal came to be perceived as a linkage between the Palestinian issue and the future of the Iraqi leadership. See his interview in *Al-Sharq Al-Awsat,* May 3, 1991, p. 8.

10. The Damascus Declaration was drafted in this spirit. See also the reporting on the first meeting of the League of Arab States held after the war and the statements made by Ismat Abdul Majid, former Egyptian Minister of Foreign Affairs and present Secretary General of the League, in *The Globe and Mail,* April 1, 1991, p. A6.

11. For an expose of the differences see "Survey," *The Economist,* September 28, 1991, pp. 3, 9; and *The New Yorker,* September 30, 1991, p. 68.

12. The quotations are from the Damascus Declaration.

13. These security measures included the prohibition of the entry of nationals of certain countries opposed to the war, expulsions, arrests and censorship.

14. For the public reaction to the war in Morocco, Algeria and Tunisia, see *Time,* February 18, 1991, p. 23.

15. Reporting from Cairo, the correspondent of the *New York Times* observed a rapidly growing shift in favor of Iraq as the war progressed. See the article by Youssef Ibrahim, *New York Times,* January 24, 1991, pp. A1, A9.

16. Wars between Arab countries and Israel are intensive and of short duration. Neither party can sustain combat unless its arsenal is immediately replenished. It requires a superpower to undertake such a task. Syria was in a predicament when the Soviets became reluctant to support it militarily.

17. For an insider account of the relations between Aoun and the Lebanese Forces, on the one hand, and Syria and Iraq, on the other hand, see Karim Paqradouni, *La'nat Watan* (A Country Under a Curse), Beirut: 'Ibr Al-Sharq, 1991.

18. For Syrian reactions to the government's policies during the crisis, see *The Globe and Mail,* February 5, 1991. p. A8, and the *New York Times,* March 27, 1991, p. A7.

19. An editorialist wrote: "If the Shah fell because Islamic society would not tolerate his being American pro-consul, the obvious question is whether the Saudi, Egyptian and Syrian leaderships do not run the same risk in the long term." *The Observer,* February 3, 1991, p. 17.

14 ISRAEL AND THE PERSIAN GULF CRISIS

Bernard Reich

The Persian Gulf crisis inaugurated by the Iraqi invasion of Kuwait on August 2, 1990, posed a major strategic-political challenge for Israel. Israel's position and response developed in phases: before the Iraqi invasion of Kuwait; during the diplomatic-political crisis; through the military hostilities (including the Scud attacks); and after the cessation of hostilities and during the attempts to create a new regional order (the period of intensive United States efforts to refocus on resolution of the Arab-Israeli conflict).

Before the Invasion

Israel's reaction to the crisis must be seen against the background and within the framework of the Arab-Israeli conflict. Salient elements include the fact that Israel has been technically at war with Iraq throughout the period since 1948, when Iraq participated in hostilities against Israel in the first Arab-Israeli war. Iraq was the only participant in that war that refused to sign an armistice agreement with Israel in 1949 after the cessation of hostilities. It also fought against Israel in the Six Day War of 1967 and the Yom Kippur (Ramadan) War of 1973 with sizable military forces. Iraq was among those Arab states that took the lead against Egyptian President Anwar Sadat's peace overtures to Israel in 1977 and 1978, and it opposed the Egypt-Israel Peace Treaty of 1979. It also supported and gave sanctuary to anti-Israel Palestinian terrorist groups. During the Iran-Iraq War (1980-1988) Israel grew increasingly concerned about Iraq's growing military strength and capability and its potential threat to Israel after the end of hostilities with Iran. Nevertheless the war was seen with mixed views.[1] There were some in Israel who saw it as an opportunity to develop a bridge to Iraq—in part because of a convergence of views that Iran was a destabilizing threat to them and to the region—while others saw a possible opportunity to renew links to Iran because of the mutually-shared concern with the threat from Iraq. Clearly neither "opportunity" proved advantageous, despite an Israeli role in the Iran-Contra activities of the Reagan administration, and an improved

Israeli relationship did not develop with Iran or Iraq. Nevertheless, Israel benefitted from the fact that two of its major enemies waged war against each other and destroyed the other's military capability. However, with the end of hostilities Iraq, with its enhanced combat experience, emerged as a more significant threat to Israel. Although Israelis generally were pleased that the war ended, and they hoped that Iraq would turn inward and focus on its massive needs of reconstruction and rehabilitation after eight years of hostilities, many (and this seemed to dominate governmental thinking) believed that Iraq was a major and growing threat and believed that it would ultimately unleash its forces on the Jewish state.

In the wake of the Iran-Iraq War, Saddam Hussein's growing ambitions, in the region and beyond, were of increasing concern to Israel, which took him seriously.[2] The worry took a dramatic turn in the spring of 1990, when Saddam Hussein threatened to "burn half of Israel,"[3] and it became an increasingly open secret that he sought and was developing an atomic-biological-chemical capability. There was also concern that much of the international community did not take Saddam Hussein's threats as seriously as Israel did.

Nevertheless, Israel was preoccupied during much of the year and a half before the invasion of Kuwait with other issues, especially the peace process that began with the proposal of Prime Minister Yitzhak Shamir for the selection of Palestinian representatives to negotiate with Israel, and the efforts of United States Secretary of State James Baker to establish some form of Israel-Palestinian dialogue. But there was also the usual political maneuvering within Israel, among and within the political parties and the political elite, in the spring and early summer of 1990. And, in the spring of 1990, there was the successful parliamentary vote of no confidence and the collapse of the National Unity Government. In June a Shamir-led Likud, right of center, and religious party government was established. There was also the large influx of Soviet Jewish immigrants which began earlier but gained dramatic momentum in 1990, leading Israelis to focus on the massive requirements of immigrant absorption. The collapse of the Soviet bloc in Eastern Europe and the concomitant "end of the cold war" led Israel to begin to rethink its position in the international system, especially its relations with the two superpowers, as well as the implications of these developments for the Arab-Israeli conflict and for the Middle East as a whole. The *intifada* that had begun in December 1987 was continuing in the West Bank and Gaza Strip and affected Israeli politics, economics and society, in addition to being a growing security threat as the level of violence increased and more Israelis were killed by Palestinians. Eventually the peace process stalled, as Baker failed to secure a formula that would allow the beginning of a dialogue between Israel and the Palestinians, and it was moribund by the time of the Iraqi invasion of Kuwait.

The Crisis: Diplomatic Responses

The Iraqi invasion and occupation of Kuwait in August 1990 and the broader Gulf crisis it spawned became the first major post-Cold War test of United States policy.[4] The Israelis were concerned about the invasion of Kuwait by Iraq, but their dominant interest focused on the reactions of the international community and especially the United States. They saw something of a parallel with a potential future attack on Israel, and this crisis might therefore provide some insight into the ability and willingness of the international system to respond. Would the United States respond and, if so, in what manner? What would be the reaction of the international community? What would be the ultimate outcome of this invasion? Among the questions raised were the value of Israel as a strategic asset in such situations and the longer term implications of the crisis for Israel and the United States-Israel relationship.

Strategic and intelligence cooperation that focused on a Soviet bloc threat had become a visible part of the special relationship between the United States and Israel in the Reagan administration.[5] With the end of the Cold War signaled by the improved relationship between the United States and the Soviet Union and the breakup of the Soviet bloc, there developed a perspective that Israel's role as a strategic asset had diminished and there was a widespread view that Israel was not relevant for potential actions in the Arabian Peninsula and the Persian Gulf. The Gulf crisis suggested a test of this perspective.

Israel did not serve as a staging area for forces, nor as a storage depot for military materiel, nor was it utilized for medical emergencies. From the outset, there was a conscious United States effort to build a broad-based international force with an Arab component to oppose Saddam Hussein, and there was a diligent United States effort to distance Israel from any such activity.[6] The obvious and stated objective of the United States was to avoid giving Saddam Hussein the opportunity to recast his aggression in terms of the Arab-Israeli conflict and to avoid giving credence to Iraqi arguments that the United States military buildup in the region was to serve Israeli interests and that Israelis were directly involved. Iraq accused Israel of joining with American forces in Saudi Arabia and of making combat planes and pilots available to the United States. Saddam Hussein tried to draw the Israelis into the crisis and thereby to mobilize Arab (and potentially Islamic and Third World) public opinion against the United States. He argued that he would not withdraw from Kuwait until all issues of occupation were resolved, including the Israeli presence in the occupied territories (that is, the West Bank and Gaza Strip). Although the charge of Israeli-American cooperation in the Arabian Peninsula was patently absurd, it struck a responsive chord in much of the Arab (and Muslim) world. Israel was determined not to be used as a tool to break the coalition. Nevertheless, Israel was concerned that it was not a full-scale partner with the United States in the crisis and that it was not part of the coalition. Israel sought to prove its utility, if not value, but was precluded from doing so by a sensitivity in Washington that its participation might drive the Arab partners from the coalition and split the consensus that had been developed against Saddam Hussein's actions. Israeli actions were discouraged.

In the short term, the focus of Washington's attention was directed to such matters as reversing the Iraqi invasion, assuring the dependable supply of oil at reasonable prices, guaranteeing the security of Saudi Arabia, ensuring the safety of American (and other) hostages in Kuwait and Iraq, establishing an embargo of Iraq, and creating the necessary international force on the Arabian Peninsula and in the waters around it to achieve these objectives. Given these goals, there was no publicly identified role for Israel; it was marginal. Israel did, however, endorse the firm and rapid American reaction to Iraq. It opposed the aggression against Kuwait as a matter of practical reality as well as of moral principle. It also adopted a clear position to deter Iraq from moving to the West. Israel established a "red line" in Jordan, making clear that the movement of Iraqi troops into Jordan, whether or not by invitation, would be regarded as an act of war, to which Israel would respond. Israel gained added credibility for its intelligence assessments and warnings that had focused on Saddam Hussein's Iraq now that Iraq clearly was a major military threat in the region.

Israel concurred with President Bush's approach to the crisis. Nevertheless, the Israelis were not fully confident that the United States would handle the situation as well as it ultimately did. Bush was not fully convincing to Israelis that he had the wisdom and judgment to go to war, if required, on January 16. The Bush-Shamir relationship had been one of political disagreement on various issues within a personal relationship characterized by a lack of positive chemistry.[7] Only in December 1990 was there a significant and apparent improvement in their personal relationship, and their meeting was a positive one; however, this may well have been primarily because they avoided the difficult issues in contention between the two states and the two leaders,[8] and they accentuated the positive support of Israel for the United States' response to Saddam Hussein.[9] The Israelis were assured that there would be no Gulf solution at their expense,[10] despite the fact that earlier the United States had joined in United Nations Security Council Resolution 672 (adopted on October 12, 1990), which condemned Israel in the Temple Mount incident, had criticized curfews in the West Bank and Gaza, the deportation of Palestinians, travel restrictions and the establishment of settlements, and had focused attention on the other issues that had been the subject of discord between the two states, at least in the Bush Administration. Despite the areas of discord, Israelis seemed reassured by the tenor and content of the December meeting and the overall American approach to the crisis.

The positive meetings and Israel's and the United States' general position during the crisis helped to allay Israeli fears and concerns about the post-war situation. However, Israelis were not certain. Israelis were convinced that the embargo would not work, that economic sanctions and United Nations resolutions would not remove Iraq from Kuwait and Saddam Hussein from Iraq. They were concerned that, in the end, Saddam Hussein might well be left in place in Iraq because George Bush would decide not to take action or would be politically and diplomatically out-maneuvered by Saddam Hussein. The latter, a "political survivor," would remain and would, as a consequence, pose a greater threat to Israel (as well as to other regional states). Israel remained uncertain about United States will and resolve, and concerned about a last-minute out-maneuvering of George Bush by Saddam Hussein. They worried about a United States misreading of Saddam Hussein and possible miscalculation. There was also concern about United States military capability, given the lack of relevant experience in recent years.

Israel benefitted from the fact that Palestinian sentiment in the West Bank and Gaza Strip generally applauded the Iraqi takeover of Kuwait, as Palestinians identified a "hero" and showed little sympathy for the deposed Kuwaitis, despite Kuwaiti political and financial support for the Palestinian cause. Notwithstanding some internal disarray and contradictory statements, the PLO voted against the Arab League resolution opposing Iraq's action and Arafat supported Saddam Hussein.[11] The articulation of terrorist threats against American targets by Baghdad-based and Iraqi-supported Palestinian groups (some of which were constituents of the PLO) gave credence to Israel's arguments about the lack of appropriate Palestinians with whom to negotiate peace.[12] These actions would make more difficult the Bush administration's ability to restart the dialogue with the PLO that had been suspended on June 20, 1990, and to resuscitate the Baker initiative to generate Israeli-Palestinian negotiations.

At the same time that some Arab leaders supported Saddam Hussein, others cast their lot with the United States and the international coalition. Some positive sentiments developed between the United States and those Arab states as they cooperated closely in response to the perceived menace. Americans and Arabs cooperating in Operation Desert Shield and later fighting in Operation Desert Storm in the Arabian desert developed a connection which may color future judgments on a number of regional issues. In this regard the positive roles not only of Saudi Arabia and other Gulf Cooperation Council (GCC) states, but also of Egypt and Syria, in cooperating with the United States-led anti-Iraqi effort, suggested a potential factor of consequence for Israel and for resolution of the Arab-Israeli conflict. The decision of Saudi Arabia to invite United States troops to help protect the kingdom, and Egypt's related efforts to organize Arab military forces in this same arena, helped to undercut assertions by Israel's supporters that Arab states would not openly join with the United States to deal with such matters.[13]

The Period of Hostilities

As a consequence of their pre-war assessments of Saddam Hussein and George Bush, and of the decisions the two leaders might make at the last minute, the Israelis were somewhat surprised by the launching of the air war but basically were pleased with the decision. The government of Israel congratulated President Bush on his determination and on the initial successes of the United States effort. However, there were concerns virtually from the outset. These revolved around the fact that Israel was not allowed to participate in the fighting and could not do so because it was denied essential intelligence and codes.[14] The United States made it clear that an active Israeli role would not be helpful, that the United States and its coalition partners could do anything the Israelis could and that, therefore, their participation was not desirable or necessary.[15] Israel's concerns were that this approach might affect negatively its relationship with the United States as well as its position within the Middle East.

The Scud missiles created a new and more somber situation in Israel.[16] There was the concrete damage caused by the Scuds as well as the psychological effect on a country that was to an extent paralyzed by the uncertainty of the attacks. There were concerns that Israel might be involved in the fighting and this might broaden the crisis to include the Arab-Israeli dispute within the parameters of the Gulf crisis. The launching of the Scuds against Israel helped to confirm Israeli attitudes about Saddam Hussein, and the reaction in the Arab world further added to the Israeli perception that the Arab world remained hostile. The attack confirmed Israeli fears and suspicions but it did not lead, as almost all assumed it would, to an Israeli military response that might have widened the hostilities. Israel carefully assessed the results and consequences of its response. There was the problem of locating the Scud targets, just as the coalition had difficulties in identifying them, and it was also unclear what Israel might be able to do that the coalition was unable to accomplish. There was also the danger of an accidental encounter between Israel and the coalition forces. At the same time, there was the concern that, if Israel chose not to respond, its defensive posture and deterrent position in relation to the Arab states might erode. It would make Israel seem weak and this would create the potential for future conflict or Arab attacks against the Jewish state. Each of these elements was part of the Israeli equation as it sought to determine its appropriate response to the missile attacks by Iraq. Nevertheless, the factors that swayed Israel against a response to the Scuds were the arrival of the Patriot missiles (a tangible way to assure that Israel would be protected despite the fact that the Patriot had a somewhat mixed record and did not fully prevent damage or casualties even after its deployment) and, even more significant, the request and cajoling of the President of the United States in a crucial telephone conversation with Shamir.[17] Bush made a quick and reportedly impassioned request to the Israelis to forego a response so as not to play into Saddam Hussein's hands.[18] Apparently, he was able to convince Shamir that if Israel responded it might lead to the breakup of the coalition and it might even allow Saddam Hussein to survive the hostilities and remain in place as a negative force in the region in the years to come. Clearly, the political dividend of being the aggrieved party and of acceding to the United States request was factored into the decision-making process. Shamir was persuaded that if Israel responded it would serve Saddam Hussein's purposes, and Shamir in turn was able to hold sway within the Cabinet to ensure that Israel would not respond.[19] Apparently he prevailed against the political arguments and military perspectives suggesting the imperative of a response. The visit of Deputy Secretary of State Lawrence Eagleburger to Israel was especially important in achieving a level of Israeli confidence in its decision. An aura of good feeling resulted as Israel's decision not to respond was welcomed in the United States and elsewhere.[20]

During the period of hostilities the government moved further to the right when Moledet (Homeland) joined the cabinet and increased the government's strength in the Knesset.[21] Although there are various possible explanations for the inclusion of Rehavam ("Gandhi") Zeevi in the Cabinet, two seemed to be the most plausible: Shamir wanted to appear to be more moderate by comparison to Zeevi, or the new composition of the cabinet would better reflect Shamir's position. Also during the period of hostilities, Shamir's domestic political approval rating and popularity increased, especially gaining support for the policy not to respond to the Scud missile attacks.

The doves in the Israeli system who were disheartened, dispirited, or disappointed by developments during the diplomatic-political phase of the crisis effectively were neutralized during the course of the hostilities. The crisis and the war did not support the perspectives and arguments of Israel's doves and it did not comport with their views of the peace process. Indeed, some of them supported the war as the best mechanism to begin a real peace process—the argument being that sometimes you must go to war to achieve peace.[22]

Israel supported the United States decision to go to war and the apparent Presidential view that at its termination Saddam Hussein should not and would not be a threat in the region. The ouster of Saddam Hussein was seen by many as an essential condition to achieve peace. Israel also chose to accept the United States position that it should abstain from combat. Nevertheless, there were tensions in the United States-Israeli relationship during the hostilities. These included differences of perspective over the participation of Israel in combat (particularly in response to the Scud attacks) and, eventually, over the cease-fire itself. However, there were other areas of discord, such as the United States administration's delay in releasing

$400 million in housing loan guarantees to Israel for Soviet Jewish immigrants, as well as a public airing of the differences between Jerusalem and Washington over settlements and housing for the new immigrants in the West Bank and Jerusalem.[23] Israel was also concerned about the joint statement of Baker and Soviet Foreign Minister Bessmertnykh on the situation in the Middle East, which raised doubts in Israel about the objectives of United States policy and the relationship of the two superpowers.[24]

After the War

The end of hostilities inaugurated a period in which the salient issue for Israel was its role as seen by Bush and Baker as they tried to reconstruct the world based on the success against Saddam Hussein. The salient question was Israel's place in the New World Order and in the new peace process. Israel's perspective on the new world order in the aftermath of the Gulf war was foreshadowed by Prime Minister Shamir in an address to the Knesset on February 4. He suggested that the lessons of the Gulf crisis and war had to be assimilated before asking Israel to accept new peace proposals. He articulated a note of caution: "We hope that now, more than in the past, the complexity of the problems in the Middle East—the cruelty of dictatorial regimes here, and that of Saddam Hussein is today the worst and cruelest of all, but not the only one—has been better comprehended and the need for us to exercise care in our policy moves better understood."[25]

In the immediate aftermath of the hostilities, Israel's position was altered positively as a consequence of the "new" Middle East created by the crisis and war. Israel's military situation improved. Saddam Hussein had been vanquished and humiliated, thereby eliminating, at least in the short term, a, if not the, major Arab military threat to Israel. Iraq's massive offensive war machine was destroyed, albeit incompletely, and its ability to wage war against Israel was significantly reduced. Iraq's non-conventional (atomic, biological, chemical) infrastructure was also damaged, and, if there were to be full implementation of the United Nations Security Council cease-fire resolution, it would be all but eliminated for the foreseeable future.[26] This clearly altered the Arab-Israeli, as well as the regional, military balance to Israel's advantage. No doubt the destruction of much of Iraq's military capability gave Israel something of a respite from the probability of war for some time to come. Arab military capabilities remained rather substantial, but without Iraq's participation, and given the new Arab order, the likelihood of a war was substantially reduced. Despite these accomplishments, the ability of Saddam Hussein to survive and to reassert his authority in Baghdad was of major concern to Israel and was seen as a worrisome factor in United States decision-making. Israel worried about Hafiz al-Assad and Syria, and the parallels between Assad and Syria, on the one hand, and Saddam Hussein and Iraq, on the other, were being increasingly discussed in Israeli intellectual as well as political circles.[27] Israel felt more secure, but only to a limited extent and probably only for a limited time.

The strategic situation was also changed by the shattering of the concept (or myth) of Arab unity, with the Arab world dividing into two, generally hostile, camps. At the same time many of the previously pro-Western (and some of the less pro-Western) Arab regimes seemed to increase their relationship with and dependence on the United States (and the West more generally). Their previously allied-with-the-Soviet Union Arab counterparts seemed to face the dilemma of having been Soviet clients and were now doubtful of the future; some, such as Syria, seemed to be shifting sides, at least on some issues.

After the end of the Gulf war, Israel was forced to re-examine its military doctrine and security concepts to take into account recent developments and consider future eventualities in light of changed regional and international circumstances. This was inevitable, no matter what the eventual outcome, and the reassessment was already in process prior to the Iraq-Kuwait crisis. The cease-fire in the Iran-Iraq War, Gorbachev's policies, and the end of the Cold War would have occasioned a reassessment, but the Gulf crisis increased the urgency and complicated the regional and international environments in which it would take place.

Among the factors which affected Israel's security dilemma were the 39 Scud missiles that were launched against it. These were the first strikes of consequence at Israel's population and civilian centers since its War of Independence (1948-49), and Israel did not respond. Israel's civilian population proved vulnerable to the missile attacks, and neither the United States nor Israel stopped the attacks before 39 were launched. The military impact on Israel was not significant, and Israel's existence was never threatened, but there were important psychological, economic and political consequences. For Israel there were a number of military questions. What if it, rather than Kuwait, had been the primary target? What would have happened if Saddam Hussein had sent a sizable force into Jordan and deployed it toward

Israel and if the Israeli-declared red line in Jordan had been challenged if not crossed? In such a case, what would have been the response (if any) of the international community of the United Nations, and also of the United States? Clearly Israel will take a closer look at its intelligence to see what mistakes may have been made, it will analyze the missile threat, and it will examine the role and effectiveness of civil defense, something which has been virtually ignored because of lack of previous real need on a large scale, since the wars generally were fought elsewhere. It will re-examine the security value of the occupied territories,[28] but the major Israeli political parties seem likely to conclude that their existing policies are appropriate.

From Israel's point of view there were other positive tangible results of the war. The war provided some "proof" of the United States commitment to Israel—the proposition that the United States would protect Israel against Arab aggression threatening its destruction. If the United States was prepared to act this way for Kuwait, what might be possible given a more significant commitment to Israel?

Israel also had gains in the political-diplomatic sphere. There was an improved relationship with the United States. Israel gained sympathy by not responding to the Scud attacks and because of the negative perceptions of the Palestinians, the PLO and King Hussein as a consequence of their articulated positions in support of Saddam Hussein against the Western alliance. The Israelis understood that this might be short-lived and it might be problematic in other ways. Nevertheless, in the short term both the PLO and the Palestinians suffered. Rethinking the role of King Hussein is part of the Israeli reassessment but there is no clear outcome. Some Israelis continue to believe that the ultimate solution to the Palestinian problem lies with King Hussein and his participation in the peace process, while others see his role as removing himself from Jordan and providing an alternative solution.[29] Israel gained, at least in the short term, greater US sensitivity to its position on negotiations involving the Palestinians, and the nature of Palestinian representation in the peace process. The Palestinian frustration factor that helped generate support for Saddam Hussein seemed to grow with his defeat. King Hussein remained separated from many Arab states but closer to the Palestinians and stronger in Jordan because of his stand on the Iraq-Kuwait crisis. The PLO clearly chose the "wrong" side—at the cost of its Saudi and Kuwaiti financial aid and of its return to a more central role in the peace process, among other negative accomplishments.

For Israel the outcome of the crisis and war suggested that the initial "track" in the dual track peace process pursued by Baker should be the state-to-state one, leaving the final settlement of the Palestinian question to a later phase. There was some anticipation of changed positions in the Arab world that might facilitate direct Israeli negotiations with Arab states previously unwilling to pursue such a course. There was also the expectation that there would be pressure on the Israelis and they understood that it was imminent. At the same time they believed there should be pressure on the Arabs to make concessions on such matters as the Arab boycott of Israel. The Israelis asked themselves and Secretary Baker if there was a new Arab world ready to deal with Israel. Was there a new consensus in the Arab world to move toward peace? They wanted a clear answer.

Although the peace process was moribund by the time Saddam Hussein invaded Kuwait, the Arab-Israeli conflict became a tool in his efforts to split the United States-led coalition and to gain Arab world support, and he had some successes in achieving his objectives. Virtually from the outset of the Gulf crisis, Saddam Hussein sought to divert attention from his aggression by calling attention to the Arab-Israeli conflict. He hoped thereby to arouse the Arab masses but also to embarrass the Arab leadership and, perhaps, to divide the coalition created to oppose his aggression against Kuwait.

The United States resisted Saddam Hussein's attempts to create a linkage between the Gulf and the Arab-Israeli issues. Among the rationales was the effort to avoid giving credence to his argument that there was a parallel between his position in Kuwait and the Israeli posture in the West Bank and in the Gaza Strip. This was successful. A series of actions and efforts made clear that there would be a sustained post-crisis effort to deal anew with Arab-Israeli issues, even if there was no formal linkage between the two questions. This was increasingly obvious to Israeli decision-makers as the crisis developed in the fall and winter of 1990-1991. Some indicators could be identified. In a speech to the United Nations General Assembly on October 1, 1990, President Bush spoke of post-crisis opportunities that might develop to deal with other regional conflicts, including the Arab-Israeli one. United Nations Security Council Resolution 681 of December 20, 1991, seemed to make clear that an international conference focused on Arab-Israeli issues would be a logical and appropriate next step in the process. Although Resolution 681 makes no explicit mention of a conference, its preamble references a statement made by the Security Council President on December 20, 1990, "that an international conference, at an appropriate time, properly structured, should facilitate" resolution of the Arab-Israeli conflict.[30]

That the administration would make a major effort on the Arab-Israeli conflict after the war became immediately apparent when Secretary of State Baker, in testimony before the Congress in early February 1991, outlined the Administration's conception of the New World Order and identified resolution of the Arab-Israeli conflict as one of its cornerstones.[31] In a speech to a joint session of Congress on March 6, 1991, in which he proclaimed victory in the Gulf war, President Bush noted:

> . . . we must work to create new opportunities for peace and stability in the Middle East. On the night I announced Operation Desert Storm, I expressed my hope that out of the horrors of war might come new momentum for peace. . . . We must do all that we can to close the gap between Israel and the Arab states and between Israelis and Palestinians. . . . A comprehensive peace must be grounded in United Nations Security Council Resolutions 242 and 338 and the principle of territory for peace. This principle must be elaborated to provide for Israel's security and recognition, and at the same time for legitimate Palestinian political rights. Anything else would fail the twin tests of fairness and security. The time has come to put an end to the Arab-Israeli conflict.[32]

Bush also noted that "By now, it should be plain to all parties that peacemaking in the Middle East requires compromise." The latter observation was seen as one that foreshadowed American efforts to achieve resolution of the problem through compromises that might have to be achieved through American pressure on the parties, especially Israel. In fact, the headline of the *New York Times* story on the speech noted "Hints at Pressure on Israel."

How do the Israelis see the peace process? In the wake of the war the Israelis expected strong pressure from the United States for some kind of process. This view developed even before the beginning of the hostilities, and the Baker visits to the region after the cease-fire were seen as part of the process and part of the pressure. The Israelis understood that they would be pressed on the parallelism of the United Nations resolutions on the Iraq-Kuwait crisis and on the issue of the occupied territories. They recognized that they would be pressed on United Nations Security Council Resolution 242 and other resolutions and on the concept of peace for territory.

Baker met with Israeli officials at the outset of his April 1991 visit to the Middle East, and it was clear that agreement had not been reached. Baker "went over differences in Arab and Israeli positions on a number of issues and made suggestions as to how to bridge the gaps in order to get a conference that would launch direct bilateral negotiations."[33] The issues in contention apparently included such matters as where to convene a conference, whether in the region or elsewhere, what powers and authority it would have or whether it would be primarily ceremonial in nature, under whose auspices it should be conducted and whether the United Nations would be a factor, which Palestinians and other Arabs could and would attend, and what prior commitments must be made by the participants. The options were varied. The question of a European role and one for the Gulf Arab states became sticking points. The areas of discord reflected both procedural and substantive points.

Baker's return to Israel in late April, on his third tour of the Middle East after the cease-fire, brought to the fore a number of issues concerning the peace process and resolution of outstanding Arab-Israeli issues. Clearly there were significant areas of discord, but the Israelis noted that "there was no atmosphere of ultimatum in our talks with Baker."[34] Both the United States and Israel sought to avoid a crisis despite differences of perspective on both the procedural and substantive levels. Part of the difference was the interpretation of what constituted procedure (or form) and what constituted substance. Baker continued to stress the need to concentrate on substance over form. Among the matters of some concern was the possible participation in the conference of states other than those bordering Israel. Israel and various observers believed that the time was appropriate to involve Saudi Arabia and perhaps Kuwait and others, given the outcome of the Iraq-Kuwait crisis. The Saudis clearly opted out of any initial conference meeting. The Saudi foreign minister, Prince Saud al-Faisal, made clear that Saudi Arabia would not be involved in any initial phase of a regional Arab-Israeli peace conference. "Participation in the meeting traditionally has been the countries that are involved directly in the peace negotiations, which are Egypt, Syria, Jordan, Lebanon and Israel."[35] He went on to say "I think this is a practical format and we will continue to support the initiatives in this manner." The Israelis understood that they would be pressed for concessions.

On the question of peace for territory there appeared to be little change in the Israeli security perspective despite the missile attacks. The argument that the missile attacks obviated the need for territory was not one that the government accepted.[36] Israelis recognized that a peace conference was probably inevitable, and from their point of view a regional conference that had no power to impose a solution but would devolve to direct negotiations with the Arab states was the preferred method. They preferred not to have an international conference at which the United Nations, which was basically seen as hostile to it, would play a major role or one at which Russia would be consequential. There was also concern about a conference where there would be an increasing escalation of pressures by virtue of the presence of a large number of states which might mutually reinforce an anti-Israeli perspective. The preference was for bilateral negotiations. The Israeli government seemed to prefer a variant of the Camp David process[37] to establish peace between Israel and the Arab states, suggesting that the Palestinians could obtain a form of autonomy within limited territory and within a time frame that would provide for the ultimate resolution of the problem.

Major concessions or major changes in Israel's policy or position did not result from the Gulf crisis and war because the latter did not generate a sea change in the region creating conditions for peace between Israel and the Arab states. Nevertheless, Israel seemed reconciled to the fact that there would be a peace process and that the United States, for a number of reasons, would seek to promote a resolution to the problem.

The Israelis seemed to understand that they must move ahead with the United States as a consequence of the crisis. However, there was unlikely to be a significant change in the policy of either major Israeli political party in this regard. Israelis seemed convinced that most of their assumptions, policies and decisions with regard to the region were reconfirmed by developments between August 2, 1990 and the cease-fire in the spring of 1991.

Within several months of the Gulf war cease-fire, the United States-Israel relationship was again characterized by discord and tension between the two states, with much of the good will built up during the Gulf crisis dissipated by disagreements over the modalities and substance of the peace process and other matters. Tensions developed as the Bush administration moved toward a linkage of proposed housing loan guarantees, essential to settle Soviet Jews in Israel, with Israeli actions concerning settlements in the West Bank and Gaza Strip (an old issue of contention) and with Israeli responsiveness on the peace process. These developments recalled previous encounters between the United States and Israel and appeared to be unaffected by the Gulf crisis.

Among the issues in contention between the two states was the matter of Israeli settlements in the West Bank, an issue of long standing difference between the two countries. In an appearance before the Subcommittee on Foreign Operations of the House Appropriations Committee on May 22, 1991, Secretary Baker, in response to a question, said: "I don't think that there is any bigger obstacle to peace than the settlement activity that continues not only unabated but at an enhanced pace."[38] Israeli leaders reacted angrily to Baker's comments that this was the largest obstacle to peace and suggested that the fault was with the Arab states who were not genuinely interested in peace. Senators and Congressmen criticized Baker's statement. But President Bush defended Baker, observing: "Secretary Baker was speaking for this Administration and I strongly support what he said and I strongly support what he is trying to do. Our policy is well known, and it would make a big contribution to peace if these settlements would stop."[39]

In some respects little changed after the Gulf war. Reflecting the views of many observers, a *New York Times* editorial on April 25, 1991, suggested "The opportunity is extraordinary. . . . The Persian Gulf war has dramatically transformed strategic and political thinking across the Middle East." This perspective provided much of the impetus for optimistic evaluations of the regional situation and the prospects for peace, and undergirded United States policy in the aftermath of the war. The view was not fully shared by Israeli politicians, who appreciated that some things had been altered, but believed that much had remained the same in terms of the prospects for Arab-Israeli peace. Many of the issues central to the United States-Israel relationship, and to the efforts to resolve the Arab-Israeli conflict, that had been impediments to progress before the crisis appeared certain to resurface after it.

In Israel, there was still skepticism after the Gulf war about whether there had been real changes in the attitudes and policies of the Arab world that ultimately might lead to peace between Israel and its neighbors. This skepticism remained after the convening of the plenary session of the peace conference in Madrid in October 1991, and the subsequent rounds of bilateral discussions in Washington in 1991-92. In 1992, there was rising concern about the attitudes and policies of the Bush Administration on matters of central importance to Israel, as manifest in the public debate over United States guarantees of housing loans that Israel sought to facilitate the integration of Jewish immigrants from the former Soviet Union. The 1992 elections in Israel, which were fought almost entirely on domestic issues, resulted in an improvement of US-Israeli relations on this matter, as the policy of the newly elected Labor government on settlements in the West Bank met the preferences of the Bush Administration in connection with the loan guarantees. Even after the elections, however, it was unclear whether Labor Party policies could lead to peace. The optimistic view that a New World Order with a lasting Arab-Israeli peace was made possible by the Gulf war was more in evidence in the United States than in Israel.

Notes

1. For a detailed examination see Bernard Reich, "Israel and the Iran-Iraq War," in Christopher C. Joyner (ed.), *The Persian Gulf War: Lessons for Strategy, Law, and Diplomacy* (New York, Westport, Connecticut, and London: Greenwood Press, 1990), pp. 75-90.

2. See Amazia Baram, "Saddam Hussein," in Bernard Reich (ed.), *Political Leaders of the Contemporary Middle East and North Africa: A Biographical Dictionary* (New York, Westport, Connecticut, and London: Greenwood Press, 1990), pp. 240-249.

3. See *New York Times,* April 3, 1990.

4. For an overview of the United States efforts in the first phase of the crisis see Bernard Reich, "The United States in the Middle East," *Current History,* January 1991, pp. 5-8, 42.

5. See Bernard Reich and Joseph Helman, "The United States-Israel Strategic Relationship in the Reagan Administrations," *IJA Research Report* (London), No. 6 (1988), pp. 1-17.

6. In an interview on Israel Television on August 22, 1990 Prime Minister Shamir noted: "The United States today also is deeply interested for Israel not to appear as an active partner in this confrontation. . . ." Foreign Broadcast Information Service (FBIS), *Daily Report—Near East and South Asia,* August 23, 1990, p. 25.

7. On the general nature of the Arab-Israeli peace efforts and the United States-Israel relationship during the first year of the Bush administration see Bernard Reich, "A Lower Priority: The Middle East Policy of the Bush Administration," in William Frankel (ed.), *Survey of Jewish Affairs 1990* (Oxford: Basil Blackwell for the Institute of Jewish Affairs, 1990), pp. 129-42.

8. See, for example, *New York Times,* December 12, 1990.

9. After private discussions at the White House, Prime Minister Shamir emerged to note: "We have been delighted to express our full support for the leadership of the President, for the policy of the United States in this recent crisis of the Gulf, and the President also expressed his support for our behavior, for our policy, and for our problems." Quoted in *New York Times,* December 12, 1990.

10. After meeting with Bush on December 11, Shamir noted: "I trust the president. He has said it several times, and he said it to me now again, that there will not be any deal at the expense of Israel." Quoted in *Washington Post,* December 12, 1990.

11. *New York Times,* August 11, 1990.

12. *New York Times,* September 18, 1990.

13. Former United States Ambassador to Israel Samuel Lewis has argued: "But the demonstration of our strategic links to the Gulf countries undermines the longstanding

Israeli argument that none of our Arab connections would ever be useful if they were needed." Quoted in *Wall Street Journal,* August 15, 1990.

14. *New York Times,* January 16, 1991.

15. *New York Times,* January 18, 1991.

16. The accounts of the Scud attacks provided by the IDF spokesman showed a total of 39 missiles in eighteen attacks. One person was killed by a missile and twelve other indirect deaths resulted from the missile attacks. Several hundred people were injured and more than 4,000 buildings were damaged.

17. *New York Times,* January 20 and 24, 1991.

18. *New York Times,* March 7, 1991.

19. *New York Times,* January 21, 1991. The cabinet decision not to respond is discussed in some detail in David Makovsky, "Behind the Velvet Glove," *The Jerusalem Post International Edition,* week ending February 23, 1991, p. 9. See also Jackson Diehl, "Israel's Moment of Truth: Restraint or Retaliation?," *Washington Post,* March 19, 1991.

20. *New York Times,* January 20 and 23, 1991. In late January, the United States Congress formally went on record in support of Israel's posture. On January 24, the Senate approved, by a vote of 99-0, a resolution condemning Iraq's attack on Israel and commending the government of Israel "for its restraint and perseverance." It also reaffirmed "America's commitment to provide Israel with the means to maintain its freedom and security." On January 23, 1991, the House approved by a vote of 416-0 a resolution condemning unprovoked attacks by Iraq on Israel, commending Israel for its restraint, and recognizing Israel's right to defend itself.

21. On February 1, 1991, the Government signed an agreement to allow Moledet to join the coalition. The party advocates the transfer of Palestinians from the West Bank and Gaza Strip. *New York Times,* February 2 and 4, 1991.

22. For example, Yael Dayan noted: "Sometimes there are wars that are necessary in order to attain peace. The Iraqi aggression is an obstacle to Middle East peace." Quoted in *Washington Post,* January 29, 1991. See also the discussion with A.B. Yehoshua in *The Jerusalem Post International Edition,* week ending February 23, 1991, p. 10.

23. See, for example, *New York Times,* February 8, 1991. The matter became an issue of significant proportions. In an interview with Reuters news agency, Israeli Ambassador Zalman Shoval accused the Bush administration of dragging its feet on $400 million in promised loan guarantees for housing for Soviet Jewish immigrants. President Bush called the Ambassador's remarks "outrageous" and Baker similarly complained in a meeting with Shoval. See *Washington Post,* February 15 and 16, 1991, for details. The guarantee was approved on February 20, 1991. See *New York Times,* February 21, 1991. The issue of settlements once again erupted during the post-war peace efforts of Secretary Baker.

24. *New York Times,* January 31, 1991.

25. Quoted in *New York Times,* February 5, 1991.

26. Clearly, full implementation of the Security Council resolution remained a concern. Iraqi responses to the various United Nations resolutions and to the inspection and reporting missions that focused on its non-conventional warfare capability in June and July 1991 raised additional concerns in Israel, as elsewhere, about the future of the region.

27. In a speech on "Israel's Security in the Post Gulf War Era," at a conference on "Regional·Security in the Middle East: Arab and Israeli Concepts of Deterrence and Defense" sponsored by the United States Institute of Peace, the Israeli Ambassador to the United States, Zalman Shoval, noted on June 18, 1991: ". . . . Syria does worry us . . . not only is she a hardliner on most questions relating to Israel and the peace process, . . . , not only does she still harbor terrorists, but her efforts to obtain additional weapons in general, and chemical weapons in particular . . . is very alarming. Meanwhile Syria is busily spending the billions of dollars she received for her rather symbolic adherence to 'Desert Storm' on purchasing missiles from North Korea." Typescript text, p. 6.

28. See, for example, Dore Gold, "Gulf Crisis Implications: New Strategic Roles for the West Bank?," *IDF Journal,* No. 22, (Winter 1991), pp. 15-20, 47-50.

29. This perspective, long held and articulated by Ariel Sharon, was restated after the Gulf war. See, for example, Ariel Sharon, "Jordan is the Palestinian State," *The Jerusalem Post International Edition,* week ending April 13, 1991. Sharon formulates the core issue in this manner: "The only real problem today is the one which has prevailed until now: the secure existence of the Jewish state west of the Jordan alongside the Arab-Palestinian state east of the river."

30. The text of United Nations Security Council Resolution 681 and the statement by the President of the Security Council on December 20, 1990, are in the *New York Times,* December 21, 1990.

31. In a statement delivered to the House Foreign Affairs Committee on February 6, 1991, Baker noted that there would be important challenges facing United States policy in the Middle East and one of these would be "to resume the search for a just peace and real reconciliation for Israel, the Arab states, and Palestinians." Secretary Baker, "Opportunities to Build a New World Order," *US Department of State Dispatch,* February 11, 1991, p. 81.

32. The full text of the speech is in the *New York Times,* March 7, 1991.

33. Department spokesperson Tutweiler as quoted in *New York Times,* April 20, 1991.

34. Quoted in *New York Times,* April 22, 1991.

35. Quoted in *New York Times,* April 22, 1991.

36. Zeev Begin, the son of the late Prime Minister and increasingly an important voice in Likud, has suggested: "It must be understood that the course of the threat to Israel's existence is a ground attack, missiles only increase this threat. . . . It is vital for our security that Israel control the entire area west of the Jordan river, all of 30 kilometers wide. If we defend our country, it will protect our people." See "Strategic Depth Still Counts," *The Jerusalem Post International Edition,* week ending March 16, 1991. In another article, Begin wrote: "We know, of course, that 'geography does not guarantee security,' but we also know that a lack of a minimum of geography guarantees defeat. If a government of Israel declares . . . that it would be ready to shrink itself back to the ridiculous pre-1967 lines 'in exchange for peace,' shortsightedness will have triumphed and peace will have been defeated." See "Chaos Into Order," *The Jerusalem Post International Edition,* week ending March 23, 1991, p. 2.

37. "In our view, the most realistic and reasonable way that could lead to peace in our area is the Camp David agreements. The intent of our peace initiative of May 1989 is this two-track approach: normalization between Israel and Arab countries, and interim arrangements with the Palestinians." Shamir interview in *The Jerusalem Post International Edition,* week ending April 6, 1991, p. 10. See also his interview as published in *Yediot Aharonot,* Pesah supplement, March 29, 1991, pp. 6-7. An English translation is in FBIS, *Daily Report—Near East and South Asia,* April 1, 1991. Zeev Begin has written: "The best vehicle is, not surprisingly, the Framework for Peace in the Middle East as agreed at Camp David in 1978." Zeev Begin, "Towards a Brave New Diplomacy," *The Jerusalem Post International Edition,* p. 8.

38. Quoted in the *Washington Post* and *New York Times,* May 23, 1991. For the text of Baker's prepared statement see Secretary Baker, "Foreign Assistance Funding Proposal for FY 1991," *Dispatch,* Vol. 2, No. 21.

39. Quoted in *New York Times,* May 24, 1991.

15 THE PALESTINIANS AND THE GULF CRISIS

Michael Simpson

The Gulf crisis was a political turning point that had a more far-reaching impact on the Palestinian Arabs than any event since the rise of the PLO in the period following the 1967 Arab-Israeli War. It created an unprecedented cleavage between the Palestine Liberation Organization (PLO) and the Arab oil-producing countries of the Gulf. In the aftermath of the war, the international diplomatic position of the PLO became too weak to sustain the organization's previous policies of insisting that all Arab-Israeli negotiations on the Palestinian issue must include the PLO directly as representative of the Palestinian people, and must be aimed at obtaining a Palestinian state, not at interim measures. In the most significant shift of an Arab position since the Sadat era, Palestinian negotiators acceptable to Israel took part in direct negotiations with Israel that were sponsored by the United States and approved by the PLO. The negotiations aimed at an agreement on autonomy in the Israeli-occupied West Bank and Gaza Strip.

Socially and economically, the crisis created a major new wave of Palestinian refugees, whose impact was most acutely felt in Jordan. It put an end to an era in which there was a large, flourishing and affluent Palestinian community in Kuwait, and diminished the size and status of Palestinian communities elsewhere in the Gulf oil-producing countries. The effects of the cut in Palestinian remittances and aid offered by Gulf states, and the new barriers to the employment of Palestinians in the Gulf region, were felt by Palestinian communities everywhere.

The Iraqi Invasion of Kuwait

When Iraqi troops invaded Kuwait on August 2, 1990, the first response of the PLO was its usual reaction to circumstances in which allies found themselves in conflict (as had happened when Iraq invaded Iran ten years earlier)—to adopt a position of official neutrality and try to position itself to become an intermediary. On August 3, at an Arab League Council of Foreign Ministers meeting, the PLO abstained (along with Jordan, Yemen, Sudan and Mauritania) during a vote on a resolution condemning the Iraqi invasion. Arafat meanwhile urged Arab mediation and offered the services of the PLO, as an organization that had enjoyed good relations with both Iraq and Kuwait prior to the invasion. The desired outcome was clearly an Iraqi withdrawal for which the PLO could obtain some credit and which would catapult the PLO to a central role in inter-Arab politics.

It soon became clear, however, that this was a conflict with no middle ground. Hints by Iraq that it would be willing to withdraw were riddled with ambiguities or made dependent on unlikely circumstances;[1] as a result, Iraq's Gulf neighbors had little hope that inter-Arab diplomacy alone could restore Kuwaiti sovereignty by inducing a voluntary Iraqi withdrawal. The fears provoked by the invasion in the governments of oil-producing Gulf countries and the United States and its western allies led to the formation of an international coalition against Iraq that was so powerful that its members had no inclination to compromise on their basic objectives: Iraqi withdrawal, the return of the ruling Sabah family, and the establishment of a new balance of power in the Gulf that would deter future Iraqi governments from any repeat effort to invade a Gulf neighbor.[1]

An economic and trade embargo was imposed on Iraq by the UN Security Council on August 6. After a visit by US Secretary of Defense Richard Cheney to Saudi Arabia, in which he urged a strong response and pledged a massive American military commitment, it was announced on August 7 that Saudi Arabia and the United States had agreed that the US would dispatch troops and planes to Saudi territory. On August 8, thousands of US troops took up position in Saudi Arabia. Egypt also promised to send troops to Saudi Arabia.

This transformation of the conflict pitted an alliance of American and Arab troops against a major Arab country for the first time. The presence of American troops in the region divided the Arab world into two camps. On the one side were the GCC countries, backed by the governments of Egypt and Syria. The GCC countries maintained that Iraq's invasion of Kuwait had to be countered by the strongest possible show of force, and that the overwhelming power of the United States made it the logical centerpiece of this coalition. On the other side were those who argued that it was an overriding factor that western troops should never be invited into a conflict opposing Arab against Arab. In this view, the political history of the Arab world in the twentieth century had been dominated by the drive for direct and indirect independence from western powers, and their renewed military involvement in the region would be an unacceptable reversal of this trend. This was the predominant position in the PLO and the Palestinian community at large.

After the announcement that American troops would be dispatched to Saudi Arabia, an emergency Arab League summit took place on August 10. At these meetings, the Gulf countries won a majority of 12 out of 21 members in support of a resolution endorsing their policies. Iraq, Libya and the PLO voted against the resolution; Yemen and Algeria abstained; and Jordan, Sudan and Mauritania expressed reservations, while Tunisia was not present.

Sympathy for the Iraqi position in the Palestinian community was greatly increased on August 12, when Saddam Hussein made a speech urging that the Gulf crisis be linked to the Arab-Israeli conflict in international diplomacy. He urged that all "issues of occupation" in the Middle East should be resolved, and that the first step should be "the immediate and unconditional withdrawal of Israel from the occupied Arab territories in Palestine, Syria and Lebanon." This should be followed by "Syria's withdrawal from Lebanon," and then by "a withdrawal between Iraq and Iran." Finally (and significantly more ambiguously), there should be a "formulation of arrangements for the situation in Kuwait" which should include "taking into consideration the historical rights of Iraq in its territory and the Kuwaiti people's choice." The withdrawals should be in order of the date of occupation, beginning with the oldest, and the same sanctions that had been imposed on Iraq by the UN Security Council should be imposed on any country that refused to withdraw.[2]

This initiative, which suddenly catapulted the Palestinian issue to the center of international attention, had the clear purpose of allowing Saddam Hussein to use the issue as a card in his international diplomacy. Among Palestinians, it generated excitement and enthusiasm as a reminder to the world that Palestinians had been under occupation for years without effective international attention being given to their situation. The PLO leadership also saw the statement as a means of moving the PLO back to center stage by involving the Palestinian cause in the issue and perhaps facilitating a role for the PLO in mediating the Gulf conflict.

Reasons for the PLO Stance

In this and subsequent actions, Arafat and leaders of the PLO were keenly aware of the currents of Palestinian politics. As had been demonstrated on many previous occasions involving major PLO decisions—involvement in the war in Lebanon, the reaction to Camp David, or the long process of change before accepting UN Security Council 242—Arafat was always unwilling to alienate strong blocs of Palestinian activists. In the earlier days of the PLO, when his movement Fateh had risen to power, he had done much to encourage the atmosphere of militant resistance that pervaded the political discourse of Palestinian nationalism. Even though Arafat finally became the Palestinian leader who accepted Resolution 242, he was always eager to show Palestinian militants that he was no enemy of theirs. Within Arafat's nationalistic constituency, there was passionate opposition to any American military intervention in the Middle East. The movements on the left of the PLO supported Iraq: the leader of the Popular Front for the Liberation of Palestine, George Habbash, declared that the Iraqi invasion had been justified by Kuwaiti economic provocations, and the Democratic Front for the Liberation of Palestine (DFLP) vehemently condemned the alliance between the Gulf states and the United States. More broadly, there was strong and visible opposition to the American military intervention and to the position adopted by the GCC countries among Palestinian communities in the occupied territories, in Lebanon and in Jordan, where an atmosphere of revived political freedom enabled active Palestinian self-expression. Iraq was regarded by Palestinian activists as the most important Arab country militarily, one that had always expressed strong support for the Palestinians and adopted a confrontationist stand toward Israel. The United States had consistently supported Israel against the Palestinians, and it was deemed unthinkable for Palestinians to take the side of a US-led coalition against Iraq. Moreover, the invasion of Kuwait occurred at an international conjuncture when Iraq was attracting increased attention among Palestinians, and the United States was particularly unpopular. In April, in an outburst of fiery rhetoric, Saddam Hussein had declared that if Israel attacked Iraq, he "would burn half of Israel"—an attitude sure to mobilize militants in the Palestinian community. At the same time, moderates within the PLO were ceasing to believe that there would be any results from a move which they had encouraged—the PLO-US dialogue, which had been broken off by the US after Arafat had refused to condemn an attempted naval raid on Israel by the Palestine Liberation Front, a pro-Iraqi faction of the PLO led by Abu al-Abbas. There was considerable resentment in PLO ranks that the major concession made by the PLO in 1988 of accepting UN Security Council resolution 242 had not been met by either US or Israeli concessions on

Palestinian self-determination. This Palestinian resentment was also expressed against Arab allies of the US—Egypt and Saudi Arabia— who had argued that a moderate PLO position would produce benefits for the Palestinians.

Although all these factors played a role, however, they do not adequately explain the PLO stance. Whatever the factors making for a rapprochement between the PLO and Iraq, the PLO also had major interests in maintaining good relations with the governments of the Gulf countries. All had provided the PLO with invaluable financial support that had helped the PLO not only to finance itself but also to set itself up as an embryonic state which sponsored economic enterprises, operated a major welfare system and financed education among Palestinians, all of them major factors bolstering PLO ascendancy in the Palestinian community. The diplomatic backing of the Gulf countries, underpinned by their economic power, had also been influential in creating widespread international diplomatic support for the PLO. This had been visible in the United Nations, and had played an important role in the European Economic Community's recognition of the importance of Palestinian rights.

In addition to these diplomatic considerations, the Palestinian communities in the Gulf were the most prosperous Palestinian communities, consisting mainly of educated people who had pulled themselves up in the world, and had surmounted refugee status. They were able, through their remittances, to offer some relief to the acute problems faced by the Palestinian people. Admittedly, the economic downturn in the Gulf in the 1980s had caused resentment among Palestinians at the ease with which they could lose jobs in the Gulf countries, and be made to return to poorer parts of the Arab world at short notice. However, the Palestinian communities in the Gulf were so large and economically comfortable that it could reasonably have been argued that the maintenance of their economic prosperity and their presence in the Gulf region was a vital Palestinian interest. It was not treated as such in PLO policy making, because calculations of this kind ran counter to the passions and political enthusiasm of most PLO activists.

The key to understanding the Palestinian reaction does not lie in the vicissitudes of international diplomacy immediately prior to the invasion of Kuwait. Much more important was the militant orientation of PLO politics, with its conviction that salvation lay in building up a strong Arab military front against Israel, and that continued US support for Israel should be met by Arab measures against the United

States, including the use of oil as a means of pressure. The existing Arab order was seen as weak and ineffective in its support for the Palestinians, and the conservative oil producers were widely blamed by Palestinian activists (even though the formal public diplomacy of the PLO avoided criticism of the Gulf states) for treating good relations with the United States as more important than the Palestinian cause.

Palestinian militance had a long history, nourished by the acute deprivation experienced by the Palestinian people. Palestinian life was still overshadowed by the 1948-49 Arab-Israeli war, when over 60 percent of the Palestinian population became refugees dispossessed by the State of Israel and not allowed to return to their homes and villages in the part of Palestine that became Israel. It is extraordinary for such high proportions of a distinct people demanding independence to be dispossessed. The political consciousness of Palestinians was inevitably dominated by rebellion against their situation of dispossession, homelessness, poverty, widespread unemployment, economic insecurity, the destructive effects of war, and the denial of independence. Education was to prove the path to survival, and Palestinians were one of the most educated communities of the Middle East, but even educated and skilled Palestinians faced enormous insecurities as a result of problems of obtaining work permits or being kept on short-term contracts or offered marginal, insecure jobs in the Arab world. The passage of time made Palestinians more, not less, convinced that their situation could only be decisively improved by Palestinian self-determination and a Palestinian homeland.

In the Palestinian refugee camps and exile communities in the Arab world, the dream of returning to Palestine became an ideal that contrasted sharply with the harsh realities that Palestinians so often faced in everyday life. Most refugees in 1949 were peasants without land who found themselves in countries without extra cultivable land for them; they dreamed of a return that would end their landlessness. For them, the State of Israel was simply a hostile power that had violently dispossessed and uprooted them, and denied them the right of return. Most other Palestinians also saw a return to Palestine as their road to a normal life, whether they were unskilled laborers competing in Arab labor markets which already had a surplus of unskilled labor; small businessmen and shopkeepers without capital or licenses to start up an enterprise; or professionals dependent on work permits from governments that would favor their own qualified citizens. Yet the power of the image of Palestine went far beyond utilitarian concerns of improving the Palestinian economic situation.

As is typical of other Eastern Mediterranean societies, the villages and towns Palestinians came from were powerful emotional anchors of their sense of identity. In refugee camps, entire villages of Palestinians often settled in the same place, so that people were living next to the same neighbors and extended family members they had in Palestine. Palestinian songs nostalgically exalted the lost homes and land; Palestinian writing, whether journalism or fiction, was dominated by the pains of exile and an overpowering sense of being the victims of injustice; and Palestinian politics focused avidly on a return to Palestine. The idea of Palestine invoked dreams, patriotism, nostalgia, yearning and passion throughout the Palestinian diaspora.

Palestinian politics became a crusade. The basic aspirations of a mass return to Palestine and the recovery of the lost land were elevated to the level of the sacred, remaining for decades almost completely beyond political criticism. In the 1960s, the PLO became the militant political movement that embodied these aspirations and asserted them as supreme goals in print, on radio, and in the political mobilization of Palestinians everywhere. Most of the refugees in whose camps the PLO based itself were refugees from the Palestinian territories that had become part of Israel in 1948; they were not enthusiastic about solutions that would not involve their return to these territories, and supported the position voiced by the PLO after the 1967 war demanding the replacement of Israel by a proposed Palestinian state that was described as non-sectarian and democratic, but whose precise political structure was never clearly defined. Just as the aims of return and recovery of the land were treated as sacred, those who supported them (Arab nationalists and their international supporters) were exalted as virtuous, those who opposed them (several western countries) were deemed malicious or misled, and those who were considered obliged to support Palestinian goals but appeared lacking in enthusiasm (many of the conservative Arab governments, unwilling to adopt a confrontationist attitude to the United States) were deemed ineffective.

Another, more pragmatic, trend also developed within the PLO after the 1967 war, but for a long time its growth was slow. The trend was characterized by advocacy of the idea of a peace settlement with Israel that would create a Palestinian state limited to the West Bank and Gaza Strip without the Palestinian territories that had become Israel in 1948. This idea gained a number of influential adherents after the 1973 Arab-Israeli war. However, pragmatists in the Palestinian community faced major problems. On the one hand, the militant atmosphere of Palestinian politics forced them to the margins, looking for avenues of quiet persuasion of the leadership away from the emotions and mass mobilization of PLO politics. There was no influential pragmatic tradition in Palestinian politics, and the movements that Palestinians admired—Vietnam and Algeria were the most popular in Palestinian political literature—were movements of armed struggle that had fought relentlessly for independence without territorial compromise. On the other hand, the adamant refusal of successive Israeli governments to countenance peace agreements that would offer even Palestinian moderates their minimum needs—a West Bank/ Gaza Strip state at peace with Israel—meant that the pragmatists appeared unable to find Israeli partners for their proposed peace settlement. Moreover, as the Palestinian pragmatic position acquired more adherents in the mid-1970s, the position of the Israeli government moved further away from Palestinian pragmatists, and, after the election of the right-wing Likud Party in 1977, became one of outright annexation of the West Bank and Gaza. Pragmatism appeared to be a trend incapable of delivering results, with neither Palestinian militants nor mainstream Israelis supportive of pragmatic Palestinian proposals.

The continued militant orientation of Palestinian politics created a major division between the PLO and a number of Arab governments. After the 1967 war, three of the four Arab governments bordering Israel accepted Security Council resolution 242, which urged a land-for-peace exchange between Arab states and Israel, and referred to Palestinians only as refugees whose situation required a solution. Syria, the fourth and most militant Arab government bordering Israel, accepted Security Council Resolution 242 in 1974, after the next Arab-Israeli war; yet it was more than fourteen years later that the PLO finally accepted the same resolution, interpreting the solution to the refugee problem as requiring Palestinian self-determination. The tension between the Palestinian tactics of armed struggle and the interests of Arab states bordering Israel was reflected in the fact that between 1967 and 1978, the armies of three of the four states bordering Israel fought the PLO militarily to try to control it (Jordan in 1970-71, Syria in 1976 and Lebanon more sporadically between 1969 and 1975). The fourth state, Egypt, made a separate peace with Israel.

The behavior of these Arab states was particularly troubling to Palestinian political activists because the maximalist aims of the PLO, and its strategy of armed resistance, required strong support from neighboring countries, as well as the willingness of Arab oil-producing countries to use their oil and financial resources as sources of pressure on the West, especially the United States. Although the

PLO gained power and popularity among Palestinians by emphasizing its specifically Palestinian character, Palestinian nationalism incorporated a strong pan-Arab element. Palestinians believed that the Palestine cause was one that had such strong support among the Arab masses that the failure of Arab governments to promote it strongly in line with the aspirations of the PLO could lead to their overthrow. This assumption had entered Palestinian political thought in the decade after the 1948-49 war, when military coups overthrew the Syrian, Egyptian and Iraqi *anciens regimes* that had been defeated; in Jordan, King Abdallah was assassinated by a Palestinian. The new, nationalist Syrian, Egyptian and Iraqi governments had then made the Palestinian cause and their commitment to it a central theme in their attempts to mobilize support in their own countries and the wider Arab world.

Even after the defeat of 1967, the political discourse of almost all Arab governments and media was strongly pro-Palestinian. Revolutions in Libya in 1969 and Iran in 1978 produced governments which made the Palestinian cause an important theme of their political mobilization, largely as Arab nationalist governments had done before the 1967 war. These developments were sufficient to make Palestinians feel that their cause was still a live, burning issue in the Arab and Islamic worlds.

In dealing with the failure of Arab governments neighboring Israel to support the Palestinian struggle, and the reluctance of the oil-producing states to make oil a weapon aganst the United States after the 1973 embargo, Palestinian militants maintained their original faith and came to the conclusion that these were temporary aberrations from a long-term trend that would favor the Palestinians. The repressiveness, unpopularity and instability of almost all Arab governments was a favorite conversation topic among Palestinians in Beirut and later Tunis, when PLO headquarters moved there after the 1982 Israeli invasion of Lebanon. Future political changes in the Arab world, in which regimes would be replaced by more popularly-rooted and therefore (it was believed) pro-Palestinian governments, were confidently predicted.

The Iraqi invasion of Kuwait and the American response to it created the sense among Palestinians that a turning point had been reached—one that would either bring about major political changes in the Arab world, or decisively confirm the trends that had been working against Palestinian nationalism, requiring major Palestinian adjustment to the new situation. Arabs had to take sides on whether they wanted a long-term military presence of the United States in the region, with its accompanying political influence on most of the states controlling Arab oil resources. They had to decide whether they were willing to participate in a US-led war against a strong Arab military power with a pro-Palestinian posture.

Although the American build-up seemed daunting, some Palestinians argued that the United States would avoid a military confrontation, opening the door to an eventual negotiated settlement, in which the Palestinian cause might be addressed. Others maintained that in the event of a war, the Iraqi army might be able to hold out. A more widespread argument was that Iraq might perform well enough in a war or attract such political sympathy in the Arab world that a new Arab political era might be launched, rather as had happened when Nasser had extricated a political victory from military defeat by Britain, France and Israel in 1956. Since nobody knew the future anyway, judgments about the likely political outcome of the crisis were often made in line with the way people thought the world worked and in which history was headed.

The Palestinian environment was one that exalted change of the established order and where the Palestinian movement was seen as part of a future tide of change. The thought that the outcome of the crisis might be a new Arab political situation favorable to the Palestinian cause appealed to the wavelength of Palestinian activists far more than the idea of calculating, self-interested diplomacy in support of a US-dominated coalition against a powerful supporter of the Palestinian cause. Palestinians who feared catastrophe were countered with the argument that they might be backing away from precisely the turning point and new political era in Arab history that Palestinians had anticipated for years.

Guided by these considerations, the PLO rejected the strategy that would have protected its Gulf interests—one of condemning Iraq and offering moral and diplomatic support for Kuwait—and instead adopted an outright no-win policy that was sure to destroy Palestinian relations with the Gulf. After the active American intervention on the side of Kuwait, it was clear that Iraq would not be able to hold on to Kuwait and rejoin the international community. If Iraq continued its occupation of Kuwait, even if it was not removed by military force, the sanctions would impoverish the Palestinian community there and eventually remove it as a significant community of the Palestinian diaspora. The PLO's sympathy for Iraq would generate anti-Palestinian feelings throughout the Gulf, and make it much more difficult for Palestinian communities to prosper there. Any other likely solution—whether the removal of Iraq by force or sanctions, or its voluntary withdrawal—

would restore sovereignty to the Kuwait government, and after the PLO's stance on the Gulf crisis, the Palestinian community was sure to become a target of Kuwaiti reprisals. Even if political upheavals happened in the Arab world, they were most likely to take place outside the Gulf region, leaving the Arab world torn by a major split, and the Palestinian cause suffering the huge obstacles of a withdrawal of Gulf support and international sympathy.

Leaders of Palestinian communities in the Gulf were particularly concerned about the prospects of a split between the Palestinians and the Gulf states. On August 20, Jaweed al-Ghussein, Chairman of the Palestine National Fund and a member of the PLO Executive Committee, declared that "it is essential to get the Iraqi forces out of Kuwait. The occupation is illegal. It is in the interests of Iraq and the Arab world for the Iraqi forces to withdraw."[3] He also stated that "the Palestinian people, without exception, stand against the occupation of fraternal Kuwait."[4] In Kuwait itself, a postwar study by a professor at Kuwait University found that "most Palestinians remained loyal to Kuwait."[5] Early in the occupation, the Kuwait office of Yasser Arafat's Fateh movement put out a flier strongly criticizing the occupation and its consequences.[6] Nevertheless, the Iraqi occupying authorities attempted to court Palestinians, in the hope of using them to assist the occupation. Arafat rejected requests for public demonstrations by Palestinians in Kuwait in support of Iraq, though smaller Palestinian organizations sponsored by Iraq were used to man checkpoints and assist the Iraqi army. In addition, the Iraqi press, radio and television played up every instance of support from Palestinians anywhere, with a regular stream of interviews with pro-Iraqi Palestinian politicians, and repeated assertions by Iraqi commentators that Iraq and the Palestinian cause were inextricably linked. All of this was designed to create the impression that Palestinians were driven by deeply-felt, passionate support for Iraq in its policy during the crisis.

In the countries of the Gulf, there was an intense increase in anti-Palestinian feeling. The Gulf countries had a strong record of offering financial and diplomatic support to the PLO mainstream led by Yasser Arafat. Kuwait in particular had been a major source of support. Arafat himself, and other leaders of his Fateh movement, had spent many years working in Kuwait, which had been one of the rare Arab countries where Palestinians could operate in relative freedom. The government had given financial support to the PLO and allowed Fateh to levy taxes on the Palestinians in the country. Support for the population of the West Bank and Gaza had come from government, non-profit and private sectors of the Kuwaiti community. Even if the Palestinian situation did not permit significant practical support, Kuwaitis expected at least the same kind of moral support for the Kuwaiti cause when Kuwait was occupied. In its public pronouncements about the Palestinian situation, the PLO had frequently emphasized the total unacceptability of foreign occupation and the right to use whatever means were necessary, including force, to end it. Its refusal to condemn Iraq, to express support for Kuwaitis under occupation, or to endorse the Kuwaiti right to use all available means to end occupation was seen in the Gulf countries as extraordinarily hypocritical.

The Road to War

In the months after the invasion, international measures of increasing intensity were taken against Iraq. During this time, Palestinian policy remained essentially unchanged. On the one hand, the PLO emphasized that Saddam Hussein would have to withdraw, and strong support was offered for the idea of Arab mediation efforts to bring this about. On the other, the PLO condemned the presence of American troops in Saudi Arabia, but refused to condemn Iraq or express solidarity with the suffering of the Kuwaiti people under occupation. It rejected the international boycott, and supported efforts to link a solution to the Gulf crisis with progress toward a solution of the Palestinian problem. Its hope was that there would be a negotiated solution to the crisis providing for an Iraqi withdrawal, and that at some point it would use its good offices to help to persuade Saddam Hussein to accept it, eventually perhaps being able to make Gulf rulers believe that it had not been such a bad thing after all for the PLO to maintain good relations with Saddam throughout the crisis.

In the autumn of 1990, major international efforts were made to bring about a negotiated settlement to the conflict in which Iraq would withdraw from Kuwait. Throughout the West, there was concern about the idea of a war being fought in the region of the world's vulnerable principal oil supply, and about the damage and casualties that would result. Opinion polls showed that the United States public was reluctant to tolerate heavy American casualties in the event of a war. The overriding requirement of any negotiated settlement, however, was that Saddam Hussein should withdraw, and the Iraqi leader was not willing to specify any realistic circumstances under which he was willing to make this move. He was willing to make gestures like the release of western hostages taken by Iraq in Kuwait; but he would not even pretend to be willing to withdraw as a ploy or gambit designed to split the coalition against him. The repeated visits to Iraq by a variety of diplomats from different countries failed to move him; instead, they created a feeling of pessimism in the capitals of the world that there could ever be a negotiated solution.

The United States stepped up its attempts to tighten international measures against Iraq and apply increased pressure. On November 8, 1991, President Bush announced a major new deployment of troops to the Gulf that would raise their number to about 400,000. In the United Nations, the Soviet Union was persuaded to back a resolution supporting the use of force against Iraq. As the cohesion of international attempts to pressure Iraq increased, and Saddam's position remained unyielding, American public opinion began to shift toward the possibility of a military solution. In Congress, however, there was still a great deal of concern about the prospect of a war, especially if it were prosecuted by the President without the consent of Congress.

Hopes for a negotiated solution rose when the United States announced early in December that Secretary of State Baker was willing to go to Baghdad to meet. The two sides could not, however, agree on the arrangements for the meeting during December, and these procedural disagreements seemed to reflect a deeper unwillingness by either side to soften its position.

As the deadline grew closer, there was increased concern in the PLO about the Iraqi position. Leaders like Salah Khalaf were increasingly critical of the pro-Iraq orientation of the organization. Late in December, PLO officials were urging Iraq to fall back on an option that did not require agreement with the US, that of making a unilateral withdrawal from most of Kuwait, in the hope that the likelihood of American military operations would be reduced if they were aimed solely at recovering the remaining area. On December 26, 1990, the Voice of Palestine in Algiers urged Iraq to take the opportunity to "withdraw from Kuwait" and stated that the Arab masses hoped "that Iraq will accept a principled withdrawal from Kuwait in order to deprive the foreign forces in the Gulf of the opportunity to ignite the war at the end of the international ultimatum."[7] At the same time, the PLO continued to oppose the launching of a war against Iraq, and Arafat's New Year message of 1991 described "the threats aimed at destroying Iraqi military and technical capability because it is set to break the barrier of Israeli superiority over our Arab nation" as a danger "threatening the existence of our Arab nation."[8]

The final failure of attempts at negotiations occurred in Geneva when Baker and Aziz met on January 9, 1991 in a dramatic context, six days before the UN ultimatum was to expire and only three days before decisive US Senate and House votes on whether to authorize the use of force against Iraq. Baker was adamant that Iraq must withdraw its troops in line with United Nations resolutions, and that the United States would accept no linkage of the Gulf issue with the Palestinian issue. Aziz repeated the standard Iraqi position. In his public statement after the meeting, he attempted to reach beyond the governments and diplomats of the world, and appeal to the Arab peoples, by talking primarily about the Palestinian problem, not about the issue of Iraqi withdrawal from Kuwait. On January 12, the Senate voted by the narrow margin of 52 to 47 to grant the President authority to use force against Iraq to remove its troops from Kuwait; the House vote was 250 to 183.

Military conflict had become inevitable. Within the PLO, as elsewhere, it was widely accepted that the United States had the overwhelming power needed to win the war. What was still an open question was whether Iraqi resistance would be strong enough, and American casualties high enough, to make the victory a Pyrrhic one, following which the United States might be much less likely ever to intervene in the Gulf again; and whether the example of the United States fighting an uneven battle against a leading Arab power would incite massive anti-American feeling throughout the Arab world that could lead to a shake-up of the existing Arab order.

Palestinian communities throughout the Arab world had been moved by the pro-Palestinian declarations of Tariq Aziz at his Geneva meeting with Baker. When war broke out, the PLO and Palestinian media vigorously attacked the United States, and expressed solidarity with Iraq. Two days after the war began, Iraq began to bombard Israel with Scud missiles, causing enthusiasm among Palestinians and movements supporting them in the Arab world. If the hope was that these attacks would provide a de facto linkage between the issues of the Gulf and the Palestine problem, causing widespread revolt in the Arab world against the United States and its Arab allies, this hope was soon disappointed. Under strong American pressure, Israel took the unprecedented step of not retaliating, and even the Patriot anti-missile protection of Israeli cities was conducted by American crews. The war, as it evolved, took the form of a worst-case-scenario for militant Arab nationalists. The incessant US aerial bombardments of dug-in Iraqi troops for a period of over one month so demoralized and disabled them as a fighting force that they were unable to put up effective resistance in the ground war, which became a rout.

Social and Economic Effects of the Gulf Crisis

In addition to being a political setback, the Gulf crisis was an economic catastrophe for the Palestinian community. It created a major new Palestinian refugee problem. Before the crisis, there were 400,000 Palestinians in Kuwait; they constituted one of the most affluent Palestinian communities. Their remittances to their families and extended families in other parts of the Arab world were an extremely significant source of revenues, and had a multiplier effect stimulating economic development among Palestinian communities throughout the Arab world.

The Gulf war put an end to the flourishing Palestinian community in Kuwait. Most members of the community left during the Iraqi occupation; others were subsequently denied the renewal of work permits or otherwise ordered to leave by the returning Kuwait government, leaving only a small proportion of the former community in Kuwait. Because the Kuwaiti dinar ceased to be a viable currency during the Iraqi occupation, there was no means of converting savings into currency of equivalent value until after the Gulf war, when the restored Kuwaiti government allowed Palestinians who had left the country to withdraw funds remaining in banks in Kuwait. In addition, the war resulted in a deterioration of the status of Palestinians throughout the Gulf, sparking a wave of non-renewal of work permits and denial of entry visas. The impact of these measures in the short, medium and long terms was sure to be severe because of the great importance of the remittances to the Palestinian community at large.

Parallel with the problems encountered by the Palestinian communities in the Gulf was the economic effect of the rift between the Gulf countries, on one hand, and Jordan and the PLO, on the other. The loss of aid was a major blow to the PLO. It also greatly worsened the situation in Jordan, where most refugees from the Gulf crisis had settled, placing demands on that country's absorptive capacity which it could not meet. The result was enormous pressure on Jordan's public services, ranging from the supply of water and utilities to education, a rapid inflation as the new surge in population outpaced the supply of goods and services, and the creation of a mood of economic desperation as a result of a rise in the already extreme unemployment rate. In a situation where Jordan needed foreign aid as never before, its rift with the Gulf cut off its most important source of this aid.

In the occupied territories, the crisis severely disrupted the economy. Apart from the pressures on employment opportunities caused by the return of residents from Kuwait, the territories suffered a decline in transfers from the Gulf. Remittances from Kuwait had been estimated at about $100 million in 1989;[9] this source of revenue vanished. Also important was the decline of the assistance that had been given by governments of the Gulf to public and non-profit institutions in the occupied territories, amounting to about $120 million in 1989.[10] During the crisis, the borders of Saudi Arabia were closed to exports via Jordan, and there was no easy way of getting Palestinian produce into other Gulf markets. The result was the loss of tens of millions of dollars of exports.

When the war began,[11] a massive, round-the-clock, indefinite curfew was imposed on the occupied territories as of January 16. Over 100,000 Palestinians were banned from commuting to jobs in Israel, and left without income. The movement of food, medicine and other supplies was constrained, and the transportation of goods and people was paralyzed. The transfer of funds to the territories was also frozen. Financial resources in the territories were so depleted that when food and dairy products were allowed to be sold, they found far fewer buyers than normal, and prices dipped severely. Even in more prosperous places like Bethlehem, the percentage of families below the poverty line was estimated by the mayor as 50 percent. The first days of the curfew were also an important period for the harvesting of winter crops, and sowing of summer crops; these processes were massively disrupted. Regular irrigation, greenhouse farming and the grazing of animals were all seriously impeded. The curfew was partially lifted in February and wholly lifted by the end of March, and Palestinians were able to return to work, usually at menial jobs which Israeli Jews had been unwilling to fill during the curfew. However, the overall costs for the local economy were enormous, and have been estimated in the $200-$400 million range. Key industries such as tourism were particularly hard-hit as the Gulf war kept tourists away from the Middle East.

This crisis exacerbated a deterioration that had already begun to take place in the economy of the occupied territories following the outbreak of the *intifada*. Gross Domestic Product in the occupied territories declined by an average annual rate in constant prices of 12 percent over the three-year period 1988-1990. On a per capita basis, in the occupied territories GNP in constant prices fell from $1,756 in 1987 to $1,147 in 1990.

The economic problems of the occupied territories that were so acute during the Gulf war revived a long-standing Palestinian concern about the vulnerability of the economic structure of the occupied territories. Israeli occupation measures had made the economic lives of the population highly dependent on the number of inhabitants working in Israel. The economic development of the occupied territories was disadvantaged by a lack of control of the major resources of the territories and by a tight Israeli system of economic control that prevented the free management of the economy of the territories. The Israeli authorities allocated a greater *per capita* proportion of water to the Jewish settler population than to the Arab population, and diverted a substantial part of West Bank water to Israel, leaving the Arab population with a shortage of water for agricultural development. A number of Israeli governmental measures, such as the imposition of barriers preventing Palestinian products from entering Israeli markets, and the tight regulation of licences, impeded the development of the local West Bank and Gaza economy. Impacting an already structurally weak economy, the Gulf crisis created a very serious situation in the occupied territories, and generated strong feelings among the population that some means must be found of improving their condition.

The PLO and American Postwar Policy

In the aftermath of the Gulf war, the PLO found its international power and prestige at their lowest ebb since the Arab League's Rabat Summit of 1974 had recognized the organization as the sole legitimate representative of the Palestinian people. The united Arab support for the PLO that had been a mainstay of its diplomacy since 1974 no longer existed. The wider international community no longer regarded support for the PLO as a necessary ingredient of good relations with oil-producing countries. Moreover, the PLO's failure to condemn Iraq's occupation of Kuwait, combined with enthusiastic Palestinian demonstrations in favor of Iraq, had lost it a great deal of international sympathy among those who had sympathized with the Palestinian argument that no people should ever be subjected to the occupation of their territory and that the denial of self-determination was intolerable.

The United States made it clear that the PLO would not be included in the peace negotiations that it planned to sponsor. Palestinians could be represented, but would be expected to fall in line with the Camp David agreements and participate in negotiations for autonomy that would defer the issue of Palestinian self-determination for subsequent negotiation years later. It soon became clear that the United States had moved closer to the Israeli position on two important issues on which it had backed Palestinian demands in discussions with Israel a year earlier. Under the new terms proposed for negotiations, only Palestinians currently living in the occupied territories would be allowed to participate, and those living in Jerusalem would be excluded.

For about six months after the Gulf war, leading up to the holding of the PLO National Council in September, the issue of whether Palestinians should join peace talks on US terms was actively debated in Palestinian circles.

The traditional PLO position was that the PLO was the sole legitimate representative of the Palestinian people. The major leaders of the PLO had been the Palestinian political leadership for over 20 years: recognition had been their consistent demand, and was not one they would give up lightly. Moreover, a great deal of PLO energy had been committed to making the idea of the PLO's representivity more than a political slogan, by rooting the PLO sufficently broadly in the Palestinian community that most Palestinians genuinely regarded it as their leadership. PLO activities went far beyond measures to mobilize Palestinians for armed struggle against Israel, and included economic, educational and welfare institutions. The movement had been careful to incorporate most of the diverse trends of thought held by Palestinians. One wing consisted of moderates urging a Palestinian state on the West Bank and Gaza Strip that would make peace with Israel; several members of Arafat's movement, Fateh, had given their lives for this belief, assassinated by more militant Palestinians. The members of the leading deliberative body of the PLO, the Palestine National Council, although chosen by the PLO Executive Committee, included many distinguished independent Palestinians who were not members of the PLO's constituent resistance movements. On the Left, Arafat tolerated and accommodated a wide variety of smaller groups with divergent militant opinions, on the assumption that it was essential to preserve the PLO from disunity.

Within the PLO, there was widespread scepticism about whether any process sponsored by the United States could lead to progress toward a significant autonomy in the occupied territories, let alone the broader Palestinian aim of self-determination. To accept the process, it was argued, would consign the PLO to inactivity, always a dangerous situation for a political movement. Military activities would have to be suspended, yet the PLO would not be allowed to participate actively in the negotiations. If the PLO were on the sidelines and no longer the major actor for a long period, it risked being regarded as irrelevant. It was in danger of being outflanked among militants by Hamas, the Islamic resistance movement that had gathered strength in recent years, and rejected the idea of autonomy negotiations. After more than twenty years of armed struggle with very ambitious aims, PLO activists found their organization's exclusion from participation in a process falling well short of traditional Palestinian aims to be humiliating.

Powerful arguments were also brought for participation in the negotiations. Among these was the belief that the Palestinian situation was so precarious that there was a need to pursue any path that might improve it. There was no alternative peaceful process in the foreseeable future with any realistic chance of success. There was no military option in a situation where the Arab world was divided, and the Soviet Union was backing rapidly away from its former position as the international supporter of Arab militance. The defeat of Iraq had devastated one of the most powerful Arab nationalist countries. If there was no Palestinian participation in the peace process, there would be no peace process. This, however, meant that Israel's Likud government would have a free hand to continue its policies aimed at annexing the occupied territories, while continuing to secure American aid by blaming the Palestinians for the lack of peace talks. Moreover, as the PLO had entrenched itself so deeply as the leadership of the Palestinians, it was argued that even if the members of any Palestinian negotiating team excluded known members of the PLO, any agreement reached would have to be undertaken in consultation with, and with the agreement of, the PLO.

The arguments for participation received added weight from the fact that the locus of Palestinian politics had shifted in ways that favored a pragmatic approach. Ten years earlier, the principal base of the PLO had been in Lebanon, in refugee camps inhabited by Palestinians who had been dispossessed in 1948, and who had no direct stake in a settlement that focused on the establishment of a state in the West Bank and Gaza Strip. Financially, the PLO had depended heavily on communities in the GCC countries, which tended to be loyal to whatever policy the PLO leadership thought appropriate. With the loss of its position in Lebanon, and now the loss of the Gulf as a major source of support, the PLO was more dependent on and responsive to two Palestinian communities that had become increasingly important in the years immediately preceding the Gulf crisis. One was the Palestinian community in the West Bank and Gaza, which had moved to the forefront of Palestinian politics through its *intifada*. The second was the Palestinian community in Jordan, which had recently enjoyed substantial freedom of expression and political support as a result of democratization in the country, and had been favorably impressed by King Hussein's refusal to adopt a pro-American stand during the Gulf crisis. Within this community, there was support for a confederal arrangement between an eventual Palestinian state in the occupied territories and Jordan, and an interest in coordination between the PLO and Jordan. The fact that Jordan supported the entry of Palestinians into peace talks was an added factor in their favor.

The arguments intensified during the spring and summer of 1991 before finally being resolved in favor of Palestinian entry into the peace talks on American terms. On September 27, the Palestine National Council authorized the PLO Executive Committee to "continue its current efforts to achieve the best conditions that can ensure success for the peace process in accordance with PNC resolutions," subject to approval by the PLO's Central Council.

On October 30, Palestinian representatives participated with the approval of the PLO in the opening of peace talks in Madrid as part of a Jordanian-Palestinian delegation. The Palestinian delegation represented Palestinians from the West Bank (except East Jerusalem) and Gaza Strip. It was led by Haidar Abdul-Shafei, a doctor from Gaza. Hanan Mikhail Ashrawi, a Birzeit University professor, was appointed Palestinian spokesperson. The Palestinian aim was to negotiate an autonomy for the occupied territories that, it was hoped, would be the first step toward self-determination and an eventual Palestinian state in the territories, possibly confederated with Jordan.

The Future of Palestinian Pragmatism

The entry of the Palestinians into peace talks on American terms was a watershed in Palestinian politics. It meant that a pragmatic political trend that had once represented a small minority of Palestinians had become a position officially endorsed by the PLO and the focus of Palestinian political hopes. It remained to be seen whether Palestinian pragmatists would in the short term be able to obtain an autonomy in the occupied territories acceptable to the majority of their inhabitants, and in the long term, whether they could achieve self-determination.

While both Palestinians and Israelis had agreed to autonomy talks, they entered them with very different priorities. The Israeli government sought pacification of the occupied territories and an end to the *intifada,* without the establishment of a hostile Palestinian entity within them. The Palestinian aim was an autonomous entity strong enough to undertake significant economic and political community development and be a stepping stone to self-determination.

Both sides agreed that the United States would play a key role as mediator, but their expectations of the United States were different. Israel wanted to be treated as part of the winning side in the Gulf war, entitled to full support as a faithful US ally (one, moreover, supported by a strong political lobby in the United States); the Palestinians expected the United States to respond favorably to their concessions to the Camp David process, and bring Israel in line with the US conception of a peace-for-territory exchange.

After the Gulf war, the United States made gestures in the direction of each side: prior to the entry of Palestinians into talks, it supported Israel on the issue of not making the PLO a partner in the talks, and not allowing Palestinians from Jerusalem to participate. On the other hand, the Bush Administration went further than previous United States governments in refusing to offer loan guarantees to Israel to support the settlement of former Soviet Jews, so long as the Shamir government continued its settlement policies in the occupied territories.

Previous American attempts to arrange an autonomy agreement· had encountered major difficulties. After the Camp David Agreement had been rejected by the Arab world, the United States had sponsored almost three years of negotiations in which Egypt had assumed the role of negotiator on behalf of the Palestinians in an attempt to reach an autonomy agreement with Israel's Likud government. These Egyptian-Israeli talks had foundered on a number of difficult issues, including the nature of the autonomous authority, the Israeli presence in the West Bank after autonomy, the status of Jerusalem, control of the resources of the area, and the status of Israeli settlements.

The negotiations arranged following the Gulf war were accompanied by more favorable expectations, partly because Palestinians were now representing the Palestinian side, and partly because the June 1992 elections in Israel replaced the Likud government with a Labor government that rejected its predecessor's objective of eventually annexing all the occupied territories. Many of the issues that had formerly caused problems were, however, sure to re-emerge as significant obstacles to an agreement. What political freedoms, movements and institutions would Palestinians be allowed to have in an autonomous entity? What kind of links would be maintained between the inhabitants of the West Bank and those of Jerusalem? What rights of military intervention would Israel be given in the event of attacks being launched against it from the autonomous region? Would these include controversial practices such as curfews, the blowing up of homes of families related to persons accused of attacks on Israel or the deportation or detention of Palestinians without trial? Would it be possible for Israel to create new settlements or expand old ones? What measure of control would Palestinians have over the water resources of the West Bank and confiscated land held by the Israeli authorities? What kind of freedom would the Palestinian entity have to regulate itself economically? Would its businesses be able to compete economically with Israeli companies, something impeded by the economic policies applied by Israeli occupation authorities since 1967?

Issues such as these could not be resolved without strong and active American mediation. An autonomy agreement was a feasible objective, since it was possible to envisage a package of proposals emerging from the negotiations that would create a Palestinian autonomy that both the Palestinian and Israeli sides could view as a significant improvement on the occupation-*intifada* impasse. Any such agreement would have to make a substantial break with the status quo that had existed in the occupied territories since 1967. A successful autonomy agreement would be one that seemed to each side to be an interim step toward the achievement of its more fundamental aims in a final agreement—self-determination, a home-land, and normal social and economic development for the Palestinians; and for Israel, final acceptance by the Arab world, security guarantees and normalization of economic relations.

Precisely because each side was sure to negotiate with one eye on the future, the terms they sought to achieve in an autonomy agreement would reflect the kind of final agreement they sought. In addition, the US itself would need to have some idea of the kind of final settlement that might follow a period of autonomy, in order to maintain a sense of direction in the autonomy talks, which were sure to require strong initiative on its part.

For most of the period between 1967 and 1990, Israel and the Palestinians each opposed the basic demand of the other for national recognition in a resolution of the Palestinian-Israeli conflict. The Palestinians refused to recognize the State of Israel, and successive Israeli governments refused to recognize the right of the Palestinians to self-determination. The Palestinians had made a move to break out of this stalemate of mutual rejection with the concession of accepting Resolution 242 in 1988, and their subsequent acceptance of American conditions for autonomy negotiations in 1991. While the Palestinian attitude to Israel had changed, however, Palestinian insistence on eventual self-determination had not. Rapprochement between the two sides depended largely on whether Israel would at some stage make a concession on the issue of Palestinian self-determination that was comparable to that made by the PLO on the issue of acceptance of Israel when it accepted Resolution 242.

Among the Palestinians, the demand for self-determination exists across the political spectrum, among moderates and militants alike. Being against Palestinian self-determination is about as popular a position in the Palestinian community as being anti-Zionist is in Israel or the wider array of Jewish communities in the world. The difference between moderates and militants in the Palestinian community is one about territorial demands (the territories Israel occupied in 1967 rather than the entire territory of mandated Palestine); about timing—whether an interim period of autonomy to build mutual confidence with Israel is acceptable; about the extent of concessions to Israel on security issues; or about whether a Palestinian state should be confederated with Jordan; there is no disagreement about the basic need for Palestinian self-determination.

In a long-term solution, the closest that the Palestinian people might come to meeting Israeli and United States objections to an independent Palestinian state would be to adopt one particular interpretation of self-determination that gained momentum in the Palestinian community of its own accord in the late 1980s and early 1990s, the idea of a confederation between a Palestinian state and Jordan. This would create one international entity, the confederation itself, that would handle foreign affairs and defense, but each of the two components— Palestinian and Jordanian—would have strong separate parliaments and state governments separate from the confederal government.

The principal obstacle to the achievement of Palestinian self-determination has been the consistent opposition of Israeli governments, both Likud and Labor. Between 1967 and 1992, the official position of both major Israeli political parties was that even if Palestinians were willing to recognize Israel, make peace with it, and guarantee its security, Israel would not accept Palestinian self-determination in the occupied territories. While the Likud Party sought to annex the occupied territories, unlike the Labor Party, which was willing to return populated areas to Jordan, the traditional Labor Party position on the Palestinian issue was seen by Palestinians as equivalent to urging them to change their sense of identity and regard themselves as Jordanian—an unacceptable idea.

The US Dilemma

The significance of the Gulf war for the Arab-Israeli conflict was that it launched a negotiating process that had not existed before between Israel and its eastern and northern Arab neighbors, including Palestinians. What the war did not do was alter the fundamental issues in the conflict, or the perception by the parties to the conflict of what these issues were. All successful negotiations on the Middle East conflict since 1973 had required major and arduous intervention by the United States. The negotiations that started after the Gulf war would not be different, except that because the easier problems had been dealt with in earlier Arab-Israeli agreements, more complex ones now had to be addressed. To give the talks the direction they would need to be successful, the United States would have to develop its own conception of the future of the region. At some point there would be a need to re-examine the issue of Palestinian self-determination and the consequences for the Middle East of attempts to avoid the issue. This point seemed likely to come earlier than later, since the issue influenced the position of the parties even on the more modest interim objective of autonomy.

In the various disputes between states and independence movements this century, one of the most endemic problems has been the unwillingness of states to recognize the strength of the sense of national identity experienced by their independence-seeking opponents. A typical blind spot has been to treat nationalism either as the creation of agitators who have obtained control of a community, as some kind of manifestation of anti-Western hostility, or simply as unnecessary for one's adversaries. For people with the kind of history the Palestinians have had, a strong sense of identity resulting in a demand for independence is entirely in the mainstream of normal aspirations by peoples of the world who believe that they are a nation.[12]

It is an international fact of life of the twentieth century that strongly nationalistic populations denied self-determination rebel against the system that denies it. Since World War II, this has been the case with Algerians, Namibians, the majority population of South Africa, and Vietnamese, among others. Israel itself was created following a rebellion against the British authorities and a war against Arab armies, in circumstances where its leaders adamantly rejected proposed peaceful solutions that did not include a Jewish state. There is no reason to believe that Palestinians denied self-determination in the long term will be more compliant or pacific than the international average.

The most serious argument against Palestinian self-determination has been the contention that self-determination would be incompatible with Israeli security. The underlying concern is that Palestinians would establish an irredentist state aimed at recovering the whole of mandated Palestine. This ignores the fact that a Palestinian state, being largely demilitarized, would lack the power to defend itself against an Israeli invasion. It is possible that if significant land and water resources were stripped from the West Bank, self-determination would fail for economic reasons; but assuming that the Palestinian entity had control of the necessary resources, Palestinian self-determination would mean that, for the first time since 1949, Palestinians would have a national stake in stability in the Middle East— an important achievement that could be lost in the event of war. By contrast, in the absence of self-determination, much of Palestinian militance in the last twenty-five years has been driven by a feeling that Palestinians have little to lose by struggle. Even those who believe that the offer of Palestinian self-determination would not lead to stability cannot seriously challenge the fact that the *denial* of Palestinian self-determination has resulted in acute instability and violence.

One concern of those opposed to Palestinian self-determination is that Palestinians might attempt after self-determination to organize an Arab coalition wielding military power against Israel. However, there is little reason to expect that a peace settlement would leave Israel less able to cope militarily with the Arab world than before. The change in the international system resulting from the collapse of the Soviet Union and the defeat of the militant Arab nationalism represented by Saddam Hussein left Israel in a more secure situation than at any time since the creation of the state. It is easy to envisage demilitarization measures, backed up by buffers of international troops, that would keep Arab armies as far away from key Israeli strategic targets as they are now, or leave Israeli troops as well-poised to intervene in the event of a major march forward by surrounding Arab troops as they are now.[13] Moreover, the international guarantees of the settlement would be expected to place Israel in a situation where its military capabilities would remain superior to those of the Arab world. In the event of a final peace settlement, therefore, the military situation need not be much different from the current one, though a major political factor stimulating Arab hostility to Israel—Israel's occupation of the Arab territories captured in the 1967 war, and its denial of self-determination to the Palestinian people—would be removed from the picture.

Apart from the security issue, several factors not directly related to Israeli security have made Israeli governments reluctant to make significant concessions to the Palestinians. The Likud governments were committed to the annexation of the West Bank and Gaza Strip, which they saw as part of Israel for historical reasons; previous Labor governments also sought to annex parts of the West Bank and Gaza Strip, and to take over land and water resources in the region, a policy greatly intensified by the Likud governments with their active settlement policies. The Labor government that came to power in June 1992 inherited a policy of opposition to Palestinian self-determination practiced by all Israeli governments, so that taking the commonly travelled path of consistency with previous policies would result in opposition to Palestinian self-determination in the long term and, in the short term, opposition to the kind of autonomy agreement that could lead to self-determination. Although such policies would perpetuate Israel's ostracism by the Arab world, many Israeli politicians either do not believe that any Israeli concessions to the Palestinians would be sufficient to overcome Israel's isolation from the Arab world, or do not consider the prospect of ending this isolation enticing enough to offer the concession of Palestinian self-determination.

From both the Israeli and American points of view, the disadvantage of this position is that it could eliminate from Palestinian politics those most willing to make peace with Israel, and those willing to seek US mediation to do it. A failure by the current pragmatic Palestinian politicians to achieve a significant autonomy agreement that could be seen as a step toward self-determination would almost certainly lead to the decline of the pragmatic tendency in the Palestinian movement. Pragmatists by definition claim that they are people who can achieve things, and get things done. There is no political position more lonely or untenable than that of pragmatists who cannot deliver the minimal requirements of their constituents. In the event of Palestinian inability to conclude a significant autonomy accord with Israel—an accord capable of attracting majority support in the occupied territories—Palestinian pragmatists would become irrelevant to active Palestinian politics. This would in effect cede the political arena to a new brand of militancy, in the form of either a revival of the strong nationalism that has characterized the PLO for most of its existence, or an upsurge in support for Hamas, the fast-growing Islamic movement on the West Bank and in the Gaza Strip.

In certain respects, the challenge posed to the United States by the demands of the Palestinians in the occupied territories after the Gulf war was a microcosm of the challenges it faced in dealing with states and peoples that had previously fallen in the Soviet or radical nationalist orbit. Would United States policy be to promote some kind of new Middle East order in which these states or peoples found benefits and a stake? Or would the US essentially adopt a *laissez faire* attitude, leaving them to be treated as losers in an arena of continuing conflict?

In the Middle East, the drawback for the United States of *not* having a new system of political relationships and *not* pursuing the resolution of conflicts would be the continued festering of the problems that existed prior to the Gulf war in a Middle East more polarized than ever before on the basis of "haves" supported by the United States against "have-nots." Among the "have-not" countries or peoples, the United States would have little or no political influence. It would be plausible to expect the growth of militant political movements seeking any means of redressing the balance of power, including new weapons technologies. As a dispossessed population with an extremely high profile in the Arab and Islamic worlds, the Palestinians could expect to be a focal point in the international political disputes that would arise in this situation, rather as they have been for most of the period since 1949.

To some, it was ironic that the Palestinians, after opposing the United States during the Gulf crisis, should subsequently have become so dependent on the United States to obtain their goals. The changed Palestinian position was, however, a recognition that the Middle East after the Gulf crisis was a different place from before, and that the advancement of militant objectives and strategies would place the Palestinians outside any realistic negotiating framework. As a result, a change in Palestinian politics long sought by the United States had arrived. The United States had repeatedly argued that Palestinian militancy was doomed to bring Palestinians to grief; that armed resistance was futile and counterproductive; and that a refusal to move from maximalist positions denied Palestinians the benefits of peace. Now that the Palestinian political leadership had accepted the peace framework advocated by the United States, US policy makers faced the challenge of showing whether the Palestinian people would be able to secure a better future following the US approach than they had by following the objectives and tactics that the US had criticized for so long.

Notes

1. In the week after the invasion, a number of Iraqi statements indicated that Iraq did not plan to keep troops in Kuwait for long. At this time, however, the Iraqi government was claiming that the main turn of events in Kuwait had been a political revolution by Kuwaitis sympathetic to Iraq; an Iraqi "withdrawal" would thus leave a pro-Iraq government in power anyway—a government that could not be forcibly removed if demands by Iraq were met that would prevent the deployment of anti-Iraqi forces in the region. After it became clear that it was impossible to create an effective pro-Iraqi government run by Kuwaitis, Iraqi hints of a withdrawal in the near term faded, and were replaced by suggestions that Iraq would withdraw after Israel withdrew from the occupied territories and Syria withdrew its troops from Lebanon.

2. Foreign Broadcast Information Service, *The Middle East and North Africa,* August 13, 1990, p. 49.

3. Foreign Broadcast Information Service, *The Middle East and North Africa,* August 20, 1990, p. 3.

4. Foreign Broadcast Information Service, *The Middle East and North Africa,* August 20, 1990, p. 2.

5. Shafiq Ghabra, *Middle East International,* April 5, 1991.

6. *Ibid.*

7. *Foreign Broadcast Information Service, The Middle East and North Africa,* December 27, 1990.

8. Foreign Broadcast Information Service, *The Middle East and North Africa,* January 2, 1991, p. 2.

9. George T. Abed, "The Palestinians and the Gulf Crisis," *Journal of Palestine Studies,* Vol. 20, No. 78 (Winter 1991), p. 42.

10. *Ibid.*

11. Most of the information in this and the next paragraph is taken from a report by the Secretariat of the United Nations Conference on Trade and Development, "Recent Economic Trends in the Occupied Palestinian Territories," TD/B/1305, 9 August 1991.

12. The Palestinian demand for self-determination dates back about seventy years. Palestinian nationalism dominates Palestinian literature and culture, and is the core recurring theme of the various Palestinian mass media. It has visibly pervaded all strata of Palestinian society.

The Palestinian people, who were the majority population of a mandated territory during the colonial era, have consistently claimed the independence that the mandate system was intended to provide populations governed by it. The terms of the mandate under which the Palestinians were placed were reviewed by British imperial committees and by the United Nations Commission that recommended the creation of Israel: all agreed that the terms of the Palestine mandate required the creation of an independent Palestinian Arab state, within the borders of mandated Palestine (i.e., Israel plus the West Bank and Gaza Strip.

13. For details of arrangements that might assist in guaranteeing Israeli security, see Valerie Yorke, "A Two-State Solution: Security, Stability and the Superpowers," in Michael Hudson (ed.), *The Palestinians: New Directions* (Washington, DC: Georgetown University Center for Contemporary Arab Studies, 1990), pp. 179-97; and Walid Khalidi, *At a Critical Juncture: The United States and the Palestinian People* (Washington, DC: Georgetown University Center for Contemporary Arab Studies, 1989), pp. 15-19.

16 TURKEY AND THE GULF CRISIS

Sherif Mardin

With the Gulf crisis, Turkey emerged to international prominence. This was unexpected, since in the past, no social transformation, political gyration or cultural somersault had enabled it to figure as a sustained focus of attention of the powers that counted or of the mass media of the West.

This previous and admittedly benign neglect, which diminished the total bargaining power of Turkey in international affairs, was perhaps the result of the peculiarly unclassifiable nature of modern Turkish society. Faithful Muslims but followers of a secular system of public law, Middle Easterners with their eyes turned to the West, superlative calligraphers of the Qur'an who had adopted the Latin alphabet, they belonged to a special category cogently described by Kemal Ataturk himself when he stated "we best resemble ourselves."

This in-between area where Turks continue to live and the demands it makes on their identity explains the intense domestic stresses of the 1970s that Turks have named the times of anarchy. The social structure of Turkey has continued to show idiosyncratic forms related to its indeterminate status. Thus, Turkey has now become the last refuge of Stalinism. The sight of a score of students running through the campus of the University of the Bosphorus chanting "Ceaucescu, we shall avenge your blood!" is not the least bizarre of the locally colored appropriations of radicalism by ardent young Turks. There are other features of Turkey, remnants of its Imperial past, consolidated and packaged by its positivistic modernism, which increase its wonderland quality. One of these is the status of the Kurds, and another is the general revival of Islam in Turkey and in the many organizations that lay a claim to its leadership. Both of these items have had repercussions within Turkish party organizations. All of these are qualities of "Turkishness" which have puzzled observers and led to many artful, fictionalized accounts of the inclinations of the Turks, some of which are recorded for posterity in the archives of western—and far western—foreign ministries.

As foreign affairs (since the 1970s) lost the quality of business transacted behind closed doors by a diplomatic caste, these tangled

275

elements of the social background of Turkey increasingly worked as vectors that have had a constraining, some would say equilibrating, influence on the elaboration of Turkish foreign policy. Among these forces, working in opposite directions, should also be cited a sizable block of the Turkish press, some of whose most deadly political marksmen are former Maoists. In a more general sense, much of the Turkish "progressive" press still professes a Jacobin, secular, "Marxisant" radicalism which, faced by the decline in the inspiration formerly provided by socialist Utopia, has bridged the gap by more than ever fastening on the US as the Great Satan.

But Turkey has also seen the revival of Islamic fundamentalism, which has joined the chorus. In addition, Turkish society is highly differentiated and its components are constantly shifting relative to one another. The unstable equilibrium of Turkish social and political forces exhibits a dynamic which makes the steering of Turkish policies a most daunting exercise. I, personally, take the internal upheavals that shook Turkey in the late 1970s and in which political parties, the press, labor unions, voluntary associations and religious groups all had a role to play, as a sign that the social forces that exist in Turkey had begun to have an influence on government. The widespread criticism of the Turkish policy in the Gulf by these same organs lends additional support to the thesis which states that the new democratic participation by Turkish citizens has had an effect on foreign policy. In fact, one can only take one's hat off to Mr. Özal who, in a country where the socio-political picture is so muddied, singlehandedly inspired and conducted Turkish policy during the Gulf crisis. His policy bears the centuries-old Turkic characteristic of decisions taken while on the move in the face of much opposition and against a moving target. But this only enhances one's admiration for a success which, in fairness, one cannot easily dismiss.

This paper is an attempt to bring into focus the extremely varied sets of factors to be found in the background of Turkish foreign policy during the Gulf crisis, namely, both the political conditions within the frame of which policy was elaborated, and the ways in which these fit into what could be described as the Grand Design of Mr. Özal, which has not been given the attention it deserves.

From the first days of the invasion of Kuwait, President Turgut Özal made three points clear. First, by declaring that Turkey could not remain a passive observer of the peace settlement that would solve the crisis, he seemed to place Turkey at the hub of a crisscrossing net of unresolved international issues—a type of foreign entanglement which, in the past, it had been a major aim of Turkish foreign policy to avoid. Second, he appeared to involve Turkey in the affairs of its Arab neighbors, which Turkish policy had also systematically avoided. Finally he had, in a sense, made clear that he was going to personally control the tiller of Turkish Foreign Policy. The ensuing moves that he initiated between August 1990 and January 1991 were part and parcel of the implementation of UN resolutions, but the specific forms of this implementation showed his imprint and were systematically opposed by the political opposition in the Turkish parliament, and this in itself, deserves an explanation.

Since 1989, there were a number of nagging domestic issues which had already set the stage for a mounting volume of recriminations directed against Mr. Özal. When Özal's majority party in Parliament since 1987 (36 percent) emerged with a mere 20 percent of the national vote in the local elections of March 1989, a campaign to the effect that Mr. Özal's Motherland Party had lost the confidence of the Turkish people had been launched by Mr. Erdal Inönü's Social Democratic People's Party and Mr. Süleyman Demirel's True Path Party. The reiterated cry for the Motherland Party to renew its mandate had not only embittered Mr. Özal but also poisoned the political atmosphere. Mr. Özal's successful campaign to be elected as President of the Republic, a success he had scored in October 1989 after having held the premiership for six years, was another bone of contention. This time Mr. Özal was accused of making the first move to change the Turkish constitutional system to a presidential regime. It was also said that he could not fill the role of President of the Republic—a role which demanded that he stand out as the symbol of the unity of the nation—in view of the meager support he had achieved in the municipal elections. This last concept of the unity of the nation is a thread that has always run through the main issues of Turkish politics and I shall have the opportunity to return to it.

There were many reservations expressed in different quarters about President Özal's policy in the Gulf, but, in fact, there was little to criticize in respect to the "correctness" of the measures Turkey had been taking under his direction. Turkey had waited until August 7, 1990 to place itself unequivocally in the allied camp by closing the flow of Iraqi pipelines crossing Turkey. (By that time Iraq had itself blocked one of them and reduce the flow of another). Turkey had also banned Turkish trade to Iraq, thus sacrificing its own trade with Iraq to the embargo. It was the Turkish parliament, not Mr. Özal, which had decided on August 12 by a vote of 216 to 151 to give the government war powers in case of an attack by Iraq. In fact, this approval by parliament was only the second option for President Özal, who had first thought of adding a Turkish contingent to allied forces, an idea which opposition from his own party had quashed. The parliament's vote had followed an agreement by NATO foreign ministers on August 11 that the Iraqi invasion of Kuwait threatened the collective security of all its members and that an attack on Turkey should be considered an attack on the alliance as a whole.

One of the arguments used against the President was that the Turkish Constitution of 1982 did not give him the authority to conduct foreign affairs. A number of leading columnists in the Turkish press also reminded their readers that Turkey had sedulously avoided involvement in the concerns of successor states to the Ottoman Empire. But opposition to the President was more than a critique of his foreign policy, it was an aspect of the political warfare between Kemalist, secular and "etatist" Turkey against what was considered the treasonable backsliding of the Motherland Party from the principles of the secular republic. Opposition to foreign policy was that very battle continued on the field of international relations. A parallel attack by conservative Muslims on what they considered his kowtowing attitude to the West made a suitable pendant to attacks coming from the republican left.

A example of the first type of secular, Jacobin Kemalist criticism emerged in the leading articles of the *Cumhuriyet,* an Istanbul daily representing "pur et dur" Jacobin secular republicanism of 1793 vintage. For some of the best known critics of *Cumhuriyet,* Kemalism—Turkish republicanism—meant opposing "imperialism," and presumably its "ferocious soldiery" as described by the author of the "Marseillaise," keeping the republic "one and indivisible" and shunning foreign entanglements. These are, incidentally, principles familiar to Americans aware of their own history. This stance, however, was accompanied by a view of the Turkish general will which these columnists believed to be personified by themselves, and by a distributive ideology bolstered by authoritarianism, which they mistakenly believed to be the authentic version of socialism. In the *Cumhuriyet* of December 13, 1990, one of these columnists, Ilhan Selçuk, expressed such views of the Gulf crisis by stating: "Today, every mother and father that sets itself against war in the Gulf is objectively an anti-Imperialist."

As to the symmetrical views of Muslim revivalists, one could follow them in the October issue of *Islam,* a monthly published by the Nakshibendi Order. In this issue, Nurettim Ayaz introduced the subject to his readers with the following words:

> With the US in the lead, the approach of the West to what western states have named the Gulf crisis—a crisis which began with the occupation and the incorporation of Kuwait but which simply constituted a pretext for the elaboration of a Middle East crisis—could be described as follows: equilibrium, raw materials and exploitation. All of which may be more clearly expressed as self-interest.

In a more general sense it could be argued that throughout the fall of 1990, a majority of Turks who could express their opinions were apprehensive about the possibility of Turkey being involved in war and supported measures against Saddam that would fall short of war.

October brought a visit of Mr. Özal to the US, during which he seems to have attempted to pry some information from President Bush as to what ultimate goal the US was pursuing. It is reported that President Bush countered this maneuver by keeping Secretary Baker by his side while he was in conversation with Özal. At the time, Mr. Özal attempted to promote a commercial agreement with the US which was "taken under consideration." His immediate gain consisted of higher quotas for textile imports. Özal's publicizing of his discussions with the American President upon his return amounted to projecting his own image as that of a major player in the Gulf crisis and as someone who had enhanced Turkey's ties with the US, a theme which caused much mirth among Turkish publicists. At this very moment Mr. Özal had to field the resignation of his foreign minister tendered on October 12. It became known that this was due to a protest at not having been fully consulted by the President. Gossip, however, had it that the minister was kept in the ante-chamber of the White House while Özal was consulting President Bush. A similar but more important crisis occurred when the Turkish chief of staff, General Torumtay, tendered his resignation on December 12. The cryptic sentence in which his resignation was worded, namely that he could not go along with principles of government which did not fit his own understanding of matters of state, was strong stuff, and in earlier times would have adumbrated a military intervention. The chief of staff had always been the arbiter of military policy and a person with crucially important political status. The resignation was an indication that he was preempted in his more cautious views concerning Turkey's role in the Gulf. What was unusual was that he played completely fair by democratic rules and refused to comment to journalists on the meaning of his sibylline phrase. The resignation of a chief of staff without accompanying rumblings in the military was in fact a signal victory for civilian rule in Turkey and for the President. That the army was indeed alarmed by Özal's policy was later to be described as contained in a report prepared by the American Embassy in Ankara at the end of December (*Cumhuriyet,* 29 December). The classical attitude of the Turkish Kemalist extreme left, which had never resisted encouraging a military coup when it suited its aims, was also relatively quiet on this occasion. Prof. Inönü's remarks, now coming from a convinced social democrat, showed a softening of the typical rebuke against "too close" relations with the US which the center-left had always had in its armory. He spoke of the General's resignation as a justified reaction caused by the fears of adventurism. December, the month during which the tension in the Gulf was mounting, brought a number of new critiques of Turkish policy. Ufuk Güldemir, the correspondent for *Cumhuriyet* in Washington, described his reservations as follows:

> From the very beginning of the Gulf crisis, Turkey gave positive signals to the US concerning [air] bases, yet, on the other hand, Turkey did not give the US an open check. Yet one gets the impression that US military bases could be used for the purpose of a preemptive strike. If this were to materialize, the party to be the aggressor would be the host of the air bases from which the planes left. (December 13, 1990)

Güldemir's questioning approach was directed to overlapping activities of NATO air tactical forces, which had come to reinforce the NATO base at Incirlik, and those of US planes with a different agenda, but using the same base. Both of these were under the allied umbrella, but who would engage in what action under what circumstances was not entirely clear. In an article on December 16, Güldemir posed a second question, namely, whether Turkey had now unnecessarily preempted its own warlike stance by making its signals too clear at a time when the US had not clearly decided for war, and was pursuing policies that could revive the implementation of methods other than war to obtain the withdrawal of Saddam from Kuwait.

December is the month of budget debate in Turkey. During the deliberations, Mr. Inönü commented on the situation with a few terse sentences in his usual telegraphic style, which I now quote: "The Prime Minister should tell us whether or not we go to war. Money, we have it or we don't but it's a problem we can solve. In war those who die don't return."

Thereupon, Mr. Inönü undertook a voyage to Jordan and Iraq on December 24-25. At the time, Inönü expressed his own views as follows:

A fundamental mistake is being made, and that is what I unceasingly criticize. We say that the occupation of Kuwait is a violation of international law and that we want the decisions of the Security Council to be observed. We share this understanding. The entire world evaluated this issue in this light. The question is in what way will Iraq withdraw from Kuwait. I say this can be done all the time protecting peace and without resorting to war. For the might of the UN is greater that the might of Iraq. (*Cumhuriyet,* December 25, 1991)

Mr. Inönü was disappointed by his encounter with Saddam. His real determination to see what were the elements that moved the Iraqi side appears from a statement made some time after his return that he had already been informed some time before his departure by one of the delegates at the International Socialist Conference he had attended that this delegate, who had earlier talked to Saddam, had told him of Saddam's absolutely uncompromising stand on the occupation of Kuwait. At the same time as Inönü was making his declaration, the general secretary of his party was publicizing the fact that he was off to organize meetings on the theme "No to War" in the Southern provinces of Turkey, the provinces that were closest to Iraq (*Cumhuriyet,* December 23). Mr. Süleyman Demirel, the leader of the center right True Path Party, showed his usual sense of humor, when shortly after the New Year he made his own assessment of the Gulf crisis. At the time he described the Turkish attitude as "war hysteria" and continued:

If war is declared those who will make the war will leave. We shall remain. Turkey was motivated by two motives when it took up its position in the Gulf: potential danger and advantage. Danger and advantage simply do not figure as items of international law. Potential danger and advantage cannot be causes for war. If we say that Saddam constitutes a danger and that we should eliminate him then Turkey can never lead a life of peace since we always will have neighbors who represent a potential danger.

Directing his remarks to Özal, he continued:

How is the world going to emerge from this? One thing is certain: we do not direct the world. So get yourself glued to the telephone, ring Bush, ring Mitterrand, ring Gorbachev. You would think war rang our door, error, it did not, we rang war's door. This development has brought out a fundamental flaw at the root of the regime. Turkey is ruled by a constitutional parliamentary regime. Democracy is the system of institutions and rules. Today the President is using powers which are those of the government. It engages itself. This is the most important reason for the gap between the people and those who govern the state. (*Cumhuriyet,* January 6, 1991)

And again:

They [the government] remind me of the tune "Don't worry, be happy." The rulers say "Don't worry" to the people, but they can't say "Be Happy."

That some people indeed were not happy with Turkey's foreign policy was demonstrated on January 13, just before the war began, when a huge demonstration against the war took place in Istanbul. Nevertheless parliament passed a resolution on January 17 authorizing the use of Turkish military bases by the multinational forces for attacks against Iraq. The opposition voted as a block against this resolution. This led to a condemnation of Turkey by Algeria, Iran, Libya, and Jordan. Spurring Mr. Demirel to comment to his caucus:

Did you see what they say: they say you are acting like an enemy. Don't do this please. History will not forgive you. So as you can see, things go round and round and eventually come back on your doorsteps. . . . Officials have begun to say that bases would be used for warlike purposes. Does that mean that planes will not bomb Iraq? So they say "don't bring up such points. Why do you muddy the waters? We shall do the necessary. Don't ask us more— It's a military secret." When we ask "did the planes cross the border?" they say: "Don't ask." From which we understand that questions are not forbidden but that answering by the government is forbidden.

With the end of the war something which even Turks only faintly perceived began to appear with a clearer definition. We may name this President Özal's "grand strategy," of which his Gulf policy was only a part. To understand this strategy of the President we have to remember Mr. Özal's deep frustrations at Turkey's application for membership in the European community having been postponed more or less indefinitely. On March 12, 1991, Özal in a declaration to a German journalist in Ankara was stating: "If the area of competence of NATO is to be extended to the Gulf, this must of necessity be discussed within the frame of Turkey's place in the European community." Özal's reference to NATO was his reply to cumulative recommendations from NATO as well as from the NATO members that Turkey should stop looking to the West and assume a role in the Gulf as best suited to Turkey's geographic position. In fact, the cards Mr. Özal had been playing in the Gulf crisis show a fairly complex game that was meant to indicate that he had other options than acceding to the EC.

In November 1990, the first meeting had taken place in Istanbul concerning a plan promoted by the President for the development of a Black Sea free trade area. The many delegates from the West who had been invited to attend the conference were made to understand that Turkey was taking the lead in providing opportunities for them for which they would have to vie, as Turkish businessmen had vied to be given a place in the European community. This was only one of Mr. Özal's aces within a more general challenge to the EC that Turkey would go it alone. Paraphrasing Cavour's *risorgimenta* formula, Özal was saying that Turkey would construct itself—and had now even inaugurated its own common market of the North. The relative blindness of these western delegations to Mr. Özal's grand plan could be seen in that two prominent guests at the Black Sea inaugural conference, the Right Hon. David Owen and Mr. Richard Perle, both advised Turkey to take upon itself the role of a policeman of the Gulf. Many Turks were outraged by these recommendations, which seemed to them to underline a lack of confidence in their genetic pool or at least a categorization of Turkey as a land of Asiatics who would be best served by remaining on their own turf. In fact, Mr. Özal was not bluffing in inaugurating his own free trade area. Turkey could indeed be an economic showcase for Bulgaria, Rumania and a number of states of the former Soviet Union.

Following that, Mr. Özal's scheme advanced to the extent of grounding a plan of economic collaboration of unprecedented scope with the Soviet Union, and approving agreements signed with the Ukraine and Kazakhstan. Mr. Özal's "grand strategy" then can be described as creating a new field for the economic expansion of Turkey—the Black Sea free trade area, the resources of which he would control, thus placing himself in a position where the barriers to EC membership would be balanced by his own gate-keeper role in the Black Sea.

At the termination of the allied war effort in the Gulf, one Turkish journalist summarized the relations between what Mr. Demirel had described as the "gap between people and government" during the crisis as follows:

> By and large intellectuals and those who were in a position to convey their feelings to the media took sides with Saddam during the Gulf crisis. . . . Why did the Turkish nation, its politicians, its doctors, its man in the street look upon Saddam with sympathy?

> What we understand now is that Turkish society saw itself as one of the community of oppressed peoples and that placing Iraq in the ranks of such people, it looked at the US as pressuring the Iraqi people and their leader Saddam.

Stating that the victory of the allies had since eroded much of this sentiment, even in Turkey, he continued:

> What I really want to underline is the following: how will the Turkish nation perceive and classify itself in the future? Will it consider itself primarily Muslim, or Turk, or Western, or Eastern, or Middle Eastern? Is it going to continue to place itself in the category of the oppressed and go on searching for alliances against the heinous West or will it work to become an integral part of the West? [Ege Cansen, *Hurriyet,* March 15, 1991.]

Throughout the Gulf war, it was clear that Turkish public opinion consisted of three segments: the protesting secular intellectual left, the man in the street who identified himself with his "Muslim brothers," and the more prosaic, brass-tacks approach of Özal and his supporters. The alliance of the first two of these segments is not surprising: *les extremes se touchent*. But despite the victory of Özal's foreign policy tack, the fundamental issue raised by Ege Cansen still remains to be answered unequivocally.

PART 4: THE ECONOMIC AFTERMATH OF THE WAR

17 THE ECONOMIC IMPACT OF THE GULF WAR

Ibrahim M. Oweiss

This paper attempts to quantify and analyze the economic impact of the Gulf crisis on Arab countries that were significantly affected by the Iraqi invasion of Kuwait and the ensuing Gulf war.

Economically, the crisis affected countries both inside and outside the Gulf region. In addition to Iraq, Kuwait and the other countries of the region, significant damage was caused to Jordan, Egypt, Sudan, Yemen, Morocco, and the Palestinian people. The adverse effects of the crisis extended to non-Arab countries such as Turkey, Bangladesh, Pakistan, India, the Philippines, and Sri Lanka.

In addition to the direct costs of military spending on confrontation and war, added economic burdens were caused by other problems: disruptions of trade, declines in remittances, the loss of belongings, the cost of displacement of people, the reallocation of returning workers to their home countries, investment expenditures to create jobs for those returning workers, the loss of income from travel and tourism and (in the special case of Egypt) the loss of almost one third of the Suez Canal earnings.

The environmental cost of the Gulf war is still to be assessed. The burning of Kuwaiti oil for about eleven months, and the largest oil spill in history of six million barrels, caused unusual damage. One report from the Gulf noted that:

> . . . the mess is catastrophic: whole estuaries lie dead under asphalt-like slabs of oil . . . . This mess isn't the only one left by the war. Some Gulf regions languish in a 'hellish daily living environment,' says the World Wide Fund for Nature . . . . The breadth of damages is indeed staggering; some problems will take decades to overcome.[1]

The burning of Kuwaiti oil resulted in a dark blanket spreading well over 1500 miles away from Kuwait with its oil acid rain. Agricultural production was adversely affected as far away as Bulgaria, Turkey, the southern Soviet Union, Afghanistan and the Himalayan region of Indian Kashmir. This kind of rain has been linked to the slow destruction of forests, crops and lakes in many parts of the industrialized world.[2]

Because of the wide range of environmental damage and the different spans of time for such effects to become fully known, there is no theoretical or practical method of assessing their cost. The cost of cleaning the oil spill in the Gulf alone was far in excess of $2.5 billion, the amount spent on the much smaller Valdez spill in Alaska resulting from the wreckage of an Exxon tanker in 1989.

In its study of the *Economic, Social and Environmental Impact of the Situation Between Iraq and Kuwait and its Consequences in the Short, Intermediate and Long Run,* the United Nations estimated the losses of remittances to the economies of certain countries as a result of the return of workers from Iraq and Kuwait, as shown in Table 1.

The preliminary estimate by the United Nations of the losses of remittances to the economies of Arab countries was in excess of $3 billion. However, the official estimate of the Egyptian government alone, according to an internal memorandum dated January 24, 1991, of the loss of revenues from remittances was $3 billion. The breakdown of this statistic was as follows: a decline of $1 billion in transfers from Egyptians working in Iraq; a decline of $1.3 billion decline in transfers from Egyptians working in Kuwait, and a decline of $0.7 billion in transfers from Egyptians working in other Gulf countries. In spite of the disparity between estimates made by the United Nations and others, the fact remains that the loss of remittances to the economies of Arab countries was very substantial, particularly in those countries which depended heavily on those revenues as the main source of their foreign exchange earnings such as Egypt, Jordan, Sudan and Yemen.

The estimates of such losses, moreover, did not take any account of the cost of displacement of hundreds of thousands of workers, nor did they include the loss of their belongings.

The Gulf crisis took its toll on the revenues normally obtained by countries exporting to both Iraq and Kuwait. The study released by the United Nations estimated the loss to Jordan alone at about 9 percent of its total foreign exchange earnings. As to the loss of revenues from tourism, Egypt and Jordan suffered more than other countries in the region. My preliminary estimate of this loss in the case of Egypt is in excess of one billion dollars, an amount which is also close to the official estimate of the Egyptian government.

Iraq

Concentrating on the adverse economic effect of the Gulf crisis on the Arab countries, it is difficult to make estimates for Iraq itself,

TABLE 1
Countries Affected by the Return of Workers and the Loss of Financial Remittances

Country	1989 Remit. ($ mil.)	1989 Remit. as % of Exports of Goods	Number of Returning Workers (thous.)	Estimated Annual Loss of Remit. ($ mil)	Loss as % of total Foreign Exch. earn.
Bangladesh	758	58.1	100	160	6.4
Egypt	4,257	113.4	500	1,270	10.2
India	2,819	17.5	300	400	1.7
Jordan	637	56.5	400	400	13.3
Lebanon	n/a	n/a	50	150	22.4
Mauritania	5	1.1	n/a	3	0.6
Morocco	1,336	40.3	n/a	n/a	n/a
Pakistan	2,010	41.0	140	300	3.7
Philippines	1,362	17.4	60	60	0.5
Somalia	20	29.5	n/a	n/a	n/a
Sri Lanka	356	22.8	100	110	4.7
Sudan	417	76.8	30	300	24.2
Syria	355	12.6	50	360	7.0
Thailand	942	4.7	10	10	0.04
Tunis	488	16.6	n/a	100	1.8
Vietnam	n/a	n/a	16	20	1.0
Yemen	438	60.8	850	450	40.3
Yugoslavia	6,290	46.4	4	23	0.1

Source: United Nations Economic and Social Council, Document E/1991/102, June 24, 1991, p. 11.

where there is no reliable recent data on national income. The loss of oil revenues may be computed at an annual rate of approximately $13 billion. The loss of economic output may be estimated at another $20 billion. Conservatively, the value of Iraq's military arsenal destroyed by the Allied forces could not be less than $40 billion. Based on interviews conducted with military experts, an estimate of the damage to Iraq's industrial base, its buildings, roads, bridges and all other forms of its infrastructure in the continuous bombing from January 16, 1991 until President Bush ordered a cease-fire on February 27 could not be less than $50 billion. The total economic loss to Iraq during the crisis could thus be very conservatively estimated at $120 billion.

Kuwait

In the case of Kuwait, provided that there was no permanent damage to underground oil reservoirs, it seemed that Kuwait would conservatively lose at least ten percent of its oil reserves as a result of the oil-well fires. This amounts to a loss of 9 billion barrels. If an average price of $20 a barrel is used, the staggering figure of $180 billion can be used as an estimate of the value of the burned oil. The cost of the loss of oil revenue during the crisis might be in the neighborhood of $15 billion. Furthermore, Kuwait pledged $16 billion[3] to the United States in support of Operation Desert Shield/Storm. The total economic loss to Kuwait should also include the cost of external diseconomies resulting from the environmental problems that the country and its neighbors are facing. The total loss to Kuwait may be estimated at more than $240 billion.

Saudi Arabia

For Saudi Arabia, there were some economic gains resulting from the rise in the price of oil in the early months of the Gulf crisis, totalling about $13 billion, but the economic losses far exceeded this. Based on interviews at the Royal Commission of Jubail and Yanbu, and the Saudi Ministry of Finance, the total economic losses can be estimated at $64 billion, as shown in Table 2.

TABLE 2
The Saudi Money Crunch:
Footing the Bill for the Gulf War

1990 expenses	[$ billion]
Cost of new weapons	13.0
Loan commitments to Soviet Union	1.5
Loan commitments to other countries	4.5
Housing and food for Kuwaiti refugees	0.8
Other costs*	10.2
Subtotal	30.0
1991 expenses	
Amount pledged to the US	13.5
Demobilization costs	3.0
Other costs*	17.5
Subtotal	34.0
Total expenses and obligations related to Gulf War	64.0

*Other costs include: the cost of the increase in oil production in a short period of time (approximately $4 billion) to compensate world markets for the loss of oil supplies from Iraq and Kuwait; the cost of environmental and other damages, opportunity cost, and wear and tear of Saudi infrastructure as a result of unusual use by heavy military vehicles and tanks as well as by the constant flow of aircraft; and other costs.

Source: David B. Ottaway, "Saudis, Said to Owe $64 Billion, Scrape to Meet Obligations", *Washington Post,* Wednesday, April 3, 1991, pp. A25–26.

Another estimate made by Prince Bandar bin Sultan, the Saudi Ambassador to the US, includes somewhat higher costs for 1990, and calculates the total financial losses resulting from the Gulf crisis at $51 billion. The breakdown is shown in Table 3.

The total cost of the Gulf crisis to Saudi Arabia could very well have been in excess of $70 billion. In addition, Saudi Arabia had to bear some added expenditures in the form of interest to be paid on its international borrowing, reflected in billions of dollars of loans arranged through J.P. Morgan in New York.[4]

It is worth noting that the Government of Saudi Arabia has run a budget deficit since the mid-1980s. In 1991, the deficit was expected to reach a record figure of $37 billion as a direct result of the Arabian Gulf crisis.

TABLE 3
Saudi Arabia's Estimated Expenditures on
Operation Desert Shield/Desert Storm

Support for US forces (8/90–12/90)	$4.00 billion
Support for coalition forces (8/90–1/91	1.00
Cost for Saudi forces (8/90–1/91)	2.00
Support for US forces (1/91–5/91)	2.00
Support for coalition forces (1/91–5/91)	0.50
Cost for Saudi forces (1/91–5/91)	0.50
Economic assistance to others	4.50
Cost for Kuwaiti refugees	1.00
Debt forgiveness to Egypt	4.00
Arms purchases (8/90–12/90)	12.00
Saudi civil defense costs	2.00
Cost of increasing oil production	4.00
Desert Storm contribution (1/91–3/91)	13.50
Total	$51.00 billion

Note: The above does not include costs such as the oil-spill clean-up and other environmental costs, the cost of slowing down the economy of Saudi Arabia during the war, costs for Iraqi refugees, continued economic assistance to coalition members, and Saudi contributions to the military support fund for Turkey and the economic support funds for Egypt and Syria.

Total costs for 1990 were approximately $34.5 billion. Windfall profits from increased oil sales in 1990 were roughly $13 billion. The estimated shortfall for 1990 as a result of the crisis was thus over $21 billion and rising.

Egypt

The net economic loss to Egypt from the Gulf crisis may be estimated at $3.5 billion. Although Egypt had some positive gains, these were outweighed by adverse effects. The gains were the forgiveness of the Egyptian military debt to the US, and the forgiveness of the country's foreign debt to other Arab countries. Other developments damaged Egypt's economy. The decline in the country's revenues from remittances may have been in the neighborhood of $3 billion, based on the number of Egyptians returning from both Iraq and Kuwait. The return of over one and half million Egyptians would require an investment of about $5 billion to create new jobs, on the assumption that at least $7500 is the capital needed to create one job.

Egypt's tourist industry was seriously affected by the Gulf crisis to the extent of approximately $1.25 billion. In addition, Suez Canal earnings decreased by about $0.5 billion. There was an overall decline in Egypt's other exports resulting from the Gulf crisis and the rise in insurance premiums. Additional costs to the government's budget arose from internal security expenditures, the increase in the wage bill, and the cost of resettling returnees at the time when the government revenues from the Suez Canal and the taxes paid by Egyptians working abroad had declined. The worsening of the government budget deficit resulting from the Gulf crisis may be estimated at about $2 billion. As the Egyptian government resorted to financing its deficit mainly by printing money, the rise in the rate of inflation added another economic burden to the majority of Egyptians, who earn fixed incomes.

Jordan

Jordan's economic losses resulting from the Gulf crisis exceeded by far the $600 million[5] of lost remittances and their multiple effects. The invasion by Iraq of Kuwait had an adverse effect on Jordan's overall trade, as goods could not be safely transported. Furthermore, the displacement of over a quarter of a million[6] Jordanians and Palestinians from both Iraq and Kuwait during the occupation and after the war added further economic burdens to the country. A rough estimate of the overall economic and financial loss to Jordan could be in the neighborhood of $2 billion. One estimate is that the overall loss to the economy of Jordan represented approximately one third of its national income.[7]

The Palestinians in the West Bank and Gaza are reported to have lost $140 million[8] in remittance earnings in the early days of Iraq's invasion of Kuwait. As a result of the overall Palestinian political position during the Gulf crisis, Kuwait's policy was not only to discourage Jordanians and Palestinians from returning to their jobs in Kuwait after the war but also to replace as many as possible with expatriates of other countries.

Yemen

In the case of Yemen, the loss of remittance earnings in the nine months following Iraq's invasion of Kuwait on August 2, 1990, was in the neighborhood of $1.5 billion. This figure kept increasing as more than one million Yemenis working in Saudi Arabia had to leave their jobs and return to Yemen in the aftermath of the Gulf crisis. Another 45,000[9] returned permanently from Iraq and Kuwait. As in other countries, the loss to Yemen's economy was far in excess of the loss of workers' remittances.

Total Losses

A summary of the total economic losses is shown in Table 4.

TABLE 4
Economic Losses to Arab Countries
Resulting from the Gulf Crisis

Country	$ billion
Kuwait	240.0
Iraq	120.0
Saudi Arabia	64.0
United Arab Emirates	4.0
Egypt	3.5
Jordan	2.0
Yemen	1.5
Morocco	1.0
Others	2.0
Total	438.0

The figure of $438 billion does not include the cost of all of those who had been affected by the Gulf crisis. A study by Elizabeth N. Offen estimated that "more than 5.5 million people from 40 countries were temporarily or permanently displaced by the Persian Gulf war of 1990/1991."[10] The present study, however, has attempted to include an estimate of the cost only of displaced persons from Arab countries.

The above estimate does not include economic losses to Arab countries which will accumulate over time because of the multiple consequences of Iraq's invasion of Kuwait. One major development was the maintenance of low oil prices resulting from the closer relations between the governments of the Gulf Cooperation Council (GCC) and the United States. Having been indebted to the United States for its military support in the Gulf crisis, the six member nations of the GCC—Bahrain, Kuwait, Oman, Qatar, Saudi Arabia and the United Arab Emirates—pursued a policy that was highly sensitive to the need of the US for relatively low oil prices, which would help to ease the economic recession in the country. With well over six million barrels a day in oil imports, the United States would benefit from low prices.[11] Because of Saudi Arabia's dominant influence in OPEC, it was reported early in 1992 that

> OPEC's production has been climbing for several months even though Iraq is still banned by the United Nations from exporting its oil. Output recently reached its highest level in more than a decade and currently exceeds 24 million barrels a day. Meanwhile the average of the basket of seven crudes used by OPEC as a price measurement has been falling. It was down to $16.57 a barrel last week; it briefly touched the $21 mark last fall."[12]

The drop in the price of imported oil of about $5 a barrel meant a loss to oil exporters and a gain to US importers of about one billion dollars a month. Lower energy prices contributed to a drop in the US wholesale price index by about 0.1 percent in 1991 for the first time in five years. According to the U.S. Labor Department, "a good portion of the improvement in 1991 came from shifting energy prices."[13] The drop in wholesale prices would make it easier for consumer spending to be directed elsewhere, facilitating economic recovery in the United States.

Concluding Reflections

The economic losses to Arab countries resulting from the Arabian Gulf crisis formed a sad contrast with the unfulfilled needs for development in the Arab world. The amount of $438 billion would have been sufficient to provide a house for sixty percent of the families[14] of the Arab world, or an adequate shelter for every family in all Arab countries. Less than one third of that amount would have been sufficient to pay for all the foreign debt owed by the Arab countries. An investment of only $20 billion dollars would have been sufficient to build the infrastructure of Sudan, helping it on the road to realizing its potential of providing the total agricultural needs of the Arab people.

It is a devastating judgment on the government of Saddam Hussein that it was the reason that these valuable human and financial resources went down the drain. More than twenty centuries ago, the ancient Greek writer Aristophanes, in his play *Lysistrata,* spoke of man's foolishness as the cause of the war and destruction which prevailed between Athens and Sparta. In the twentieth century, with its enormous leaps in science and technology, it was still possible to find an Arab leader who could bring ruin to his own country as well as the dreams, hopes and aspirations of the Arab people. Whatever the effects of his actions on the rest of the world, the Arabs were the only big losers, economically and otherwise.

References

Aspin, Les, Chairman of the House Armed Services Committee, *Sharing the Burden of the Persian Gulf: Are the Allies Paying their Fair Share?,* Washington, DC: House Armed Services Committee, April 8, 1991.

Association of Arab American University Graduates, "The Arab World and the Gulf War," *Arab Studies Quarterly,* Vol. 13, Nos. 1 and 2, Winter/Spring, 1991, Normal, Illinois, U.S.A.

Egypt. Government of Egypt, Internal Memorandum, January 24, 1991, Cairo, Egypt.

Overseas Development Institute, *The Impact of the Gulf Crisis on Developing Countries,* Briefing Paper, London, March 1991.

United Nations, Economic and Social Commission for Asia and the Pacific, Document OES/R/7.2, Oct. 24, 1990, Bangkok.

United Nations, Economic and Social Council, Document E/1991/102, June 24, 1991, New York.

United Nations, United Nations Conference on Trade and Development, "Economic Consequences of the Present Crisis", Document TD/B/1272, September 22, 1990.

Notes

1. John Wells, "The Legacy of War: The Battles are Over, But Gulf Environment Still Fights for its Life," *Wall Street Journal,* October 15, 1991, pp. 1, 10.

2. *Ibid.*

3. Representative Les Aspin, Chairman of the House Armed Services Committee, *Sharing the Burden of the Persian Gulf: Are the Allies Paying their Fair Share?,* Washington, DC, April 8, 1991.

4. *Wall Street Journal,* September 24, 1991, p. A14.

5. *Foreign Affairs,* Vol. 69, No. 5 (Winter 1990/91), p. 24.

6. *New York Times,* June 16, 1991.1

7. Parker L. Payson, "Figure it Out," *The Washington Report on Middle East Affairs,* Vol. X, No. 2 (July 1991), p. 55.

8. *New York Times,* August 27, 1990, p. 8.

9. *New York Times,* June 16, 1991.

10. Elizabeth N. Offen, *The Persian Gulf War of 1990/1991: Its Impact on Migration and Security of States* (Cambridge: Massachusetts Institute of Technology, Department of Political Science, December 1991), p. 1.

11. It should be noted, however, that lowering the price of oil does not serve the long-run economic interest of the United States, as internal production keeps falling. This production reached its lowest level in 30 years, according to a January 1992 report of the American Petroleum Institute. Lowering the price of oil, therefore, increases US dependency on foreign oil, and discourages the development of alternate sources of energy.

12. James Tanner, *Wall Street Journal,* January 14, 1992, p. A2.

13. *Washington Post,* January 10, 1992, p. C1.

14. Assuming that the typical family size is 5 in the Arab countries, there are approximately 40 million families in the Arab world from the Atlantic to the Arabian Gulf. Assuming that the cost of a prefabricated house is $18,000, then the amount drained by the Gulf crisis would have been sufficient to provide single-family housing for each of 24 million families, representing 60 percent of the total number of Arab families.

18 AFTER THE WAR: THE BUSINESS OUTLOOK IN THE GULF

Nemir A. Kirdar

Iraq's invasion of Kuwait came at a time when there were encouraging signs that the Gulf region was emerging from the long recession that had afflicted it since the mid-1980s. Oil prices and oil revenues, which had fallen steeply since the early 1980s, seemed to be levelling out, with good prospects of rising through the 1990s. Although by the mid-1980s the great infrastructure boom which followed the oil price rises of the 1970s had virtually come to an end, much industrial diversification had been subsequently carried out, with signs that private enterprise and initiative were beginning to be more prominent. Exports of petrochemicals, aluminum and other industrial products were picking up, and international investors were starting to explore joint venture opportunities. Moreover, at the end of the 1980s, the GCC represented an increasingly mature market in which consumers had become more educated, more sophisticated and more discerning. Expectations were rising rapidly and populations were becoming more youthful, introducing a powerful dynamic into the region. Share prices in the emergent stock exchanges of Bahrain, Saudi Arabia, Kuwait and Oman had reached new highs. Even the depressing effect of the Iran-Iraq war on trade and investment in the area was beginning to dissipate. Perhaps only the banking system was experiencing real difficulties, largely, I believe, because of mistaken lending policies and failure to identify appropriate lines of business in the 1980s — a subject to which I will return later.

The Gulf war, of course, interrupted these developments in the Gulf, although it did not, I think, bring them to an end: indeed, the massive reconstruction needs of Kuwait continue to provide a strong stimulus to economic activity. Undoubtedly, there has been a negative impact on domestic and external confidence in the area which will check, at least for a time, both domestic and external investment in the region. Hopefully, the speedy and successful end to the war, and the liberation of Kuwait will lead to a rapid revival of that confidence. The destruction of a major part of Kuwait's oil production and distribution facilities is an enormous loss, which seems likely to hang over the region for some years to come. Fortunately, because of its previous wise investment policies, Kuwait has substantial foreign assets on which it can draw to finance reconstruction of its infrastructure and its oil wells. Moreover, if and when political confidence is re-established in the region, foreign oil companies will also play a part.

Destruction was not confined to Kuwait's oil wells and refineries. Highways, ports and the airport were also extensively destroyed. So too were many public buildings and hotels, as well as many privately owned factories and trading premises. By the time Kuwait has been rebuilt, the estimated cost will have been at least $60 billion; some estimates put it as high as $100 billion.

The war has also inflicted further damage on the region's banking system. Iraq's invasion of Kuwait on August 2, 1990 led to an immediate flight of deposits from the region's banks as depositors sought safety in London, New York and Switzerland. It is reported that Bahrain's domestic banks lost 15 per cent of their deposits in the first two weeks, whilst the Offshore Banking Units (OBU's) lost 12 percent—at least $11 billion in all. Saudi Arabia's commercial banks also lost deposits heavily, as did banks in Qatar and elsewhere. All told, the flight of bank deposits from the Gulf amounted to at least $20 billion, and was probably much in excess of this. Many domestic banks had to cut their scale of operations, and some foreign banks exited from the area or reduced their presence drastically. Unfortunately, if understandably, international banks withdrew their credit lines to banks in the region.

However, "out of crisis come opportunities." It is evident that the region is facing another reconstruction boom, although not, of course, on the scale of the one in the 1970s and early 1980s, since destruction has been largely confined to Kuwait. (I leave aside Iraq since it is difficult to see how reconstruction of that country can easily or quickly be financed.) After the war, the region showed signs of once again becoming a honey pot for Western exporters, who were queuing up to cash in on the bonanza. With much of the West in or close to recession, and with construction activities being particularly depressed, there was no shortage of industrial capacity throughout the world to meet Kuwait's needs. A bigger problem was likely to be the availability of labor since Kuwait has lost a large proportion of its immigrant labor force. It will be a challenge and, indeed, expensive to persuade people of skill and quality to work in a still unstable Gulf.

It is important to note, however, that the Gulf region is able to meet many more of its industrial needs today than was the case in the 1970s and early 1980s. Areas of regional production include petrochemicals, pharmaceuticals, plastics, construction and refurbishment equipment, aluminum, water and sewage equipment, cables and rubber products and some electronics. In recent years, Gulf companies have even looked to increase exports of some of their products to Europe, Asia, and North and Latin America. This means that the Gulf region itself will get a much larger spinoff from reconstruction activity in Kuwait than was the case during the primary construction boom of the 1970s, when the industrial development of the region was virtually non-existent.

In addition to the need to reconstruct Kuwait, a further stimulus will stem from the intention of the countries of the region to take greater responsibility for their own defense. The creation of a regional security structure is a target, backed up by a substantial arms package from the US. Saudi Arabia is also expected to increase its own defense expenditure substantially over the next few years. Although, of course, most of the sophisticated defence equipment will come from the US, the UK and other Western powers, there is sure to be a substantial spin-off for local economic activity. The Arab Organization for Industrialization—basically a military manufacturing partnership among Egypt, Saudi Arabia, the UAE and Qatar—has also been revived. It is expected to receive an infusion of funds from the Gulf States to enable it to manufacture or assemble such defense equipment as armored cars, artillery rockets and other missiles, jeeps, electronic equipment, and possibly training planes—all under US, British and French licenses.

All of this suggests that the region is likely to witness a sustained burst of economic activity in the next few years. Indeed, the antecedents of such a boom in activity could already be seen in Saudi Arabia during the crisis itself. The influx of 350,000 Kuwaiti exiles created a "mini-boom" in housing with its allied demand for household and other goods; and the presence of over half a million foreign troops in the Kingdom created a major market for many consumer goods, including bottled water, soft drinks and portable air conditioners. Although such demand was by nature temporary, it maintained economic activity and income at a level that might otherwise not have been reached.

One cannot of course talk about the Gulf without referring to oil. Although the wilful destruction of a large proportion of Kuwait's oil wells and refineries was a massive loss for Kuwait, the region's total production of oil was maintained by Saudi Arabia's willingness to increase its own output. Within four months of the invasion, Saudi Arabia had lifted its output from 5½ mbd to over 8mbd. With oil prices also being significantly higher, Saudi Arabia's revenue from oil almost tripled from its mid-year level. Much of the extra revenue was pledged to the governments that came to the defense of Saudi Arabia and also to friendly countries in the region, such as Turkey and Egypt, that suffered economic damage as a result of implementing the economic embargo of Iraq. As a result, probably not a great deal of this extra revenue percolated through to the private sector, although the great improvement in the Saudi government's finances may have helped sustain the confidence of the private sector which was initially hit by the Iraqi threat to the Kingdom.

However, it seems likely that the expansion of Saudi Arabia's oil production will not be a short-term affair. Leaving aside the destruction of Kuwait's oil wells and the possible long-term embargo on Iraq's exports, which Saudi production will make up, there are signs that the Saudi government intends to assert its position in OPEC and to maintain much of its higher production for some time to come. This would mean substantial extra investment in oil facilities to bring production back to the sustainable levels of a decade ago. The revenue received from the higher level of oil exports would put the Saudi government back in the driver's seat in the promotion of economic development. Although this is to be welcomed, it is also to be hoped that the rise in rents and other costs associated with further basic development of the Kingdom will not work against the diversification of the private sector, which in the last few years has seen industries and services develop which appeared to be totally uneconomic in the booming construction years of the 1970s.

I come now to the impact of the Gulf war on the region's banking and financial systems. As I indicated earlier, Iraq's occupation of Kuwait precipitated a loss of confidence in the commercial banks, leading to a massive loss of deposits. Many of the banks had to cut their scale of operations and even consider relocating themselves in Europe and elsewhere. Paradoxically, however, the shock to the Gulf's financial system may well result in long term beneficial results.

The dynamic economic explosion that took place in the Gulf as a result of the escalation of oil prices in the 1970s inevitably created new dimensions of demand for financial products and services. On the one hand, individuals and institutions emerged with phenomenal levels of wealth and income in search of investment opportunities. On the other hand, industrial and commercial enterprises sprang up, looking for capital. Clearly, an efficient, effective financial intermediation system was urgently required.

Although in the 1970s and 1980s numerous banks were established in the Gulf, it cannot be said that they adequately filled the need referred to above. Most of the banks that were established took the form of commercial banks, largely engaged in deposit-taking and lending activities. Paradoxically, some of the larger of these banks ended up by taking deposits from the Western banking system and lending them to third world countries, that is to say, intermediating between wealth holders in the Western world and governments in poorer countries outside the Gulf. Unfortunately, the experience of many of these banks ended in grief. With many of the poorer countries being unable to service their debts, serious loan losses not only sapped the profits and capital reserves of the Gulf banks, but also exhausted the energies of their human resources.

Unfortunately, the financial needs of the Gulf remained largely unfilled. New enterprises in the Gulf, needing to raise capital, could not expect their needs to be met by the commercial banks. Nor were there other institutions that could fill the role. Indeed, despite many years of experience in the Gulf, I do not know of any professional entity which specializes in raising capital for new or even ongoing privately-held concerns.

As a result of the Gulf crisis, we may now see a radical change in this situation. For a time at least, banks will be more concerned with rebuilding their liquidity than with profitability. The shock to the deposit base of the Gulf banks, plus the longer-term deterioration in their profit and capital positions, will inhibit a return to the traditional commercial banking business of deposit-taking and short-term lending. But, as I have suggested earlier, the reconstruction of Kuwait and the prospect of rising oil revenues will provide the basis for a further rise in incomes and wealth in the Gulf States. Although governments in the region will undertake a major part of the expenditure on infrastructure and repair of oil facilities in Kuwait, private sector activity will also be given a boost. Hence the need for effective regional financial intermediation will be all the greater, and it will be surprising if the banks do not now take the opportunity to adapt themselves to the new circumstances. What are required in the region are more investment banks, i.e., banks whose main function is to raise capital in equity or debt form for businesses or governments, not banks whose main function is deposit-taking and short-term lending.

Of course, in recent years some of the commercial banks in the Gulf have aspired to convert themselves into investment banks, but this has proved a good deal easier said than done. It requires a careful identification of the local market's needs for finance; an identification of the appropriate products and services, with the appropriate know-how and experience; and the capacity to design the organizational structure and the terms and conditions necessary to attract the talents and resources required. Needless to say, a prerequisite of the emergence of an effective investment banking industry is a receptive and encouraging legal and regulatory framework. Unfortunately, such a framework does not exist in many Gulf States today. Investment banks have played a crucial role in the development of the US, Britain, Japan and Europe in the past, and it is clear that the Gulf itself requires the services of such institutions today. Hopefully, Gulf financial institutions will survive and we will not see serious insolvencies. Capital markets, mergers and acquisitions, and venture capital are likely to be the order of the day—a very desirable development in an overbanked region.

Out of crisis often comes opportunity. Iraq's destruction of Kuwait dealt a huge blow to confidence, domestic and foreign, in the Gulf, and also created massive physical damage. But the Gulf is the source of a major part of the world's oil and gas. This ensures, for as far as we can see into the future, substantial income and wealth in the Gulf. Much of this should be retained in the Gulf to finance the reconstruction and very necessary diversification of the region's resources. But much, too, will have to be channelled abroad to build up the region's assets overseas. Here, too, the services of investment banks will be required. Kuwait's wisdom in maintaining foreign earning assets is a living example which cannot be overstated.

The Gulf crisis and the willingness of many countries to come to Kuwait's assistance have demonstrated how important the region is to the rest of the world. The fact that two thirds of the world's known oil resources are to be found there ensures that plenty of business opportunities will be generated in the region for many years to come.

19 OPEC AND THE GULF CRISIS

Charles K. Ebinger
John P. Banks

1. Introduction

The dangers and complexities of maintaining a cohesive and functioning oil cartel were never more apparent than in 1990. The Iraqi
invasion of Kuwait was oil politics taken to its most brutal extreme
and will fundamentally alter the structure and traditional role of the
Organization of Petroleum Exporting Countries (OPEC) in global oil
markets. Nevertheless, rumors of OPEC's possible demise are
premature. Despite the violent consequences of OPEC's political
failure to resolve the problem of Saddam Hussein and his search for
economic security, regional political dominance, and oil market
hegemony, the likelihood after the Gulf crisis was that OPEC would
emerge strengthened, albeit in a very different form.

The underlying impetus for the invasion was economic. In 1988,
with Iraq's defeat of Iran in the Gulf War, Iraq clearly emerged as the
dominant military power in the Gulf. The war, however, left Iraq
deeply in debt and in need of generating revenue to rebuild its society. In
addition, Iraq had been plagued by rampant financial mismanagement—
Baghdad's non-Arab external debt of $60 billion was the world's
third largest behind Mexico and Brazil, and its annual short-term
debt service was estimated at $6-$7 billion. Just prior to the invasion,
Iraq had failed to meet payments on its debt, some of which had been
rescheduled for a third time only six to nine months earlier.

The chronic OPEC over-production and the steady fall in prices
over the first two quarters of 1990 posed a grave threat to Iraq's
financial and economic health. The outcome of the July 25 OPEC
meeting was the final straw; though the trade press made much of the
difference between Iraq's demand for oil at $25 per barrel and the
support of the rest of OPEC for $20 per barrel until a compromise
was worked out at $21 per barrel, in reality, Iraq knew that prices
could not be sustained at $20 per barrel in the wake of previous
OPEC over-production and the likelihood that the agreed quotas
would not be implemented. At the time of the meeting, spot prices
were finding it difficult to achieve stability at $15-$16 per barrel.
Indeed, during the first seven months of 1990, the spot price for

OPEC's seven most widely traded crudes averaged $16.84 per barrel versus the $18.00 per barrel target price. In July, it had fallen to $15.68 per barrel with the prospect of further decline. This prospect was clearly intolerable to Iraq, especially in light of the fact that Baghdad's long-term development plans after the Iran-Iraq war seem to have been drawn up on the assumption of an oil price level of at least $20 per barrel.

In addition to Iraq's preponderant military power, Baghdad knew that in OPEC councils its 100 billion barrels of oil reserves placed it on a par with the UAE (98 billion), Iran (93 billion), and Kuwait (97 billion, including its share of the Neutral Zone). Nevertheless, it was still far behind Saudi Arabia's official figure of 255 billion barrels (at least 285 if recent discoveries of light crude reserves are included).[1]

Thus, although Iraq offered immediate reasons for the invasion of Kuwait—repudiation of war debt, gaining direct access to the Persian Gulf, disgruntlement over Kuwait producing oil from the Rumaila field, and the desire to recover the nineteenth province—there can be no doubt that Iraq's primary motivations were first, to stop the levels of production by Kuwait and the UAE, which exceeded their quotas, and second, to emerge as the principal challenger to Saudi Arabia's domination of the world petroleum market in the 1990's, thus guaranteeing some degree of financial and economic security. Although Iraq clearly miscalculated the impact that the invasion of Kuwait would have in galvanizing world opinion against it, the invasion was not the act of a "madman," but a cold, calculated decision that, by a single stroke, Iraq would achieve its longstanding goal of becoming the dominant force in the Gulf.

Saddam Hussein's gambit did not work, but he clearly decided that the opportunities were worth the risk. With the acquisition of Kuwait, Iraq overnight would have boosted its reserves to 194.5 billion barrels, nearly 20 percent of the world's total; acquired a near-term production capability of 5.7 million barrels per day (mbd) and the prospect of being a 9.5 mbd producer in the 1990's versus 10 mbd for Saudi Arabia; gained control of 5.2 billion barrels of oil reserves in the neutral zone, and 400,000 barrels per day of production—output that in the current market was Japan's single largest crude supply source; and gained control of significant upstream investments in a dozen countries, major downstream world class refineries, significant retail markets in Western Europe, and sizeable investments in petrochemicals and tankers, not to mention the prospect of solving its debt problem by seizing an estimated $100 billion in Kuwaiti assets abroad.

Iraq realized that during the 1990's, at least five and possibly more OPEC countries would cease being significant oil exporters and that the locus of world oil power would reside clearly in the Gulf. The acquisition of Kuwait, combined with Iraq's raw military power, would enable Iraq to emerge as the dominant power in the Middle East and a significant world actor, never to be held economic hostage again.

2. An Emerging OPEC Order: August-December 1990

The United Nations trade embargo on Baghdad removed an estimated 4 mbd from world oil markets (including Kuwaiti output).[2] In the immediate aftermath of the invasion and subsequent embargo, there was concern over potential supply shortages. With the approaching winter heating season, there was a perception that a shortfall would emerge, and the fear of severe market imbalance jolted prices to $31 per barrel by August 22.

In the quest to determine where additional supplies would come from, it was not clear in the several weeks following the invasion that other oil producers, principally OPEC members Saudi Arabia, Venezuela, and the UAE, had the spare capacity to increase production in order to replace the supply shortfall. Not only were there questions concerning the technical capability of these countries to boost production, but there were also doubts concerning their political will to undertake such an endeavor. Iraqi foreign minister Tariq Aziz warned OPEC against raising production, and the Iraqi government newspaper *al-Jumhuriya* bluntly stated on August 22 that "the new Iraq owns a big share of the world oil reserves that will establish it as a regional power that is worth taking into consideration."[3]

As Saudi Arabia took steps against Iraq, US and other Western forces began simultaneously arriving in the kingdom, and Riyadh shut down the IPSA II pipeline, which transported Iraqi oil to the Red Sea. In fact, Saudi Arabia had privately already set in motion contingency plans to increase production. On August 16, Saudi Arabia publicly called for an OPEC meeting to authorize member countries to boost oil output, and Venezuela announced its support on the following day. Riyadh's proposal called for an increase in production to meet the supply shortfall and stabilize markets.

Once again, however, OPEC was divided. The price hawks were

opposed to any production increase, because they were reaping benefits from the higher prices, as were all member countries. They saw no economic reason to jeopardize the windfall. Algeria, Indonesia, and Nigeria all claimed that it was too early to consider a production increase, that no unilateral decisions should be taken, and that oil stocks should be drawn down first. Venezuela declared that it would temporarily raise production by 500,000 barrels per day to help offset the supply shortfall, but that this additional output would be placed in storage and await official OPEC approval to export.

The most severe attack on the Saudi proposal, however, came from Iran. Iranian President Ali Akbar Hashemi-Rafsanjani stated that "OPEC members have no right to commit treachery against their people in favor of the global oil devourers," and called on the industrialized world to use huge oil stockpiles instead of increased OPEC production to meet the expected demand/supply shortfall.[4] Large oil stocks throughout the OECD nations had contributed to the downward pressure on OPEC prices all through 1990, and some OPEC members hoped that if these stocks were drawn down during the crisis, OPEC would have fewer problems following the crisis.

Nevertheless, the simple fact was that those who possessed the spare capacity were in favor of raising production. Saudi Arabia was estimated to have extra output capacity in the short term of 7.65 mbd and 8.2-8.5 mbd in the long term. By year-end, it was estimated that the UAE could increase production 600,000 barrels per day above quota, Venezuela 500,000 barrels per day, Libya 217,000 barrels per day, and Nigeria 289,000 barrels per day.

Indeed, near the end of August, without an official meeting to sanction increased production, any country with the spare capacity to raise output was doing so. Saudis were producing 6-6.5 mbd and were rumored to have concluded September contracts for 7.4 mbd. Nigerian production reached 1.8 mbd (quota of 1.61 mbd), and Libya's output neared 120,000 barrels per day in excess of its quota.

Riyadh was attempting to preserve some semblance of a united and operational OPEC by going through official OPEC procedures and succeeded in convening a meeting in Vienna on August 26-29. Under the leadership of the Saudis, the UAE and Venezuela, OPEC fashioned an agreement in which members were allowed to increase output according to excess capacity with no specified volume limitations. Priority for the additional output was given to the developing countries, owing to their greater susceptibility to oil price and supply disruptions. The agreement, however, was only temporary "until such time as the present crisis is deemed to be over,"[5] and specific provisions mandated that OPEC revert back to the July 1990 resolutions. Iraq and Libya refused to participate.

Pumping up the Volume

Despite initial opposition, OPEC increased production significantly after the August agreement. Following a decrease in output to 21.9 mbd in the third quarter, production averaged 23 mbd in the fourth quarter of 1990. In December, OPEC crude oil production averaged 23.86 mbd, with Saudi Arabia's production reaching 8.3 mbd—in August the kingdom's output had been 5.5 mbd. In early November, the Saudis announced that they were accelerating their expansion program, increasing production capacity to 10 mbd by 1995 instead of 2000 at the cost of $75 billion, five times the original cost estimate.

By the end of the year, the UAE and Venezuela were producing at 2.35 mbd, and Libya and Nigeria also increased production during the fourth quarter of 1990. Even Iran had joined in boosting output, despite earlier strenuous objections. Tehran increased the volume of oil shipped to the Far East by 760,000 barrels per day in the fourth quarter and also secured substantially improved price terms for increased volumes shipped to Japan. Iranian light was increased by $0.60 per barrel, and Iranian heavy was increased by $1.40 per barrel.

3. The New Order

How will the events of 1990–91 affect OPEC? Three fundamental factors will probably characterize the new OPEC: the rising dominance of the Saudi-led subgroup; a growing focus on economic considerations in OPEC decision-making; and increasing producer-consumer cooperation.

Although the locus of power within OPEC had been shifting toward the high-reserve, large-volume, market-oriented Gulf states and Venezuela since 1986—driven primarily by increasing demand for OPEC oil—Iraq's invasion of Kuwait and the Gulf war inexorably accelerated this process.

The market destabilization and price volatility resulting from the invasion of Kuwait were anathema to this coalition. The August accord was an attempt to reinstitute some stability and predictability to markets and symbolized the solidarity and prominence of the coalition, presenting the low-volume, limited-reserve members with a *fait accompli*.

Moreover, from an intra-OPEC political standpoint, the August 1990 agreement signaled that the Saudi-led group was willing to abandon the traditional unanimity required in all OPEC policy decisions. The meeting was procedurally converted to the status of a Monitoring Committee meeting, thus removing the requirement that any action be approved by every member. The Saudis gave notice that they were willing to discard their consensus-building *modus operandi*. In addition, the weak opposition of price hawks such as Algeria, Libya, and Iran to Iraq's actions in 1990 will serve to discredit these players and diminish their influence at least in the near term.

The August agreement represented a political as well as economic decision. Saudi Arabia and the UAE were directly threatened by Iraq's willingness to resort to brutal force. Their decisions to support wholeheartedly the worldwide condemnation of Iraq, to allow hundreds of thousands of foreign troops into the Gulf, to cut off Iraqi pipeline exports, and to increase production in order to stave off a potential serious shortfall in supplies were clearly provocative to Iraq, but were calculated political decisions to confront Baghdad and guarantee their own survival. The invasion and subsequent war forced the market-oriented Gulf states to band together and abandon the non-confrontational, consensus-building approach. The close cooperation and mutual assistance that emerged among Kuwait, Saudi Arabia, Qatar, and the UAE further enhanced the power of this OPEC subgroup.

Clearly, such provocative steps were contemplated only under the diplomatic and military aegis of the United Nations coalition. With strong international support, the high-reserve, large-volume coalition had gained significant stature. The devastation of Saddam's military machine meant that the willingness and ability of this subgroup to undertake economic decisions without intimidation, fear of reprisals, or political-military repercussions were likely to continue.

The new OPEC focus on economic and market factors in setting policy was likely to have an impact on the relationship of OPEC with the consumer countries. After August 1990, OPEC (minus Iraq) and the industrialized consumer countries moved closer together. The widespread military and political support that Western nations provided to Saudi Arabia, Qatar, the UAE, and Kuwait linked the interests of producers and consumers in confronting a common enemy and attempting to restore stability to the troubled Persian Gulf. Support from the consumer countries was not limited to the political and military realms. On January 11, 1991, members of the International Energy Agency (IEA), representing the major industrialized countries, agreed to a plan designed to stabilize the global oil market in the event of a shortfall caused by hostilities. The plan included a drawdown from government and private company stocks of 2 mbd, with another 400,000 barrels per day to be backed-out by conservation measures, and 100,000 barrels per day to be made available from fuel switching and surge capacity. IEA member countries were to arrange their own plans to meet the overall 2.5 mbd target. After the outbreak of the Gulf War, the IEA announced that its members were ready to implement this contingency plan, releasing 2.5 mbd of oil to world oil markets within 15 days.

For its part, OPEC demonstrated a willingness to bolster the new-found cooperation through increased production in an attempt to stabilize prices, as well as through Saudi and Kuwaiti pledges to contribute $27 billion to the US costs of operations Desert Shield and Desert Storm. In addition, the industrialized countries that participated in the liberation of Kuwait have played a significant role in the rebuilding of that country, cementing the relationship even further.

OPEC cooperation was a theme raised frequently in the course of 1990, owing in part to the deteriorating market condition. OPEC Secretary General Subroto indicated early in the year that the financial requirements of expanding OPEC capacity in the 1990's would necessitate investment from the consumer countries. In October, OPEC President Bousseha called for greater cooperation between producers and consumers to achieve a consensus on appropriate oil price levels in the future. Even Iran, in the midst of criticizing the OPEC decision to boost production after the invasion, called for a meeting between the IEA and OPEC to work out a shared plan to address market concerns. Shaikh Ahmad Zaki Yamani, the former Saudi oil minister, in a speech delivered in March 1990, had taken the call for a new cooperative spirit one step further, arguing for a "trilateral dialogue between the governments of the consuming countries, the producers—members and non-members of OPEC— and the oil companies."[6]

4. Whither Prices?

How will these developments affect price levels? After the Gulf crisis, the interests of the consumer and producer countries seemed likely to move closer together, and the support of the United Nations coalition, including most of the major consumer countries, was likely to result in a vast improvement in the stature of the high-reserve, large-volume producers, making it easier for them to dominate the price hawks whose influence was on the wane. The interests of the ascendant OPEC sub-group—stable oil markets and moderate price levels—coincide with those of the consumer nations. Thus, the Saudi-led subgroup will enjoy growing influence and will be empowered to pursue policies designed to achieve these goals. With Saudi Arabia, Venezuela, and other producers having invested large sums of money to raise production capacity in order to stabilize oil markets and capture a larger share of the rising demand for OPEC oil, there is little incentive for them to roll back their production and have it sit idle. Indeed, although Saudi Arabia has professed its desire to see strict quota adherence and prices at the established $21 per barrel reference mark, it also has indicated that it will not unilaterally sacrifice production increases and revenue for the good of OPEC, thus tending to depress prices below the $21 target. An estimated $50 billion in war-related costs provides Riyadh with an additional incentive to preserve prices at this level.

Saudi Arabia wasted no time after the war in wielding its new-found power in OPEC councils. At the March 12, 1991, OPEC Monitoring Committee meeting, Saudi Arabia orchestrated an agreement to reduce the cartel's output by 5 percent and set the quota ceiling at 22.3 mbd (down from 22.49 mbd) in an effort to bolster prices. In addition, prior to the March meeting, Saudi production was estimated at 8.4 mbd, and officials indicated that they would not accept a quota below 8 mbd—the quota that Saudi Arabia was ultimately assigned and significantly above its prior quota of 5.38 mbd.

Although much has been made of the potential destabilizing impact of returning oil production from Iraq and Kuwait, this is a factor whose significance should not be exaggerated. In particular, for Iraq, the return of oil exports to the world market was delayed indefinitely by the continuation of the UN embargo. The debate in the Security Council concerning the mechanics of allocating a certain percentage of Iraqi oil export revenues to reparations would need to be resolved for Iraqi production to have an impact on prices.

In the event of a resumption of Iraqi imports, Saudi Arabia and the Gulf states were in a stronger position within OPEC after the Gulf war to force Baghdad to comply with conservative pricing and production policies. Indeed, the Saudis were in the unique position of being able to control 300,000-400,000 barrels per day of Iraqi export capacity through the Saudi pipeline system. If discussions concerning postwar security arrangements were to lead to the permanent presence of western allied forces in the region, the political standing of Saudi Arabia and its Gulf allies would be even further enhanced. It was most ironic that Saddam's move into Kuwait, initially designed to catapult Iraq into a leadership role in OPEC and world oil markets, would thus have created an OPEC in which Iraq had little, if any, influence in the near term.

In the long term, however, both Iraq and Kuwait faced the daunting task of rebuilding their war-ravaged societies, and reestablishing oil production and export capacity was the only route to generating sufficient revenues to accomplish this. If Iraq were forced to pay substantial war reparations, it would have an even stronger incentive to raise production. Eventually, therefore, increased Iraqi and Kuwaiti production could place downward pressure on prices.

The behavior of Iran was another important variable in determining the direction of oil prices. The destruction of most of Iraq's military and Iran's neutrality and efforts at mediation during the war improved Tehran's stature in the Gulf and the Middle East at large. Initially, there was considerable concern that Tehran might decide to parlay this new-found influence into a campaign to gain more power within OPEC, boosting output and forcing the sub-group to contend with more over-production. In addition, it was feared that Iran might also attempt to bolster its standing by drawing attention to the close relationship of the Arab and western members of the UN coalition and rouse anti-western, anti-Gulf state sentiments in the Arab world.

During and immediately after the Gulf crisis, however, Iran showed increasing signs of a wish to cooperate with GCC countries. Iran and Saudi Arabia commenced discussions on reestablishing diplomatic relations, and Riyadh received great cooperation from Tehran in arranging the March 1991 Geneva agreement. Iran also decided to open an interest section in Egypt, ending years of cool relations between the two countries, and refused to take any overt military role in the rebellion inside Iraq following the end of the Gulf War even through Saddam Hussein's forces were killing Shiite brethren.

Iranian cooperation with the Gulf war victors was clearly part of a concerted effort to guarantee a political role in the postwar balance of power. This might portend stable oil prices, if Teheran adhered to the policy direction of the Saudi-led sub-group and became more incorporated into the OPEC locus of decision-making. Longer term, in the aftermath of the Gulf crisis, Iran still needed to generate revenues to rebuild its shattered economy in the aftermath of the Iran-Iraq war, and there remained considerable debate about the outcome of an internal political power struggle between the Islamic fundamentalists and the more Western-oriented moderates. These factors had the potential to translate into more aggressive posturing and lobbying for higher quotas by Iran, thus increasing supply and depressing prices.

After the crisis, a near- to mid-term price in the $18-$22 per barrel range for OPEC oil not only loomed on the horizon, but seemed to be in OPEC's long-term interest. Prices much above this range would stimulate a response similar to that exhibited in the period 1980-1985: increased non-OPEC production, the rising use of alternate fuels, and greater utilization of energy conservation. Price levels below this range would depress revenues and cause intolerable financial and economic pain for all players, similar to the effects experienced in the 1986 price collapse.

In the event of a re-entry into the market by both Iraq and Kuwait, if OPEC were to push for a higher price without a number of producers cutting back on current output to make room for Kuwaiti and Iraqi production, the specter of a price collapse below $15 per barrel would become a reality. Over the longer term, a real potential exists for Baghdad and Tehran to exert greater influence over production and pricing policies, a role they believe is justified owing to huge oil resources and high output capacity. The almost certain divisions within OPEC that might follow such a revival of the influence of Iraq and Iran would lessen the organization's control over prices and inevitably lead to a decline in prices.

After the Gulf crisis, there remained a myriad of unresolved diplomatic, economic, and political issues that could lead to other confrontations. The world had witnessed the human, financial, and environmental consequences of failed oil diplomacy: it was incumbent upon the international community, particularly the Gulf states, to guarantee that oil politics did not again deteriorate to such a violent conclusion. In particular, assured access to Middle Eastern oil reserves would never be secure unless the United States used all its diplomatic leverage to help effect a comprehensive peace plan for the region. And if projections of US oil import dependency of 11-12 million barrels per day by 2000, coming increasingly from the Persian Gulf, were to materialize, future crises of even greater magnitude could be the result.

Notes

1. Reserve figures are not absolute and are subject to debate. The figures cited here are accepted industry estimates.

2. *Middle East Economic Survey (MEES),* August 13, 1990, p. A2.

3. *MEES,* August 27, 1990, p. A6.

4. *MEES,* August 27, 1990, p. A4.

5. Text of OPEC's Vienna Agreement, August 29, 1990. Reprinted in *MEES,* September 3, 1990, p. A4.

6. Address by Shaikh Yamani to a meeting of the Institute of Petroleum in Glasgow on March 8, 1990, reprinted in *MEES,* April 2, 1990, p. D1.

CHRONOLOGY OF THE GULF CRISIS

May 1990–June 1991

Compiled by Tim Lake*

May 1990

May 28. Sixteen members of the Arab League convene in Baghdad in an emergency session requested by Iraq and the PLO seeking a unified Arab policy toward Israel and its supporters. Iraqi President Saddam Hussein suggests using Arab oil as a lever to force changes in US policy towards Israel.

May 30. The Arab League issues a communique which threatens unspecified "political and economic measures" against countries that recognize Jerusalem as the capital of Israel. The communique also criticizes US Congressional support for Israel's claim to Jerusalem.

According to an Iraqi radio report on July 19, 1990, Iraqi President Hussein delivers a speech criticizing Arab oil producing countries who fail to abide by OPEC production quotas. Hussein states at one point that, "This is in fact a kind of war against Iraq" and that "this enormous drain on our economy derives from a lack of vision or a failure by those directly concerned locally to view matters from a pan-Arab angle."

June 1990

June 19. The Bush administration notifies Congress of a 4 billion dollar arms sale to Saudi Arabia. Congress does not block the sale within 30 days, thus making the sale law.

June 26. In a personal message, Iraqi President Hussein warns Kuwait to curb its excess oil production because of its negative impact on Iraq and OPEC's vital interests. Iraqi deputy Prime Minister Saadoun Hammadi tells Kuwaiti officials that prices should be raised from $14 a barrel to $25. The UAE is also accused of overproduction.

Iraqi deputy Prime Minister, Saadoun Hammadi, criticizes OPEC pricing policies in a news conference in Kuwait and states, "I do not consider $25 per barrel a high price by any standards."

July 1990

July 10. Five Persian Gulf oil producers—Iraq, Saudi Arabia, Kuwait, UAE and Qatar—agree on a Saudi-sponsored proposal for Kuwait and the UAE to cut their oil output down to 1.5 million barrels per day with the promise of higher allotments later. The agreement

---

* With the assistance of Robert Engle and Simone Manigo-Truell.

Because of differences in time zones, the date on which some events occurred was different in the Middle East from the date in the United States. For example, the air war against Iraq was launched at a time that was the evening of January 16, 1991, in the United States, but the early morning of January 17 in Iraq. This chronology dates events according to the time zone in which they took place (i.e., January 17, in the above case).

calls for a stricter enforcement of the previously-set 22.5 million barrels per day production ceiling for all OPEC producers. Agreement is intended to push market prices up to the November 1989 target price of $18 per barrel from the prevailing price of $14 a barrel.

July 16. Iraqi Foreign Minister Tariq Aziz delivers a letter to the Arab League accusing Kuwait of stealing oil worth $2.4 billion from the Rumaila field inside Iraqi territory and building military installations on Iraqi territory. The letter also accuses Kuwait and the United Arab Emirates of deliberate overproduction of oil to reduce oil prices and complains that the two Gulf states had declined to cancel Iraqi debts from the Iran-Iraq war.

July 17. Iraqi President Hussein threatens to use force against Arab oil producers who fail to curb excess oil production and fall in line with previous OPEC quota agreements. Hussein states that some Persian Gulf states had stabbed Iraq in the back "with a poison dagger" and that "if words fail to protect Iraqis, something effective must be done to return things to their natural course, and return usurped rights to their owners."

July 18. A US State Department spokesman states that the US remains "strongly committed to supporting the individual and collective self-defense of our friends in the Gulf, with whom we have deep and longstanding ties."

July 19. The Kuwaiti government counters Iraqi charges of oil theft by informing the Arab League that Iraq has been digging oil wells on Kuwaiti territory.

July 21. Iraq begins deployment of approximately two armored divisions of about 30,000 soldiers toward the Iraqi-Kuwaiti border.

July 23. Egyptian President Mubarak, Jordan's King Hussein and Iraqi Foreign Minister Aziz meet in Alexandria, Egypt in an attempt to diffuse tension over dispute.

The US Joint Task Force Middle East is placed on alert.

July 24. The United States dispatches two aerial refueling planes to the United Arab Emirates and sends six combat vessels to the Persian Gulf region. Bush Administration officials justify the move as a signal to Iraq that the US is prepared to use force to defend the flow of oil through the Strait of Hormuz. The Bush administration releases statements warning Iraq against "coercion and intimidation."

Egyptian President Mubarak travels to Kuwait, Iraq and Saudi Arabia in hopes of bolstering mediation efforts.

July 25. Thirteen OPEC oil ministers meet in Geneva. The Iraqi oil minister, Issam Abdul-Rahim al-Chalabi, repeats the call for an oil price of $25 per barrel.

Egyptian President Mubarak announces that Kuwait and Iraq have agreed to hold talks in Jeddah, Saudi Arabia.

Iraqi President Hussein and Iraqi Foreign Minister Aziz meet with US Ambassador to Iraq April C. Glaspie. Hussein sends a message to US President George Bush expressing Iraq's desire to end the crisis peacefully and avoid confrontation with the United States. Hussein reportedly states that he felt "betrayed" by the deployment of US forces in the Gulf the day before. According to Iraqi accounts, Glaspie states that the US has ". . . no opinion on the Arab-Arab conflicts, like your border disagreement with Kuwait."

July 27. OPEC reaches agreement on production quotas, reaffirming much of the July 11 agreement, and increasing the reference price to $21 per barrel from $18 by the end of 1990.

July 28. Iraq and Kuwait open talks in Jeddah to discuss outstanding territorial issues and recent Iraqi allegations against Kuwait. The Iraqi newspaper *al-Jumhuriya* states that "whoever comes to meet the Iraqi side . . . must be prepared to erase the harm and the aggression against Iraq, and be ready to respond to Iraq's legitimate rights."

July 30. Iraq concentrates an estimated 100,000 troops with 300 tanks, 300 heavy artillery pieces and bridging equipment near the Kuwaiti border.

August 1990

August 1. The Iraqi delegation led by Izzat Ibrahim, Revolutionary Command Council (RCC) vice chairman, walks out of talks in Jeddah after a single two-hour session. Kuwait reportedly refuses to write off Iraqi debts and relinquish disputed territory. No agreement is reached.

August 2. Iraqi troops launch an invasion in the early morning hours deep into Kuwaiti territory, taking Kuwait City by midday. An estimated 700 Kuwaitis are killed. Iraq claims the invasion to be an act of support for a Kuwaiti coup to overthrow Emir Jabir al-Ahmad Al-Sabah. Members of the Kuwaiti ruling family, including the Emir, take refuge in Saudi Arabia.

The United Nations Security Council passes Resolution 660 condemning the invasion and calling on Iraq to withdraw its forces from Kuwait.

President Bush condemns the invasion and orders a near-total economic embargo on Iraq. The US freezes Iraqi and Kuwaiti assets and coordinates efforts to freeze Iraqi and Kuwaiti assets with a number of European allies. The Soviet Union suspends all deliveries of military equipment to Iraq and condemns the invasion.

Iraq freezes debt payments to the US and warns other countries not to come to Kuwait's assistance, saying that the Iraqi armed forces "will make Iraq and Kuwait a graveyard for those who launch any aggression." Iraqi radio stations announce the formation of a new provisional government in Kuwait.

Iran issues a statement condemning the invasion and demands an Iraqi withdrawal. The statement also warns that intervention by foreign countries will destabilize the region further.

Israeli defense minister Moshe Arens warns that any movement of Iraqi troops into Jordan would provoke an Israeli military response.

August 3. Iraq mobilizes 60,000 troops south of Kuwait City towards the Saudi border. President Bush warns against expansion into Saudi Arabia and terms the "integrity of Saudi Arabia" as one of America's "vital interests." Both the US Senate and the House pass measures in support of the US embargo.

US Secretary of State James Baker, who had been in the Soviet Union during the invasion, issues a joint-statement with Soviet Foreign Minister Edward Shevardnadze in Moscow strongly condemning the invasion and calling for a complete withdrawal of Iraqi forces.

The Arab League Council of Foreign Ministers votes 14 to 0 with five abstentions to condemn the Iraqi invasion of Kuwait. Those abstaining are Jordan, Yemen, Sudan, Mauritania, and the PLO Libya walks out of the meeting, and Iraq is ineligible to vote.

The Gulf Cooperation Council (GCC) issues a separate statement condemning the invasion of Kuwait.

August 4. Saudi Arabia is said by unnamed US officials to be mobilizing air and ground forces in case of attack. The European Community imposes sanctions on Iraq, including embargoes on oil and arms.

Jordan's King Hussein refers to Iraqi President Hussein as "a patriotic man who believes in his nation and its future and in establishing ties with others on the basis of mutual respect." Iraq issues a list of nine members of the "free provincial government of Kuwait."

President Bush consults with senior advisors at Camp David and reportedly makes decision to consult King Fahd of Saudi Arabia about military options to protect Saudi Arabia.

PLO chairman Yasser Arafat travels to Cairo and Baghdad to discuss a joint PLO/Libyan peace plan, which is believed to stipulate that the Kuwaitis agree in principle to compensation to Iraq, to a settlement of border disputes, to leasing the two islands of Warbah and Bubiyan to Iraq, and to the replacement of Iraqi troops in Kuwait with a joint PLO/Libyan force, and free elections in Kuwait.

China begins an arms embargo against Iraq.

August 5. An American delegation led by US Secretary of Defense Cheney is dispatched to Saudi Arabia to meet with Saudi King Fahd. President Bush states that an Arab solution "obviously has failed."

Japan orders a ban on all imports of oil from Iraq and Kuwait and halts all commercial relations with Iraq.

August 6. The United Nations Security Council passes resolution 661 by a vote of 13 to 0 imposing a worldwide trade embargo with Iraq and occupied Kuwait. Cuba and Yemen abstain.

Iraqi President Hussein summons US charge d'affaires Joseph Wilson in Baghdad and expresses the intention of keeping Kuwait.

Several hundred Westerners are taken from hotels in Kuwait and transported by bus to Baghdad.

An American delegation led by US Secretary of Defense Cheney meets with Saudi King Fahd in Jeddah to discuss the possible deployment of US troops and the shutting off of the trans-Saudi Arabia Iraqi pipeline to the Red Sea.

Iraq voluntarily reduces most of its oil flowing through Turkish pipelines.

PLO Chairman Arafat meets with Egyptian President Mubarak in Alexandria, Egypt to discuss a joint Libyan/PLO peace initiative.

August 7. President Bush orders the deployment of US aircraft and troops to Saudi Arabia after receiving approval from Saudi King Fahd. The US declares that Saudi Arabia is under "imminent threat" from Iraqi troops positioned in southern Kuwait.

US Secretary of Defense Cheney travels to Egypt and Morocco to consult leaders about an Arab role in the multinational force.

Turkey effectively cuts off all Iraqi oil traveling through its pipelines. Iraq cuts approximately 75 percent of its oil flowing through Saudi Arabian pipelines to 200,000 barrels per day.

Iraqi President Hussein vows to "pluck out the eyes of those who attack the Arab nation" and states that "we would rather die in dignity than live in humiliation, and vow to fight until death."

August 8. Iraq announces that it has permanently annexed Kuwait. The US warns that use of chemical weapons would provoke a "severe" military response. President Bush delivers a speech to justify the deployment of troops, stating that "to assume Iraq will not attack again would be unwise and unrealistic." Bush calls the mission a defensive one, ruling out an immediate invasion of Kuwait.

Jordan's King Hussein states that his government still recognizes the Al-Sabah monarchy as the legitimate government of Kuwait. He also states that Jordan will not allow foreign military forces on Jordanian territory.

Britain announces its intention to send forces to defend Saudi Arabia. Pakistan reportedly makes a commitment to send troops.

Egyptian President Mubarak states that he will not order Egyptian troops to Saudi Arabia unless they are part of an all-Arab force. Mubarak also calls for an emergency Arab Summit within 24 hours.

August 9. Iraq officially closes its borders, baring departure of all foreigners except diplomatic personnel. Iraq also orders diplomats in Baghdad to close their embassies in Kuwait by August 24.

The Pentagon states that the Iraqi military are consolidating their forces and "seem to be in a defensive posture."

The United Nations Security Council unanimously pass Resolution 662 declaring Iraq's annexation of Kuwait "null and void."

Arab leaders and representatives gather in Cairo for an Arab League summit. Official negotiations are postponed until August 10 after an Iraqi delegation arrives unexpectedly and demands the Kuwaiti seat.

Jordan agrees to abide by the embargo and closes the port of Aqaba to Iraq.

France announces the intention of sending forces to Saudi Arabia and the Persian Gulf under independent command.

Saudi King Fahd states that the presence of foreign troops will be "temporary" and that they will "leave here as soon as the Kingdom so demands."

Hundreds of protestors critical of the US presence in Saudi Arabia demonstrate outside US embassies in Khartoum, Sudan and Sanaa, Yemen.

August 10. Twelve out of twenty-one Arab League members pass a resolution condemning the Iraqi invasion, renouncing the annexation of Kuwait, and agreeing to send an Arab military force to Saudi Arabia alongside coalition forces. Iraq, Libya and the PLO vote against the resolution; Yemen and Algeria abstain; Jordan, Sudan and Mauritania express reservations; Tunisia is not present.

Iraqi President Hussein calls on Arabs and Moslems to "rise and defend

Mecca, which is captured by the spears of the Americans and the Zionists." Hussein attacks the "Emirs of oil" as "traitors," and states that "the American forces came and Saudi Arabia opened its doors to them under the false pretext that the Iraqi army will move toward them. It means there are plans for aggressive intentions."

August 11. The first Egyptian troops arrive in Saudi Arabia. Egyptian President Mubarak says he sees "no hope" for a peaceful solution. Morocco is also said to be sending troops.

August 12. Iraqi President Hussein states that all "issues of occupation" in the Middle East should be resolved before Iraq would withdraw forces from Kuwait. His proposal calls for Israel to withdraw from all the lands seized during the 1967 war and for Syria to withdraw its forces from Lebanon. Hussein suggests using an all-Arab force excluding Egypt to replace the forces already in Saudi Arabia. The Bush administration "categorically rejects" the proposal.

President Bush orders US forces in the Gulf to "interdict" Iraqi oil exports and imports. Bush cites Article 51 of the UN charter to justify the order. US Secretary of State Baker says the United States is acting at the request of the deposed Kuwaiti Emir.

Demonstrations against US involvement occur in Mafraq, Jordan; Sanaa, Yemen; and Sidon, Lebanon.

August 13. Jordan's King Hussein meets with Iraqi President Hussein in Baghdad.

Pakistan agrees to send troops to Saudi Arabia.

August 14. President Bush says he is willing to offer financial aid to Jordan to ensure Jordan's compliance with the UN embargo of Iraq.

The first Syrian troops arrive in Saudi Arabia.

Iraqi President Hussein delivers a letter to Iranian President Ali Akbar Hashemi Rafsanjani offering to withdraw troops from Iranian territory, to recognize Iran's disputed pre-war borders and to release all prisoners of war. The Iran-Iraq war effectively ends.

August 15. President Bush delivers an address denouncing Iraqi President Hussein, stating that he is a threat to the Arab Nation. Bush adds that ". . . we are talking about maintaining access to energy resources that are key not just to the functioning of this country, but to the entire world. Our jobs, our way of life, our own freedom and the freedom of friendly countries around the world would all suffer if control of the world's great oil reserves fell into the hands of that one man, Saddam Hussein."

The US State Department refers to foreigners in Iraq and Kuwait as "restrictees."

August 16. US naval forces in the Persian Gulf region formally begin a policy of interdiction of commercial shipping to and from Kuwait and Iraq.

President Bush meets with Jordan's King Hussein in Washington. Bush announces that Jordan intends to adhere to the UN-sponsored economic embargo of Iraq.

Iraqi President Hussein accuses President Bush of being a "liar" intent on "plundering" the Arab world's oil wealth and warns that American troops who clash with Iraqis "will go home in shrouded coffins."

August 17. President Bush decides to call up tens of thousands of Army, Navy and Air Force reserves for active duty.

Permanent members of the UN Security Council met with representatives of the Military Staff Committee to discuss coordination of naval forces in the Gulf and the enforcement of sanctions. This meeting is the first of its kind in the history of the UN.

The speaker of Iraq's parliament announces that Iraq will not release citizens of "aggressive nations" until the threat of war against his country ends.

August 18. US warships in Persian Gulf fire warning shots across the bows of two Iraqi oil tankers.

The UN Security Council unanimously adopts Resolution 664 demanding that Iraq immediately release all detained foreigners in Kuwait and Iraq.

The Iranian news agency reports that Iraqi forces have begun withdrawing from Iranian territory.

August 19. Iraq orders westerners in Kuwait to go to three hotels for relocation to strategic military and civilian sites. Iraqi President Hussein says he will free all foreign nationals if the US withdraws its forces from Saudi Arabia and the worldwide embargo against Iraq is lifted. The US dismisses the offer.

August 20. President Bush refers to Americans and other foreign nationals detained in Iraq and occupied Kuwait as "hostages." Iraq announces that it has moved an undisclosed number of

Westerners to military sites and other potential targets to discourage attacks by US forces.

Iraqi troops in Kuwait are estimated at 160,000 and are still seen to be in a largely defensive posture.

August 21. The Western European Union, a military group including nine EC member nations, agrees to send navel forces to the Persian Gulf.

August 22. The US State Department announces its intent to try to evacuate nonessential personnel and dependents from the US embassy in occupied Kuwait.

President Bush orders the first mobilization of approximately 40,000 reserves.

August 23. US embassy personnel and dependents leave occupied Kuwait by car and travel to Baghdad.

An estimated 15,000 to 25,000 people protest in Islamabad against the deployment of US and Pakastani troops in the Gulf.

August 24. Iraqi troops surround several embassies in Kuwait. Iraq prevents US personnel and dependents who had left Kuwait from leaving Baghdad.

August 25. The UN Security Council passes Resolution 665 by a vote of 13 to 2 authorizing forces in the Gulf to "use such measures commensurate to the specific circumstances as may be necessary . . ." to enforce trade sanctions against Iraq. Cuba and Yemen vote against.

August 26. The government of Saudi Arabia orders Saudi ARAMCO to begin increasing oil production to make up for lost Kuwaiti and Iraqi production.

Soviet Foreign Minister Shevardnadze states that the Soviet Union has no plans to use military means to enforce the embargo on Iraq.

August 27. The United States expels 36 Iraqi Embassy personnel from the US and places strict travel restrictions on remaining Iraqi personnel.

August 28. Iraqi President Hussein states that all women and children detained in Iraq will be allowed to leave.

August 29. In a public interview, Iraqi President Hussein vows to hold onto Kuwait and claims that "Kuwait is an Iraqi province."

OPEC ratifies an agreement to increase production to make up for lost Kuwaiti and Iraqi oil production.

August 30. Thirteen members of the Arab League gather in Cairo for an emergency meeting. Eight members, Algeria, Iraq, Jordan, Mauritania, Sudan, Tunisia, Yemen and the PLO, boycott the proceedings.

August 31. The Bush administration announces its intention to forgive $7.1 billion of Egypt's military debt to the United States pending congressional approval.

UN Secretary General Javier Perez de Cuellar begins talks with Iraqi Foreign Minister Aziz in Baghdad.

September 1990

September 1. Talks between UN Secretary General Perez de Cuellar and Iraqi Foreign Minister Aziz end without an agreement.

Twelve of thirteen Arab League representatives renew their condemnation of the Iraqi invasion and annexation of Kuwait. They call on Iraq to pay reparations to Kuwait and allow foreigners to leave.

September 4. US Secretary of State Baker proposes in testimony before Congress a new "regional security structure" in the Gulf similar to NATO to "contain" and "roll back" Iraq. Baker announces that the Bush administration is planning for a long-term military presence in the Gulf even if Iraq withdraws from Kuwait.

September 5. US Secretary of State Baker qualifies remarks made to Congress a day earlier, stating that the US is not advocating a "NATO of the Middle East."

September 6. After meeting with US Secretary of State Baker in Jeddah, Saudi King Fahd agrees to commit "billions" of dollars to the US to help defray the military costs. Fahd also agrees to permit 50,000 more Egyptian and Syrian troops onto Saudi soil if desired by those countries.

September 7. US Secretary of State Baker meets with Kuwaiti Emir Jabir al-Ahmad Al-Sabah in Taif and secures a $5 billion commitment for 1990 to pay for US military operations and for compensation to countries that have incurred losses from the embargo of Iraq.

September 8. Presidents Bush and Gorbachev arrive in Helsinki for a superpower summit. Iraqi President Hussein suspends charter flights carrying hostages through Jordan because of Jordan's complaints of being overwhelmed by the volume of flights.

September 9. Presidents Bush and Gorbachev issue a joint statement reaffirming the August 3 US-Soviet joint statement and their support for UN

Security Council Resolutions 660, 661, 662, 664, and 665. The text states that "our preference is to resolve the crisis peacefully . . ." and that "We must demonstrate beyond any doubt that aggression cannot and will not pay."

September 11. US Secretary of State Baker meets with Soviet Foreign Minister Shevardnadze in Moscow to discuss security arrangements in the Middle East.

September 12. The Muslim World League meeting in Mecca passes resolutions approving Saudi Arabia's decision to call in US troops, but also calls for a replacement of US troops by a pan-Islamic force as soon as possible.

September 13. The UN Security Council passes Resolution 666 by a vote of 13 to 2 imposing strict controls on humanitarian food aid to Kuwait.

September 14. Japan offers an additional $4 billion in military and economic aid in support of the coalition against Iraq.

Iraqi troops storm diplomatic compounds of France, Canada and Belgium in occupied Kuwait.

US Secretary of State Baker meets with Syrian President Assad in Damascus.

September 15. Iraq opens the Saudi-Kuwaiti border, allowing approximately 10,000 people to leave over a three day period.

September 16. President Bush states on Iraqi television, "Perhaps your leaders do not appreciate the strength of the forces united against them. Let me say clearly, there is no way Iraq can win."

The UN Security Council passes Resolution 667 by a vote of 15-0 condemning the Iraqi violations of the diplomatic missions of Belgium, Canada, France, and the Netherlands.

September 17. Saudi Arabia and the Soviet Union formally reestablish diplomatic relations after a 52-year hiatus.

Twelve European Community countries expel Iraqi military attaches and restrict the movements of the other Iraqi diplomats in direct response to the Iraqi raids on Western diplomatic compounds in Kuwait City.

September 18. Saudi Arabian Foreign Minister Saud al-Faisal says his country would welcome the presence of Soviet troops on Saudi soil if Moscow decided to join the forces allied against Iraq.

September 19. Saudi Arabia abolishes the residence and employment privileges extended to Palestinians and Yemenis because of their stand in regard to the Gulf crisis.

The price of oil hits $32.35 per barrel (Brent exchange) and $28.80 (Dubai).

September 20. Saudi Arabia halts oil deliveries to Jordan.

September 22. The government of Saudi Arabia announces the expulsion of most Iraqi, Jordanian, and Yemeni diplomats.

September 23. Iraqi President Hussein threatens to destroy oil fields in the Middle East and attack Israel if sanctions begin to "strangle" Iraq.

September 24. French President François Mitterrand proposes a four stage comprehensive peace plan for the Middle East, saying, "If Iraq were to affirm its intention to withdraw its troops and free the hostages, everything would be possible."

The UN Security Council passes Resolution 669 ordering the Sanctions Committee to examine aid requests by countries adversely affected by the UN-sanctioned embargo of Iraq.

September 25. The UN Security Council passes Resolution 670 by a vote of 14 to 1, extending the economic embargo to air travel and calls on member nations to detain Iraqi ships in their ports. Cuba votes against.

US networks broadcast parts of the 76-minute speech by Iraqi President Hussein in response to President Bush's 8-minute speech on Iraqi television on September 16.

At the end of his four-day trip to Tehran, Syrian President Assad and Iranian leaders declare they are in "full agreement" in their opposition to the Iraqi invasion of Kuwait and the US deployment in the Gulf.

September 27. The Bush Administration notifies Congress of a $7.3 billion arms sale to Saudi Arabia, scaled down from a $20 billion request. The White House discloses that this package will be followed by a second package in January taking into account Saudi Arabia's longer term needs.

October 1990

October 1. In a speech at the UN, President Bush states that Iraq's withdrawal from Kuwait could lead to "opportunities" for peace between Israel and Arabs. He also says that his position on an unconditional Iraqi withdrawal has not changed and that even if Iraq did withdraw, its chemical and other weapons capabilities would still be a problem.

The US House of Representatives passes a resolution by a vote of 380 to 29

approving the deployment of troops by President Bush.

October 2. The US Senate passes a resolution by a vote of 96 to 3 approving President Bush's decision to deploy troops to the Gulf.

October 4. Special Soviet Envoy Primakov meets with Iraqi President Hussein and urges Iraq to withdraw from Kuwait.

October 8. Israeli security forces clash with rock-throwing Palestinians near the Haram al-Sharif (Temple Mount) in East Jerusalem. Israeli authorities report 19 Palestinians dead.

October 10. The price of oil hits $40.75 a barrel (Brent) and $35.10 (Dubai).

October 12. The UN Security Council unanimously passes Resolution 672 condemning Israel for the October 8 killings and requests the UN to send a mission to the region to report on the incident.

October 14. The Israeli government states that it will not accept the UN mission to investigate the October 8 killings.

October 15. President Bush refers to Iraq's actions in Kuwait as "Hitler revisited." Bush warns that atrocities in Kuwait could result in trials similar to the Nuremberg trials following World War II, holding Iraqi President Hussein accountable for war crimes.

October 16. The Japanese cabinet adopts a plan to send thousands of troops as part of a UN Peace Cooperation Corps to Saudi Arabia. They would be barred from the threat or use of force.

October 19. Iraq announces a rationing program for gasoline and engine oil as of October 23 citing shortages in chemical additives due to the economic embargo.

October 24. The Middle East News Agency (MENA) reports that Kuwait, Qatar, Saudi Arabia, and the UAE have all decided to cancel Egypt's debts totalling an estimated $7.7 billion.

October 25. The US Congress approves the sale of $7.3 billion in sophisticated arms to Saudi Arabia as well as $37 million for Bahrain. The Bush administration agrees to support a provision allowing up to $1 billion in additional military support for Israel. Congress also approves President Bush's request to cancel $6.7 billion of Egypt's military debt.

October 27. The Soviet Union unexpectedly requests the UN Security Council to postpone voting on a resolution condemning Iraq.

October 28. Iraqi President Hussein abolishes gasoline rationing and fires oil minister Abdul-Rahim Chalabi.

October 29. The UN Security Council passes Resolution 674 by a 13 to 0 vote condemning Iraq for "mistreatment and oppression" of Kuwaiti citizens, and states that Iraq "is liable for any loss, damage or injury" that it causes in Kuwait. Yemen and Cuba abstain.

Soviet President Gorbachev calls for a new Arab initiative to resolve the crisis, reiterating that a military solution is "unacceptable."

Secretary of State Baker states in testimony to Congress, "We will not rule out a possible use of force if Iraq continues to occupy Kuwait."

October 30. Iraqi President Hussein orders his military commanders to be on "extreme alert."

October 31. Egyptian President Mubarak rejects Soviet President Gorbachev's call for a new Arab initiative to resolve the crisis saying it would result in a summit of insults. The Syrian government also rejects the idea.

November 1990

November 3. The Iraqi Government announces proposed terms for resolution of the Gulf crisis, including the withdrawal of all non-Arab forces, allowing for an Arab solution, and a guarantee that Iraq would not be attacked militarily. Iraq reiterates that any settlement would exclude the return to power of the exiled Kuwaiti government, and rejects the idea that the issue of Israeli occupation can only be dealt with after an Iraqi pullout from Kuwait.

November 4. US Secretary of State Baker makes the first stop in Bahrain of an eight-nation tour to sound out allies on the use of force to remove Iraqi troops from Kuwait.

The first part of a 15,000-man Syrian armored division begin arriving in Saudi Arabia.

November 5. US Secretary of State Baker and Saudi King Fahd meet in Jeddah and formally agree on a framework for command and control over American and Saudi military forces in case of war.

November 6. In Geneva at a UN conference on global warming, Jordan's King Hussein warns that in the event of war the world would suffer an ecological catastrophe with oil-field fires that would blacken the sky for hundreds of miles.

November 7. The United States contends that it did not need a mandate from the UN for the use of force because Article 51 of the UN charter allows member states to ask for assistance in fighting aggression against them.

Japanese Prime Minister Kaifu abandons his bid to send a Japanese UN Peace Cooperation Corps to the Gulf because of national and Parliamentary opposition to Japanese involvement in military conflict abroad.

November 8. President Bush orders the deployment of an additional 200,000 troops to the Persian Gulf area over two months, increasing the total US force to 430,000 to ensure an "offensive military option." Bush states that this increase is intended to be a signal to Iraqi President Hussein that the United States is serious about forcing a withdrawal.

Soviet Foreign Minister Shevardnadze states that force against Iraq cannot be ruled out as an option.

Iraqi sources reveal that Iraqi President Hussein has dismissed Army Chief of Staff Nizar Khazraji and replaced him with the younger General Hussein Rashid, the commander of the defense of Basra during the Iran-Iraq war.

November 11. In a radio broadcast, Moroccan King Hassan calls for an emergency Arab summit to avert war.

November 14. President Bush tells Congressional leaders that he has not changed his Gulf policy, and that he has not decided to take military action.

November 15. A joint statement is issued by Syrian President Assad and Egyptian President Mubarak claiming

that Iraq is setting "impossible conditions" for the realization of an emergency Arab summit.

Soviet President Gorbachev warns Iraq that an "immediate and unconditional withdrawal from Kuwait" is the only way to avert a military solution to the Gulf crisis.

In a CNN interview, President Bush says the withdrawal of Iraqi forces from Kuwait should be followed by a UN effort guaranteeing the elimination of Iraq's chemical weapons arsenal and a halt to its nuclear program.

US and Saudi forces carry out their first joint military exercise, Imminent Thunder, an amphibious landing about 100 miles south of the Kuwaiti border.

November 17. Egyptian President Mubarak urges the US to give Iraq three months to consider withdrawing its forces from Kuwait.

US Secretary of State Baker "dismisses a similar call for delay" put forth by Soviet Foreign Minister Primakov.

President Bush embarks on an 8-day foreign tour.

November 18. Iraq promises to release all foreign hostages between December 25 and March 25 "unless something should occur to disturb the atmosphere of peace."

November 19. Iraq announces an increase of troops in Kuwait and Southern Iraq by 250,000 to approximately 700,000.

November 21. President Bush arrives in Saudi Arabia and meets with Saudi King Fahd and Kuwaiti Emir Jabir al-Ahmad Al-Sabah. Bush calls for UN hearings on the treatment of Kuwait, stating, "I feel that we should take action (on the resolution) before November 30." (On December 1, Yemen is due to replace the US as the chair of the UN Security Council).

President Bush cancels a meeting with Jordan's King Hussein due to Hussein's anti-American speech at the opening session of Parliament.

November 23. President Bush meets with Syrian President Assad in Geneva, wrapping up an 8-day trip which includes a stop in Saudi Arabia, Bush's first trip to the Middle East since the August 2 invasion. No joint statement is made. Bush states that he is "determined" to keep the Palestinian question separate from the issue of the occupation of Kuwait.

November 26. In his strongest public statement to date, Soviet President Gorbachev warns that if Iraq does not withdraw from Kuwait and release all foreigners, it will be subject to the effects of a "tough resolution" in the United Nations.

November 28. The PLO is unable to find enough support to force a UN Security Council vote on a resolution proposing a Geneva Conference on the Palestinian question. The US, fearing a veto on this issue might threaten the coalition against Iraq, tries to keep the Palestinian resolution from coming to a vote before a vote authorizing the use of force.

November 29. The UN Security Council passes Resolution 678, which states that, unless Iraq fully complies with all previous security council resolutions and withdraws all of its forces from Kuwait by January 15, member states "may use all necessary means . . . to restore international peace and secu-

rity in the area." The vote passes by 12 to 2, with Yemen and Cuba dissenting and China abstaining.

November 30. President Bush proposes sending Secretary of State Baker to meet with Iraqi President Hussein before January 15, and invites Iraqi Foreign Minister Aziz to Washington for "consultations" during the week of December 10.

Iraq refrains from furnishing an official response to Bush's offer, but issues an official statement rejecting UN Security Council Resolution 678, calling the resolution "illegal and invalid."

December 1990

December 1. Iraq publicly "accepts the idea of the invitation and the meeting" proposed by President Bush.

Saudi Arabia formally announces the cancellation of Egypt's estimated $4 billion debt.

December 2. Iraq test-fires two Scud missiles for the first time since April.

December 4. The Democratic Caucus of the US House of Representatives approves a non-binding resolution that demands that Congress give "affirmative approval" before any US offensive military operations in the Gulf. The vote in the Caucus is 177-37.

December 5. A joint statement is issued in Baghdad by Jordan's King Hussein, Vice-President Baidah of Yemen, PLO Chairman Arafat and Iraqi President Hussein expressing the need for "inter-Arab dialogue"

Israeli Foreign Minister David Levy warns that Israel may attack Iraq if the US fails to force withdrawal from Kuwait and the dismantling of Iraq's military might.

December 6. Iraqi President Hussein states that all foreigners are to be released "promptly" and that Iraqi forces have completed their preparations to defend against attack.

December 8. In an interview on US television, Iraq's Foreign Minister, Tariq Aziz, says Iraq would not insist on the phrase "linkage between the resolution of regional issues and the situation in the Gulf," but that the United States would have to recognize that problems existed before the Iraqi invasion of Kuwait and that all UN resolutions pertaining to the area had to be implemented.

Iraq rejects the proposed dates for a meeting with US Secretary of State Baker (December 21 and 22, and January 3), and rather suggests January 12 as an alternative.

December 10. Soviet Foreign Minister Shevardnadze states that public opinion in the Soviet Union would not permit Soviet President Gorbachev to deploy even a token force in the Gulf.

Israeli Prime Minister Shamir warns against efforts to solve the Gulf crisis at the expense of Israel.

December 12. Iraqi President Hussein replaces Defense Minister Gen. Abdul-Jabbar Shanshal with Maj. Gen. Saadi Tuma Abbas. Abbas, at age 51 the younger of the two, is renowned in Iraq for successfully directing the Iraqi defense of Basra against Iranian attacks in 1982.

Algerian President Benjedid arrives in Baghdad for talks with Iraqi President Hussein.

December 13. The last American detainees arrive in Frankfurt. Included is the skeleton staff of the US embassy in Kuwait (Ambassador W. Nathaniel Howell and 4 staff members).

December 14. Iraqi President Hussein and President Bush state that US-Iraqi talks are "on hold."

December 15. Iraq cancels Foreign Minister Aziz's trip to the US, and states that "Iraq alone" will set a date for US Secretary of State Baker's trip to Baghdad.

December 16. British diplomats close their embassy in Kuwait.

December 18. President Bush states that a return to the status quo before the Iraqi invasion would be "unacceptable." Bush asserts that an International Peacekeeping Force (including a US naval presence) will be necessary in the Gulf region, regardless of whether Iraq withdraws from Kuwait and/or complies with the UN resolutions. The President cites the need to control Iraq's nuclear and chemical weapons capabilities as one reason for a continued international presence in the region.

December 20. The UN Security Council unanimously adopts Resolution 681, which calls for the use of UN Personnel to monitor the condition of Palestinians in the occupied territories, and "deplores" the deportation of Palestinians from the territories. In a separate statement, the Council (including the US) supports the idea of a Middle East peace conference. This is the first time the US has consented to allow the UN a role in a Middle East peace conference.

Soviet Foreign Minister Shevardnadze resigns.

December 22. The GCC convenes its 11th annual summit meeting in Doha,

Qatar. This summit meeting is the first top-level meeting of the regional defense and economic cooperation organization since the invasion of Kuwait. The agenda includes devising a strategy to liberate Kuwait and discussing ways to protect the region from future aggression.

December 24. Iraq recalls its ambassadors to the US, the United Nations, and "leading European countries" for consultations regarding the Gulf crisis.

In a televised interview, Iraqi President Hussein marks Tel Aviv as Iraq's first target if war breaks out.

December 25. At the close of their meeting, GCC leaders release a communique calling for Iraq to comply with UN resolutions, and "pay compensation for all damage caused" (by the invasion) or "face war." The communique also supports the proposal of an International Peace Conference (on the Palestinian Question), and states that "the GCC welcomes Iran's wish to improve ties."

December 26. Israel asserts that it will not launch a preemptive strike against Iraq, but reserves the right of massive retaliation if Iraq attacks (including missile attacks).

Iraq and the United States resume diplomatic contact with a view to arranging a dialogue.

Iraq test-fires a surface-to-surface missile.

December 31. Sudan calls on Iraq to withdraw completely from Kuwait.

January 1991

January 2. NATO announces its intention to send 42 German, Italian and Belgian jet fighters from the Allied Command Europe Mobile Force to Turkey.

Jordan's King Hussein orders 80,000 troops to deploy in defensive positions along the Jordan valley facing Israel.

January 3. President Bush proposes a meeting in Geneva of Secretary of State Baker and Iraqi Foreign Minister Aziz between January 7-9. Bush states that there will be "no negotiations, no compromises, no attempts at face-saving and no rewards for aggression."

January 4. Iraq accepts the proposal for talks between Foreign Minister Aziz and US Secretary of State Baker in Geneva on January 9. President Bush states that he is not willing to allow Baker to travel to Baghdad, saying that the US has "exhausted that option."

January 5. President Bush states in weekly radio address, "Each day that passes increases Saddam's worldwide threat to democracy."

January 8. President Bush delivers letter to Congress formally requesting authorization for the use of force against Iraq in accordance with UN Resolution 678.

January 9. Talks in Geneva between US Secretary of State Baker and Iraqi Foreign Minister Aziz fail to bring progress. Aziz rejects letter delivered by Baker from President Bush to Iraqi President Hussein, explaining in a news conference that the "letter is not compatible with the language that should be used in correspondence between heads of state." Aziz also states Iraq's intent to attack Israel in case of an attack by US-led forces on Iraqi forces. Baker in the news conference states, "I heard nothing that suggested any Iraqi flexibility."

Iraqi President Hussein declares in Baghdad as the Geneva talks fail that Iraq is "ready for a showdown" with foreign forces and warns, "We will make them swim in their own blood."

President Bush in a news conference states that "the choice of peace or war is really Saddam Hussein's to make."

January 10. Most western embassies close down operations in Baghdad.

US Secretary of State Baker and Lt. Gen. Howard Graves, Assistant to the US Joint Chiefs of Staff, meet in Riyadh with Saudi King Fahd and discuss possible military operations.

January 11. The US Congress opens a debate on whether or not to authorize of the use of force against Iraq. After meetings between US Secretary of State Baker and Saudi King Fahd, Saudi and US officials confirm Saudi approval of the use of American forces against Iraq, stating that notification but no further consultation is needed before launching an attack.

Twelve European Community foreign ministers hold a meeting with UN Secretary General Javier Perez de Cuellar in Geneva and endorse a plan designed to assure Iraq of peace and security if Iraq withdraws unconditionally from Kuwait.

January 12. The US Congress passes a resolution authorizing the use of force in accordance with UN Resolution 678 and the War Powers Act. The Senate votes 52 to 47 for the resolution, while the House votes 250 to 183.

President Bush says if there is war, it will come "sooner rather than later."

The US closes down its embassy in Baghdad, though diplomatic relations formally remain intact. The State Department orders the expulsion of all but four Iraqi diplomats from Washington.

Egyptian President Mubarak reportedly indicates to US Secretary of State Baker that he is prepared to use Egyptian forces for offensive action against Iraq. Syria's Foreign Minister states that Syrian troops "are there for defensive purposes, and that up to this moment this is the case."

January 13. After meeting with Iraqi President Hussein, UN Secretary General Javier Perez de Cuellar says that "only God knows" if there will be war.

January 14. The UN Security Council discusses a last-minute French-sponsored peace proposal which includes an international conference on the Palestinian question. The proposal fails to reach a vote.

January 15. The UN deadline passes for Iraq to withdraw its forces from Kuwait. In a public speech, the UN Secretary General makes a personal appeal to Iraqi President Hussein to avoid a conflict by giving up Kuwait.

January 17. Coalition forces from four countries, the United States, the United Kingdom, Saudi Arabia, and Kuwait, launch a massive air assault in the early morning hours on military targets in Iraq and Kuwait. Iraq offers little resistance.

President Bush states that the goal "is not the conquest of Iraq; it is the liberation of Kuwait." Bush also expresses his intention to destroy Iraq's nuclear and chemical capabilities.

The Turkish Parliament authorizes US fighters and bombers to launch air strikes from the Incirlik air base.

January 18. Jordan's King Hussein calls for a temporary cease-fire, during a news conference in Amman.

The highest judicial body in Saudi Arabia, the Council of Ulama, issues a decree (*fatwa*) sanctioning a holy war against Iraq and calls on all Muslims and "those assisting them" to evict his forces from Kuwait.

January 18. Iraqis launch 8 Scud missiles with conventional warheads towards Israel, landing in Tel Aviv and Haifa and injuring fifteen people. Israeli Ambassador to the US Zalman Shoval states that Israel reserves the right to respond to the attack.

One Scud missile fired toward Dhahran, Saudi Arabia is shot down by a US Patriot missile.

January 19. Four more Scud missiles strike Israel, slightly injuring fifteen. The US delivers several batteries of Patriot missiles to Israel.

January 20. General H. Norman Schwarzkopf, commander of US forces, states that coalition forces have "thoroughly damaged" Iraqi nuclear reactors.

Iraqi President Hussein delivers a short speech calling on supporters to carry out holy war against Iraq's enemies and to "target their interests everywhere."

January 20-21. Iraq launches ten Scud missiles toward Saudi Arabia, nine of which are reported to be shot down by Patriot missiles. One falls harmlessly into the sea.

January 21. Pentagon officials report 14 allied planes and 17 Iraqi planes lost. The total number of allied sorties for five days is reported at 8,100.

January 21. Six Iraqi Scud missiles are launched towards Saudi Arabia. Patriot missiles intercept at least one. No casualties reported.

January 22. Iraq is reported to have set fire to two Kuwaiti oil refineries and the Wafra oil field in Kuwait.

Israel asks the United States for $3 billion for expected war damages and $10 billion in additional aid over five years to help resettle Soviet Jewish immigrants.

January 23. An Iraqi Scud missile strikes apartments outside Tel Aviv, killing 3 and injuring 96.

January 24. Iraq closes off border with Jordan.

The UN Security Council discusses a call for a cease-fire by five North African countries, Morocco, Algeria, Libya, Tunisia, and Mauritania.

Canadian forces join the air campaign, switching from a defensive to an offensive role.

January 25. Iraq is reported to have released millions of gallons of Kuwaiti crude oil at the port of Mina al-Ahmadi into the Persian Gulf.

American Patriot missiles intercept seven Iraqi Scuds above Tel Aviv and Haifa. Debris from the missiles kills one and wounds 42. One Iraqi Scud strikes Riyadh, killing one and wounding 30.

20,000 demonstrate outside American and French embassies in Nouakchott, Mauritania.

January 26. 75,000 demonstrators gather in Washington calling for an end to the war.

Pentagon announces that at least two dozen Iraqi aircraft have fled to Iran since the start of the war.

January 27. The US bombs oil installations in Kuwait in an attempt to halt the flow of oil into the Persian Gulf.

Egyptian Minister of State for Foreign Affairs, Boutros Ghali, states that Egypt "is not in favor of a change of government" in Iraq.

January 29. The Pentagon states that 90 Iraqi aircraft have gone to Iran. Iran expresses the intent to keep Iraqi aircraft until the war is over.

PLO guerrillas launch numerous short-range missiles from southern Lebanon toward four settlements in northern Israel, missing the targets. A PLO spokesman in Sidon terms the attack as a "defense of Iraq and its people." Israel launches reprisal raids near Tyre, killing five.

January 30. Iraq launches a raid with approximately 1,500 troops a few miles into Saudi territory. Coalition forces drive back Iraqis to the town of Khafji near the border. Eleven US Marines are killed and two wounded. At least 24 Iraqi tanks are destroyed.

US Secretary of State Baker and Soviet Foreign Minister Alexander Bessmertnykh issue a joint statement in Washington reiterating a commitment to UN Security Council resolutions related to the Gulf. The statement also says that both ministers agree that "in the aftermath of the crisis in the Persian Gulf, mutual US-Soviet efforts to promote Arab-Israeli and regional stability, in consultation with other parties in the region, will be greatly facilitated and enhanced."

January 31. US, Saudi and Qatari forces oust remaining Iraqi forces from Khafji. A Saudi source estimates 12 Saudis and 28 Iraqis killed. Ameri-

cans estimate 17 Iraqi tanks and armored vehicles destroyed.

Iraqi Deputy Prime Minister Saadoun Hammadi arrives in Tehran to discuss possible peace initiatives with Iranian, Yemeni, and Algerian officials. France sends a special envoy to discuss proposals, but expresses the intention not to meet directly with the Iraqi delegation.

February 1991

February 3. Secretary of Defense Richard Cheney suggests in an interview that the United States and its allies will continue economic sanctions after Iraq withdraws from Kuwait.

Moroccan authorities permit at least 300,000 demonstrators to gather in the streets of Morocco showing support for Iraq and demanding withdrawal of coalition forces from the Gulf. No major incidents are reported.

February 4. Iranian President Rafsanjani announces that he has presented "ideas" to Iraq for peace and warns, "any exclusion of Iran from negotiations would mean genuine security could not be achieved." The State Department issues a statement rejecting any mediating role for Iran.

February 5. The number of coalition sorties to date totals over 47,000. President Bush states that he is "skeptical" that the air war will be enough to move Iraqi forces out of Kuwait.

Syrian forces enter combat for first time, repelling a small Iraqi incursion into Saudi territory.

The Soviet Union and Turkey send envoys to Iran to discuss Rafsanjani's proposal to mediate.

The Iraqi Petroleum Ministry announces

that all sales of gasoline to the general public are halted citing "technical damage to oil installations."

February 6. Thirteen more Iraqi aircraft fly to Iran, bringing the total to 147 since January 17.

One Scud missile strikes Israel injuring seventeen, bringing the total to 30 Scuds fired at Israel since the outbreak of war.

February 9. Iraq formally severs ties with the United States.

Soviet President Gorbachev states in Moscow, "The logic of the military operations, the character of the military operations, is creating a threat of going beyond the limits of the [UN] mandate."

February 12. Soviet Special Envoy Primakov meets with Iraqi President Hussein in Baghdad.

February 13. US planes bomb a building in Baghdad killing numerous Iraqi civilians. Iraqis claim 400 dead and claim the building to have been an air raid shelter. US authorities refer to the building as a military target, though acknowledging the loss of civilian life.

February 14. US officials release a statement estimating the destruction of 1,300 of 4,280 Iraqi tanks, 800 of 2,870 armored personnel carriers and 1,100 of 3,110 artillery pieces in Kuwait and southern Iraq.

February 15. Iraq offers to withdraw from Kuwait, provided that Israel withdraws from "Palestine and the Arab territories," that eleven UN Security Council resolutions are rescinded, including the embargo, that US and other forces withdraw from the region within one month of a cease-fire, and that

"Iraq should not incur any financial expenses in this regard." Iraq also demands that all debts of Iraq "should be written off."

President Bush rejects the offer outright, referring to the proposal as a "cruel hoax." The Soviet Foreign Minister refers to the statement as an "encouraging" decision. Eight Arab foreign ministers in the coalition (excluding Morocco) issue a statement in Cairo rejecting the offer.

February 16. The Soviet Union in an official statement formally rejects the Iraqi offer for withdrawal.

Eight Arab countries in the coalition, Egypt, Syria, Saudi Arabia, Kuwait, Bahrain, Oman, Qatar and the United Arab Emirates, agree on a postwar security plan including the maintenance of an Arab peace-keeping force in the Gulf and the establishment of a new development fund of up to $15 million for poorer Arab countries.

February 17. Soviet President Gorbachev meets with Iraqi Foreign Minister Aziz in Moscow and presents a detailed plan for an end to the war.

February 19. President Bush states that the Soviet proposal "falls well short of what would be required."

Schwarzkopf claims that the Iraqi military "are on the verge of collapse." An Iranian newspaper quotes an Iraqi official as putting Iraqi casualties at 20,000 dead and 60,000 wounded.

February 20. US-led forces intensify incursions into Kuwait, taking over 500 Iraqi prisoners.

February 21. Iraqis agree to Soviet proposal calling for a cease-fire and the "full and unconditional withdrawal of Iraqi troops from Kuwait." The proposal includes the release of prisoners of war immediately after a cease-fire, a timetable for withdrawal, the removal of UN economic sanctions after two-thirds of Iraq's forces have withdrawn from Kuwait, the lifting of UN Security Council resolutions after complete withdrawal, and the monitoring of withdrawal by non-combatant UN forces.

The United States does not accept the proposal.

February 22. President Bush delivers an ultimatum demanding that Iraq make an "immediate and unconditional withdrawal from Kuwait" by 12 noon Eastern Standard Time on February 23 or face a ground attack.

After the statement by President Bush, the Soviet Union revises its proposal, calling for the withdrawal of Iraqi forces from Kuwait within 21 days and from Kuwait City within 4 days. The proposal includes the release of all prisoners of war within three days after the cease-fire, the lifting of all UN Security Council resolutions after withdrawal, and the stipulation that the supervision of the cease-fire and troop withdrawal be conducted by parties to be determined by the UN Security Council.

Iraqi troops increase the destruction of oil wells, setting fire to over 100 in a 24-hour period.

February 23. Iraqi Foreign Minister Aziz officially accepts the revised Soviet proposal in Moscow. The deputy chairman of the Iraqi Revolutionary Command Council, Izzat Ibrahim, states in Baghdad that Iraq "will pay no attention" to the US ultimatum.

At 8 p.m. EST, US-led forces launch a massive ground offensive into southern Iraq and occupied Kuwait. Allies encounter minimal resistance and capture at least 14,000 Iraqi soldiers. Approximately 270,000 French, British and American troops move with relative ease into southern Iraq west of Kuwait in an attempt to outflank Iraqi forces in the Kuwaiti theater. US Marines, with allied air and artillery support, launch the brunt of the attack into southern Kuwait with GCC, Egyptian, and Syrian forces on the far eastern flank. The forces reach the Burgan Oil field a number of miles south of Kuwait City by the next day.

February 24. The Soviet Union releases a statement critical of the US decision to launch a ground offensive, stating that the US lost a "very real chance for peace" with the Soviet proposal.

Egyptian police break up a demonstration of approximately 2,000 anti-war student protestors at Cairo University. An estimated 100,000 Yemenis gather outside the presidential palace in Sanaa denouncing Egyptian and Syrian involvement in the war.

February 25. Allies continue to advance on Iraqi positions in Kuwait and Iraq, nearing the encirclement of Republican Guard forces north of Kuwait.

Baghdad Radio announces that it has ordered a withdrawal of Iraqi forces from Kuwait "as a practical compliance with Resolution 660." The White House releases a statement doubting Iraqi intentions, saying that "Saddam Hussein's forces will fight their way out of retreating" and that "we will consider retreating combat units as a movement of war."

An Iraqi Scud missile hits US barracks

in Dhahran, killing 28 and wounding 98.

At least 8,000 Cairo University students protesting the war clash with Egyptian police, injuring dozens.

February 26. US-led forces complete their encirclement of Iraq's army. President Bush states that "The liberation of Kuwait is close at hand." Allied forces take control of Kuwait City.

Kuwaiti Emir Jabir al-Ahmad Al-Sabah declares martial law in Kuwait for a period of three years.

Iraqi President Hussein publicly announces an immediate pullout of forces from Kuwait but claims a "dignified" victory.

Allied planes bomb Iraqi soldiers stuck in a traffic jam on the road leading out of Kuwait toward Iraq.

February 27. Coalition forces take Kuwait City, and US forces reach the banks of the Euphrates River 100 miles south of Baghdad.

President Bush announces that "Kuwait is liberated," and orders allied forces to suspend attacks effective midnight Eastern Standard Time. Bush states that a permanent cease-fire is contingent on an end to hostilities by Iraq; the immediate release of all coalition prisoners of war, third-country nationals, and Kuwaiti detainees; the informing of Kuwaiti authorities of the location and nature of all land and sea mines; and full compliance with all pertinent UN Security Council Resolutions. Bush also calls on the Iraqi government to designate military commanders to meet within 48 hours with coalition commanders.

February 28. President Bush announces

that Iraq has agreed to designate military leaders to meet with coalition commanders to formulate the details of a permanent cease-fire. Only two minor cease-fire violations are reported.

March 1991

March 1. Cease-fire proceedings are delayed due to "technical details."

March 2. US forces are reported to have destroyed or captured 140 retreating Iraqi tanks and armored vehicles that fired on US forces in southern Iraq.

The UN Security Council passes Resolution 686 by a vote of 11 to 1 with 3 abstentions dictating terms to Iraq for a formal cease-fire. Terms include the return of all POWs and Kuwaiti detainees, Iraqi acceptance of liability for war damages and the rescinding of the Iraqi annexation of Kuwait. Cuba votes against, while China, India, and Yemen abstain.

Various sources report Basra to be in a chaotic state.

March 3. Iraq formally accepts all conditions for a temporary cease-fire after a two-hour meeting between coalition and Iraqi military commanders in Safwan, Iraq. Iraqi Foreign Minister Aziz delivers a letter to the United Nations expressing willingness to comply with Resolution 686 and asks the Security Council to consider rescinding its economic embargo of Iraq.

Refugees fleeing Iraq into Iran, Kuwait and Syria report continued turmoil in various cities and towns in southeastern Iraq.

Iraq releases ten allied prisoners as a goodwill gesture. The Bush Administration estimates Iraqi POWs at 60,000 to 70,000.

March 4. Refugees report increased anti-government resistance in several cities including Basra, Nasiriyah, Karbala, Amarah, Samawah, Diwaniya, and Kut. A number of refugees claim that the uprising has been led by the Islamic Revolutionary Party of Iraq, headed by Muhammad Bakr Hakim.

March 5. US military sources in Saudi Arabia report clashes between Iraqi Republican Guard troops and Shiite Muslims in at least thirteen cities. The co-president of the Iraqi Kurdistan Front, Jalal Talabani, while in Damascus, claims that there has been a Kurdish takeover of Irbil in northern Iraq.

The Iraqi government annuls its annexation of Kuwait and agrees to release stolen Kuwaiti assets.

Iraq frees the last 35 allied prisoners of war.

In Damascus, the Foreign Ministers of Egypt, Syria, and the Gulf Cooperation Council (GCC) reach an agreement on a postwar defense arrangement.

March 6. President Bush delivers a speech to Congress, saying that the US "commitment to peace in the Middle East does not end with the liberation of Kuwait." Bush restates the call for a comprehensive settlement based on Security Council Resolutions 242 and 338, and states that a solution must provide for Israel's "security of recognition, while giving the Palestinians legitimate political rights."

Eight Arab foreign ministers from the GCC countries, Egypt, and Syria meet in Damascus and reach agreement approving the use of Egyptian and Syrian troops in the Gulf as a "nucleus of an Arab peacekeeping force" as part of the postwar defense arrangements.

Refugees and US military sources report decreased activities by the Iraqi resistance and increased control by pro-government forces in Basra.

According to Kurdish leader Talabani, Iraqi Kurdish guerrilla commander Mas'ud Barzani announces his intention to commit thousands of troops to the Kurdish uprising in north.

March 7. Iraqi newspapers *al-Thawra* and *al-Iraq* issue harsh warnings against insurrectionists. Secretary Cheney states that insurrections have spread to more than two dozen towns and cities in central and southern Iraq. Cheney also states, "we do not want to see any changes in the territorial integrity of Iraq, and we do not want to see other countries actively making efforts to encourage changes."

Kurdish leaders in Damascus claim the capture of several towns in northern Iraq.

March 8. Iraqis release first 1,100 of about 5,000 Kuwaiti civilians detained during the war.

During Friday prayers, Iranian President Rafsanjani urges Iraqi President Hussein to "submit to the will of the people" and share power with Iraqi opposition groups.

March 11. More than 20 Iraqi opposition groups convene in Beirut to discuss means of toppling the Iraqi government. Turkish President Turgut Ozal announces that Turkish officials have met with Talabani, leader of the Patriotic Union of Kurdistan, and Muhsin Dezayee of the Kurdish Democratic Party. Dezayee states that Turkey pledged "to defend us in international forums."

March 12. Insurrections are reported in Baghdad for the first time after the war. The US issues a statement confirming violence in Baghdad. The Kurdish opposition claims control of nearly 75% of the Kurdish north, and reports raids on Mosul.

President Bush issues a warning to Iran not to attempt to annex territory from Iraq. Bush also criticizes the use of Iraqi helicopters to quell rebellions and states that it could delay the withdrawal of American forces from the region.

March 14. Kuwaiti Emir Jabir al-Ahmad Al-Sabah returns to Kuwait.

US Secretary of State Baker ends talks with Syrian President Assad and leaves the Middle East for Moscow asserting that the initial steps for a regional peace in the Middle East are being taken.

March 15. Gen. Schwarzkopf warns that US forces will shoot down any Iraqi fixed-wing aircraft that take off, considering them a violation of the cease-fire agreement.

March 16. In a national address, Iraqi President Hussein promises democratic political reforms with multi-party elections. No timetable is mentioned.

March 17. Allied military commanders meet with Iraqi military commanders in Safwan and warn Iraqis against moving any combat aircraft within Iraq.

March 20. A US fighter plane shoots down an Iraqi warplane in northern Iraq.

Heavy fighting continues between government forces and Kurdish rebels in and around Kirkuk.

Iraqi parliament speaker Saadi Mahdi Saleh directly accuses Iran of aiding "saboteurs."

March 21. Fighting between Kurds and the government is confirmed in Mosul for the first time since the beginning of the insurrection. Kurdish leaders claim control over Kirkuk. Heavy fighting continues in Karbala.

March 22. A US fighter downs another Iraqi plane.

March 23. Iraqi President Hussein reshuffles the Iraqi cabinet, adding four Shiites, including Saadoun Hammadi as Prime Minister. Tariq Aziz loses the position of Foreign Minister, but retains his role as Deputy Prime Minister.

March 24. The US army repositions units in Iraq, driving north 60 additional miles into the Euphrates River valley.

March 26. US officials reaffirm US neutrality in Iraq, stating "We don't intend to involve ourselves in the internal conflict in Iraq."

US workers plug the first oil well of the estimated 800 damaged and burning in Kuwait.

Kurdish forces seize an Iraqi military base in southern Kirkuk.

Saudi Arabia refuses a US request to host the headquarters for the US Central Command in the Gulf.

March 30. Iraqi government forces make significant advances on Irbil and reportedly take much of Kirkuk.

The Arab League convenes in Cairo for first meeting since the outbreak of war. The Iraqi delegate, Saad Qassim Hammoudi, asserts that "There is no revolution in Iraq" and accuses Iran and Israel of covert activity supporting the insurrection. GCC Secretary General Abdullah Bishara discloses that the GCC plans to discontinue aid to Jordan and the PLO for their support of Iraq during the crisis.

April 1991

April 1. Baghdad Radio claims government control over the Kurdish centers of Kirkuk, Irbil, Dohuk, and Zakhu.

April 2. Turkish President Ozal makes an appeal to the United Nations Security Council for assistance in dealing with the estimated 220,000 Iraqi refugees who have fled to Turkey.

April 3. The UN Security Council adopts Resolution 687 dictating final cease-fire terms to Iraq by a 12 to 1 vote with two abstentions. Cuba votes against while Yemen and Ecuador abstain. The resolution requires Iraq to recognize the international borders between Iraq and Kuwait established in a 1963 agreement; provides means for the establishment of a demilitarized zone six miles into Iraq and three miles into Kuwait; requires Iraq to destroy or remove all chemical, biological and nuclear weapons and their related components, and forbids the future development of such weapons; and creates a fund for payment of compensation to which Iraq must contribute. The resolution also lifts the prohibition of foodstuffs but retains the arms embargo.

April 5. The UN Security Council passes resolution 688 by a 10 to 3 vote, with two abstentions, condemning Iraqi repression and killings of Kurds and Shiites.

President Bush orders an airlift of humanitarian aid to Kurdish refugees fleeing Iraq.

April 6. Iraq accepts terms for a permanent cease-fire as stipulated in UN Resolution 687, effectively ending the Persian Gulf War.

April 7. Secretary of Defense Richard Cheney in an interview suggests that UN forces might establish safe zones for refugees in northern and southern Iraq.

April 8. US forces begin withdrawing from southern Iraq.

April 11. The UN Security Council declares the cease-fire to be officially in effect and sets the timetable for the implementation of the cease-fire terms.

April 14. The remaining US military forces in southern Iraq begin withdrawing back to the UN-established demilitarized zone along the Iraqi-Kuwaiti border.

April 16. President Bush orders the mobilization of US forces into northern Iraq in order to establish refugee camps for the Kurds.

April 17. US and allied troops begin entering northern Iraq.

April 19. US and Iraqi military commanders meet near the Iraqi-Turkish border to discuss arrangements for a security zone for Kurdish refugees in northern Iraq. No agreement is reached though the US expresses intent to continue relief operations.

April 24. Patriotic Union of Kurdistan leader Jalal Talabani claims that Kurdish rebels have agreed "only in principle" on terms for Kurdish autonomy with the Iraqi government.

May 1991

May 2. Allied forces in northern Iraq move 35 miles further eastward, doubling the size of the security zone.

May 8. Egyptian President Mubarak announces a decision to withdraw Egypt's forces from the region.

May 13. UN officials begin taking over relief efforts in northern Iraq from allied forces with the establishment of a humanitarian relief center in Dahuk. A small firefight breaks out between Iraqi and British troops, injuring two Iraqi soldiers.

The Iraqi government agrees to permit 400 to 500 UN security force members to enter northern Iraq to protect returning Kurdish refugees.

Kurdish leader Mas'ud Barzani claims "broad agreement" with the Iraqi government on autonomy for the Kurds, but notes unresolved points on territory and oil rights blocking a final agreement.

May 22. US and Iraqi military officials reach agreement on security arrangements for Dahuk in northern Iraq.

The US Defense Intelligence Agency issues a statement estimating that roughly 100,000 Iraq soldiers were killed during the war.

May 29. President Bush proposes significant arms limitations for the Middle East. The proposal includes a freeze on surface-to-surface missiles, a ban on materials for nuclear weapons, a ban on chemical weapon use, and "collective self-restraint" for weapons suppliers.

May 30. The Chairman of the US Joint Chiefs of Staff, General Colin Powell, visits northern Iraq and states that allied forces intend to pull out soon from the area.

June 1991

June 15. The last allied troops withdraw from Dahuk.

June 26. The Kuwaiti government ends martial law in Kuwait. Kuwaiti Crown Prince Saad Abdullah Al-Sabah commutes death sentences of 29 people convicted of collaboration with the Iraqis.

The US and others accuse Iraq of concealing equipment for nuclear weapons research from United Nations inspectors.

June 28. Iraqi soldiers fire shots near a UN nuclear inspection team filming the movement of nuclear weapons research equipment in Baghdad. President Bush states that there is "incontrovertible evidence" of violations by Iraq of the cease-fire terms because of its failure to cooperate with UN officials.

Tim Lake, who compiled this chronology, has been a research associate at the University of North Carolina at Greensboro since 1991. He previously worked as a publications assistant at the Center for Contemporary Arab Studies, Georgetown University, where he was a student in the Master's program. During the summer of 1990, he was Department of State intern in the Political Section of the US Embassy in Riyadh, where he was a member of the Embassy's task force that responded to the invasion.

CONTRIBUTORS

Abbas Alnasrawi is professor of economics at the University of Vermont. He earned his Ph.D. in economics from Harvard University. During the 1950s he worked for the Central Bank of Iraq and the Iraqi Ministry of Finance. Among Dr. Alnasrawi's many studies dealing with the economics of the Middle East are *Financing Economic Development in Iraq: The Role of Oil in Middle Eastern Economy; Arab Oil and United States Energy Requirements;* and *OPEC in a Changing World Economy.*

John Duke Anthony is President and Chief Executive Officer of the National Council on US-Arab Relations and adjunct professor of Middle East Studies at the Defense Intelligence College. He holds graduate degrees from Georgetown University and the Johns Hopkins School of Advanced International Studies. He is the author of *Arab States of the Lower Gulf: People, Politics, Petroleum* and *The Middle East: Oil, Politics, and Development,* as well as numerous publications dealing with the Persian Gulf and the Gulf Cooperation Council.

John P. Banks is senior associate at International Resources Group, Washington, DC, where his specialty is the economic and political analysis of US and international energy issues. He received his Master's degree from Georgetown University's School of Foreign Service. He has testified before Congress on OPEC and global oil markets, and is a consultant on energy projects funded by the US government in eastern Europe, Kazakhstan and Kyrgyzstan. He is a frequent contributor to *Oil and Gas Journal* and *Octane Week.*

L. Carl Brown is Garrett Professor of Foreign Affairs at Princeton University. His publications include the books *International Politics and the Middle East: Old Rules, Dangerous Game; The Tunisia of Ahmed Bey;* and *Psychological Dimensions of Near Eastern Studies* (co-editor). He is also the author of numerous articles about the Middle East. He received his Ph. D. from Harvard University, and spent six years as a US Foreign Service officer prior to his doctoral work.

Michael C. Dunn is senior analyst of The International Estimate, Inc., and Middle East Editor of its biweekly newsletter, *The Estimate*. He received his Ph.D. from Georgetown University, where he teaches regularly as an Adjunct Professor. He is the author of numerous articles in periodicals on strategic and military issues affecting the Middle East, subjects about which he has also lectured frequently. Apart from strategic and military issues, one of his major fields of specialization is the history of Islam.

Charles K. Ebinger is vice-president and group manager for energy of International Resources Group, Washington, DC, and senior associate of the Center for Strategic and International Studies (CSIS), where he served as director of the Energy and Strategic Resources Program from 1982 to 1987. Dr. Ebinger, who received his Ph.D. from the Fletcher School of Law and Diplomacy at Tufts University, has also held positions as a senior consultant to Putnam, Hayes and Bartlett, and as foreign affairs officer in the Office of International Affairs of the Federal Energy Administration.

Shamlan Y. Al Essa is a professor of political science at Kuwait University. He obtained his Ph.D. in political science from the Fletcher School of Law and Diplomacy at Tufts University. The author of *Manpower Problems in Kuwait,* as well as a number of articles on Kuwait and the Gulf, Dr. Al Essa has acted as a consultant to the Gulf Cooperation Council. He was a founder, and is currently vice-president, of the Center for Child Evaluation and Development in Kuwait.

Hani A. Faris is a research associate at the Institute of Asian Research at the University of British Columbia. After receiving his Ph.D. in political science and comparative politics from the University of Calgary, Dr. Faris taught at Kuwait University for seven years as assistant professor of political science. His publications include *Conflict and Confessionalism in Lebanon* and *Arab Nationalism and the Future of the Arab World* (editor), as well as several papers concerning political and development issues in the Middle East.

Xiaoxing Han is a visiting assistant professor in the Department of Government at Georgetown University, where he received his Ph.D. He was previously Lecturer at the Institute of West Asian and African

Studies in the Chinese Academy of Social Sciences. He received his graduate degree from the Chinese Foreign Affairs College. He has written in Chinese and English on a variety of topics, including Chinese policy in the Middle East, the comparative political systems of Egypt and China, and the politics of Islam.

Jo-Anne Hart is assistant professor of political science and a research associate with the Center for Foreign Policy Development at Brown University. Dr. Hart, who received her doctorate from New York University, has written widely on issues affecting Gulf security and threat reduction, and on Middle Eastern politics. A member of the Persian Gulf Study Group sponsored by the Council on Foreign Relations, Dr. Hart is engaged in research on American military policy in the Gulf region in the past decade.

Michael C. Hudson is professor of international relations and government and Seif Ghobash Professor of Arab Studies at Georgetown University, where he served as Director of the Center for Contemporary Arab Studies from 1976 to 1989. He received his Ph.D. in political science from Yale University. Dr. Hudson's studies of the Middle East include *Arab Politics: The Search for Legitimacy; The Precarious Republic: Political Modernization in Lebanon;* and *The Palestinians: New Directions* (editor). He has also authored numerous papers and articles on international relations affecting the Middle East and on Arab politics.

Ibrahim Ibrahim is Director of the Center for Contemporary Arab Studies. He received his M.A. from the University of Heidelberg and his D.Phil. from Oxford University. Prior to joining the Georgetown University faculty, Dr. Ibrahim was advisor to the Ministry of Foreign Affairs in the United Arab Emirates. He has also taught at Warwick University and the American University of Beirut. His publications include *Arab Resources: The Transformation of a Society* (editor and contributor), and many articles on the recent history and current political developments of the Middle East.

Nemir A. Kirdar is the founder, President and Chief Executive Officer of INVESTCORP, an international investment bank, established in 1982, which operates out of Bahrain, London and New York. He currently serves as Chairman of the Advisory Council of the Center for Contemporary Arab Studies, Georgetown University, and is a member of the Board of Visitors of the University's School of Foreign Service. He is also a member of visiting committees at Harvard University and Fordham University, New York. Mr. Kirdar obtained his M.B.A. from Fordham University, and completed the Senior Managers Program at Harvard University. Prior to establishing INVESTCORP, he had been Vice President and Director of Long Range Planning for the Middle East, and then Gulf Division Executive, at Chase Manhattan Bank.

Sherif Mardin is Chair of Islamic Studies in the School of International Service at American University. He received his Ph.D. in political science from Stanford University and his M.A. in international relations from the Johns Hopkins School of Advanced International Studies. His publications include *The Genesis of Young Ottoman Thought* and *Religion and Social Change in Turkey*. He has written extensively in English, French and Turkish on the politics of Turkey.

Phebe Marr is senior fellow at the Strategic Concepts Development Center at the National Defense University. She received her doctorate in History and Middle Eastern Studies from Harvard University. Dr. Marr's research has centered on the modern political history of Iraq, and on political instability in the Middle East, particularly the Persian Gulf. In addition to her many articles on the Gulf, her publications include *The Modern History of Iraq; The Gulf, Energy and Diplomacy;* and *Ideology and Power in the Middle East.*

Yelena S. Melkumyan is a senior research scholar at the Institute of Oriental Studies in Moscow, where she obtained her Ph.D. in 1971. Dr. Melkumyan's research has focused mainly on the modern history of Kuwait and its relations with the Arab world. Her numerous publications in Russian about the Gulf area include *Social-Political Development and Foreign Policy of Kuwait (1960–1989),* and several articles on Kuwaiti development, the Gulf Cooperation Council, and regional security problems in the Gulf.

Augustus Richard Norton is senior research fellow at the International Peace Academy in New York and professor of political science at West Point. He earned his Ph.D. from the University of Chicago. In 1989, as a Fulbright Research Professor at the Norwegian Institute of International Affairs, Dr. Norton researched the issue of peace-keeping, especially in Middle East settings. In addition to writing extensively on the Middle East for major newspapers, he is the author of *UN Peacekeepers: Soldiers with a Difference*.

Ibrahim M. Oweiss is a professor of economics at Georgetown University. His numerous publications include *The Political Economy of Contemporary Egypt* (editor and contributor); *Arab Civilization* (co-editor); and *The Dynamics of US-Arab Economic Relations in the 1970s* (editor and contributor). He has written extensively on oil pricing and on oil revenues and Arab development. He earned his doctorate in economics from the University of Minnesota. Dr. Oweiss also served for one year as first undersecretary of state for economic affairs for Egypt and has also been chief of the Egyptian Economic Mission to the United States.

Bernard Reich is professor of political science and international affairs at George Washington University. He also serves as Chairman, Advanced Area Studies (Middle East–Fertile Crescent) at the Department of State's Foreign Service Institute. His works include *Quest for Peace: United States-Israel Relations and the Arab-Israeli Conflict* and *The United States and Israel: Influence in the Special Relationship*. He has published numerous articles on Middle East politics and international relations in the Middle East and is the editor of the Nations of the Contemporary Middle East series for Westview Press.

Michael Simpson is Director of Publications at the Center for Contemporary Arab Studies, Georgetown University. Formerly the Assistant Editor of the *Journal of Palestine Studies*, he is the editor of the volume *United Nations Resolutions on Palestine and the Arab-Israeli Conflict, 1981–1986*. He specializes in the political economy and society of the contemporary Middle East, and has written articles on a variety of issues, including technology transfer, stereotypes of the Arab world, and US-Arab relations.

INDEX